Acting Like a Woman in Modern Japan

Theater, Gender, and Nationalism

Ayako Kano

palgrave

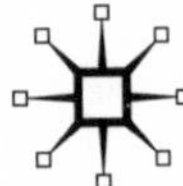

ACTING LIKE A WOMAN IN MODERN JAPAN

First published 2001 by PALGRAVE™
175 Fifth Avenue
New York, N.Y. 10010 and
Houndmills, Basingstoke, Hampshire RG21 6XS.
Companies and representatives throughout the world

PALGRAVE is the new global publishing imprint of St. Martin's Press LLC Scholarly and Reference Division and Palgrave Publishers Ltd (formerly Macmillan Press Ltd).

ISBN 0–312–23997–1 hardback
ISBN 0–312–29291–0 paperback

Library of Congress Cataloging-in-Publication Data
Kano, Ayako, 1966-
Acting like a woman in modern Japan : theater, gender, and nationalism / by Ayako Kano.
p. cm.
Includes bibliographical references and index.
ISBN 0–312–29291–0 (alk. Paper)—ISBN 0–312–23997–1
1. Kawakami, Sadayakko, 1871–1946. 2. Matsui, Sumako, 1886–1919. 3. Women in the theater—Japan—History—19th century. 4. Women in the theater—Japan—History—20th century. I. Title.
PN2928.K375 K36 2001
792'.028'0820952—dc21

2001032762

A catalogue record for this book is available from the British Library.

Design by Letra Libre, Inc.

First edition: September 2001
10 9 8 7 6 5 4 3 2 1
Printed in the United States of America.

Contents

List of Illustrations vii
Preface ix

Part I
Setting the Stage

Chapter 1 Acting Like a Woman 3
Chapter 2 Modern Formations of Gender and Performance 15

Part II
Kawakami Sadayakko

Chapter 3 Wifeing the Woman 39
Chapter 4 Straightening the Theater 57
Chapter 5 Reproducing the Empire 85

Part III
Matsui Sumako

Chapter 6 A New Woman 123
Chapter 7 A New Theater 151
Chapter 8 Feminists and Femmes Fatales 183
Epilogue Revealing the Real Body 219

Notes 231
Bibliography 283
Index 313

List of Illustrations

Cover illustration	Actress Matsui Sumako in the title role of Maurice Maeterlinck's *Monna Vanna*	
Illustration 2.1	Geisha from *Engei gahō* (September 1910)	16
Illustration 2.2	Actresses of the Teikoku Gekijō training institute, *Engei gahō* (September 1910).	17
Illustration 2.3	Male actors in a performance of Gerhart Hauptmann's *Lonely People. Onnagata* Ichikawa Enjaku as Anna Mahr is pictured on the top left and bottom right. *Engei gahō* (December 1911)	20
Illustration 3.1	Kawakami Sadayakko as a wife, bottom right, with Kawakami Otojirō on top. *Engei gahō* (October 1908).	43
Illustration 4.1	Triptych of Kawakami troupe's *Sino-Japanese War.* Kawakami Otojirō as war reporter is making a speech in front of General Li. *Onnagata* Ishida Nobuo as the Japanese maiden is crouching behind the hero. Courtesy of Waseda University's Tsubouchi Shōyō Memorial Theater Museum.	63
Illustration 4.2	Triptych of Kawakami Troupe's *Sino-Japanese War.* Courtesy of Waseda University's Tsubouchi Shōyō Memorial Theater Museum.	65
Illustration 4.3	Kawakami Sadayakko surrounded by actresses of her "platoon." *Engei gahō* (October 1908).	82
Illustration 5.1	*Geisha and the Knight* at the Paris World's Fair 1902 [*sic*]. Kawakami Otojirō as the samurai, far left; Sadayakko as the geisha, third from left. Courtesy of Waseda University's Tsubouchi Shōyō Memorial Theater Museum.	87

Illustration 5.2	Kawakami Sadayakko as a Western lady, and as a Japanese woman. *Engei gahō* (October 1908)	91
Illustration 5.3	Kawakami troupe's performance of *Dumb Travel,* with Kawakami Sadayakko as an English actress, below right, and as the goddess of peace, above. *Engei gahō* (October 1908)	105
Illustration 5.4	Kawakami troupe's performance of *Othello,* with Kawakami Otojirō as Othello, center. *Engei gahō* (February 1910).	108
Illustration 5.5	More scenes from *Othello,* with Kawakami Sadayakko as Lady Tomone. *Engei gahō* (February 1910).	109
Illustration 6.1	Matsui Sumako dressed in kimono. Courtesy of Waseda University's Tsubouchi Shōyō Memorial Theater Museum.	136
Illustration 6.2	Matsui Sumako in *manteau.* From *Peony Brush.*	137
Illustration 8.1	Matsui Sumako in the Tarantella dance scene from *A Doll House. Engei gahō* (October 1911). In the insert on the upper right, she is dressed in a *manteau,* ready to leave the house.	193
Illustration 8.2	Matsui Sumako as Magda. Courtesy of Waseda University's Tsubouchi Shōyō Memorial Theater Museum.	206
Illustration 8.3	Matsui Sumako as Magda with *manteau.* From *Peony Brush.*	207
Illustration 9.1	Kawakami Sadayakko as Salomé. Courtesy of Waseda University's Tsubouchi Shōyō Memorial Theater Museum.	221
Illustration 9.2	Matsui Sumako as Salomé. Courtesy of Waseda University's Tsubouchi Shōyō Memorial Theater Museum.	222
Illustration 9.3	Magician Shōkyokusai Tenkatsu as Salomé. Courtesy of Waseda University's Tsubouchi Shōyō Memorial Theater Museum.	223
Illustration 9.4	Comic strip of *Salomé. Engei gahō* (June 1915).	226

PREFACE

THIS BOOK WAS HATCHED OVER TEN YEARS AGO and its growth took place in coffee shops and libraries in three cities, Tokyo, Ithaca, and Philadelphia. The idea came to me while writing an undergraduate thesis on the adaptations of Japanese theater by Bertolt Brecht, William Butler Yeats, and Benjamin Britten. As I neared the completion of that thesis, I became increasingly conscious of the fact that its pages were dominated by men: There was one striking female figure, but she was portrayed on stage by a man, and all the playwrights and composers whom I discussed were also men. Sipping my scalding cup of coffee at a donut shop near Keio University in Tokyo, I resolved to myself that in graduate school, I would study Japanese theater and *women*. That is what I set out to do when I arrived at the Ph.D. program in Comparative Literature at Cornell University in the fall of 1989.

My first explorations in identifying the presence of women in Japanese theater yielded mildly interesting results. I translated *Kamabara,* a comic *kyōgen* play, which features a strong female character chasing her lazy husband around the stage, threatening to hack him to pieces with a sickle and driving the man close to committing suicide with that same instrument. The translation was eventually published as *The Sickly Stomach* in *Traditional Japanese Theater: An Anthology of Plays,* edited by Karen Brazell (Columbia University Press, 1998). The play, however, ends exactly where it started, with the wife chasing her husband off the stage. And the wife is portrayed on stage by a man, according to the conventions of *kyōgen.* This did not seem a very encouraging sign for a progressive change in women's status, in theater or in society.

My search for women in Japanese theater also led to the works of a few female playwrights, including those of Enchi Fumiko. Although best known as a novelist, Enchi wrote a number of interesting plays in her youth, and I was able to translate one of them, *The Storm* (Arashi), which deals with abortion and sexual antagonism between women and men. But I was still disappointed: It seemed that the equivalent of a Murasaki Shikibu or a Yosano Akiko, famous for their prolific production in prose and poetry respectively, was not to be found in the realm of drama. Was my attempt at feminist criticism of Japanese theater doomed to engage, once again, only with works by men, staged by men?

The connection between Japanese theater and feminism was an elusive one, with one important exception. All accounts of Japanese women's history mentioned the Japanese premiere of Henrik Ibsen's *A Doll House* in 1911, and the discussion of women's issues it occasioned. I started researching the reception of *A Doll House* in Japan, reading the commentaries by members of the feminist literary journal *Seitō* and contrasting them with the reception of the play in Germany and the commentary by feminists in that country. Soon, my attention was drawn to the Japanese actress who premiered the role of Nora, the heroine of *A Doll House* who abandons her husband and children in order to find her true self. The actress, Matsui Sumako, was one of the first women in modern Japan to be trained in European acting techniques, and she had left her husband in favor of a married man who was also her teacher and director. Surely, I thought, this actress must have been a fierce and forthright feminist. Surely, I had found my perfect topic, my link between Japanese theater and feminist studies.

The actress turned out to be a much more complex character than I had anticipated. She was the target of intense gossiping and personal attacks both while she was alive and after her death. Her director-lover was the one who came across in the historical accounts as the true artist and true feminist, a martyr to the cause who was seduced by the femme fatale, Matsui Sumako. This was a puzzle, I felt, that was worth a closer look. A casual look at other actresses of the time pointed to the same puzzle. Why were actresses such controversial figures, and why were their relations to feminism so vexed and difficult? The attempt to answer this question eventually turned into my Ph.D. dissertation. I focused on two pioneering actresses in modern Japan, Matsui Sumako and Kawakami Sadayakko, and explored their relation to the process of nation-building. A small part of this early exploration was published as "The Roles of the Actress in Modern Japan," in *New Directions in the Study of Meiji Japan,* ed. Helen Hardacre (Leiden: E. J. Brill, 1997).

In the years since, my interest in the figure of the actress developed and diversified in several directions. These new areas of exploration formed the basis of two articles, "Japanese Theater and Imperialism: Romance and Resistance," in *U.S.-Japan Women's Journal,* English version, no. 12 (1997), and "Visuality and Gender in Modern Japanese Theater: Looking at Salome," in *Japan Forum* 11, no. 1 (1999). These new explorations, further revised and refined, found their way into chapters 5 and 9, while chapters 4 and 7 were newly written.

What follows, then, is the result of ten years of research and countless cups of coffee.

It is also the result of countless acts of guidance and friendship by many people. I owe many thanks: to Brett de Bary, J. Ellen Gainor, and Biddy Martin for supporting the beginnings of this project at Cornell University; to Karen Brazell, Victor Koschmann, and Naoki Sakai for stimulating seminars and reading groups; to Kanai Yoshiko, Ehara Yumiko, and Ueno Chizuko for their feminist work in Japan; to Mike Bourdaghs, Joanne Izbicki, Beng Choo Lim, Joseph Murphy, Robert Steen, and Jan Zeserson for friendship during and beyond graduate school; to Ikeda Shinobu, Chino Kaori, Wakakuwa Midori, and other members of the Image & Gender Group, as well as Nakano Toshio and Iwasaki Minoru of the Workshop in Critical Theory for opportunities to share my work in Japan; to Norma Field, Carol Gluck, David Goodman, Barbara Molony, Jennifer Robertson, Barbara Sato, and Kathleen Uno for their intellectual guidance and inspiration; to my colleagues at the University of Pennsylvania, especially Linda Chance, G. Cameron Hurst, Hiroko Kimura-Sherry, William Lafleur, and Cecilia Segawa-Seigle, for the daily camaraderie; to Toshiyuki Takamiya for providing an academic home base at Keio University; to Sabah Al-Ghandour, Regina Bendix, Ann Farnsworth-Alvear, Laura Grindstaff, Demie Kurz, Mary Martin, Barbara Savage, Matthew Sommer, Emily Thompson, and Liliane Weissberg for their friendship at the University of Pennsylvania; to Julia Paley for our writing alliance; to all of my students for keeping me excited about teaching as well as about my research; to my junior colleagues Dina Amin, Sara Davis, Noriko Horiguchi, Maki Morinaga, and Seiko Yoshinaga for their intellectual companionship; to Diane Moderski and Peggy Guinan for holding it all together; to Fuji Shuppan, Shinshokan, Yūshōdō and the Tsubouchi Shōyō Memorial Theater Museum at Waseda University for permision to reproduce photographs; to the Spencer T. and Ann W. Olin Foundation, the Mellon Foundation, the Department of Comparative Literature and the East Asia Program at Cornell University, the Research Foundation, the School of Arts and Sciences, the Trustees Council of Penn Women, the Center for East Asian Studies, and the Department of Asian and Middle Eastern Studies at the University of Pennsylvania, for fellowships, grants, and leave-time that made this research possible; to the Harrington family for always welcoming me; to my parents, Eisuke and Miyoko, for always being there; to my sister Rie for always surprising me; and to my best friend and partner, Lewis E. Harrington, for more than I can ever express.

Part I

Setting the Stage

CHAPTER 1

ACTING LIKE A WOMAN

ACTING LIKE A WOMAN DOES NOT COME NATURALLY. It has to be taught, learned, rehearsed, and repeated. It does not arise from a moment of inspiration, but from many years of persistent inculcation. In an acting woman, the cultural and social desires of an age are concentrated, molding her every gesture, every glance. In turn, her movements and words, watched and heard, applauded and critiqued, enforce and revise those desires. Of all acting women, it is the professional actress who most clearly embodies the fantasies and fears of the age. Hence, at the most general level, this book is about acting like a woman in modern Japan, while at the most specific level it is about two actresses who were pioneers in channeling and shaping new desires in a rapidly changing society.[1]

In the past decade, it has become almost fashionable to say simply that "gender *is* performance."[2] Whatever sexual difference might exist on the biological level, gender difference is a cultural and social construct that may be understood as "performance." Thus, one might say, "gender exists only in so far as it is perceived; and the very components of perceived gender—gait, stance, gesture, deportment, vocal pitch and intonation, costume, accessories, coiffure—indicate the performative nature of the construct."[3] Gender is, in this view, a performance that is learned, rehearsed, and given to an audience to be perceived. It is presumably also a performance that can be given differently, with different gestures, intonation, accessories, for a substantially different effect on the audience.[4]

Yet this notion of gender as performance must be somewhat qualified. First, to say that gender is performance can make the whole problem of "being a woman" and "acting like a woman" seem like a question of costume choice: "If you don't like your gender, change into a pair of pants!" Most people would agree that a change of costume might make you a different kind of woman, but that you would be a woman nonetheless. Part of the problem, then, is that despite feminist attempts to separate gender from sex, gender continues to be construed in binary terms: feminine or masculine, woman or man.

Another part of the problem lies with the metaphor of "performance" itself: What does it mean to say that gender is performance? If we are performing gender, are we doing so consciously or unconsciously? Are we entirely free to choose how to act, or is there a prior script that constrains our performance? How far should we take the metaphor of performance?[5]

One answer would be: not too far. In *Bodies that Matter,* Judith Butler clarifies this point: Saying gender is performative is different from saying "that one woke in the morning, perused the closet or some more open space for the gender of choice, donned that gender for the day, and then restored the garment to its place at night."[6] So it is more complicated than keeping skirts in one closet and a pair of pants in another. Butler stresses that the *performativity* of gender has little to do with the *theatricality* of gender, and that by performativity she means something much closer to a "reiteration of a norm."[7] However, in an earlier essay, "Performative Acts and Gender Constitution," and in her subsequent book *Gender Trouble,* Butler's emphasis had been on the possibility of interpreting and enacting gender differently, not confined to the norm: "[G]ender is an 'act,' as it were, that is open to splittings, self-parody, self-criticism."[8] This emphasis on the fluidity of gender had been the main cause of the wide-ranging enthusiasm that greeted *Gender Trouble.* The enthusiastic (mis)reading of the idea of the performativity of gender was what led Butler to clarify her position subsequently in *Bodies that Matter,* declaring that "this act is not primarily theatrical."[9]

This rejection of "theatricality" is based on an understanding of theater in which an actor is "performing" consciously while on stage but stops doing so when offstage. What would happen to her theory of gender as performance if a different theory of performance were employed? Moreover, if we take seriously the double meaning of "to act," and consider that even when offstage, one is acting in daily life with varying degrees of consciousness, then that understanding of theatricality would not diverge as much from Butler's notion of performativity.[10]

Butler writes about gender: "Its theatricality gains a certain inevitability given the impossibility of a full disclosure of its historicity."[11] I choose to read this as an invitation for a not entirely impossible project: the *partial* disclosure of gender's historicity, in the service of a recovery of gender's theatricality. In other words, since gender appears as if it is inevitable and unchangeable only because its historical "origin" remains hidden, to uncover at least part of the historicity of gender is to open up possibilities for gender to be more playful and, indeed, more theatrical.

Such is the purpose of this book. By scrutinizing a specific historical moment in a specific location, I wish to add a few brushstrokes to the often highly abstract portrait of the relationship between gender and performance. At the same time, by sifting through some of the sedimented historicity of gender, I hope to add a few handfuls of sand in the direction that would dislodge gender's inevitability. The locale is Japan, the historical moment is the turn of the previous century, a moment in which both gender and performance, as well as the relationship between them, registered a recognizable shift. From my vantage point at the turn of another century and at a moment in history in which the performativity and theatricality of gender can be glimpsed again—inside and outside theory books, on stage, on screen, and in the streets—I aspire to trace the beginning of the modern definition of gender and to hasten the demise of understanding "acting like a woman" as that which comes naturally.

The historical link between theater and prostitution is documented in many areas of the globe. Japan is no exception. Advertising their sexual services through sensual and sensational dances, certain women had made the stage their showcase by the early seventeenth century. When scandals and riots involving the ruling classes ensued, the authorities blamed the sellers, rather than the buyers: From 1629 to 1891, women were officially prohibited from performing in theaters. Initially they were replaced by young men, the *wakashu,* akin to the boy-actors in English theater of the Elizabethan period.[12] It soon became apparent, however, that these boys were as prone to igniting scandals and riots as the women, and they were banned from the stage as well. It thus fell upon adult male actors to carry the stage, and to carry the female roles in particular.

Applying thick white powder and rouge to their faces, donning elaborate costumes and heavy wigs, forcing their shoulders back and walking with bent knees, these actors, called *onnagata,* or *oyama,* cultivated a style of acting that represented idealized femininity by concealing one set of somatic signs and inscribing another. So highly valued was their portrayal of femininity that women from the pleasure quarters began to imitate them. Femininity was a set of signs that circulated from the pleasure quarters to the theater and back.[13] Prostitution continued to be associated with the theater, with the male actors available as sexual partners for male patrons, but the practice of *onnagata* eventually led to the development of a stylized art and made idealized femininity something that was represented by men.

All of this started to change in the late nineteenth century. But how and why did this change occur? In the years between 1629 and 1868, Japan was to a large extent politically isolated from the rest of the world, maintaining limited commercial relations with a few nations. When a new political regime seized power in the Meiji Restoration of 1868, a period of state-building and nation-building commenced, the gates were opened to Western influence, and women entered the theater as part of this process. Yet the introduction of women to the stage was no simple matter.

Theater was one of the most conspicuous sites for the new government to display Japan's legitimacy as an advanced nation, one that could not only avoid colonization by nations such as the United States, Britain, Germany, and France, but one that would eventually become a colonial power itself. Theater was also one of the most visible components of diplomacy—when Japanese government officials traveled to London, Berlin, and Paris, for instance, they were ushered to the opera houses for cultural entertainment. But where were the Japanese opera houses to which European and American visitors could be invited? One possibility was the *noh* theater, designated as official music (*shikigaku*) under the Tokugawa government, but the slow and dignified movements of *noh* actors tended to put the uninitiated spectator to sleep. The *kabuki* theater, on the other hand, was popular, eye-catching, and entertaining, but it had its own problems. William Elliot Griffis aptly described the condition of Japanese *kabuki* in his journal dated April 12, 1871:

> The house was crowded. The acting was fair. The play was full of love and murder, with many amusing incidents. . . . Clandestine meeting of wife and old lover. Jealous husband detects paramours. Murder of the guilty pair. The husband finds that the pipe-mender [i.e., the lover] is his dear friend in humble disguise. Remorse. Commits *hara-kiri*. Finale. . . . The interest centers in the bloody scene, when heads, trunks, blood, and limbs lie around the stage promiscuously. The deliberate whetting of the sword with hone, dipper, bucket, and water in sight of the frantic guilty pair, the prolongation of the sharpening and the bloody scene to its possible limit of time—twenty minutes by the watch—make it seem very ludicrous to me, though the audience look on breathless. During this time all talking, eating, and attention to infants cease. . . . The theatre is large, but of a rather primitive order of architecture. . . . As a rule, the better class of Japanese people do not attend the theatres for moral reasons, and as examples to their children. The influences of the stage are thought to be detrimental to virtue.[14]

These were precisely the concerns that led to a government-led effort to reform the theater. With the support of the ruling elite and the explicit purpose of raising the status of theater so that it would reflect Japan's new status in the world, the Theater Reform Society (Engeki Kairyōkai) was founded in 1886. Replacing *onnagata* with actresses was among the top items on the group's agenda, along with improving the quality of plays and building modern theater buildings.[15]

Among the first results of theater reform was the improvement in the status of actors. Before the Meiji Restoration, actors had been legally designated outcasts, and despite the great popularity and prestige of a few theater practitioners, most were seen as no better than "river-bed beggars" (*kawara kojiki*). In 1871 the status of "untouchable" (*eta*) and "non human" (*hinin*) was abolished, and freedom of choosing one's occupation and residence was declared. Actors were freed from their social status as outcasts and outlaws and were incorporated into the newly established status of the common people (*heimin*). The government also issued an order in 1882 to require all actors to be licensed by the state (specifically the police) and to pay taxes.[16] It is also customary in theater history to regard the emperor's attendance of a *kabuki* performance in 1887 as a ground-breaking event that legitimized the *kabuki* theater in the eyes of the state and confirmed the status of actors as cultural representatives of the nation, rather than social outcasts. This imperial spectatorship (*tenran kabuki*) is cited as the Theater Reform Society's major concrete achievement.[17]

The Theater Reform Society's efforts were part of the general effort at "reform" (*kairyō*) that preoccupied various sectors of society: reform of clothing, reform of hair style, reform of dining habits, reform of education, reform of housing. It was no coincidence that these were the same years in which the government was trying to revise unequal treaties with various Western powers.

Like theater, women were the target of reform as well as spectacles on display. When intellectuals and government officials traveled abroad in the early years of the new regime, they could not help but notice that women were prominent in social settings in Europe and the United States. Women were ushered first through doorways, danced with men in public, and commanded attention as hostesses at parties.[18] This was terribly shocking, but it showed that women needed to be shown in public in Japan as well. In November of 1883, the government initiated a series of Western-style balls at the newly built Rokumeikan mansion, with politicians and their companions, among them current and former geisha, awkwardly waltzing in long gowns. Pulled by their own wishes for greater roles in society, women were also pushed into the limelight as part of government policy.

In the midst of these social, cultural, and political changes stood actresses. During a time when the public regarded women's performance as synonymous with sexual entertainment, these women trained their bodies and minds in order to enter a profession that consisted of nonsexual performance. Challenging the prerogative of the *onnagata* to represent feminine beauty, these women sought to prove that women could act, that they could act like women, and that they could do so better than men. Among those pioneering women who achieved fame and notoriety as performers in the years known as the Meiji (1868–1912) and Taishō (1912–1926) periods were Kawakami Sadayakko and Matsui Sumako. The former was a former geisha who turned to acting while touring the United States with her husband and their ragtag band of performers. The latter was one of the first actresses trained in a school dedicated to the methods of modern acting and attracted a great deal of attention for her conduct on and off stage.

It is their careers that constitute the core of this book.

What did the increasing visibility and popularity of women like Kawakami Sadayakko and Matsui Sumako signify? Did it contribute to the advance of women into the public sphere by placing women's bodies on stage and giving them a voice? Or did it signal the repressive institution of a definition of gender as naturally grounded in the body rather than constituted in performance? As actresses gained prominence, male performers of female roles did not disappear from the stage, but their significance changed. No longer regarded as the embodiment of ideal femininity, their presence was debated, derided as backward, decadent, even perverse. The rise of the actress, then, brought with it a marginalization of the *onnagata*.

The emergence of the actress and the marginalization of *onnagata* in modern Japan was both a liberating and repressive phenomenon. A definition of "woman" grounded in the physical body was necessary if feminist arguments speeding the rise of the actress were to make any sense. This definition of "woman" was hammered out as part of a contentious process through which Japan became a modern nation-state, and that necessarily excluded certain polymorphous possibilities. This definition was essentialist and expressivist: A certain essence of womanhood was thought to reside in the physical body, and this essence was thought to be expressed outwardly in appearance and behavior. Theatrical performance was also thought to be an expression of this essence. What was lost, negated, repressed in this formation of an essentialist and expressive definition of gender was an earlier model of gender as theatrical accomplishment, which for example saw the *onnagata* as the ideal of womanhood.

The emergence of the actress in modern Japan thus embodies a complex process. The shift in the relationship between gender and performance in fin-de-siècle Japan moved in two directions at once: While it gave rise to feminist discourse, in which theater was involved as a vehicle, it also led to a rigidly essentialist definition of gender, to which theater also contributed.

An instructive parallel can be drawn between the changes taking place in modern Japanese theater and in Renaissance-Restoration theater in England.[19] In both instances, a tradition of using male performers of female roles was replaced by the emergence of the actress.[20] Though much uncertainty remains about the status of gender and sexuality in the Renaissance English theater's use of boy-actors for female roles, the emergence of the actress in Restoration theater can claim many similarities with the Japanese case. It seems to have been "both reactionary and subversive, questioning as well as reinforcing traditional dramatic female stereotypes"—simultaneously allowing women a voice on the public stage as well as leading to greater objectification and heightened voyeurism of the female body.[21] The same assessment could be made about Japanese actresses after the Meiji Restoration.

Part of what makes the Japanese case interesting is that here the transition from male performer of female roles to actress took place in the modern era, about a century ago. This means, first of all, that many primary materials are available, if not always easy to locate, and this study makes extensive use of them. It also means that the rise of the actress in Japan is occurring as part of the process of modern nation-building, state-building, and empire-building, a process in which Japan is situated as the latecomer and emulator. The European and North American stage and society are being actively studied, imitated, even parodied. In this context, it is interesting to note that studies of three famous European actresses in the fin-de-siècle, Sarah Bernhardt of France, Ellen Terry of Britain, and Eleonora Duse of Italy, arrive at some of the same conclusions as my study of Japanese actresses—that the increased importance of women on stage parallels the increased objectification and even repression of women in society.[22] The Japanese case stands out, however, because of the increased complexity of the multiple changes occurring simultaneously. It is the temporal conjuncture between the rise of the actress, the decline of the *onnagata,* and the process of transculturation in the context of nation- and empire-building that distinguishes the Japanese case and renders the Japanese actress a unique embodiment of changes going on at various levels: changes in the role of performers in the theater, in the role of women in society, in the role of Japan in the world. This inquiry is therefore situated at the confluence of theater studies, feminist studies, and Japan studies.

Theater, like other cultural practices, powerfully shapes our ideas about gender, sexuality, sex.[23] Theater has also historically been a site for nation-building, as well as a virtual public sphere.[24] Yet, with a few notable exceptions, English-language scholarship on Japanese theater has concentrated on premodern genres, under the unspoken assumption that modern Japanese theater amounts to not much more than an imitation of European theater. Recent scholarship on the Japanese novel has amply demonstrated, however, that such assumptions are misguided and that *modern* Japanese cultural practices offer rich loci for understanding the complexities of cultural colonization and postcoloniality.[25] This book seeks to supplement these readings of modern Japanese culture by paying attention to practices that are nonverbal or quasiverbal—dance and song, gesture and costume—and by focusing on the body, along with language, as the contested locus of modern transculturation.[26]

An incident comes to mind as a perfect illustration of the status of the early twentieth century in the overall history of Japanese theater. In early

1998 I had the chance to catch the tail end of a major exhibit entitled *Japanese Theater in the World,* sponsored by the Japan Foundation in collaboration with the Tsubouchi Memorial Theatre Museum. I arrived at the Japan Society in New York on the day before the exhibit closed and spent a blissful afternoon walking through the various galleries, taking copious notes. I was perplexed, however, by the fact that while the catalogue made reference to a section on "Japan in the Modern World: *Shingeki,*" I could not find any exhibits under that rubric. Frustrated, I inquired of a staff member where I could find the section "Japan in the Modern World." "Oh, we took that exhibit down early," came the reply. Seeing my disappointment, the staff member added consolingly: "It was just a bunch of photographs anyway." Disappointed, I went back to contemplating the mysterious *noh* masks, gorgeous *kabuki* costumes, and outlandish *butō* posters: men acting like gods, men acting like women, men acting like ghosts. I could see how "men acting like men" and "women acting like women" would seem slightly less compelling.[27]

While gender and Japanese literature is finally becoming a topic of discussion and research both in Japan and in the United States, gender and Japanese *theater* remains a less-studied topic.[28] Significant scholarship has elucidated the relationship of prostitution, male same-sex relations, and *kabuki* in the Edo period (1603–1868),[29] while questions of gender performativity and sexuality have been explored with respect to the Taishō period and after (1912-), especially in the all-female Takarazuka theater.[30] My topic is situated chronologically between these two: What happens to the relationship of gender, sexuality, and theater in the transition to the modern period? Between the all-male *kabuki* theater in which idealized femininity is portrayed by men, and the all-female Takarazuka theater in which idealized masculinity is portrayed by women, this book focuses on the early years of the so-called modern theaters of *shimpa* and *shingeki,* in which women portraying women is taken to be the self-evident and rarely questioned norm.

By uncovering the historicity of the essentialist definition of gender in which we are still trapped, we can resist the all-too-familiar essentialization of Japanese "womanhood" as unchanging and continuous. In order to move beyond the assumption of such an unchanging and transhistorical femininity, then, we might start from the idea that categories such as "woman" and "femininity," mean radically different things in different historical times.[31] Thus, starting from an assumption of the radical discontinuity of gender categories in history, the first line of inquiry would delineate the specifically *modern* formation of gender categories.[32] The modern formation of the category "woman" is closely related to that of the category "citizen" of the modern nation-state, and this relationship is beginning to be examined by a few scholars in Japan.[33] My analysis builds on theirs and adds to them the consideration of theater as a space in which the construction of gender and of nationhood proceeded simultaneously.

Yet this kind of questioning of the historicity of categories is not sufficient: Their imbrication need also be analyzed and exposed. Therefore, this study also attempts to deal with a process that might be called "the reproduction of imperialism." Here the pun works with three meanings of the word "reproduction": first, reproduction as replication, that is, how Japan became an imperial power within the context of Western imperial aggression towards Asia; second, reproduction as representation, that is, how imperialism is represented in discursive practices; and third, reproduction as gendered labor, that is, how women's bodies become involved in imperialism. There are many interlocking questions to be considered. How do the logics of imperialism, colonialism, and Orientalism replicate themselves in relation to Japan? What is the role of culture and gender in this process? Cultural practices such as theater, literature, journalism, and scholarship produce collective fantasies and imagined communities. How do people imagine themselves to be members or subjects of a nation when they never meet most of the other members of the nation face to face? And how do people imagine themselves to be members of a colonial empire, how do people place themselves within a hierarchy of the center and the periphery? How do cultural practices shape these images and fantasies and thus contribute to imperialism and colonialism? And what is the role of gender in reproducing imperialism? An empire needs subjects, and subjects need to be reproduced. What can we say about gendered labor, gendered production, and gendered reproduction in the empire? How is imperialism reproduced, as both geopolitical logic and cultural representation, through women's bodies? This present study seeks to be a part of an emerging scholarly effort to answer many of the above questions.[34]

The following pages will take readers into the historical milieu of Meiji Japan. Starting with a survey of the debates surrounding the emergence of the actress in the early twentieth century, chapter 2 maps out a shift taking place in the Meiji period that defined gender and performance in a way that necessitated the presence of the female body on stage, and relates the shift to the building of Japan as a modern nation-state. Analyzing the various debates for and against the replacement of *onnagata* by actresses, the chapter shows that the debates are structured by assumptions about the nature of woman and the nature of theater. It then outlines the modern formation of the definition of woman as a gender grounded in the body, and of the definition of theater as a type of desexualized performance, and shows how the process of forming categories of gender went hand in hand with theater reform.

Part II and Part III feature two pioneering actresses, Kawakami Sadayakko and Matsui Sumako, respectively. Carefully sifting through biographical representations *of* them as well as theatrical representations *by* them, these chapters analyze how these two women embody the tensions and complications of the modern formation of gender and performance.

Kawakami Sadayakko (1871–1946), discussed in Part II, lived a colorful life as geisha, actress, and mistress, performing in the United States and Europe around the turn of the century and becoming the first woman to perform in modern Japanese theater. Yet Sadayakko's acting is too often dismissed as amateurish and her life portrayed merely as a string of relationships with powerful men. Her career is often subsumed under the name of her husband, Kawakami Otojirō. This is true of the standard theater histories as well as the more recent accounts of her life from the perspective of "women's history." Chapter 3 examines the various biographers' attempts to fit Kawakami Sadayakko's life as geisha, actress, and mistress into the mold of the ideal wife and shows where these attempts break down. It is in the tension between the attempts at what might be called "wifeing" and aspects of her life that refuse to conform to this "wifeing" that the ideology of the "good wife, wise mother" becomes most visible.

Moving from the actress as woman to the actress as performer, chapter 4 delineates Kawakami Sadayakko's participation in a process that I call "straightening" theater. This concept is derived from the principles of "straight theater" (*seigeki*) advocated by the Kawakami troupe: a theater that focuses on dialogue and realistic action, shunning the stylized song and dance of the Japanese performance tradition. Straightening, however, went beyond simply removing elements of song and dance: Concomitant with its downplaying the citationality of speech and action was its rejection of the citationality of gender. Hence the rejection of the male performer of female roles in favor of using actresses such as Kawakami Sadayakko. Straightening theater was a multifaceted process producing what amounted to a "homosocial theater" of fighting men, exemplified by the play *Sino-Japanese War,* staged by the Kawakami troupe in 1904. Drawing on recent theorizing on citationality, homosociality, and direct and indirect speech and action, this chapter draws further theoretical connections between gender and performance

Finally, chapter 5 examines the performances by Kawakami Sadayakko, drawing on unpublished archival scripts. The most intriguing of these roles are "travel plays" and "colonial plays": the former include *The Geisha and the Knight,* staged by the actress and her troupe while touring the United States and in Europe, as well as *Around the World in Seventy Days* and *Dumb Travel,* which capitalized on these experiences of world travel. The latter, including versions of William Shakespeare's *Othello* set in Taiwan and of Wilhelm Meyer-Förster's *Alt Heidelberg* set in Korea, address Japan's emerging colonial relationship to its Asian neighbors. None of these plays and adaptations have been studied in any detail either by Japanese scholars or by others. While several scholars have traced the reception of Sadayakko's performances in Europe and the United States, so far there has been very little analysis about the significance of this actress and her performances in the context of Japan's emergence as a nation-state and as a colonial empire. Moreover, an analysis of these plays shows that contrary to the attempts to straighten theater, it was the nonstraight elements of song, dance, and melodrama that attracted the audience to the theater.

Matsui Sumako (1886–1919), the focus of Part III, was the first professionally trained actress in modern Japan. Most of the conventional accounts of this actress focus on her torrid love affair with director Shimamura Hōgetsu, and her spectacular suicide after his death. Chapter 6 critiques these conventional representations, analyzing the underlying ideologies about gender and sexuality encapsulated in the labels of "New Woman." It sets the representations of her against her self-representation in her memoir.

Chapter 7 positions Matsui Sumako in the process to form "New Theater." New Theater involved new ideas and practices such as faithful adherence to the playwright's intentions, well-trained interpreters shunning commercial success and placing themselves at the service of the play, and spectators regarding the performance as a serious text to be read and appreciated without sexual involvement with the performers. These ideas, akin to what Jacques Derrida has called the "theater of logos," become clarified through debates between practitioners of New Theater, Tsubouchi Shōyō, Osanai Kaoru, and Shimamura Hōgetsu. This chapter analyzes these debates and relates Matsui Sumako's training as an actress to these emerging ideas of New Theater.

Chapter 8 discusses the theatrical roles performed by Matsui Sumako: feminist roles such as Nora in Henrik Ibsen's *A Doll House* and Magda in Hermann Sudermann's *Heimat,* and femme fatale roles such as Oscar Wilde's *Salomé* and Gerhart Hauptmann's *The Sunken Bell.* While Matsui Sumako's enactment of *A Doll House* has drawn some critical attention because its timing coincided with the founding of Japan's first feminist literary magazine, the other plays have hitherto been studied only from the perspective of the reception of European drama in Japan. The controversies surrounding Matsui Sumako's career illuminate a larger argument: These roles embodied the modern definitions of womanhood and theater, while their performances also pushed the boundaries of these definitions.

Finally, since the competition between Matsui Sumako and Kawakami Sadayakko reveals the process of the modern formation of gender and performance most clearly, the epilogue examines the competing performances by the two actresses before concluding the book.

Unless otherwise indicated, all translations from non-English languages are mine. In accordance with East Asian practice, Japanese surnames precede given names (or pen names), excepting Japanese writers whose English-language works have been cited. The surnames are used in references, with the exceptions of some writers and artists whose stage names and pen names are used instead, in accordance with Japanese convention.

CHAPTER 2

MODERN FORMATIONS OF GENDER AND PERFORMANCE

BETTER THAN MEN?: THE ACTRESS DEBATES

IN THE FINAL YEARS OF THE REIGN OF MEIJI EMPEROR (1868–1912), a new kind of woman appeared in the pages of *Engei gahō* (Theater graphic), a theater magazine featuring many photographs and sketches as well as performance reviews and essays. First published in 1907, the magazine had been including in almost every issue a page or two of photographs of the most popular geisha of the day. Dressed in Japanese kimono or Western dress, these women had shared the same space with male actors. But in the last years of the Meiji era, a new breed of women started appearing on these pages, arrayed in composite photographs, symbolically announcing that henceforth actresses, not geisha, were to be featured and contraposed with male actors. These photos thus announced the beginning of a new era, the era of the actress as modern woman and modern performer.

The rise of the actress to theatrical and social prominence, however, was not as easily accomplished as the replacement of one photo by another. In the two decades surrounding the turn of the century, roughly bordered by the beginning of Kawakami Sadayakko's career and the end of Matsui Sumako's life, the print media in Japan featured numerous articles debating various aspects of what was called "the actress question" (*joyū mondai*). Not only was "the actress question" a part of larger discussions about the status of women and the status of theater, but these discussions were a part of the process of building Japan as a modern nation-state. At stake was Japan's cultural legitimacy as a civilized nation that deserved equal treatment by the Western powers. A modern nation-state required modern subjects, gendered, educated, and integrated into the family as a unit of social organization.[1] Theater was one of the

2.1 Geisha from *Engei gahō* (September 1910)

most visible spheres in which to assert cultural legitimacy, as well as one of the most effective tools for educating the modern subject for the modern nation-state. Hence the significance of debates about women and the theater at this juncture in Japanese history.

The debate over the "actress question" usually took the form of asking whether or not Japanese women were physically suited to be actresses and whether or not the newly trained actresses would be superior to the male impersonators of female roles, the *onnagata*. The debate focused on whether or not these "men acting like women" could, and should, be surpassed by "women acting like women." It is of course problematic to define *onnagata* as "men acting like women" since such a formulation assumes a binary opposition of gender that may not have been functioning in pre-Meiji Japan. It is arguable that *onnagata* as well as the *wakashu*—young men who served as sexual partners to adult men—constituted a separate gender in Tokugawa Japan.[2] For the most part, however, the debates of the 1890s to 1910s adopt

2.2 Actresses of the Teikoku Gekijō training institute, *Engei gahō* (September 1910).

the modern vocabulary of a binary opposition, according to which *onnagata* are described to be men acting like women, and actresses are described to be women acting like women.

One schema of the time categorized the various responses to the question "Do we need actresses?" into three groups: the pro-actress group, which says actresses are necessary (*joyū hitsuyō ron*); the anti-actress group, which says they are unnecessary (*joyū fuhitsuyō ron);* and the eclectic group, which says they are necessary for some kinds of plays but not for others in which *onnagata* are more appropriate (*danjo heichi ron*).[3] In all of the answers, for and against actresses, for and against *onnagata,* we can detect shared assumptions about the nature of woman and about the nature of theatrical performance.

It is not surprising that the most powerful arguments in favor of actresses came from those who welcomed the entrance of women into a realm of larger social responsibilities. Those who argued that actresses are necessary, according to writer Minaguchi Biyō, simply declare that "it is a matter of course that a woman should play a woman [*onna ga onna ni naru*], that it is unnatural for a man to play a woman [*otoko ga onna ni naru*]."[4] This writer concludes that once this statement is made, there is nothing more to be added to the argument. However, for such a statement to make sense, there have to be certain shared assumptions already in place, not only about what it means to be a "woman" or a "man" but also about what it means to "play" and what it means to be "natural" or "unnatural." In other words, Minaguchi's statement belongs to an episteme in which "man" and "woman" stand for mutually exclusive identities from which the act of "playing" proceeds. A normalizing judgment considers this "playing" to be "natural" if it conforms to the various traits and behaviors deemed proper to that identity.

Nonetheless, in the statement it is deemed unnatural, but *not impossible,* for a man to play a woman. Moreover, the Japanese verb "*ni naru*" leaves the line between "play-acting" and "becoming" ambiguously permeable. Hence, it is possible to read the second half of the line as: "[I]t is unnatural [but not impossible, since such cases exist] for a man to become a woman." And with this reading, the tautology of the statement begins to unravel: The very stability of the boundary of "woman" versus "man," "becoming" versus "playing," begins to break down. Indeed, it was precisely because such men acting like women were socially visible that one needed to argue over whether or not women could act like women. In other words, "acting like a woman" was contested territory.

Those who favored introducing women onto the Japanese stage based their arguments on the premise that there is some kind of essence that is naturally expressed by a woman through her body. One of the strongest feminist advocates of actresses was Tamura Toshiko, a novelist who had dabbled in acting at one point in her life and whose writings portrayed powerful emotional bonds between women. She believed that *onnagata* only expressed limited aspects of women and that it was a foolish and "perverse art" (*hentai geijutsu*). She reflects on the great lengths to which the *onnagata* of the past would go in order to preserve the illusion of femininity even in their daily lives: claiming any illness to be due to "female trouble" (*chi no michi*), walking about in the Tokugawa equivalent of high-heeled shoes (*takai bokuri*), gingerly clinging to male attendants.[5] Tamura calls these efforts "utterly ridiculous" and not worth the trouble:

> No matter how much these ancient *onnagata* suffered for the sake of their art, it's not like they left us any special artistic techniques to portray women on stage. Just by wearing female wigs they were made into beautiful women, roughly imitated simple expressions of women's grief, anger, joy, and left us these as "patterns." That's all.[6]

In Tamura's opinion, if only women had been acting during all this time, there would have been more interesting, complex, and natural plays (*shizen na shibai*), instead of the set patterns (*kata*) handed down from generation to generation. This association of *onnagata* with stilted and stifling "patterns" and of actresses with authentic "nature" goes further: Tamura suggests that even the "crippled" plays (*katawa na shibai*) of the *kabuki* tradition left to us by *onnagata* can convey "a sense of truth" (*shin to iu kanji*) when performed by women. It may be good for actresses to study and perform these plays, precisely in order to break the "patterns" from the inside.

According to Tamura, while actresses may learn something from performing *kabuki,* it is in modern and "Western" plays that actresses achieve their greatest triumph: "[T]he role of an awakened woman [*jikaku shita onna*], or a woman with a modern education and a scientifically developed brain, would not be comprehensible to male actors raised in the Japanese *kabuki* theater."[7] Comparing the portrayal of two "New Women" characters in European plays, i.e., actress Matsui Sumako's portrayal of Nora in Ibsen's *A Doll House* with *onnagata* Ichikawa Enjaku's portrayal of Anna in Gerhart Hauptmann's *Lonely People,* Tamura sees the former as having clearly triumphed over the latter. And here she focuses on the voice as the conduit of inner emotion to external form:

> The male actor who performed the role of Anna Mahr tried to portray an educated and complicated woman by using a low voice—in the end, he had to resort to his natural male voice, which sounded unnatural [*otoko no fushizen na jigoe*]. The role of Nora, too, would be difficult for an *onnagata* to perform . . . the part after she becomes self-aware could never be performed by a man. It is because a woman speaks at the top of her naturally thin voice [*hosoi onna no ji no koe*], and dares to let the sound of fury resonate, that the two words "self awareness" echo in the audience's hearts. It wouldn't work if a man were to use a feminine falsetto [*onna no tsukuri goe*].[8]

This feminist concludes that "A male impersonator of female roles might be able to portray a woman's weakness to a certain extent, but there is no way he could portray her strength."[9] In Tamura's view, then, a woman and her voice are naturally thin, but she can convey a woman's strength by raising her natural voice; a man, on the other hand can convey a woman's weakness by manipulating his voice, but as soon as he tries to convey a woman's strength, he reverts back to his natural masculinity.

The above view about the female voice is echoed by another woman writing in favor of actresses in modern plays: playwright and theater critic Hasegawa Shigure.[10] Hasegawa's argument is complex, advocating the use of actresses for modern plays, but the use of *onnagata* in *kabuki* plays: "Old

2.3 Male actors in a performance of Gerhart Hauptmann's *Lonely People. Onnagata* Ichikawa Enjaku as Anna Mahr is pictured on the top left and bottom right. *Engei gahō* (December 1911)

plays [*kyūgeki*], however, should be played by *onnagata* as they have been in the past. This may be just a matter of being caught in old traditions, but since [the art of *onnagata*] has developed to such an extent already, it would break the hard-wrought harmony to introduce actresses at this point."[11] While this view is closest to that of the "eclectic position" (*danjo heichi ron*) discussed later, Hasegawa also stresses that for "modern plays [*kindai geki*] that portray women living in the self-awareness of a new age, the actress is absolutely necessary."[12] Hasegawa points out that there are two instances in which *onnagata* simply cannot measure up to actresses: One is vocal, the other is visual. The first instance refers to plays that require singing: Unlike the chanting of the *kabuki* theater, where a stylized male voice has been accepted as portraying femininity, in Western-style songs the male voice cannot be disguised. The other instance encompasses plays that require Western dress: Unlike the long-sleeved kimono, a dress would reveal the large hands and feet of *onnagata,* and, as Hasegawa puts it, "seeing that, one's enthusiasm fades."[13] The more body parts are exposed in a performance, then, the more advantage accrues to the actress.

These and related arguments in favor of introducing women to the stage reveal the assumption that there is some kind of essential femaleness that is naturally expressed by a woman through her body and her voice, and that the straightforward expression of such essence is the basis for a woman's liberation as well as the basis for her theatrical portrayal of such liberated women. A straight line is drawn from what is understood to be woman's essential nature, through what is described as a natural expression, to the performance on stage. Womanliness is the basis and starting point of this performance, rather than the result or end point of performance. The body is both the medium of this expression as well as the locus of woman's essential difference from man.

Now we turn to the adversaries of actresses. Those who argued that actresses are unnecessary usually based their judgment on physical criteria, especially the observation that women, specifically Japanese women, lacked the physiological and congenital qualities necessary to perform on stage. Japanese women were said to be too short, their voices too soft, their hips too large and unshapely.[14] Others added that Japanese women's noses are too flat, their faces not striking enough, and their gestures not forceful enough.[15]

The speciousness of the biological difference argument can be demonstrated by an argument, actually made during this time, that shifts the focus away from the body and onto the social context. The playwright Mayama Seika, for instance, takes up the issue of the shortness of Japanese women, seen by many critics as an unalterable and therefore incorrigible drawback for women aspiring to act on stage. Instead of focusing on the incorrigible body, however, Mayama looks at what surrounds it. He blames the architectural features of the Japanese stage, with its lateral beams, its great width, and its relatively low ceiling, which trick the audience into always measuring the performer's height against the stage dimensions, and thereby accentuate the shortness of the actress. The solution is to build a different kind of theater with a stage that is tall and not too wide and that is also small enough to benefit from women's softer voices.[16] Another solution is for actresses to learn to disguise their shortness. Just as *onnagata* have learned through long study and training how to disguise their tall physiques, actresses should be able to create the illusion of height, too.[17] But this kind of emphasis on architecture and artistic illusion over physical features was a minority viewpoint. Most anti-actress arguments concurred that "it seems a universal social rule that in general women are inferior to men in appearance."[18]

An even more serious blow against actresses, as described by the anti-actress faction, is that Japanese women's mental and psychological capacities are insufficient for the difficult task of acting. Kojima Koshū mentions the "simple brain operations" (*tanjun na nōryoku*) and "monotonous psychological functioning" (*henka ni toboshii shinteki sayō*) of women, which combine to make them inferior to men:

> An undistinguished role might be best performed by a woman who can seduce the audience with her feminine form [*katachi*] and appearance [*sugata*]. But for a role with a complicated personality, a role requiring portrayal of tormented suffering, or a role animated by intense passion, a woman with her simple brain operations and monotonous psychological functioning could never do justice. These roles would require the artistry of an *onnagata* who has the male's brainpower and psychological functions.[19]

In other words, a woman can look like a woman, but it takes a man to really *act* like a woman!

The most damning verdict against the mental capacities of Japanese women came from novelist Morita Sōhei.[20] Morita believes Japanese women to be lagging behind men "in all abilities" by about five or six centuries.

> For the time being at least, I doubt that any women, not only actresses, could measure up to men. In academics, for example, I do not even dream that women could be compared to men. I cannot help but believe thus, especially when I hear recent reports about grades at the women's universities and so on. Therefore, to make actresses appear together with male actors is like putting two kinds of people of utterly different status on stage together: there is no way it could result in a coherent art.[21]

According to this argument, not only do present-day performances prove that actresses are unable to measure up to *onnagata* in *kabuki* theater, with its long tradition and set patterns, but the fundamental inferiority of women to men would mean that actresses would also inevitably fail in any kind of new play that might be written in the future.

These assertions against the prospect of actresses point to several underlying assumptions: First, women are by nature inferior to men in physical as well as mental qualities; second, women's natural inferiority directly and naturally leads to their inferiority as performers, disqualifying them from the stage. Yet when these assumptions are compared to the assumptions underlying arguments in favor of actresses, certain similarities emerge. Both those arguing for actresses and those arguing against actresses align women with what they are "essentially," "physically" and "naturally."[22] This is set against the male *onnagata*'s "patterns," his "art," or "artifice." The difference is that the pro-actress faction values woman's natural expression, rooted in her body, over the *onnagata*'s artificial one, while the anti-actress faction values the *onnagata*'s superior art over woman's inferior nature, also rooted in her body.

This becomes even clearer in the arguments from the eclectic position. There are those who argue that actresses are good and necessary for some plays but not for others, that *onnagata* are more appropriate for *kabuki* plays. Minaguchi Biyō dismisses this position as pure nonsense: "If actresses are appropriate for the stage, *onnagata* should be abolished entirely; if *onnagata* are sufficient, why go through all the trouble to train actresses?"[23] But many others argue that it is indeed appropriate to use actresses for some plays but a shame to abolish *onnagata* entirely; that *onnagata* are sufficient and appropriate for *kabuki* plays, but that women should be trained for appearances in more modern plays. This had been the gist of Hasegawa Shigure's argument when she declared that *onnagata* were suitable for *kabuki* whereas modern plays called for actresses. Another advocate of eclecticism is novelist Yanagawa Shun'yō: He starts out by declaring boldly, "the question no longer is whether or not to train actresses in our country,"[24] but then goes on to explain why we should stick to *onnagata* for the "old plays" (*kyūgeki*). His view, shared by many others, is that the art of the *onnagata* in *kabuki* has had such a long history and has reached such a refined state that actresses would never be able to measure up, much less surpass it.

Most of the critics advocating eclecticism agree that *onnagata* and actresses should *not* appear on the same stage together. This practice was indeed seen in various theaters at the time, often because of the difficulty of training actresses: *Onnagata* were still needed to fill the minor female roles when not enough actresses were available. Objections by critics of this practice betray the assumption that the *onnagata* may be more skilled, but that the actress would offer a more natural presentation of female roles:

> No matter how good the actress and how skilled the *onnagata,* the two should not appear together on the same stage. They would only undermine each other's strong points, and would only displease the audience. No matter how skilled the *onnagata,* he could not bear comparison if placed side by side with a real woman. That a real woman would more closely resemble a real woman goes without saying.[25]

The *onnagata* might be more skilled, but the actress is more real. Women are to nature as *onnagata* are to art. Both feminist arguments in favor of actresses and misogynist arguments against actresses share this basic assumption.

This essentialist and expressive understanding of gender was a modern one, in contrast to the theatrical and performative understanding of gender exemplified in *kabuki.* Eventually the pro-actress faction overwhelmed the anti-actress faction, yet the victory was an ambivalent one. It confirmed the definition of womanhood as an essence naturally grounded in a woman's body, a definition that would also justify the reduction of woman to *nothing but* her body.

WORSE THAN GEISHA?: SEX AND ACTING

There is another dimension of the actress debate that merits attention: the dimension of the sexual relationship between performers and audience members. For instance, one of the most intriguing arguments in favor of actresses comes from writer Kema Namboku. Admitting that his opinion is "daring" (*daitan*), he proposes that actresses are needed in today's theater because *onnagata* have lost the sexual appeal associated with their profession in the past: "After all," he points out, "in the old days, *onnagata* were male prostitutes [*iroko*]."[26] The context for such prostitution was the custom of male same-sex relations and the close relationship between actors and patrons in the *kabuki* theater. *Onnagata* wore special headgear to disguise their masculine shaved foreheads, as well as kimono with long sleeves like those worn by young women.[27] All this, says Kema, has changed in modern times. Today, *onnagata* have short haircuts and wear western clothes—silk hats and frock coats—in their daily lives, and even when they appear on stage, they seem to lack the long black hair and the soft breasts that the *onnagata* in the past seemed to have. Kema laments "Today's people are more skeptical than people in the past. No one today is as gullible as to think that anyone wearing a long-sleeved kimono is a woman."[28] If *onnagata* insist on cutting their hair short, he concludes, we need actresses to take their place.

This is indeed a "daring" argument. It opens a whole new can of worms, raising questions about the sexual status of impersonators in premodern times, about the status of the feminine characteristics that these impersonators *seemed* to have in the past but have lost in modern times, about the status of the sexual attractiveness of *onnagata* acting like women, which can be replaced by the sexual attractiveness of actresses acting like women.

What is striking, though, is that this can of worms is put away in a closet, as it were, almost as soon as it is opened. Kema's argument is remarkable because it is precisely around this time that the questions he raises are becoming unmentionable, if not unthinkable.[29] An article appearing in the same magazine in the same year, 1912, illustrates this point. In this article, the argument about the sexual attractiveness of actresses is turned around into an argument against allowing women on stage: The writer Nakayama Hakuhō claims that men and women sharing the stage would lead to lewdness either among the performers or among the audience. Nakayama worries about the impact of actresses on morality and decency:

> If an actor and an actress were to take each other's hands on stage, and sit close enough that their knees touch, would not the real sensations of the performers themselves be excited, even before those of the audience? You cannot have a theater with actresses only, but if men and women were to act together, we would not be able to watch it with comfortable interest.[30]

The significant term here is "real sensations" (*jikkan*), the sensations of actual physical arousal that love scenes presented by real men and women on stage would provoke. Another significant phrase is "comfortable interest" (*anshin shita kyōmi*), which implies a state directly opposed to "real sensations." It is a state of interested yet detached appreciation of the scene portrayed, and this is presented as the proper relationship of performer to audience. Nakayama denies the possibility of an all-female theater, which was soon to be actualized in the form of the all-female Takarazuka theater, but leaves the status of the all-male *kabuki* theater unquestioned.[31] Unquestioned also is the status of love scenes in *kabuki* performed by men. In light of Kema Nanboku's opinion, discussed earlier, we might well ask: Are real sensations aroused when *men* act together on stage? Nakayama does not even raise the question, much less answer it, and thus the question of sexuality in premodern theater is put safely away into the closet.

What is revealed in these arguments for and against actresses? One is the shared assumption that overt sexuality may have been part of the attraction of the premodern theater but that modern theater is, or should be, different. The world of *onnagata* as one of male prostitution is seen as the world of old theater, set against the modern theater. And while the old theater is associated with male same-sex relations, the modern theater is associated with the threat, or promise, of heterosexual arousal. Most importantly, while the sexuality of the old theater becomes unmentionable and is eventually disavowed, the sexuality of the new theater becomes an object of constant surveillance and constant incitement.

This is where the "worse than geisha" argument is heard: Actresses are compared to geisha as well as prostitutes and are judged by the degree to which they can differentiate themselves from those women engaged in sex work.[32] Thus Kuwano Tōka, author of a book-length treatise on the actress question, devotes a whole chapter on the question "Are actresses any different from geisha?"[33] He lists the various similarities between actresses and geisha: their lack of education, their loose sexual morals, their dependence on male patrons, their vanity, and their desire to ensnare rich men. In some ways, says Kuwano, actresses are even worse than geisha and are nothing but "high class prostitutes" (*kōtō inbai*) who sell themselves to their patrons.[34] Kuwano concludes:

> Once upon a time, geisha robbed clients away from prostitutes [*baishunfu*] by stooping to their level. Now, retribution is upon them, as geisha lose their

> clients to actresses. The reason that geisha dominated prostitutes in the beginning was that geisha kept up the appearance of not being prostitutes. This appealed to the tastes of hypocritical men of the time. But now, geisha have lost their superficial purity which was their only weapon, and have become no different from prostitutes in name or in fact. Thus their dominance is gradually weakening, and they are being surpassed by actresses, whose superficial purity can still deceive society for a while.[35]

Are actresses better than geisha or worse than prostitutes? Answers vary. What is clear from these documents is that an actress is valued in so far as she can distance herself from sex work, but that she is constantly suspected of being no different from those women who sell sexual performances.

It is significant that this entire debate on actresses is taking place against the background of nation-building. This becomes clear in the arguments of several critics. If, as these critics insist, it goes without saying that a real woman would be better to perform women's roles, why should there be any need for *onnagata?* This is indeed Minaguchi's viewpoint, and he reluctantly admits that the *onnagata* has a bleak future: Considered "from the perspective of the national theater [*kokugeki*] of Japan in the future,"[36] something as unnatural as men acting as women would not be allowed. Minaguchi insists that he is not pro-actress at heart, that personally he believes men to be superior to women in the artistic realm, and that the *onnagata*'s art is unique to Japan and should be shown abroad as well. Minaguchi's tone betrays his aversion to the theater of the future in which it is assumed that men should play men and women play women. He is resigned to lay aside his personal preferences, however, for the sake of the good of the national future. *Onnagata* could survive, he muses, as an antique art (*ko bijutsu*), protected and preserved like the *noh* theater.[37]

A similar tone of reluctant concession pervades writer Kojima Koshū's argument for partial use of actresses. While admitting that actresses should be used in modern plays (*kindai geki*), where female protagonists are often more central, where dialogues are crucial, and where it may be advantageous to have female voices expressing the nuances of female psychology,[38] he casts doubt on the status of such kinds of plays in Japanese society:

> How many people in Tokyo at this moment have any wish to see modern plays? Probably about ten thousand. In a place like Osaka, probably less than one thousand. Thus, modern plays are part of a limited problem concerning only those few who want to see progressive [*shimpo shita*] plays like those performed in the West [*taisei*], or those few who are making great efforts to perform these plays in Japan.[39]

Although Kojima uses the language of the enlightened intellectual impatiently waiting for the nation to come to its senses—"How long will Japanese theater maintain its status quo? When will the majority of Japanese spectators open their eyes and start singing the praises of the so-called modern play?"[40]—his tone suggests that his sympathies may lie elsewhere. Kojima concludes that while actresses may be necessary for modern plays centering on dialogue, for the present and near future, *onnagata* will be more valued than the actress.

All the opinions surveyed so far have one trait in common: They assume that men and women are fundamentally different and that difference is fixed at the level of the body by nature. This assumption underlies both the argument that women should perform women's roles because for a man to do so would be unnatural, and the argument that women should *not* perform because they are naturally and physically inferior to men. And while the argument in favor of actresses privileges the naturally female body over the artifice of performances by *onnagata,* and the argument in favor of *onnagata* reverses this hierarchy by privileging the skill of the *onnagata* over the physical characteristics of the female body, the fundamental premise remains the same: The *onnagata* is aligned with art and performance, the actress with nature and the body.

The assumptions structuring the actress debates reveal a specifically modern definition of theater—as the performance and reception of dramas that express inner meanings through transparent signifiers—and a modern definition of woman—as a stable category based on the alignment of biological sexual difference, social gendering, and heterosexual coupling. Although the categories of modern theater and modern woman are inherently unstable and mutually imbricated, the effort to separate them and stabilize them has called for repeated acts of coercion, exclusion, and violence, and therein lies the significance of uncovering the historicity of these categories.

THE MODERN FORMATION OF WOMAN: FROM PERFORMANCE TO BODY

The formation of modern categories of gender and performance should be seen as a contentious process that took place in the decades following 1868, decades shaped by the effort to build a nation-state that would not only resist being colonized by the West but would itself become a colonizer of other nations. On the one hand, gender was produced and regulated as a fixed category through medical discourse about biological sexual difference, as well as legal and political codes such as those forbidding crossdressing and those excluding women from participation in politics. This went hand in hand with the institution of the norm of heterosexuality, a norm that both assumed and constituted the binary division between men and women. Such a norm was consolidated through the pathologizing of homosexuality as "perverse" and "unnatural," supported by the translation of European writings on sexology and the influx of Christian religious influence.

It can be argued that before the Meiji period, what we now think of as biological sex and cultural gender were aligned radically differently from today.[41] For instance, in an eighteenth-century treatise on proper behavior for women, *Onna daigaku,* biological motherhood counts for little in the definition of ideal femininity. If a wife is unable to have children, for example, she can adopt the child of her husband's mistress. Biological motherhood is not crucial to a woman, since its absence does not necessarily threaten the status of the wife, and its presence does not necessarily elevate the status of the mistress. Further, the absence of physical capability for biological motherhood does not prevent anyone, including a man, from being able to represent ideal femininity. If anything, the capacity for biological motherhood is associated with lack of femininity: Female sex does not guarantee feminine gender, and might indeed be antithetical to it. This is why some scholars conclude that during this period, "Sex was perceived as subordinate to gender."[42] This is in stark contrast to the modern definition of woman, shaped in the period under investigation here, in which *gender is perceived as subordinate to sex,* the former derived from the latter and grounded on it. Before the modern period, feminine gender was thought to be achieved by subordinating the female sex, by training and cultivating the body to match the ideal of femininity. And that ideal of femininity could be represented by a man acting like a woman, the *onnagata* of the *kabuki* theater.

By contrast, medical and scientific discourse during the Meiji period emphasized the physical basis for the difference between men and women. In 1875 (Meiji 8), the first translation of a European scientific text on sexual difference was published, and the next two decades saw the publication of over a hundred texts on sexology, including translations, adaptations, academic treatises, and popular guidebooks.[43] Many of these books would start with a description of male and female sexual organs, move on to discuss sexual desire, and the mechanism of conception and childbirth, and would often include an injunction against masturbation.[44] After surveying various sexological writings from the 1870s to the 1890s, feminist scholar Ueno Chizuko summarizes how the diverse kinds of Meiji discourse on men and women became homogenized by the 1890s:

> Among the theories of gender of this period, what eventually won out was the "theory of different rights for men and women" [*danjo iken*], or at best the theory of "equal status with a difference" [*sai aru byōdō*].[45] This argument, which legitimizes the sexual division of labor inside and outside the home under the guise of scientific principles, was not to be questioned for another century.[46]

Thus, what became hegemonic was the idea that the gendered division of labor is grounded in scientifically observable sexual difference.

The question of whether or not there "really exists" biological sexual difference between men and women has always been embroiled in gender ideology. Biological research is not free from cultural bias, and the language of biology reproduces cultural assumptions about gender. For this reason, feminist scientists have claimed that the question of purely biological, noncultural sexual difference is unanswerable.[47] For the purpose of my argument here it suffices to say that it was at this point in history that the *discourse of biological sexual difference* between men and women became predominant in Japan, and this served to create the category of "woman." Biological sexual difference became aligned with other kinds of difference, but then it was seen as the natural basis for treating women as a category of bodies that are different from and inferior to male bodies.

Along with medical and scientific discourse about biological sexual difference, legal, educational, and political discourse all contributed to a gendering of the social sphere. Historians have pointed out that in the Edo period preceding 1868, it was social class, rather than gender, that most strongly defined a person's status in society.[48] The new government after 1868 ostensibly "leveled" the class hierarchy, unifying the general populace into one class of "common people" (*heimin*). At the same time, the government started issuing various laws and pronouncements that addressed women in all classes, differentiating them from men.[49] This is of course not to suggest that class hierarchies ceased to exist and to powerfully shape people's experiences; nonetheless, it is significant that in the Meiji period, legal, political, educational, and other discourses installed a category of woman that would cut across class differentiations.

For example, the strict dress codes that prevailed in Edo society, detailing clothing and hairstyles allowed for each class, were no longer applicable. The government encouraged Western dress and short haircuts for all men for the sake of progress and civilization. When some women decided to cut their hair, however, the government responded swiftly, outlawing short hair for women in 1872. This double movement shows that the government was promoting the construction of a certain kind of a modern national subject, but that this subject was assumed to be male. All men might henceforth be equal in theory, but women were a different story. The same law of 1872 made it illegal for men to dress like women and for women to dress like men, thus drawing a stricter line between the genders.[50]

To say that the government promoted the construction of a modern national subject that was assumed to be male is not to say that women were ignored by the government, but that its policies became explicitly gendered in the 1880s and 1890s.[51] Another powerful way to construct "women" as a category was the educational system. Four years of elementary education were made mandatory for all children in 1872, but in a move structurally parallel to the banning of short hair for women, in 1879, the education ministry decided to institutionalize women's education as separate from men's education beyond the elementary level. In 1899, each prefecture was ordered to establish at least one higher school for girls, and these schools adopted a curriculum stressing the domestic arts. The educational policy was to produce the "good wife, wise mother" (*ryōsai kenbo*), identifying the role of women as helpmates and reproducers of the loyal male subjects of the nation-state.[52]

The ideology of women as "good wives, wise mothers" was now used to justify the explicit exclusion of all women from politics. Whereas previously there had been various venues for women to participate in local politics, depending on their different positions in society, now, women were prohibited from participating directly in the political process yet were expected to contribute to the nation indirectly by serving the men in their lives. Starting in 1890, women were barred from political meetings and from forming political organizations.[53] These legal, educational, and political discourses produced and controlled a category of "woman" that cut across all classes and that was set in opposition to "man."

The third aspect of the formation of the category of woman can be located in the realm of sexuality. Scholars such as Furukawa Makoto and Gregory Pflugfelder have pointed out that up until the 1900s, male-male sexual relations in Japan were regarded under an interpretive code of "male love" (*nanshoku*), which is quite different from the code of homosexuality in Westernized modernity. "Male love" was not condemned as unnatural or immoral; it was on equal terms with "female love," and there were sustained debates about the merits of each. Male-male sexual behavior was something that a man might engage in for various reasons at various moments in his life: It coexisted with heterosexual behavior.[54]

In the Meiji period, the introduction of Western medicine, sexology, and Christian dogma brought with it the idea that homosexuality is unnatural and pathological. By the end of Meiji, male homosexuality was interpreted through the code of "perverse sexual desire," and this marginalizing and pathologizing of male homosexuality went hand in hand with a new emphasis on heterosexuality. Monogamous marriage between husband and wife became the new ideal and the proper conduit for sexuality, promoted through the popular sexology texts mentioned earlier. This new norm of heterosexuality both assumed and constituted the binary division of gender. In other words, by positing heterosexuality as the norm, the division between male and female became absolute, and by positing the natural division and complementarity between male and female, heterosexuality became normalized. Thus it became "self-evident" that a woman is a woman, that one cannot act like a woman unless one is a woman, and that even if one does act like a woman, one cannot really be a woman unless one really is a woman.

In this way, the performative dimension was purged from the definition of gender. Of course, as the very existence of debates concerning "acting like a woman" indicates, and as the more recent theatrical as well as theoretical renaissance of interest in "gender as performance" illustrates, this dimension could never be purged completely. Let us then look a little further into the relationship between theater and gender definitions.

One of the more visible signs of the changing definition of "woman" in the modern period is the change in the basis for what is considered ideal feminine beauty. This change corresponds to a shift in the site of definition of femininity from performance to the body. In the Edo period, the ideal of womanhood was represented by performance: the *onnagata* in *kabuki* theater who specializes in women's roles.[55] Various scholars have pointed out that the pictorial representation of the late Edo period hardly distinguishes between the beauty of women and the beauty of young boy actors. In woodblock prints they are depicted with the same kinds of facial features and with the same kinds of hairstyles and clothes, the contours of their bodies concealed beneath layers of kimono. Often it is only the title of the print that distinguishes women from *onnagata*. The feminine beauty of the *onnagata* had little to do with the anatomical body of the actor; it had everything to do with the way he dressed, moved, gestured, and danced—in short, with the way he performed.[56] And women, especially those in the pleasure quarters, imitated the *onnagata*'s performance as the ideal of feminine beauty, copying his kimono patterns, his hairstyle, his carefully contrived gestures.

In the decades following 1868, changes in clothing from kimono to Western-style dress helped shift the focus of feminine beauty from performance to the physical body. Western dress not only revealed the contours of the wearer, but it exposed hitherto hidden body parts such as the arms and the legs as well. In general, it seemed to draw attention to the body beneath the surface. In the 1910s, the popularization of cinema also contributed to the shift of focus: Cinematic close-ups of *onnagata* drew attention to body parts hitherto concealed through movement and distance, such as the prominent Adam's apple and the bony hands.[57] The visibility of the *onnagata*'s body contributed to the *onnagata*'s downfall: No longer disguised through clothing, movement, and distance, he lost the ability to achieve the ideal of feminine beauty and was replaced by the actress, whose body now became the privileged sign of womanhood. The 1629 ban on women acting on stage was rescinded in 1891, and actresses gradually began to gain prominence.

It ought to be noted that women had continued to perform even after the ban of 1629. There were women who were hired to perform plays and to teach song and dance to the ladies in the mansions of feudal lords (*okyōgenshi*), and there were even small troupes of female *kabuki* players (*onna yakusha*) at the margins of the theater world in the Tokugawa period.[58] After the Meiji Restoration, some of the former *okyōgenshi* who lost their feudal patronage turned to acting on the public stage. The most celebrated was Ichikawa Kumehachi, who apprenticed with the famous *kabuki* actor Ichikawa Danjūrō IX, learned most of his repertoire, which consisted of heroic male roles, and became known as "lady Danjūrō." In a later twist that illustrates the endless circle of citation of performed femininity, Kumehachi's performances became the model for the impersonation of female roles by male actors in *shimpa:* Famous *shimpa onnagata* such as Kitamura Rokurō idolized her and copied her speech patterns.[59]

Geisha comprised another group of performing women who persisted after the ban of 1629. And geisha, because of their training in music and dance, found themselves interpellated to the public stage as the demand for actresses became increasingly louder. In November of 1891 (Meiji 24), a mere three months after the rescinding of the ban against women's performance, the Seibikan troupe led by Ii Yōhō staged the first "male and female co-production reform theater" (*danjo gōdō kairyō engeki*). Six women, all former geisha, participated in this 15-day run. Yoda Gakkai, a theater reformer who advocated abolishing *onnagata,* was the advisor to the troupe and wrote the *kabuki*-style play that they performed. Chitose Beiha, one of the geisha, continued to appear in a few other performances, but the Seibikan theater quickly folded due to internal squabbling. None of the women performers were heard from much thereafter.

The figures of Ichikawa Kumehachi, Chitose Beiha, and other women like them represent an important subplot in the story about the rise of actresses in modern Japan. Significantly, women like Ichikawa Kumehachi and Chitose Beiha were usually called "female players" (*onna yakusha*) or "female actors" *(onna haiyū*), but hardly ever "actresses" (*joyū*).[60] This difference is not trivial: *Onna yakusha* and *onna haiyū* imply that the standard actor (*yakusha, haiyū*) is male and that the female (*onna*) variant is an aberration or an imitation. That terms such as "*otoko yakusha*" or "*otoko haiyū*" are never used for male (*otoko*) actors further supports this asymmetry. *Joyū,* on the other hand, is symmetrical, at least lexically, with *danyū,* the male counterpart.

Thus it is Kawakami Sadayakko, or alternatively Matsui Sumako, rather than any "female players" or "female actors" before them, who are considered by most theater historians to have been the first generation of actresses. This suggests that the definition of actress involves more than a woman performing.[61] The rise of the actress involves not only a shift in performers' sex from male to female, but also a shift in performance convention itself, as well as a shift in the characteristics of the performed feminine gender. It is because they acted in new kinds of plays, different from *kabuki* plays, and because they represented new kinds of women in these plays that Kawakami Sadayakko and Matsui Sumako are considered the first generation actresses.

THE MODERN FORMATION OF THEATER: FROM SHIBAI TO ENGEKI

In the years between the 1860s and the 1910s, there occurred a shift in the realm of theater as well, a shift that interacted with the formation of "woman" and prepared the way for the emergence of actresses. This shift can be roughly labeled as the shift from "*shibai*"[62] to "*engeki,*"[63] or from the theater before modernity to the theater of modernity.[64] "*Shibai*" literally translates as " being on the lawn," referring to the fact that premodern performances often took place on lawns adjacent to temples and shrines. In defining "*shibai,*" some scholars have pointed to the coalescence of locale, theater building, and performance, as well as to a mode of experiencing theater that involves multiple senses, such as drinking, eating, smoking, conversing with neighbors, hanging out with actors, and occasionally paying attention to the proceedings on stage.[65] "*Engeki,*" in contrast, literally means "extending drama," and carries with it connotations emphasizing the literary aspects of the play and the mimetic aspects of acting it out. The shift from "*shibai*" to "*engeki,*" then, is a process of localizing and narrowing in temporal and physical scope, of shifting from theater as a participatory experience that involves multiple senses to theater as a text to be read aloud on stage and heard in silence by audience. The chapters that follow will trace some of the most salient aspects of the formation of theater in Japanese modernity, delineating the process of "straightening" and the crystallizing of the later ideology of the "New Theater."

In order to analyze the shift to the modern definitions of theater, however, the definition of "early modern" theater needs to be clarified and refined first. Charting the shift from medieval to early modern theater will allow us to go further in charting the shift from early modern to modern theater. For instance, theater historian Moriya Takeshi discusses the formation of two characteristic elements of the performing arts of the early modern period, covering the two and a half centuries from 1603 to the 1868: the "show business" (*kōgyō*) system and the "school master" (*iemoto*) system.[66] These two systems are analyzed as interlocking systems that share the same material base and provide evidence of the formation of a mass society in early modern Japan.

The "show business" (*kōgyō*) system is defined as "a system in which performers without specified patrons perform their arts in a specified place with the aim of profit, and in which an unspecified audience may attend the performances by paying money."[67] In other words, the system includes the existence of a group of *performers* not bound to specific patrons, as in the medieval period, but earning profit through their performances; a population of *theatergoers* with the money and leisure necessary to pay for performances as entertainment rather than being invited or obligated to attend them as part of political or religious rites; and a specific and at least semipermanent *facility* set aside for performances rather than the makeshift stages of the medieval period. Moriya likens the "show business" system to a store in which performances can be bought as if they were commodities. The semipermanent space specifically set aside for performances was called "*shibai*," and Moriya notes that a publication in 1825 lists 132 such facilities, distributed widely in the major towns of the archipelago.

The "*iemoto*" system, on the other hand, is defined as "a system in which a certain number of teachers are employed to educate students in the arts, following a unified curriculum, awarding licenses with fees according to the level of the progress of the students, and in which the students feel these licenses to be valuable."[68] This system involves the existence of performers who no longer aim to advance their own artistry but primarily function as *teachers;* a population of *students* with the time and money to choose to become students in these arts; and a *space* within the homes of townspeople where the arts can be practiced and displayed. In other words, this system is most similar to that of a school, in which performance art is treated like a skill that can be studied by anyone. The room set aside in the homes of townspeople was called "*zashiki*" (tatami-lined room), and Moriya points out that the formation of the *iemoto* system depended on the "material apparatus"(*busshitsu teki na sōchi*) that made possible the installation of tatami-lined rooms, specifically the change from wooden roofs to shingled roofs that keep out rain.[69]

It is the public half of the interlocking system that interests us in particular: the "show business" system of public production of the performing arts (*gekijō geinō*), which is also often metonymically called "*shibai,*" according to the performance facility that characterizes it. The *iemoto* system, on the other hand, is a realm of private learning and enjoyment of the arts (*shitsunai geinō*), and while not unimportant for the formation of the modern theater, its function is more mediated and indirect. To summarize, the three most salient aspects of *shibai* were the ambivalent status of the actor at the margins of social order, the location of the performance in a theater building within a special district set aside for the theater, and the implication of multisensory pleasure in the theatergoing experience. Chapter 4 and chapter 7 will deal with how these aspects would shift in modern theater. The status of actors would change to that of a professional with special skills, the performance would become a spatially and temporally bounded event, cut off from the milieu of the pleasure quarters, and the theatergoing experience would change to that of a silent communion with the interior meaning of a play.

This, then, was the situation of the theater in 1868, when the event known as the Meiji Restoration created the conditions of possibility for the formation of the "modern" theater. Theatrical performance in post - 1868 Japan was targeted by repeated attempts—initiated by government officials, business leaders, intellectuals, and theater practitioners themselves—to purge it of sex, prostitution, and other unsavory elements that would detract from its purpose as cultural showcase and pedagogical institution for the modern nation-state.[70] The modern theater was to be an exalted theater based on inner essences, expressed and perceived through the transparent significations of the actors' voices and bodies. Such transparency was to be guaranteed by reforms in acting techniques and the language of dramas, and transparency also required the replacement of *onnagata* by actresses, because acting like a woman was now only possible for a "real woman." The stability of the categories of gender and performance could only be maintained by repeated sanctions, enforcing particular definitions of womanhood or theater and excluding all deviating definitions. And yet the very fact that such repeated acts of coercion and exclusion were needed perhaps points to the inherent instability of the categories and divisions and perhaps suggests the fundamental imbrication of gender and performance.

Part II

Kawakami Sadayakko

Chapter 3

WIFEING THE WOMAN

WHO WAS KAWAKAMI SADAYAKKO?

Kawakami Sadayakko is conventionally portrayed as a woman who stole the stage by accident.[1] She is pictured as a woman who became an actress under duress, who had neither much training nor talent in acting, and whose success can be attributed mostly to her relationships with powerful men. In the standard texts of Japanese theater history, she is dispatched in a few lines. She is usually mentioned, briefly and nonchalantly, as arguably having been Japan's first actress in the modern period, and certainly the first to gain recognition outside of Japan. Her name is usually subsumed under that of her husband, Kawakami Otojirō.[2]

For example, in a volume entitled *The Complete History of Japanese Theater* (Nihon engeki zenshi), references to Sadayakko are sprinkled sparsely in a chapter that pays close attention to the "Achievements of Kawakami," by which is meant those of Kawakami Otojirō. These references are reticent when it comes to Sadayakko's contributions to theater history. Her early success in the United States and Europe are dismissed easily:

> [B]y displaying dubious pseudo *kabuki* [*iikagen na kabuki magai no mono*] to foreign countries, Kawakami's and his wife Sadayakko's names became famous; yet we can perceive no meaningful achievements, and it may be more accurate to say that they rather embarrassed themselves [*haji o sarashite kita*].[3]

Her role as pioneering actress in modern Japan is also often elided in these references, and attention is shifted to what came after her:

> The word "actress" is conventionally applied beginning with the Actress Training Institute, which Kawakami Sadayakko opened and then handed over

> to the Imperial Theater. But it is Matsui Sumako who should properly be called the pioneering actress [*senkuteki joyū*] of the new age, since the Imperial Theater's main purpose was *kabuki* training.[4]

Thus Sadayakko, who launched the Actress Training Institute but was herself not trained by it, is deftly excluded from the group signified by the word "actress." She is also seen as belonging to the world of *kabuki* rather than to the modern theater of the "new age."

In theater history and women's history, Kawakami Sadayakko is a figure at the margins, a glamorous but distracting footnote. A closer look at this footnote, however, reveals a more complicated and interesting picture. Two processes, the modern formation of gender and the modern formation of performance, operate in and around the figure of this actress, defining the context and manner in which the figure speaks to us. The term *figure* is appropriate here, since we are dealing with representations and reminiscences outside of which Kawakami Sadayakko is not available to us. Even accounts that present themselves as the most authentic are shaped in a particular way, and shape the figure of Sadayakko in a particular way while presenting her to us.

For example, the chapter on Sadayakko in a theater historian's *Genealogy of Actresses* (Joyū no keizu) starts with a description of how the writer visited the Yoshichō pleasure quarter district, where Sadayakko used to work as a geisha.[5] Interviews with old geisha take up much space in the subsequent account, and the account as a whole conveys less about Sadayakko the actress than about the writer's familiarity with the milieu of the pleasure quarters and his nostalgia for a now-lost part of Tokyo. Another historian's aptly titled *An Anecdotal History of Modern Japanese Actresses* (Monogatari kindai Nihon joyū shi) begins with reminiscences of the writer's elementary school days when he lived across the street from the mansion of Fukuzawa Momosuke, Sadayakko's patron and lover, and how as a young boy he always wondered about the existence of a small theater building on the premises.[6] Having established the sense of long-standing acquaintance with his subject, the historian assembles an anecdotal history of Sadayakko's life from various sources, including *Genealogy of Actresses* cited above. Sadayakko's biographies thus often evolve into conglomerations of myths and rumors.

And yet, a closer look at these various representations and reminiscences of her and *by* her reveal the tensions and contradictions produced by the modern formations of gender and performance. These tensions and contradictions show us the limits of the modern formations in which we are still trapped, and paying attention to them allows us to situate Kawakami Sadayakko at the intersection of major changes occurring in Meiji Japan: changes in the role of women in society, the role of theater in the nation, and the role of Japan in the world.

This chapter considers various responses to Sadayakko's life in order to highlight the tension between the feminine ideal of the "good wife, wise mother" and Sadayakko's stubborn refusal to conform to this ideal—an ideal that emerges and begins to become dominant in her lifetime, shaping biographical representations of her both during her lifetime and after. The next chapter analyzes Kawakami Sadayakko's involvement in the movement to modernize theater, and to create what was called "straight theater" (*seigeki*). Although this movement is described by historians as her husband Kawakami Otojirō's main achievement, Sadayakko's involvement as an actress was an inextricable, though ambivalent, part of process. Chapter 5 investigates Kawakami Sadayakko's performances in various plays, both inside and outside Japan. These performances both embodied and contributed to the process of Japanese nation-building and empire-building, a process for which theater was a showcase as well as pedagogical tool.

WIFEING AND THE IDEOLOGY OF THE GOOD WIFE, WISE MOTHER

Here, I would like to introduce a new term that captures the contradictory and contentious process of the definition of woman as gender. I will call this process "the wifeing of woman." Many scholars have elucidated the ideology of "good wife, wise mother," which was adopted as state educational policy in the 1890s, and which, many argue, persists to the present day.[7] The "good wife, wise mother" ideology was initially an ideal that affirmed the importance of women within the family. In contrast to Confucian ideology, which saw women as "borrowed wombs" for the purpose of bearing male heirs to the household, the recognition of women's roles as wives and mothers was a progressive ideal. It soon became a narrow and oppressive ideology, however, institutionalized in the legal codes and inculcated through the education system. It defined womanhood in narrow terms, controlled women's behavior and their energies, and marginalized those who failed to fit the ideal.

It has been pointed out that the Meiji state actually focused more on motherhood than on wifehood as the crucial function for Japanese women.[8] Although it is this motherhood ideology that has been most lucidly critiqued by feminists as continuing to the present day,[9] my focus here is on the less-discussed "wifehood" aspect. What I call "wifeing" is a view that defines women always in relation to the "ideal wife" position and that regards women as complementary to men and ultimately incomplete without men.

Historian Vera Mackie points out a similar phenomenon with regard to women who joined the socialist movement in modern Japan: "While women in mainstream society were constructed as helpmates to the militarist state, women in the socialist movement were constructed as 'wives,' as supporters of male activists, who were addressed in gender-specific ways in socialist writings."[10] Even women who were not actually married to male socialists were metaphorically called "wives." Though evidence suggests that many young women in fact came to participate in the socialist movement on their own, accounts of these women tend to describe their activities as having been shaped by familial, romantic, or marital relations with socialist men, and "this emphasis on familial connections tends to obscure the independent political commitment of many of these women."[11]

It is my contention that this ideology of wifeing, which became dominant during Kawakami Sadayakko's lifetime, continues to shape up to the present day the manner in which the actress is perceived and portrayed in theater history books and in biographies. Both those writing about Sadayakko as a contemporary as well as those writing about her as a historical figure tend to measure her against the ideal wife in a lifelong monogamous heterosexual union: virginal before marriage; faithful to her husband in marriage; and chaste as a widow after his death. Yet Sadayakko's life did not fit this mold at all. Her life seems almost deliberately designed to contradict it: She was a geisha with numerous patrons before her marriage; she became a popular actress while being married and was seen as sexually suspect due to her profession; she did not bear any children, although she adopted two children later in life; and finally, after her husband's death, she became the mistress of a former patron. In the failure, or refusal, of Sadayakko's life to fit the mold of the "good wife, wise mother," in the tension between the process of wifeing and the irrepressible abundance of social and sexual liaisons that characterized Sadayakko's life, we may glimpse the contradictions inherent in the process of gendering the modern nation-state.

THREE ROLES OF GEISHA, ACTRESS, MISTRESS

Geisha, actress, and mistress—these are the three consecutive occupations, all situated at the margins of society, that comprised Sadayakko's life.[12] As an actress she joined the ranks of the former "river-bed beggars," but even before and after her career as an actress she was located at the edge of bourgeois respectability, first as geisha and later as mistress to a married man. These three occupational roles were not only marginal in themselves, but the boundaries between them and the boundaries between each of them and adjacent social categories were permeable. Hence, much anxiety circulated among these categories and along these boundaries.

For example, a geisha is considered to be better than a prostitute (*shōfu*) because she presumably sells her performance rather than her body, but she is

3.1 Kawakami Sadayakko as a wife, bottom right, with Kawakami Otojirō on top. *Engei gahō* (October 1908).

not considered a full-fledged artist (*geijutsuka*) because presumably her body is also on sale to select customers. Thus a geisha needs to constantly distinguish herself from a prostitute while at the same time maintaining a pose of sexual availability not ostensibly required of an artist. An actress (*joyū*) is often seen as not much different from a geisha and is in direct competition with actors who impersonate female roles (*onnagata*). Thus an actress needs to distinguish herself from a geisha by emphasizing her art over their sexual appeal while at the same time proving herself superior to the *onnagata* by emphasizing her natural sex over his artifice. A mistress is in a more secure position than a geisha, but her status is less secure than that of the legal wife (*seisai*). Thus a mistress needs to defend her position against both the short-term competition from a geisha and the long-term confrontation with the legal wife.

The geisha occupies a marginal and elusive position in Meiji social hierarchy.[13] While ostensibly making a living by relying on conversational and artistic skills to entertain men at teahouses, they were also expected to have financial and sexual arrangements with steady patrons. Some historians go so far as to say that there were no fundamental differences between geisha and prostitutes, except that geisha were more expensive.[14] Like registered prostitutes, many geisha were sold into the business; the manager bought them from their families for a lump sum advance that had to be worked off by the woman. If a geisha was lucky, her debt would be paid off by a wealthy patron, and she could retire from the business as his mistress or wife. If not, she would continue to work and struggle to maintain her clients. There were derogatory expressions such as "tumbling geisha" (*korobi geisha*) or "indiscriminate tumbler" (*mizuten*) for geisha who sold their sexual services easily, but some have suggested that this was simply a tactic on the part of the employers to sell the sexual services of their "non-tumbling" geisha at a higher price. Scarcity raises the price of a commodity: A geisha could become more expensive by being marketed as difficult to attain sexually. When a commodity is more expensive and less accessible, its buyers tend to come from higher social and economic ranks, and some of the geisha became mistresses and even wives of high-ranking government officials and business leaders in the Meiji period. This in turn raised the status of the geisha, which raised their price further.

In 1888, the year after Sadayakko started working, over 10,000 geisha were registered in the whole nation; they came in different ranks and price-ranges, but the upper ranks were prized as accomplished and expensive commodities. Sadayakko belonged to the Yoshichō group of geisha, second in ranking after the Yanabashi and Shimbashi group. The price of a geisha from the Yoshichō district was 50 sen to 80 sen, about 50–80 percent of the cost of monthly tuition at Tokyo University.[15] Like all geisha, Sadayakko was trained in the performing arts: song, dance, playing instruments. The geisha in Meiji thus combined the elements of sexual circulation and artistic occupation but could not be reduced to either. She is located between the prostitute and the actress, more valued for artistry than the former, but less than the latter. She is also located between the prostitute and mistress, circulating less than the former, but more than the latter.

The status of mistress, which Sadayakko entered in her later years, was also changing. Until 1883, a mistress (*gonsai*) was recognized legally as having the same status as wife, a situation that was finally changed due to pressures from enlightenment intellectuals and feminist activists in favor of monogamy and wifeing. The practice of men of means keeping mistresses continued, however, with the legal status of the kept woman now less certain. When Sadayakko became the mistress of the business tycoon Fukuzawa Momosuke, she transgressed against the wifely ideal in two ways: She gave up her own status as legal widow of Kawakami Otojirō, and she entered into direct competition with Fukuzawa Momosuke's legal wife. As mistress, Sadayakko may have been financially secure, but she was in a socially and discursively unstable situation.

If these three categories of geisha, actress, and mistress are charged with ambiguity, then one can easily imagine that a woman who moved through all three categories would present a biographer with interesting challenges. Reading the various narrative representations of Sadayakko's life, one notices that it is indeed around these three categories that some of the most intriguing interpretive differences emerge. In particular, one notices diverging explications of Sadayakko's alleged motives in proceeding from one stage of life to another: from geisha to actress, from actress to mistress. Much rhetorical energy is expended in making these transitions seem natural, psychologically motivated, and logically coherent. It is in those places that one detects the stresses of trying to fit Sadayakko's life into a developing paradigm of feminine ideal, the stresses of wifeing. Significantly enough, the role of "wife" does not receive special attention in these biographies because it is not considered an occupation. Wifehood is the unquestioned ground on which the various roles of Sadayakko are played out, and against which they are compared.

FOUR QUESTIONS ON LOVE AND ACTING

The most controversial aspects of Sadayakko's life, as described by the biographers, can thus be condensed into the following questions and answers. Question 1: Why did she marry Kawakami Otojirō? Question 2: Why did she become Fukuzawa Momosuke's mistress after her husband's death? Question 3: Why did she start acting? Question 4: Why did she stop acting?

The first two questions concern her "private life" or relationships with men, the last two questions concern her "public life" or acting career. As will be explained below, the first two questions are often answered in a way that explains Sadayakko's life through the logic of romantic love; the last two questions are often answered in a way that subordinates her acting career to that of her husband. Moreover, all four questions arise out of the process of "wifeing" in which the biographers attempt to fit Sadayakko's life into a neat narrative of lifelong heterosexual monogamous union. And all four questions obscure the material conditions motivating and constraining a woman's choices in the Meiji period. Instead, the questions are answered by ascribing explanatory force to internal psychological feelings. As a result of the rhetorical emphasis on these questions and as a consequence of the efforts to answer them through recourse to psychological rather than material motives, Sadayakko's career is obscured from our view. Her life is discussed in terms of her private relations to men, and her performances are discounted because of her initial reluctance to act in public. The following biography will show how the process of wifeing works.

The subject of our biography was born as Koyama Sada, the twelfth child of a Tokyo merchant in 1871 (Meiji 4). At age seven, she was adopted by Hamada Kame, a former geisha who managed a geisha house in the Yoshichō district in Tokyo. There is some difference of opinion as to why Sada became a geisha. Either she was "sold" to the geisha house by her parents, like many female children of impoverished households, or she was somehow attracted to the world of geisha as a child and requested to be adopted by Hamada Kame. Depending on which explanation is accepted by the biographer, Hamada Kame is portrayed as either a shrewd businesswoman or an affectionate surrogate-mother. In 1887 (Meiji 20), at the age of 16, Sada became a full-fledged geisha, with the nickname "Yakko." It is said that Itō Hirobumi, who was then prime minister, was her first patron and sexual partner. It is at this point that the biography shades into mythology, since matters such as patronage of geisha are not on public record. Yakko became quite famous in the pleasure district, due to her good looks and her taste for "Western" and "masculine" activities such as horseback riding and swimming in the ocean. She is also said to have had numerous lovers, among them the best *kabuki* actors and *sumō* wrestlers of the time.

She met and married Kawakami Otojirō, an actor performing political and satirical skits, sometime around 1890 or 1891—the biographies differ slightly on exactly when. It is said that at this point she was already involved with a young student named Iwasaki Momosuke: This affair fell apart when Momosuke married the daughter of Fukuzawa Yukichi, a prominent entrepreneur and intellectual. As Fukuzawa's son-in-law, Momosuke was sent abroad to study, and broke off relations with the geisha for the time being. After Otojirō's death in 1911 (Meiji 44), however, Sadayakko became Momosuke's mistress.

This is where the first set of questions arises: Why did Sadayakko marry Kawakami Otojirō? And why did she become Fukuzawa Momosuke's mistress 20 years later? In answering the first question, most critics would like to prove that Sadayakko married Otojirō because she was in love with him.[16] A typical account depicts the geisha feeling attracted to the young actor's passionate disposition and his masculinity: When contrasted with this "wild and virile" man, her other lovers, such as the *onnagata* Nakamura Fukusuke, rapidly lost their charm.[17] Others counter that the marriage was motivated by more complex factors. For example, one text represents Sadayakko as marrying Otojirō out of spite, because she was spurned by Fukuzawa Momosuke.

Did she or did she not truly love him? This becomes the crucial question. This question, however, hides other kinds of questions. One might argue that the vocabulary of romantic love as well as the vocabulary of psychology disguises the material forces that would motivate a geisha's marriage. After all, the fate of a geisha who cannot find someone to marry her and thus buy her off at an early age was quite predictable: decline of popularity with advance in years, high likelihood of infection by venereal disease, and eventual destitution in old age. Becoming a mistress was a common option, but it had the disadvantage of lower social status and little legal protection. Marriage was the prize sought after by most geisha, as a ticket that not only gave them a way out of their social condition but also promised them the best chance of a secure position in the years to come. These material considerations are apparent in Sadayakko's own explanation of her marriage:

> It was in Meiji 23 (1890) that I married Otojirō. I was at that time a geisha in Yoshichō, working under the name of Yakko. So some may think that it was one of those affairs between an actor and a geisha, and that we just hitched up, but that was certainly not the case. I was in fact brought to the Hamadaya in Yoshichō as an adopted daughter, so my adoptive mother would always say to me: "I feel so sorry to make you earn money; if you were to become someone's mistress [*mekake*], I would feel bad for you and your parents." So I think she was intending to give me a husband, no matter how scrawny or poor.[18]

The phrase "one of those affairs between an actor and a geisha" refers to the common practice of geisha and *kabuki* actors entering into relations for various lengths of time. Since both geisha and *kabuki* actors are associated with the selling of sexual favors, such affairs are likely to have been regarded as financially motivated and as transitory in nature. Many of the accounts about Sadayakko's early life mention the practice of "actor buying" (*yakusha gai*) in which a geisha would use her earnings to purchase the favors of a *kabuki* actor. Even when such overt commercial transactions are not involved, the liaison of a geisha and a *kabuki* actor was likely to have been regarded as less formal and binding. By distinguishing that kind of affair from her marriage to Otojirō, Sadayakko is here bringing her relationship closer to the ideal wifeing model. It also mattered that Otojirō was an actor whose social status could be distinguished from that of the professional *kabuki* actor. After all, he had started out as a political activist of the People's Rights Movement, and was performing skits and plays that had a political message.

> At the time, Kawakami was performing *The True Records of Itagaki Taisuke's Travails* [Itagaki Taisuke sōnan jikki] at the Nakamuraza in Torigoe, and my [surrogate] mother went to see it. She told me, "It's very interesting, and you should definitely go see it," so we went together to the theater. This is when I saw Kawakami for the first time. Then, when it was time for Kawakami to go abroad, mother promised him that I would marry him, without my knowing it. After all the arrangements had been made, she asked me if I had any objections. But I myself was of peculiar taste, and did prefer student types, and

> I also thought someone like Kawakami would not stay an actor all his life. And with my status, even if I wanted someone serious, they would probably not marry me, so I decided I wanted to be with someone who was rather mysterious and incomprehensible. So I said, as long as Mr. Kawakami wants me, I shall accept him, and so this match was made.[19]

The "student-type" (*shosei*) refers to a category of young men who are perceived as involved in some kind of intellectual endeavor. They need only be loosely affiliated with a school—Otojirō was for a while a custodian cum auditor at Keiō University—and they are defined more by their outlook and demeanor than by their particular institutional status. What made Otojirō a "student type" was the public perception that his kind of theater was more verbal, political, and intellectual than the *kabuki.* It also meant that he was not perceived as a full-time actor, that his acting was simply a temporary preoccupation. This is why Sadayakko thought he "would not stay an actor all his life." Someone like Otojirō might well have become a politician or an entrepreneur: He did indeed run for national elections twice in 1898 (Meiji 31), and his theatrical ventures were driven by the entrepreneurial instincts of a businessman.[20]

But Sadayakko's words also tell us something else: She did not expect that she would marry someone who was not also in some way marginal, though he might eventually make a name for himself. Although she had many patrons, they were either rich men of high status who would only want her as a mistress or men on the margins of society, just like her. Although it was not uncommon for geisha to become legal wives of upper-class men—Prime Minister Itō Hirobumi's wife was a former geisha, for instance—it seems that Sadayakko is voicing a newly emerging understanding that good wives are made of good daughters, i.e., virgins. The new emphasis on virginity as a desirable female trait would soon be traceable in other locations, for example in debates on the pages of the feminist journal *Seitō.*[21] The geisha, valued for sexual expertise in the older paradigm, would be devalued in this newly developing paradigm of wifeing.

Sadayakko's memoir thus describes the marriage of a geisha and a "mysterious and incomprehensible" man, a man outside of the legible categories of society. As such, her marriage does not fit the model of wifeing. Yet the memoir also reveals Sadayakko's negotiation with the wifeing model, underscoring its increasing hegemony. And the portrayals of her marriage to Otojirō as a love story follow the model and perpetuate it to this very day.

As for the question of why she became Fukuzawa Momosuke's mistress after Otojirō's death, the various answers reveal that what is at stake is the ideology of lifelong monogamous romantic love characteristic of wifeing: If Sadayakko was truly in love with Otojirō, how could she love Momosuke? And if she truly loved Momosuke, was her marriage to Otojirō simply one of convenience? Her love for Otojirō and her love for Momosuke must be seen as mutually exclusive if the thread of wifeing is to be maintained. And this is what happens in the narratives about Sadayakko's love life. For example, the narrative that presents the actress as marrying Otojirō out of spite depicts her as eventually coming to deeply love her husband and as becoming Fukuzawa Momosuke's mistress in order to *punish* her former patron. But, the text coyly tells us, the relationship with the patron was now purely formal and nonsexual: "there was no carnal relationship between them; no matter how much Momosuke wanted her, Sadayakko refused to comply with his wishes."[22] Obscured again in these types of answers to the question "Why did she become a mistress?" is the material difficulty for a widow to support herself financially, a difficulty only beginning to be recognized by the government as possibly contradicting with the ideal of "good wife, wise mother" ideology.[23]

The strain of discursively transforming a former geisha into an ideal wife can result in accounts that take the exact opposite tactic. Sadayakko elicits this kind of response from several biographers, who ascribe to Sadayakko an insatiable sexual desire and who see such desire as the one-size-fits-all answer to all questions concerning her life decisions. Perhaps the best example is Ezaki Atsushi's floridly titled *The True Records of Kawakami Sadayakko: A Fiery Woman Who Spanned the World* (Jitsuroku Kawakami Sadayakko: sekai o kaketa honoo no onna), which, counter to its title, turns out to be a pseudo-pornographic novel containing elaborate descriptions of Sadayakko's sexual encounters with various men. Although the woman constructed by this text is the antithesis of the monogamous and faithful "good wife," she is, nonetheless, defined by her relations to men. The difficulty of wifeing Sadayakko occasionally produces this type of reaction.[24]

For another ten years from the time of her marriage, Sadayakko primarily performs the role of Kawakami Otojirō's wife. This gives rise to the second set of questions concerning her life. How and why did she begin acting? Most biographies contend that she started acting because she had no other choice: In 1899, at the beginning of the Kawakami troupe's tour of the United States, Sadayakko was told that without an actress the performance would fail, and thus her acting career "officially" started at this point. "Unofficially," however, her career had started the moment she became a geisha. She was trained in the various arts associated with stage performance: dance, song, playing musical instruments. Her own memoirs remind us that she had also participated in numerous amateur theatricals organized among the geisha houses. She always took on male roles, according to her own reminiscences.

> I actually love performing male roles. There was a theater called Yurakukan in Hamachō, with which Mr. Shibusawa [Eiichi] was associated. At that time I was a geisha, and I was asked to perform at their opening ceremony: I performed the

> battle scene of Soga Gorō. After that, at the end of every year, they would organize charity performances. We geisha would buy about one thousand-yen worth of tickets from our own pockets, and would enjoy acting in these performances. On those occasions, we had much ado, rehearsing our plays, selling our tickets. From that time, I have always liked performing male roles, and was happy to take on all kinds of male roles that others disliked. I performed Gorō's battle scene, Tadanobu, I'ichi Hōgen, Gorō's encounter scene, Izaemon, Hachiman Tarō, Kudō's encounter scene—all roles of older men, or of fierce battles. I was especially proud of performing battles in which I would slit my stomach while standing up. I was quite a tomboy, you see.[25]

These kinds of performances by geisha are a little-known aspect of the performance of theater by women prior to the emergence of modern professional actresses. Although these were women who were not specifically trained to be actresses, they were certainly professionals in certain kinds of performance. The "parody" of *kabuki* by geisha, though never intended to be in competition with the real thing, must have amounted to a fairly sophisticated spectacle. It shows that acting was part of Sadayakko's life as a geisha as well. Moreover, Sadayakko's performance of stomach-slitting heroes in these theatricals perhaps foreshadows her acting of male roles later in her life. These lines then, help us see a certain kind of continuity in Sadayakko's life, one that belies the attempts to narrate her beginnings as an actress as a wholly passive and serendipitous one.

Not only had Sadayakko performed in these kinds of amusements while she was still a geisha, but she had also prepared herself well for her "debut" in the United States. A few months before she first performed in San Francisco, she had warmed up in rehearsal performances in Japan:

> Then we started final preparations for departure. I intended to go abroad only to help out as Kawakami's wife, but just in case I should be required to perform on stage in America, we held rehearsal performances [*keiko shibai*] in Himeji. The play performed was *Demon Quelling in Taiwan* [Taiwan oni taiji], with Yamamoto and Fujikawa in leading roles, supported by Tsusaka, Takanami, Nogaki, Wada, Kawakami's younger brother Isotarō, and others. As the finale, I danced *Dōjōji,* and this was indeed the first time I stepped on the stage as a professional actor [*haiyū*].[26]

This episode, too, is often left out of biographies, which tend to emphasize the fact that Sadayakko began acting not out of her own desire to act, but as a last resort, when it became clear that the troupe would not survive without her. Moreover, the likelihood that she started acting out of necessity is used to characterize her acting style as passive: The lack of agency in making the decision to act is seen as detrimental in the subsequent series of acts.

Her passivity is then used to explain why she quit acting six years after her husband's death. The answer to the question "Why did she stop acting?" becomes the exact reverse of the answer to the question "Why did she start acting?" In other words, if one sees Sadayakko as not being truly willing to begin acting, one may consider it natural and logical that she would be very eager to stop acting. For example, one account represents her as losing all interest in performing after her husband's death, and thus deciding on a graceful exit: "She had no regrets. She chose her happiness as a woman over the stage. When Otojirō died, her life as an actress was over."[27] Thus, paradoxically, an ascription of agency occurs where it had been previously denied. She is seen as having chosen to end her career, though she is not seen as having chosen a career in the first place.

If, however, one takes seriously the possibility that Sadayakko chose to perform and that she may have indeed been eager to *continue* performing, then one can start considering the forces that pressured her to stop performing. Consequently, her retirement can be seen as involving more complex negotiations with the forces around her. An interview with Sadayakko shortly after Otojirō's death reveals some of these complicated forces that the actress had to negotiate. At this point, she fully intended to continue acting, despite these complications:

> Once my husband left this world, it would have been more proper for me to have stopped acting. And I wanted to stop, too, yet it seems I am still destined to go on. Various circumstances and complicated relationships have developed, which will not allow me to leave the stage for another four or five years. And I have been thinking: in this day and age, someone like myself, immature in the ways of the arts, cannot please the audience no matter how much effort I put into recapturing the good old plays. The audience shall tire of me very quickly. This being the case, it would be better for me to go abroad once again while I am not yet behind the times, observe the developments over there, study new plays, and introduce them to this country. This would be a wiser way, both from my own standpoint, and also as a way of serving the theater world, if my ideas would be of some interest. This is why I suddenly decided to go abroad. I plan to stay there for about a year and a half.[28]

This last tour abroad was not to be realized. First, there were objections from the male leaders of antiprostitution groups who feared that her performances abroad of plays such as *The Geisha and the Knight,* discussed in the next chapter, would "hurt Japan's dignity."[29] A later plan failed when the Japanese Foreign Ministry would not permit the tour, in response to the tightening of U.S. immigration laws—another installment in the saga of the tortuous relationship of Japanese performers and the Japanese nation-state's position in the international arena.[30]

Depressingly clear evidence of the resistance that Sadayakko's career faced after her husband's death is found in a survey conducted by *Shin engei* (New performing arts) magazine in 1916. A call for readers' letters in the March issue asked: "How should we dispose [*shobun*] of Sadayakko?"

> It's not that we think Sadayakko is a nuisance to our theater world. But there are those who say it's time for her to retire, to quit while she is ahead. On the other hand, there are those who say it's too early for her to retire. Should we make her retire or not? If we make her retire, what should we make her do? If not, what would we have her do? WE ASK FOR THE IMPARTIAL JUDGMENT OF OUR WISE READERS.[31]

The May issue announced that 3,853 replies were sent in.[32] The prize-winning entries featured in the magazine all advocated her retirement from the Japanese stage. The winner of the first prize (ten yen in cash) pronounced his impartial judgment: "There is no future for Sadayakko. I only wish for her to maintain the kind of beauty that would not soil the past."[33] The winner of the second prize helpfully hinted that while it may be impossible for her to maintain her reputation in Japan, she might be able to form a vaudeville troupe and tour cities in Europe and the United States.[34] Other entries suggested other occupations: managing actresses at the Teikoku Gekijō theater, operating a hotel or inn, or returning to the geisha business.[35] Not a single entry cited by the magazine advocated her continued performance on the Japanese stage.

Sadayakko retired from the stage in 1917 at the age of 46. Despite her multifaceted career during the six years after Otojirō's death and despite her directorship of a children's theater group that lasted until 1932, narrative accounts of Sadayakko's career are often abruptly terminated with the death of her husband. Descriptions of his funeral and her grief, accompanied by some comments about the inseparable unity of the couple, finish off the narratives. For instance, *Kawakami Otojirō, Sadayakko,* a compilation of contemporaneous newspaper clippings, covers the period from 1883 (Meiji 16) to 1911 (Meiji 44), that is, from Otojirō's early career in politics through the whole span of his career as actor and up to his death. The volume does not cover Sadayakko's career after her husband's death, and the last entry is dated a month after Kawakami's funeral in 1911.[36] The ideology of wifeing is thus reproduced by scholarship as well.

The autobiographical texts published shortly after the Kawakamis' return from their first tour abroad are equally patriarchal in their structure. Their *Records of Travels* (*Man'yūki*) was published in 1901 and is widely cited by historians and theater critics.[37] The narrative voice of the account is presented as being that of Kawakami Otojirō, and Sadayakko is presented as sitting silently next to him. Her silence, indicated in parenthetical "stage directions," supports his narration, as in the following example:

> Well, [Sadayakko's] *Dōjōji* was for some reason a great success after that Chicago performance; everyone kept calling for Sadayakko, only for Sadayakko. So while we were in that country, I lost all my clout. But now that we are back in Japan, the land that considers man superior and woman inferior [*danson johi*], I can walk tall again. (Sadayakko sits by his side and merely smiles.) When we performed *Dōjōji* at the ambassador's ball, so many newspaper reporters came—not just from Washington, but also from Boston and New York.[38]

This autobiographical volume was initially serialized in the newspaper *Chūō Shimbun* earlier that year.[39] There are numerous differences in phrasing between this serial and the book published later, suggesting that the Kawakamis' recollections were perhaps recorded by shorthand, then transcribed by different people for different publications. One may imagine that at the scene of the initial enunciation, Sadayakko had a more active voice. The process of recording, transcribing, and editing gradually reduced her to a quiet and supportive presence sitting beside her talkative husband. In the process of turning the newspaper series into the book, several sections were entirely deleted. One notices that among these sections are precisely those places where Sadayakko speaks up about her own experiences, such as her observation on the strangeness of funerary customs in the United States and her acceptance of an award by the New York Actress Club. This staging of the vocal husband and the silently smiling wife exemplify the notion that Sadayakko can be subsumed under her husband's name. Thus, in the way they organize the available data, these historical sources also reflect the process of wifeing and help to reproduce it.

Since the 1970s, several collections of women's biographies have sought to recover the history of women's accomplishments. Ironically, representations of actresses such as Sadayakko and Matsui Sumako, penned by female novelists and historians, are often quite negative. It seems that there is a strange species of normalization at work in these "women's history" texts, one that seeks to impose an ideal of womanhood on the woman being described. The ideal may be a modernized one, stressing career-orientedness and personal ambition rather than obedience to the patriarchs, yet the imposition of an ideal, even a feminist ideal, leads to the abjection of women who do not fit the ideal. Actresses are often found to be too emotional and impulsive to please these female novelists and historians. Sometimes, these negative views betray the writer's own bias against women who do not fit the traditional ideal of femininity. Women who are perceived as selfish, for example, are generally discussed in negative terms. And actresses often turn out to be the most "selfish" women of all.[40]

Novelist Sugimoto Sonoko, for example, summarizes Sadayakko's personality as selfish and strong-willed, yet lacking in modern intelligence and consideration.[41] She criticizes the actress for not displaying the required devotion and social skills of a wife, such as supporting her husband by placating disgruntled troupe members, and for not taking care of the troupe members by speaking up on their behalf to her husband. According to Sugimoto, there are no indications that Sadayakko performed these wifely services, and all evidence points to a self-centered and crude woman: She scolded her husband in front of others; she kept her finances separate from his in later years; and she was shunned by Otojirō's disciples, who even performed a separate funeral for him after his death. Sugimoto speculates, "There must have been some cause on her side to precipitate such behavior."[42] Sugimoto goes on to question Sadayakko's attitude toward her profession, citing an episode first recorded by female theater critic Hasegawa Shigure: Sadayakko would demand grilled fish to be cooked for her during intermission, even if it caused the smell of fish to drift to the stage. "This is a story that not only reveals the selfishness of her character, but also casts doubt on her self-awareness as a theater professional who ought to think of the stage first. Even from such a trivial anecdote, we must, unfortunately, sense one of the limitations hidden in Sadayakko's essence."[43] The fact that Sadayakko initially had no desire to become an actress is interpreted as a sign of her indifference toward her profession, and Sugimoto claims that this explains why Sadayakko retired from the stage after her husband's death and why she failed to leave a legacy in theater history. This extraordinary account ends with the lines:

> Though she was a pioneer, gracing the first page of the history of actresses, Kawakami Sadayakko left nothing behind as her legacy. The illusory light that she radiated for a certain period of time was nothing more than the intense reflection from the sun that was her husband, Kawakami Otojirō. It is sad to have to conclude thus, but it is an inescapable fact.[44]

The wifeing of Sadayakko thus culminates in the image of her as a pale moon glowing in the light radiated by her husband-sun.

Marukawa Kayoko's biographical essay is slightly more charitable towards its subject, but the conclusion is similar to Sugimoto's: Sadayakko's success is the result of her associations with great men, not the fruit of her own efforts.[45] This is also suggested by the title of her essay "From Famed Geisha Patronized by the Prime Minister in a Single Leap to the First International Actress" (Saishō o patoron to shita meigi kara ichiyaku kokusai joyū ichigō e). It sets up the impression that Sadayakko's career was jump-started and fueled by her patrons and protectors, rather than driven by her own desires and designs: "Being loved by great men with grand ambitions, Sadayakko did not fight her fate."[46]

Despite all these attempts by biographers and theater scholars, Kawakami Sadayakko's life cannot be confined to the narrow path of lifelong monogamous romantic love: of chastity before marriage, of faithfulness during marriage, and celibate widowhood after the husband's death. As geisha, actress, and mistress, she broke all these rules. Or, rather, she lived in a time when the rules were just being hammered into place, and the tensions in attempts to pin her life down to the narrow path reveal tensions inherent in the path itself.

Let us remember that the "good wife, wise mother" ideology had started out as a potentially progressive ideal that affirmed the importance of women. In contrast to the premodern view of women as no more than "borrowed wombs," the recognition of women's roles as mothers and wives was a significant step forward. The ideology became institutionalized from the 1890s onwards and became increasingly oppressive during Sadayakko's lifetime. Needless to say, however, the lives of the majority of women in Japan during this time were far removed from the ideal of the "good wife, wise mother" in any version. For one thing, it was an ideal that could, for the most part, be realized only by women of the upper samurai class. And even within the samurai class, whose values were being disseminated into the rest of society, there were many contradictions and contestations. For the lower classes, chastity before marriage only became a norm in late Meiji, while for many widows, it was not economically feasible to remain unattached. Thus the figure of the "good wife" in a lifelong monogamous, heterosexual marriage was a narrow ideal that had little to do with the material reality of many women.

Wifeing was necessary precisely because of this gap. This is indeed why we can perceive the contradictions inherent in the ideology of "good wife, wise mother" precisely at those points where Kawakami Sadayakko's life resists wifeing, and insists on charting a different, complex, and challenging course.

CHAPTER 4

STRAIGHTENING THE THEATER

SHIMPA AND STRAIGHT THEATER

WHILE WIFEING SHAPES THE IMAGE OF KAWAKAMI Sadayakko as woman, as a performer she is usually defined in relation to the genre of "*shimpa.*" The word translates as "new school drama," and the standard encyclopedia definition explains that it was a kind of hybrid genre, a step between *kabuki* and truly modern theater. For this reason it is a genre that illuminates the contours and contradictions in the transition to modern theater.[1] Kawakami Sadayakko's involvement in *shimpa,* however, is more than a little complicated, not the least of all through the structure of wifeing. The discussion in this chapter will center on the theatrical developments in Kawakami Sadayakko's time, yet many of these developments are credited to her husband, Kawakami Otojirō. Even those activities that would have been impossible without Sadayakko's consent and support, perhaps even initiative, are attributed to her husband. My assumption, however, is that Sadayakko both embodied and enabled the changes occurring in Japanese theater at this time, and that there is an agency in her involvement that is too often edited out of historical accounts of the modernization of Japanese theater. For these reasons, this chapter will use the signifiers "Kawakami" or "the Kawakamis" or "the Kawakami troupe" to refer to a joint enterprise, with full recognition of both partners' contributions.

Moreover, though modern theater in Japan as a whole developed in a direction suggested by the Kawakami troupe's performances, what is now called "*shimpa*" in conventional theater history was to veer off in a direction different from either modern theater or Kawakami's theater. *Shimpa* eventually began incorporating more and more elements reminiscent of *kabuki,* such as the use of *onnagata,* music, dance, and melodrama.

For these reasons, it seems to make sense to call Kawakami's theater by a name other than "*shimpa.*" While some have proposed the term "*shin'engeki*" for Kawakami's genre, that term pulls us too closely towards "*shingeki,*" the younger, more serious, and arguably quite different genre to be discussed in Part III. And while "*shin'engeki*" and "*shingeki*" have more in common with each other than either has with "*shimpa,*" it might be best to reshuffle these categories and come up with a designation that will accurately capture the substance of the Kawakami troupe's efforts.

The Kawakami troupe engaged in what I would like to call the "straightening" of Japanese theater. The straightening of theater is a process that is usually simply seen as part of the inevitable "modernizing" of theater, or of "making theater more realistic." Yet these well-worn formulations ought to be scrutinized: What exactly does it mean to make theater more modern, more realistic? What is involved in such a process? What is erased in such a process? And what is the correlation, if any, between the straightening of theater and the straightening of gender?

Globally, straightening is a process in which one dominant mode of theatrical representation, originating in Europe, comes to hold center stage as the universal mode, pushing other, local modes into the wings.[2] More locally, straightening is a process in which *kabuki* is labeled as "old theater," is regarded as archaic, decaying, and associated with femininity and homosexuality, in contrast to the new and vigorous modern theater, associated with masculinity and homosociality. *Kabuki* is abjected as decadent and "queer" and manages to survive only by disavowing certain parts of its queerness and by calcifying into a "traditional" and "classical" genre representing the nation's past. Meanwhile, modern theater is straightened into an apparatus that builds a national community made up of national subjects—*male* national subjects. Most relevant for us, Kawakami Sadayakko's involvement in this process points to straightening as the promoting of women as actors and the boosting of expectations that women should act like women and men should act like men. And it suggests how such a dichotomized understanding of gender buttresses a theater of masculine subjects and feminine wives, of warriors and their helpmates—or, alternatively, their seducers.

KABUKI AS QUEERED THEATER

What can we accomplish by calling *kabuki* "queer" in these pages? "Queer" is a condensed term that allows us to do two things: We could unpack it, or we could use it to link to another condensed term quickly. My wish here is to do both: to unpack what was "queer" about *kabuki* and to contrast it with what was "straight" about modern theater. At the turn of the nineteenth century, many aspects of *kabuki* became coded as "queer" and abjected. What was desirable was that which was opposed to *kabuki,* and this became coded as "straight theater" (*seigeki*). "*Seigeki,*" written with a set of characters that could be also translated as "correct," "pure," theater, is a term used by the Kawakami troupe to translate the English term "straight play," referring to spoken drama. But if we fully play on the double meaning of "straight," "non-straight," and "queer," we might actually begin to see how the various elements of theatrical representation, gender, and sexuality, all worked together.

The verb "*kabuku*" had been used since the middle ages with the meaning of "to slant," "to bend," or "to tilt," but had come to be used by the beginning of the Tokugawa period as a slang for any action that defied the conventions and the proper rules of behavior: unusual and extravagant ways of dressing, for example, or roaming the streets and engaging in acts of violence.[3] Even when "*kabuki*" came to be more closely associated with the theater and the word came to be written with the characters for song (*ka*), dance (*bu*), and mime (*ki*), the association with slanted, outrageous behavior persisted: "In the eyes of the shogunate early *kabuki* was another form of rebellious non-conformism, perverse in its eroticism, transvestism, outrageous costumes, and hybrid mixture of religious elements with licentious contents."[4] In other words, one could say, early *kabuki* was queer theater.

Kabuki was queer, however, not only in its association with norm-breaking behavior and anti-establishment attitudes; it was also queer in its association with homosexual practices. Even after repeated attempts by the government to curb homosexual prostitution by actors, the sexual aspect never disappeared from *kabuki.* An account in an Edo guidebook suggests that the audience continued to be titillated to the extreme by the sight of the male actors:

> When these youths, their hair beautifully done up, with light make-up, and wearing splendid padded robes, moved slowly along the runway, singing songs in delicate voices, the spectators in front bounded up and down on their buttocks, those in back reared up, while those in the boxes opened their mouths up to their ears and drooled; unable to contain themselves, they shouted: "Look, look! Their figures are like incarnations of deities, they are heavenly stallions!" And from the sides others called: "Oh, that smile! It overflows with sweetness. Good! Good!" and the like, and there was shouting and commotion.[5]

Yet it is important to note also that homosexual practices in Tokugawa Japan were not necessarily "queer" in the contemporary sense. In fact, they could possibly be seen as constituting one major part of the hegemonic sexual constellation during the Tokugawa period, and at least one scholar has argued that homosexual behavior was *normative.*[6]

Calling *kabuki* "queered theater" highlights those aspects that "complicate hegemonic assumptions about the continuities between anatomical sex, social gender, gender identity, sexual identity, sexual object choice, and sexual practice."[7] While we risk being anachronistic if we see *kabuki* at the end of the nineteenth century as self-consciously queer in this sense, we would be equally anachronistic if we were to view *kabuki* of that time through eyes clouded by the "straight-laced" image of national theater that it enjoys today. Today's *kabuki* almost entirely disavows its historical ties to homosexual practices, presenting itself as "high art," yet such an image of *kabuki* as national theater has only been proposed since the late nineteenth century and only consolidated since 1945.[8] It is difficult, from our present vantage point, to conceive of the extent to which *kabuki* was threatened at the turn of the previous century—by the charge that it was old-fashioned, decadent, too violent, too erotic, too spectacular, too risqué, too bent, too queer. Even in 1928, a scholarly discussion of *kabuki* would point out the association of *onnagata* with homosexuality with a strange combination of nostalgia—viewing it as embodiment of artistic refinement—and repulsion—viewing it as example of sexual perversity:

> Until the middle of Meiji, *onnagata* lived a daily life strangely filled with subtle shadings [*myō ni in'ei ni tonda nichijō seikatsu*]. It is not so far in the past that we could see many an *onnagata,* already well advanced in age, saunter gracefully into the dressing room with eyebrows already plucked, face powdered white, red undergarment flashing beneath long-sleeved kimono. The fact that *onnagata* bathed apart from the men, and that some *onnagata* would immerse themselves in even more bizarre homosexual relations [*kikai naru shudō kankei*] and become transformed both physically and psychically—these bespeak the strangeness of the life of *onnagata.*[9]

The scholar laments the deterioration of the *onnagata*'s art in the modern period and attributes it to the decline of male same-sex relations: "*Onnagata* used to have their own peculiar, illusory, and perverse sex lives [*tokushu na gen'ei-teki na hentai-teki na sei seikatsu*] . . . but the decline of male-male relations [*nanshoku*] has influenced the acting of *onnagata.*"[10] By the 1920s, male-male sex is already understood under the framework of "perversity" (*hentai*), but *kabuki* is still carrying memories of a previous framework, in which male-male sex is central to the art of the *onnagata.* It was in the preceding decades, the 1890s to 1910s, that *kabuki* was "queered" in the modern sense. It was during that time that *kabuki* was repudiated as "queer" in order to install the "straight," that is, the hegemonic constellation connecting "anatomical sex, social gender, gender identity, sexual identity, sexual object choice, and sexual practice."[11] And to this hegemonic constellation we can now add gendered performance.

A THEATER OF FIGHTING MEN: SINO-JAPANESE WAR PLAY

As a way to illustrate what the straightening of theater meant in concrete terms, let us look at a play in which Kawakami Sadayakko did *not* appear, but with which she was closely associated. This was the *Sino-Japanese War* (*Nisshin sensō*) performed by the Kawakami troupe in 1894–1895. The various aspects of this play and its production illustrate some of the fundamental principles of the straightening of theater. The play is also a paradigmatic example of the representation of Japan as a growing empire coming into violent contact with its neighbors.

This play has never been published, and neither have any of the other plays performed by the Kawakami troupe discussed in this chapter. About 80 hand-written scripts used by the troupe are stored in the Kawakami Archives at Waseda University's Theater Museum.[12] Although the general academic neglect of modern Japanese theater has hitherto consigned this material to obscurity, these scripts are crucial for understanding how theater functioned to construct Japan as modern nation-state and as colonial empire.

When the Sino-Japanese War broke out in August 1894, a number of theater troupes in Japan competed with each other in portraying the war. In an age before news-film and television, theater was one significant medium through which the civilian population could experience the sights and sounds of the battlefront. *Kabuki* was ill-suited to the task of representing this modern war, since it conventionally staged battles through gracefully choreographed movements punctuated by carefully composed tableaux. Moreover, newspaper reports suggest that *kabuki* at this time was already suspected of decadence and lack of masculine discipline and therefore unsuitable for showing Japan's first modern battle against its former role model, China. The newspapers report that many troupes asked for permission to perform plays about the war but that most had been turned down by the censors. The *Miyako Shimbun* of August 16, 1894, reports the reasoning of the censors as follows: "[T]he old school actors [i.e., *kabuki* actors] tend to care only about being beautiful and about gaining popularity among the ladies. Therefore, there is concern that they might damage the fighting spirit of our nation."[13]

This is when Kawakami Otojirō's troupe of actors scored a coup by being allowed to stage their version of *Sino-Japanese War*. They thereby inaugurated a new mode for theater to represent and reproduce imperialism and concomitantly changed the course of the history of Japanese theater. The *Miyako Shimbun* article cited above explains:

> In contrast, although they [i.e., the Kawakami troupe] are viewed as little better than new commoners [*shin heimin*],[14] they are literate and have some deep

> thoughts of their own. It is thought that their acting would inspire the military with its valor and excitement. We hope that members of this troupe, bearing such an honor, would acquit themselves well, without becoming slack [*dajaku*],[15] and without so much as a rumor of love affairs.

On August 19, 1894, the Kawakami troupe announced their upcoming production:

> With the purpose of enhancing the luster of national prestige, and of inciting the fighting spirit of our troops, we have arranged the Sino-Japanese War into a spectacular play. We strive to make the audience feel as if they were in the midst of the battlefield, and could see in front of their very eyes the valiant generals and brave soldiers battling like dragons and fighting like tigers. We humbly beg all of our fellow patriots under heaven to bring their true feelings of loyalty for our country, and come see this grand and magnificent new spectacle.[16]

The logic suggested here is consonant with the logic expressed in the "actress-*onnagata*" debates discussed in chapter 2. *Kabuki* actors are here associated with slackness, lack of military spirit, and sexual liaisons between performers and patrons. That liaison is represented here as involving male actors and female fans, though in practice it would have been both heterosexual and homosexual. It was feared that *kabuki* acting might inflict damage to the national military spirit by dissipating in sexual liaisons those precious energies that ought to be saved for the battlefield. In contrast, the new species of actors are perceived as being masculine and nonsexual, and therefore suited to representing, and thereby further inciting and inflaming, patriotic fervor and military valor. The actors in these new groups were mostly former students and political activists with limited training in the arts but an unlimited supply of enthusiasm and energy. These were men behaving like men in a *homosocial,* rather than either a heterosexual or a homosexual, field of action.

Kawakami's theater emerged thus as a theater of a nation at war, whereas *kabuki* was a theater of *Pax Tokugawana.* Kawakami's theater established its cultural and political legitimacy by repudiating the *kabuki,* in which not only *onnagata,* but all actors stopped short of being vigorous and masculine enough. The use of white powder in the *kabuki* actor's makeup became a synecdoche for the genre's connection with women and effeminacy. By contrast, straightening theater was about men acting like men; it meant the removal of that makeup, the presentation of the naked face. This new kind of theater was intended to incite the fighting spirit of the Japanese troops and of the whole nation—it thus assumed and imagined that the nation was a homogeneous unit and that whether one was fighting on the front, fighting on stage, or sitting in the auditorium, one was a member of it. The theater troupe on

4.1 Triptych of Kawakami troupe's *Sino-Japanese War.* Kawakami Otojirō as war reporter is making a speech in front of General Li. *Onnagata* Ishida Nobuo as the Japanese maiden is crouching behind the hero. Courtesy of Waseda University's Tsubouchi Shōyō Memorial Theater Museum.

stage was a stand-in for the troops in the field, and the audience was also caught up in the battles as it viewed itself as a nation at war, as part of a group of fighting men.

The plot of *Sino-Japanese War* follows the adventures of two Japanese newspaper reporters in China as they are caught in the military confrontation. The reporters are captured and tortured by Chinese troops, and one of them dies in prison. The other reporter is dragged before General Li, commander of the Chinese military. Here the reporter proceeds to lecture the General, and thus the audience, about the situation in Asia and the backwardness of China, justifying Japan's decision to go to war. The reporter is treated kindly by a prison guard, who turns out to be a Japanese expatriate in disguise. The play ends with the capture of Beijing by Japanese troops and triumphant shouts of "Banzai!"

The script borrows freely from two French plays: *Michel Strogoff* by Jules Verne (1828–1905), which depicts a battle between Russians and Tartars; and

La Prise de Pékin (The capture of Peking) by Adophe D'Ennery (1811–1899) which depicts the capture of Peking/Beijing during the Opium War. Various scenes are patched together from both plays, including the depiction of battle from the former play, and, from the latter play, a speech given by a *London Times* reporter in front of the Chinese Emperor, as well as the episode in which a Chinese guard frees French officers from prison.[17]

This play and its production exhibit the process of wifeing on many levels: in its portrayal of female characters, in its treatment of romance, and in its lack of actresses. The female characters play a small but critical role in the play, and their importance lies in their supplementary and auxiliary nature. There are ladies of the Japanese Red Cross, who visit the Japanese troops bearing gifts from the Empress herself. There is also a "Chinese" girl wandering around the battlefield, but she, too, turns out to be a loyal Japanese woman in disguise. The effect of all this, one suspects, is to show the audience that every Japanese subject, man and woman, upper class and lower class, is involved in the war effort. Women may help the war effort by aiding the men.

It is noteworthy in this respect that there are no love scenes in *Sino-Japanese War:* There are no overt expressions of romance at all. The Chinese/Japanese girl is rescued by the Japanese reporter, but there are no hints of romance in their relationship in the script. The play is all about glorifying Japanese military victory, and when women do appear, as in the case of the Red Cross ladies who help Japanese soldiers, or, by way of contrast, in the case of the prison guard's Chinese wife who mistreats the Japanese prisoners, their roles are secondary to this main purpose. Women can either support or hinder the war effort, but the masculine military subject is the true hero. The female characters in effect play the role of the "ladies auxiliary" of the Japanese military, and the process of wifeing is clearly operative here as well.

One might also speculate on the effect of the absence of "real" women from the stage itself, since all roles in this play were performed by men. *Sino-Japanese War* came before any concerted effort on the part of the Kawakami troupe to introduce the use of actresses. Moreover, in a troupe lacking the highly trained male *onnagata* found in *kabuki,* it may be logical that the women's roles were doubly marginalized.

Aside from gender difference, there is another kind of difference that is carefully negotiated in this play: that between the Japanese and the Chinese people. The depiction of Japanese and Chinese characters in the play reprises the Orientalist paradigm, with Japan playing the role of the civilized West and casting China as the backward Orient. Pictures of the production of this play show that the Chinese soldiers are visually Orientalized, while Japanese soldiers are visually Westernized: The former equipped with pig-tails and straw hats, the latter sporting Westernized uniforms and imperious Kaiser-style beards.[18] The Japanese characters are depicted in the drama as being loyal and

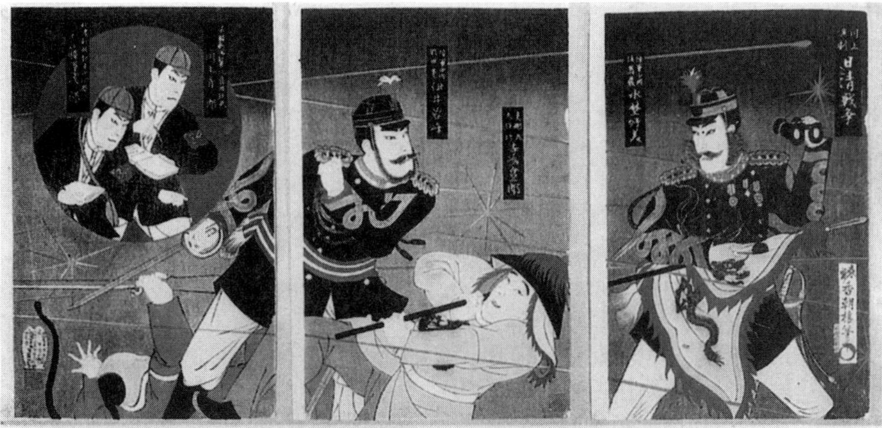

「日清戦争」錦絵（明治27年浅草座）

4.2 Triptych of Kawakami Troupe's *Sino-Japanese War.* Courtesy of Waseda University's Tsubouchi Shōyō Memorial Theater Museum.

courageous, from the commanders at the top to the foot-soldier at bottom. The Chinese are depicted as being inefficient fighters, easily bribed, and cruel in the treatment of prisoners. The only decent Chinese prison guard turns out to be actually a Japanese man in disguise.

This kind of "enemy turns out to be a loyal servant" plot device is familiar from *kabuki* and is also a twist on an original scene from *La Prise de Pékin.* Ideologically, however, the revelation of the true identity of a disguised character moves in two separate directions. On the one hand, it underscores what the play wants the audience to believe to be the essential difference between Japanese and Chinese moral nature: If you are a decent man, you must be Japanese. The device also reminds the audience that "we are all Japanese and we are in this war together." On the other hand, it raises the uncanny and disturbing possibility that Japanese and Chinese people are perhaps not so different, since one can pass for the other. Passing, disguise, and espionage are constant threats in war, and a popular theatrical theme as well.[19] This theme of sameness and difference is reiterated in *Korean King,* discussed in the next chapter. That chapter will also show that the ethnic difference managed by this sleight-of-hand in *Sino-Japanese War* was not (yet) legible outside of Japan, where Western eyes would regard both China and Japan as uncivilized.

Sino-Japanese War, then, was pure jingoistic propaganda intended from the outset to rouse the Japanese fighting spirit. But the main reason for the popularity of the play was to be found in the realistic representation of battle scenes. These battle scenes worked powerfully on the audience, interpellating masse as a national people engaged in a national battle. One felt that one was part of a unity, stretching from the auditorium seat all the way to the frontlines of the war. This was a theater of a nation at war, and the nation was represented—as well as imaginatively constructed—by these scenes. Firecrackers were used to simulate canon blasts, and actors entered into real fistfights on stage. The newspapers reported frequently of actors being "wounded in action," receiving gashes from stage fights. They also reported that audience members would sometimes become so excited by the battle scenes that they forgot that they were seeing a play. The *Miyako Shimbun* of September 4 reports that during one battle scene, two men in the audience suddenly jumped on the stage shouting "You pig-tail Chinese, you won't get away with this!" and proceeded to punch the actors representing Chinese soldiers. These kinds of reports only further enhanced the reputation of the play as a realistic representation of the war.

The new mode of acting begun by the Kawakami troupe thus served the function of representing the Sino-Japanese War as a current event, delivering news, excitement, and militaristic inspiration to the audience. This is clear when compared against the rather pathetic attempts of *kabuki* to represent the same war. At the Kabukiza theater, a play was being performed by Ichikawa Danjūrō IX, the greatest actor of his generation. Danjūrō dressed up as a sailor and used sticks of dried fish to demonstrate the movements of the Japanese navy's battleships: He tried, in other words, to portray the war by *talking* about it.[20] Not surprisingly, this play was a flop. Significantly, it was after this point that *kabuki* abandoned attempts to deal with contemporary events and instead began devoting its energies to preserving the canonical plays and the performance conventions as they stood at the end of the nineteenth century. Having lost the competition to represent the Sino-Japanese War, *kabuki* mutated into a "classic" theater.

The Sino-Japanese War was the first major triumph for the modern Japanese nation-state, and *Sino-Japanese War* was the first major triumph for the new, modern, masculine kind of theater. It was natural that the Kawakami troupe, when it embarked on a tour of the United States and Europe from 1899 to 1900, would desire to showcase this play abroad. And naturally the troupe was planning to use an all-male cast as it had done in Japan. But as we shall see in the next chapter, something funny would happen on the way to the stage in San Francisco.

INDIRECT AND DIRECT SPEECH AND ACTION.

Let us shift back again to a more general discussion of what the straightening of theater entailed. As its etymological origins in the English term "straight play" suggest, "straightening theater" at the most fundamental level was a matter of reducing performance to spoken drama by eliminating the distractions of music and dance. Yet this had deeper implications having to do with the other meanings of "straight": It amounted to the repression of the citationality of words, of gestures, and of gender, as we shall see.

In the specific context of Meiji Japan, this also involved a shifting of borders between performance genres. The dominant genre of *kabuki* had combined elements of drama, dance, and music; the very letters of the word, "ka-bu-ki," stood for "song-dance-mime," signifying the amalgamation of these elements. In the early Meiji period, through contact with Western categorization, Japanese theater practitioners began to recognize these as potentially separate elements and began to discuss reorganizing them into separate performance practices.

For example, in *kabuki,* dialogue was intoned, chanted, or sung: There was no way to simply "speak" a line without "singing" it to some extent. Yet theater practitioners, such as members of the Kawakami troupe on tour in Europe and the United States, witnessed that "song" could be separate from "speech" and that something like "opera" as a sung genre was separate from the "straight play" as a spoken genre. The same was true about dance. In *kabuki,* there is no movement or gesture that is not choreographed: Every action on stage is carefully coordinated as a dance. In the West, the Kawakami troupe could see that "ballet" as a dance genre was separate from "straight play" as a nondance genre. Song and dance thus constituted genres separate from spoken drama. Hence, the Kawakamis coined the term "*seigeki*" (literally a translation of "straight play") to designate the kind of theater they would advocate as the theater of the future in Japan.

The advocacy of "straightening theater" was initially expressed in the form of deprecation of song and dance, and Kawakami Otojirō's 1903 article "Actors Don't Need to Dance" is the first of such expressions.[21] One of the earliest indications about what was meant by "straight theater," this article argued that there is no need for actors to learn traditional dances, and no need to follow the traditional movement patterns of *kabuki:*

> If you go abroad, you'll find that in every country there is a clear distinction between dance [*butō/dansu*] and drama [*engeki/dorama*]. Dance is performed in revues [*yose*], and is not something that drama actors perform. Actors [*haiyū*] only need perform that which is their vocation. There is no need for actors to learn how to dance—they should rather devote all their energies to drama.[22]

A year later, Kawakami elaborated on the injunction against song and dance. He argued that the kinds of song and dance currently used in theater are unnatural and unsatisfactory, and that the unembellished "intonation of words" (*gengo no yokuyō*) and "pacing of movement" (*dōsa no kankyū*) should be sufficient to create beauty.[23]

What "straightening" as a rejection of song and dance implied was what is conventionally referred to as "realism": The understanding of spoken drama and its performance as a transparent medium expressing a content that lies beyond the medium. The radical nature of "straightening" can be fully understood, however, only by thinking more about the nature of "song" and "dance" and the nature of speech and action on stage.

What is dance? What is the component that the Kawakami troupe tried to resist by emphasizing the unembellished pacing of movement? We might start with the definition of dance as "extraordinary nonverbal movement with intrinsic value."[24] The "nonverbal movement" component of the definition is, for the moment, self-explanatory, though determining the precise border between verbal and nonverbal might eventually prove troublesome.[25] The "intrinsic value" also makes sense if we subscribe to the Kantian definition of beauty as the object of disinterested satisfaction, not tied to any representation of a purpose.[26]

It is the "extraordinary" in the definition that catches our attention. What is extraordinary, and what is ordinary? Following the theorization of Naoki Sakai, we could say the "ordinary" is "direct action," i.e., a bodily action that is in unity with the performative situation: "Direct action involves synchronization and coordination among all participating elements—bodily movement, verbal utterance, and performative situation. It is further characterized by the absence of musicality and other formalizing agents."[27] An "extraordinary" action, then, is that which is *not* direct action, that which does *not* match the performative situation.[28] Dance in this sense is "extraordinary" in that it is "indirect action." Unlike direct action, dance as indirect action is restored behavior that can be repeated by another person, or at another moment. A choreographed fight (*tate*) found in *kabuki* is an example of indirect action, or dance. When the Kawakami troupe broke into real fistfights on stage, "real" in the sense that they caused each other physical injury, they were coming closer to direct action, the repudiation of dance.

What is song, then? What is the element that the Kawakami troupe sought to reject by stressing the unembellished intonation of words? If we were to borrow the terms above, song would be defined as a kind of "extraordinary vocal movement with intrinsic value" and would be characterized as "indirect" rather than "direct."[29] There are aspects of song that would make it count as "direct," but when the Kawakami troupe rejected song, it was rejecting those aspects that would count as "indirect." A *kabuki* actor narrating, intoning, and chanting about battles with sticks of dried fish was clearly "indirect speech." What would have been Kawakami's counterexample of direct speech?

The shout of "You pig-tailed Chinese, you won't get away with this!" uttered by an excited spectator? The shout of "Shut up, you pompous Japanese!" that might have answered it, coming from an excited actor on stage? The question leads to other questions, eventually leading us to the shifting nature of the divide between "direct" and "indirect" that will be discussed below. Suffice it to say here that in the *Sino-Japanese War,* a production of fighting men who refused to be seen as queer, the men repudiated dance as indirect action and therefore *punched* each other in more direct action; they repudiated song as indirect speech and therefore *shouted* at each other in more direct speech.[30]

Kawakami's statements and practices for rejecting song and dance were confrontational declarations of independence from *kabuki,* and reactions from the *kabuki* world were swift and caustic. Especially virulent was criticism of the Kawakami troupe's performances of historical plays, such as *The Transfer of Edo Castle* (Edo-jō akewatashi), dealing with the transfer of power from the Tokugawa Shogunate to the Meiji government. Major *kabuki* performers complained that the amateurish actors of the Kawakami troupe did not know how to hold a sword or how to climb in and out of palanquins in style, that the lack of dance made them look less dignified, and that the lack of music made their speech monotonous and hard on the ears.[31] While straightening worked well in portraying contemporary battle scenes, it proved difficult to extricate the movements and speech of the samurai and the aristocrat from the patterns of movement and speech refined over hundreds of years in *kabuki* representation.

Moreover, it was difficult to resist the appeal of song and dance. As the next chapter will show, Kawakami Sadayakko's success as the dancing geisha of *Dōjōji* attests to the irresistible strength of song and dance and points to the intractability of this aspect of straightening theater. In the Kawakami troupe's performance of *Hamlet,* it was Ichikawa Kumehachi's dancing in the "play within the play" scene that stole the show. In their *Othello,* it was the "clown's dance" (*dōke odori*) and "Chinese theater" (*shina geki*) inserted as entertainment in the banquet scene that most amused the audience. These *divertissements* caused at least one observer to lament that "the enjoyment of sophisticated punch-lines and clever innuendoes is something that can only be expected of critics and other persons of leisure; the common spectator, it seems, attends the theater in order to abandon thought."[32] The aspect of melodrama (drama with "melos" or song) also kept creeping back into Kawakami performances of various plays.[33] Elements of dance, song, music, and melodrama were never far from Sadayakko's performances, and neither were they ever fully purged from "*shimpa*" as a genre. Moreover, after her husband's death, Sadayakko would appear in even more blatantly melodramatic adaptations of operas such as *Tosca* and *La Traviata.* Though the amount of real "singing" involved in these productions is uncertain, the implication is clear: It was almost impossibly difficult to purge theater of song and dance.

Why was this so? What prevented straightening theater from achieving truly direct speech and direct action? What made song and dance so intractable, so difficult to expel from the stage? Part of the answer lies in the nature of the difference between "direct" and "indirect." Let us now take a closer look at this question of "direct" and "indirect" speech and action.

REPUDIATING CITATIONALITY OF SPEECH, ACTION, GENDER

It is easy to see that in the language of *noh,* puppet theater, and to a certain extent *kabuki,* there is no clear distinction between dialogue and narration. Neither is there a clear articulation of tense and person. A character might refer to himself in the third person, narrate a tale in past tense, and then slip into a reenactment in present tense. Or a character's words might be voiced not by the actor embodying that character but by a chorus or by a chanter-narrator. In *Voices of the Past,* Naoki Sakai argues that before the eighteenth century in the space that we now call Japan, one finds that there was no clear differentiation of direct and indirect speech, either. Direct speech is the form: *"I am Atsumori" he said.* Indirect speech, on the other hand, would take the form: *He said that he was Atsumori.* In classical Japanese, such as the language of the *noh* theater, there are few grammatical rules by which direct and indirect speech are clearly distinguished.[34] For example, there is no systematic use of quotation marks and syntactical markers, which would distinguish direct and indirect speech. Thus in the *noh* theater, Atsumori might confusingly introduce himself by chanting something that might be translated as: *He is Atsumori, he said.*[35]

In eighteenth-century discourse, differentiation between direct and indirect speech begin to be indicated. The best example is the script of puppet theater (*ningyō jōruri*). The difference between direct and indirect speech in the puppet theater is not necessarily marked by grammar, or in the script. The difference is primarily marked by the chanter of the puppet play, who *sings* the sections that are indirect speech (narration or *ji*), but *speaks* the direct speech (dialogue or *kotoba*). For example, a line that is undifferentiated on the page might look like this: *Chūbei impatiently asks why she is so late.* A chanter can differentiate the line, so that it sounds like indirect narration followed by direct dialogue: *Chūbei impatiently asks "Why's she so late?!"*

In puppet theater, however, all the lines are voiced by the chanter, and though he can make certain lines sound like direct speech, everything he says is filtered through his voice. So in that sense, although the chanter can make his words sound like direct speech, the words are not coming from the characters themselves and are therefore ultimately indirect speech. Several centuries later, French critic Roland Barthes would characterize this split between the enunciating body (the chanter) and the body of the enunciated (the puppet) as follows:

> Western spectacle is anthropomorphous: gesture and speech (not to mention song) form but a single tissue, conglomerate and lubricated like a unique muscle that sets expression going without ever dividing it: the unity of movement and voice produces *the one* who acts; in other words, it is in this unity that is constituted the person of the personage, that is, the actor. In Bunraku [i.e., the puppet theater], however, no one is on stage, or, more precisely, no person has taken up position there. The (personal) corporal illusion disappears, not because the actors are made of wood and cloth . . . but because the codes of expression are detached from one another, pulled free from the sticky organicism in which they are held by Western theatre.[36]

This discontinuity of codes frees the entanglement of voice and gesture, and results in a "total spectacle, but divided."[37]

In *kabuki,* with the use of human actors rather than puppets, more and more lines are spoken by actors and sound even more like direct speech. There is still some overtly indirect speech, in the occasional use of the chanter and in the way the actors declaim their lines in a stylized and musical manner.

What happens in the process of straightening theater, then, is that the speech becomes more and more direct. In modern theater, the chanter disappears completely, and the lines spoken by actors sound even more like direct speech. Because of a new style of acting, the words sound as if they are coming directly and spontaneously from the interior of the bodies on stage. But even here, where the words seem to come directly from the characters, the words are in fact memorized and rehearsed, and not totally spontaneous. They are, in that sense, indirect speech. It is only in contrast to the more indirect kinds of speech (of *noh, kabuki,* and puppet theater) that they seem more like direct speech.[38] And even if the actors are speaking *ad libitum,* as they did in many scenes in the Kawakami troupe's plays, their speech can be construed as being direct only in contrast to the more indirect, rehearsed kinds of speech.

Direct speech, in the strictest sense, does not exist, since pure direct speech would deny the materiality of the body that must produce the speech. No matter how direct speech may seem, there is the interference of the body, which separates speech from its putative origin in consciousness. There is also the interference of language itself: We are never totally in control of the language we speak, since language pre-exists us, eludes our control, and makes our speech not entirely our own—we somehow always end up mouthing clichés, even at the moment of our most sincere, honest expression. The unrehearsed barbs and expletives that undoubtedly accompanied the battle scenes of *Sino-Japanese War* were indeed more direct than the rehearsed speech delivered by aper reporter to the Chinese general, but they were not pure direct ıre direct speech would be a totally unprecedented, unmediated expression, the unity of enunciation and enunciated, a form of enunciated in which the enunciation is fully present, not just as a trace.[39] And, this is an impossibility.[40]

Most of the above statements about speech on stage also apply to direct and indirect action on stage. Pure direct action is an impossibility: "the immediacy of a direct action, with its proclaimed absence of formalization, is in fact a result of complex mediation."[41] The directness of direct action is conceivable only within a certain discursive formation in which it is *constructed* as direct action.[42]

The differentiation between direct and indirect speech, direct and indirect action, then, is not a fixed line, but a relation of "différance."[43] Sakai explains this relation of différance between direct and indirect as follows:

> Only differences exist, differences that give rise to oppositions without which neither "natural" behavior nor ritualized gesture would exist. There is no such thing as natural behavior in itself or direct speech in itself. Therefore "natural" behavior and direct speech are possible only when ritualized and formalized action and speech have been introduced as their opposites. There could be neither direct speech nor nonformal behavior without these oppositions.[44]

The différance between direct and indirect, then, has to do with the différance between the real and the imitated, the original and the citation, the spontaneous and the rehearsed. What does this différance have to do with gender?

The différance between direct and indirect is analogous to the différance between femininity understood as real, truthful essence on the one hand, and femininity understood as masquerade, mimicry, and performativity on the other hand. Psychoanalyst Joan Riviere sums up the relation when she points out:

> Womanliness therefore could be assumed and worn as a mask, both to hide the possession of masculinity and to avert the reprisals expected if she was found to posses it. . . . The reader may now ask how I define womanliness or where I draw the line between genuine womanliness and the "masquerade." My suggestion is not, however, that there is any such difference; whether radical or superficial, they are the same thing."[45]

Feminist philosopher Luce Irigaray also declares that "one must assume the feminine role deliberately," deploying such a strategy of mimicry in order to "convert a form of subordination into an affirmation, and thus to begin to thwart it,"[46] and also in order to avoid adopting the position of the male subject and thus perpetuating it.[47]

We could then summarize these ideas as the "there is no *there* there" theory of femininity,[48] an understanding of gender as fundamentally a matter of citing and imitating external norms rather than as a matter of expressing inner essences. Theorist Judith Butler brings together the metaphors of acting, miming, citing, and performing by proposing a thought experiment: If gender attributes are not *expressive* but *performative,* then these attributes constitute the very identity they are said to express or reveal:

> The distinction between expression and performativeness is crucial. If gender attributes and acts, the various ways in which a body shows or produces its cultural signification, are performative, then there is no preexisting identity by which an act or attribute might be measured; there would be no true or false, real or distorted acts of gender, and the postulation of a true gender identity would be revealed as a regulatory fiction.[49]

Moreover, if gender can be construed as a "stylized repetition of acts," it would also mean that gender can be acted differently and that possibilities for transformation can be found "precisely in the arbitrary formation between such acts, in the possibility of a failure to repeat, a de-formity, or a parodic repetition."[50]

If straightening theater was a way for theater to deny its own indirectness, its own citationality, this also went hand in hand with denying the indirectness, the citationality, the performativity, of gender. In straightened theater, gender is no longer a pattern to be cited but becomes an identity to be expressed. It becomes a theater of "direct gender." Just as the indirectness and citationality of speech and action is carefully concealed in modern theater, so is the indirectness and citationality of gender. This is clear when one looks at the increasing importance of actresses and the nature of their performances, to which we now turn.

TRAINING ACTRESSES

After returning from her second trip abroad, during which she observed the training of actresses in Paris, Kawakami Sadayakko declared that "having seen how actresses there are highly educated and well-read, and how society welcomes them and heartily supports their development, I wish to exert myself behind the scenes in Japan, since it is too much to hope for myself, and would like to train accomplished actresses, who might come to be called the Sarah Bernhardts of Japan."[51]

In 1908 (Meiji 41), she opened the Imperial Actress Training Institute (Teikoku Joyū Yōseijo), Japan's first acting school for women. Funding for the school came from the Imperial Theater (Teikoku Gekijō), and financial heavyweights such as entrepreneur Shibusawa Ei'ichi and Sadayakko's former patron Fukuzawa Momosuke. The former's speech at the opening ceremonies conveyed the optimism of a businessman whose social status had moved to the center of power in the Meiji period, and connected his own rising status to the enterprise he was supporting.[52] Pointing out that merchants, women, and actors have traditionally been held in low esteem by society, he expressed the hope that actresses, as women and actors, would rise up in the same way as merchants did.[53] This connection to the world of commerce was to haunt this particular school for actresses, but that connection resurfaces in later contexts as well.

The rules for the Imperial Actress Training Institute were formulated to insure that the women schooled there would be regarded as artistic professionals rather than as the equivalent of geisha or worse. Each student was required to have two guarantors; students were forbidden from performing outside the institute (at private parties for example); tuition was free but after two years of training all students were required to act professionally at the Imperial Theater for two years; those students leaving the institute before the end of the two year term were required to pay back tuition as well as a high fine and publish an apology in the newspapers. The last stipulation also applied to "students who would use the arts acquired at the institute to operate as geisha."[54] This rule addressed the fact that such students-turned-geisha were not uncommon. Despite its strict rules, the Institute came under immediate attack:

> Even before the opening ceremonies were over, the applicants to the Actress Training Institute have become the targets of ridiculing and castigating voices. Contemporary thinking might have freed us from the denigration of actors as river-bed beggars, yet any ordinary lady [*ippan no shukujo*] would still find it insulting to be an actress. Thus it may be inevitable that candidates for actresses would be regarded as tomboys [*otenba*].[55]

The first generation of would-be actresses often *did* come from the geisha quarters, a fact that was seen as sufficient reason to suspect the propriety of the school: The Actress Training Institute was branded "Detention Center for Hussies" (*abazure shūyōjo*) in the *Yamato Shimbun* the day after its opening.[56] Actresses continued to have a hard time and continued to be seen as no different from geisha. Mori Ritsuko, an actress-in-training who came from an upper-class background, was expelled from the alumnae association of her alma mater; her younger brother committed suicide rather than live with the shame of being taunted by his classmates about his sister's occupation.[57] The actresses of the Imperial Theater would be compared to actresses of the Literary Society, discussed in further detail in chapter 7. The former would be continuously associated with the glitter and glamour of the geisha world while the latter would try to define themselves as striving students and serious artists.

Despite Kawakami's earlier injunction against mixing music and dance with straight drama, the curriculum of the Actress Training Institute included training in Japanese and Western dance, Japanese and Western music, instructions in traditional Japanese instruments such as the flute, drums, and *koto,* chanting (*gidayū*), and the study of both "new and old theater," meaning both *kabuki* and modern plays. This curriculum was without doubt designed to answer the demands of the Imperial Theater. When the Imperial Theater opened in 1911, women began performing there in a new genre of *kabuki*-style spectacles, called "actress plays" (*joyū geki*), many of them written by Masuda Tarōkaja (1875–1953), the author of *Dumb Travel,* which is discussed in the next chapter.[58] These plays closely resembled the kinds of spectacles for which Kawakami Sadayakko had been applauded abroad and reviled at home ten years earlier. Ironically, the training of actresses led to the popularization of the kind of spectacular combination of music, dance, drama, and romance that the straightening of theater had meant to purge.

A manuscript of a peculiar one-act play entitled *Actress Training Institute* (Joyū Yōseijo) is preserved in the Kawakami collection at Waseda University's Theater Museum. It depicts the opening ceremony of the institute, with a long-winded speech by Sadayakko that puts the assembled dignitaries and students to sleep. The play ends with her fuming exit. I have been unable to find records of this play's performance, but it seems like another example of the Kawakamis' penchant for parodying their own ventures. It might also stand as a reminder that straight speech alone was hardly riveting to watch on stage: Without the song and dance, Sadayakko could not hold the audience's attention, and at some level, she was aware of that fact.

KAWAKAMI'S THEATER REFORMS

Straightening theater was a process of dissociating theater from the world of *kabuki* and pleasure quarters and associating it with the world of business and the military. It sought to alter the relationship of actor to audience from one based on the prostitute-client transaction to one based on the idea of men working together to serve the nation. Let us now turn to some more specific aspects of straightening as envisioned and practiced by the Kawakami troupe.

While touring the United States in 1900, Kawakami Otojirō was asked, at a banquet hosted by President William McKinley, what he thought of American theater. In his autobiography, Otojirō presents himself as proudly launching into an impromptu speech, after confirming that what was requested of him was a frank reply rather than a diplomatic one. This speech would foreshadow the Kawakami troupe's efforts to reform Japanese theater. Speaking in the first person singular "*watakushi,*" but most likely summarizing the general views of his troupe, Otojirō first replied that he was impressed by the grandeur of the theater building and the size of the stage, and that he was amazed by the sets and "the sophisticated machinery that allows the stage scene to be transformed in myriad ways through lighting." Switching to the plural, Otojirō then spoke on behalf of the Japanese people (*wareware nihonjin*): "In everything we saw and heard, there was not a single thing that did not become the source of amazement for us as Japanese." All of these things—the large size and structure of the theater building and the stage, the use of electric lighting—the Kawakami troupe would later attempt to replicate in Japan.

The most significant comment about the direction of Kawakami's theater reform, however, concerned the theme of the plays:

> Next, looking at the plot of the plays, we were surprised to find that more often than not they approach the realm of the licentious [*waisetsu ni chikai*]: four out of five acts end with a man and a woman embracing and kissing each other. Kissing between men and women may be an old custom in your country or in Europe, and therefore nothing to wonder about, but to us Japanese it does look quite peculiar [*ika ni mo fushigi*].
>
> Our theater tends to value the kind of tragedy that shows a hero who is loyal to his nation and obedient to his lord, who risks his life for the sake of filial piety [*kō*] and sacrifices his life for the sake of righteousness [*gi*]. Plays in your theater, on the other hand, revolve around women from beginning to end [*ichi mo onna no tame ni mo onna no tame*]. "How can a man win the attention of a woman, and how can he buy her love?" Your theater seems to provide material to study these questions and to interpret these problems. That is the impression we receive and we find it simply astounding [*tada shingai ni taenu*].[59]

This response was typical of Kawakami Otojirō's aversion to romantic love scenes. It is not clear whether he objected primarily to theater plots revolving around women instead of men, or to theater plots revolving around romance instead of loyalty, or to the overt physical expression of sexuality instead of subtle suggestion of it. It may be that it was not clear to him, either; what is clear is that he wanted men fighting and risking their lives as the focus of his theater plots, "the kind of tragedy that shows a hero who is loyal to his nation and obedient to his lord."

The Kawakami troupe chose plays that centered on the exploits of male heroes rather than those focusing on couples or on women. Most often these choices are explained as strategic moves for rendering the new brand of theater respectable in the eyes of society and for distinguishing it from *kabuki*. Yet exactly why should these moves render theater more respectable?

Straightening theater meant distancing theater from the realm of the licentious and feminine, and moving it into alignment with righteous and manly pursuits. It entailed moving the theater away from the pleasure quarters, cutting off the conventional ties that bound the theater to the milieu of licensed prostitution. It also involved running theater along a modern management model, one in which personnel, resources, and time would be allocated rationally and efficiently, and one in which masculine subjects would enact masculine scenes in order to educate others to act masculine.

Kawakami Otojirō's aversion to geisha has been noted by theater historians. Whatever his behavior might have been in private life, and though he married one himself, Otojirō seemed to believe that geisha exerted a corrupting influence on social morale, and since he insisted that theater was a form of education, he refused to ever perform any play that had a geisha as a main character.[60] This is ironic, since the *shimpa* we know of today, that is, the *shimpa* after Kawakami, takes many of its sources from the world of the geisha. The later development of the genre veered off from Kawakami's proposals in many ways. It eventually began incorporating more and more elements reminiscent of *kabuki,* such as the use of *onnagata,* music, and melodrama.[61]

Despite advocating the training and use of actresses to replace *onnagata,* Otojirō's stance toward women, romance, and gender relations in general seems to have continued to be characterized by ambivalence. This might explain some of the tensions in the plays performed by the Kawakami troupe, between an emphasis on gender differentiation between men and women on the one hand, and a diluting of the depiction of heterosexual romance in favor of homosocial relations on the other hand. If one were to borrow the classic formulation of dramatic conflict found in discussions of the puppet theater and of *kabuki,* that between passion (*ninjō*) and obligation (*giri*), the Kawakami plays highlight obligation every time and are almost eager to push passion offstage.[62]

Shortly after coming back to Japan, the Kawakamis publicized their proposals for theater reform. These proposals were clearly derived from the experiences and observations gathered while touring abroad. These covered shortening performance time, altering the structure of the theater building and scenery, and elevating the status of actors. It argued for replacing complicated sets with painted backdrops and abolishing the *kabuki*-style walkway (*hanamichi*); using electricity to show a natural change of scene (from day to night, for example); and raising the intellectual level of both actors and managers.[63]

These proposals pushed further certain movements already under way in Japan to reform theater by confining and regulating the extent and effect of performances. Such efforts to discipline theater had been most monumentally visible in the reform of theater buildings. The dismantling of the "theater districts" was one such example. Historically, the organization of theater districts (*shibai machi* or *shibaya machi*) can be traced back to the Tokugawa government's use of theater and pleasure quarters to attract more inhabitants to Edo in the 1600s.[64] These theater districts were established outside of the norms and laws of the city and marked as places of "excess." They were places inhabited by members of the "non-human" (*hinin*) class, set apart from and below the social hierarchy of the majority; where upper-class spectators disguised themselves before entering the auditorium; "where people gave up their status temporarily, leaving it, as it were, at the theater door."[65] The dismantling of the theater districts was heralded by the relocation of the Moritaza theater to the city center of Tokyo in 1872 (Meiji 5).[66] The disintegration of the theater district went hand in hand with the extraction of the theater from the local environment. Theater was now confined to a building, cut off from the area establishments, the teahouses (*shibai chaya*) that handled tickets, transportation, and meals, and especially the quarters for licensed prostitution. These so-called "pleasure quarters" had been so closely associated with the theater district as facilities for the amusement of city dwellers in the Tokugawa period[67] that it could be said that "the theaters were variants of the pleasure quarters and the pleasure quarters were variants of theaters" (gekijō ni yūkaku no hentai o mi, yūkaku ni gekijō no hentai o hakken suru).[68]

When the Moritaza theater was rebuilt and renamed the Shintomiza theater in 1878 (Meiji 11), it incorporated many features of the theaters of Europe and the United States: chairs instead of floor seating, artificial lighting, and a proscenium stage.[69] The new building was an example of modern theater architecture that separates, confines, and *rivets* the bodies of spectators that visit its premises. Similar changes could be found with the building at the Kabukiza in 1889 (Meiji 22),[70] and the Yūrakuza in 1908 (Meiji 41).[71] In these modern buildings, theatergoers were no longer able to move about during the performance, no longer able to eat and drink while conversing with their neighbors. They were now assigned to seats fixed onto the floor and compelled to gaze at the stage in rapt attention, as the artificial lighting focused their vision and the architecture of the proscenium framed the stage as a picture in front of them.

When Kawakami built the Teikokuza theater, which opened on February 27, 1910, it was a crowning moment in his career and the culmination of straightening efforts.[72] The Teikokuza theater was a western-style theater with mostly chair seating and electric lighting. It still had two floors of *tatami* seating, and included a *kabuki*-style walkway (*hanamichi*) and turning stage as well as an orchestra box.[73] Eating in the auditorium was forbidden, and smoking was discouraged. *Around the World in Seventy Days* was one of the first plays performed there, and it used grand scenery, panoramic photographs, and lighting changes (*anten*).[74] At the time of its opening, the Teikokuza theater was the most "Western" and modern in Japan.[75]

While space is the most visible aspect of the abstracting and localizing that attends the straightening of theater, time is another aspect in which there is a significant parallel shift. *Kabuki* performances in the Edo period could last from dawn to midnight, and when combined with the time required for transportation to and from the theater, attending a performance could easily turn into a three-day affair.[76] In the Meiji period, there was much discussion that this leisurely pace did not fit with the busy lives of the modern urban workers. Kawakami, for instance, proposed five to six hours of performance total, with a dozen minutes of intermission—barely enough to stand up and stretch, certainly not enough to eat a meal or pay a visit backstage. Some proposals went even further. For example, Hatoyama Kazuo, a lawyer, proposed that performances be reduced to a couple of hours:

> Today's performances usually begin around 4 P.M. and last until 11 P.M., or begin at 10 A.M. and last until 4 P.M. If one wants to see a complete performance, it takes a whole day. So I tend to shy away from going to the theater: I may really wish to go, but finding such a long stretch of free time is impossible. And yet, I would want to see the whole performance, like everyone else, not just see part of it, right? So I wish they would shorten the intermissions, and show us performances that conclude in two or three acts. Those could be shown in two hours in the morning, or three hours in the afternoon. That way, it becomes easier to catch a show: someone like myself might peek in when a court hearing has been postponed from morning to afternoon, or a traveler might catch one act when he has missed his train. That would work just fine. From now on, people will place more value in time, so there is real need for reform.[77]

While theaters began reducing their performance hours, government regulations also cut down the hours allowed for performance. Thus, show time changed from a special duration set apart from the mundane flow of daily life to a slice of the homogenized time of the modern clock and calendar: It was cut down to fit in the interval between two court hearings, or between two trains.

Thus, the straightening of theater involved the shortening of theater performances and the construction of a theater building that fixes the audience and focuses vision. Yet Kawakami's plans for straightening theater were even more comprehensive, extending to the rationalization of production and management. Let us look more closely at Kawakami's efforts at theater reform.

In 1904, Kawakami proposed the following five principles to the theaters where the troupe would be performing:[78]

Hours of performance: open curtain at 5:30 P.M., close at 10 P.M., for a total of four hours of performance; reduce intermissions to 30 minutes.

Ticket prices: reduce to one-third of previous price; introduce system of selling tickets directly to public, rather than through tea houses.

Food and drink: prohibit eating and drinking in the seats; only allow food and drink in the promenade and tea houses.
Transportation: hire rickshaw pullers for the theater and sell tickets for them before the end of performance
Scenery: stop using the painters of *kabuki* scenery and mainly use Western-style painters.

Besides confining performance in temporal terms—about a third of the typical *kabuki* performance duration—these principles were designed to make theater independent from the tea houses, the ushers, the pleasure quarters, and various other providers of services that surrounded the theater building. This was part of the general formation of modern theater as a physical experience quite different from that of *kabuki.* In *kabuki,* a spectator had to negotiate with the tea houses to buy tickets and pay extra for being shown to one's seat, for checking in one's shoes, for buying food, drink, and seat cushions. In Kawakami's reformed theater, the spectator's relationship to the performance was rationalized, localized, and extricated from social relationships.

The response to Kawakami's reforms was an immediate attack from those who would lose business under the new system: A group of ushers beat up Kawakami's deputy, the head scenery painter also threatened to cause disturbances, and the dispute could only be resolved after Kawakami paid off these parties.[79] The *Yomiuri Shimbun* of January 18, 1904 contained a scathing anonymous attack against the reform efforts. The critic accused Kawakami of merely seeking fame and fortune rather than true improvement of theater arts:

> Even if performed from the crack of dawn to midnight, good acting is still good acting [*myōgi wa myōgi nari*]; Danjūrō would still be Danjūrō. Even if the fees for checking in shoes were abolished, bad acting would still be bad acting [*setugi wa setsugi nari*]; Otojirō would still be Otojirō. No matter how beautiful its binding and how low its price, a dull book is still a dull book [*sessaku wa sessaku taru ga gotoku*]. No matter if gratuities [*shūgi*] were abolished, an ugly whore is still an ugly whore [*shūgi wa shūgi taru ga gotoshi*].[80]

This anonymous attack contrasts Kawakami Otojirō's acting with that of Danjūrō, the most famous *kabuki* actor at that time. The concluding pun on the homophone "*shūgi*" deftly reestablishes the connection between theater, commercial exchange, and prostitution that Kawakami Otojirō had worked so hard to sever. One also notices, however, the metonymic substitution of the book for the performance in the penultimate sentence, a suggestive metaphor whose significance will become even more apparent in Part III.

Not satisfied with reforming practices at theaters where his troupe would be engaged to perform, the Kawakamis proposed their own system of tour performances, called "Reformed Theater Management" (*kakushin kōgyō*):

> The new management system I have conceived this time is the following: five or six troupes from distant places like Tokyo, Osaka, Yokohama, Kobe, Nagasaki, Nagoya, would form a union. Say we want to perform *Chūshingura:* we would prepare the scenery and props together. After first performing in Tokyo, for example, we would send all the equipment to Osaka, and have the troupe there perform *Chūshingura.* After Osaka, they would send the equipment on to Yokohama, or to Kobe, or wherever the play should be performed next. Thus we would have a united contract and circulate equipment from troupe to troupe, performing the same play at each place. In that way, we would be able to afford better scenery, props, and costumes, and since the performance expenses would go down substantially, we could also reduce the ticket prices. The audience would find it easier to come to our plays, and the managers might end up making more profit, too.[81]

Putting this idea into action, the Kawakamis organized a total of five troupes, called "platoons" (*gun*). Thus the "troupes" were turned into "troops" and were incorporated into a new multisegmented machine, geared both toward theatrical and military maneuvers, "in such a way that the maximum quantity of forces may be extracted from each and combined with the optimum result."[82] The military metaphor was not lost on the audience, some of whom responded with short satirical poems (*senryū*), published in the October 1908 issue of *Engei gahō:*

> Hatsu kōgyō ikusa gokko de futa o ake.
> [The first performance opens with war-games.]
> Gundanchō Kawakami shōgun to hiyakasare.
> [Platoon leader Kawakami is teasingly dubbed The Shogun.]

As these poems also show, one of the most successful of the performances under this reformed management system was a play called *Dumb Travel,* in which Sadayakko and a few fellow actresses were the main attraction.

> Debagame wa nigun no hō e kata o ire.
> [Peeping Toms support the Second Platoon.]
> Dai nigun dōken ron o jitsugen shi.
> [The Second Platoon makes equal rights a reality.]

Significantly, although the Reformed Theater Management sought to rationalize theater and make it more masculine and militaristic, it turned out that it

4.3 Kawakami Sadayakko surrounded by actresses of her "platoon." *Engei gahō* (October 1908).

was the spectacle of women performing that gathered the most audience attention and that consequently financed the whole venture.

HOMOSOCIAL THEATER

What straightening theater aimed to achieve, then, was something that might be called "homosocial theater." Here the term "homosocial" is deployed at the intersection of its usage by two theorists: Eve Kosofsky Sedgwick and Naoki Sakai. The former characterizes homosociality as the construction of male bonding and sexual homogeneity through the misogynist appropriation of women as well as the homophobic disavowal of homoeroticism, and hypothesizes the potential unbrokenness of a continuum between homosexuality and homosociality, although its visibility for men is radically disrupted in Western society.[83] On the other hand, Naoki Sakai sees homosociality as characterizing the "construction of national, ethnic, and cultural homogeneity through the spectacularization of the outsiders," but also sees that gender differentiation and gender politics operate powerfully in such a construction.[84] In the context of Japan in the period under discussion, homosociality attains a particular hue, due to the recent memory of "unbrokenness" of the continuum between homosociality and homosexuality in the Tokugawa period, combined with the gender politics at work in the construction of the Japanese nation in the Meiji period. "Homosocial theater" is a theater focusing on masculine national subjects, in which women are appropriated and wifed as mere mediators of relations between them; a theater in which heterosexual relations are subdued and secondary, only serving to consolidate homosocial relations; a theater in which men's relations with men are also carefully purged of any hint of sexuality, and in which this bond between men is figured as "obligation" (*giri*) and "loyalty" (*chūkō*); a theater in which a heterosexual relation is also reduced to a facsimile of this homosocial bond; a theater where the model man is a loyal national subject and soldier, and the model woman is an obedient wife and comforter. All of this is evident in *Sino-Japanese War* and is more evident in the plays discussed in the next chapter.

Straightening theater as "homosocial theater" also aims to create a "sameness" in society, and to that end seeks to manage various kinds of difference and deploy them for a unified national cause. For example, in straightened theater, gender difference is managed by distribution among different bodies. Women should act like women and men should act like men. This distribution is not completed in the process of straightening, since there are not enough women who can act. Thus men continue to act like women, and eventually, because of other considerations, some women begin to act like men, showing how the system of distribution is an unstable one.[85]

Difference in sexuality is managed by diluting the sexuality of actors through the magic formulae of the concepts of loyalty and obligation. By stressing the homosocial, rather than the homosexual aspects of military culture, and by diluting romance all together, straightening theater works to control sexuality without stressing heterosexuality.[86] The fluidity that characterized premodern *kabuki*'s "intertextuality"—understood as the regime of possible channels between genders and sexualities—is thus framed onto the bodies of males and females, closing off the kinds of polymorphous desires that were previously possible.[87]

Ethnic and linguistic difference is managed by having the main characters turn out to be Japanese in disguise. The most striking instances occur in *Sino-Japanese War,* where various Chinese characters turn out to be loyal Japanese, and in *Around the World in Seventy Days,* discussed in the next chapter, where an Indian princess turns out to be Japanese as well. This trick of "transformation," of showing the true nature of someone as a plot device, is here employed for the sake of building an imagining and imagined community: "We are all Japanese underneath." It is a useful gimmick in constructing this imagined sameness.

Politically, difference is managed by making theater represent the empire: benevolence on top, loyalty on bottom, everyone bound primarily by ties of obligation (*giri*) and secondarily by ties of sentimentality (*ninjō*).[88] The empire is a homosocial one, in which an attempt is made to turn everyone into loyal subjects: Teach them to speak Japanese, give them Japanese names, educate them to act like Japanese.[89]

The Kawakami troupe did not start out as an organ of the Japanese imperialist state but rather as a purveyor of bitingly satirical antigovernment burlesques, associated with the People's Rights Movement. It was the success of the production of *Sino-Japanese War* that turned the Kawakami troupe from populism to imperialist nationalism. One could say along with Sinologist Takeuchi Yoshimi that the energies of ethnic nationalism reflected in the People's Rights Movement were absorbed by the state nationalism and imperialism evidenced in the Sino-Japanese War and later the Russo-Japanese War, and that the Kawakami troupe's peregrinations merely followed this general trend.[90] Yet the People's Rights Movement was also intrinsically homosocial in that it was, like the French Revolution and the Enlightenment values, on which it was modeled, contingent on the definition of "man" as masculine. Such a definition of humanity as made up of upstanding male citizens always requires the abjection of "non-man": slaves, women, queers. This is why straightening theater attempted to purge the queer, the different, the indirect, in order to create an imagined community of the same—a politically, linguistically, ethnically, and sexually homosocial community.

CHAPTER 5

REPRODUCING THE EMPIRE

TRAVELING PLAYERS AND ORIENTALIST PLAYS: THE GEISHA AND THE KNIGHT

It was in 1899 that a troupe of about 20 actors embarked on a world tour, led by Kawakami Sadayakko and her husband Otojirō. It seems that Sadayakko's role in this troupe was an ambiguous one at the outset: She did participate in rehearsal performances in Japan, yet there were no concrete plans for her to perform abroad. Upon arriving in San Francisco in May 1899, however, she found out that the theater conventions of the United States expected her to take on a much more central role.

> One thing came as a surprise to me: on the way to the hotel, I could see photographs of myself blown up larger than life plastered at every street-corner! When I asked the promoter what that was supposed to mean, he told me, "in this country, performers [*haiyū*] must be female." I argued that it was a big mistake, that I had not come as a performer, that it was Kawakami who would perform, and that the play would be *Sino-Japanese War* [Nisshin sensō]. But I was told, "No, that just won't do. Americans don't know the difference between Japan and China—they think it's the same country. If you perform a play like that, nobody will come see it. And you've got to have an actress. You've got to have a woman." So there was nothing I could do; I had to become a performer and act.[1]

This was an early hint of the multiple roles Sadayakko would come to play in the United States and Europe, not only as a woman who by virtue of being a woman was superior to male impersonators, but also as an "oriental" woman representing her nation in relation to the West. A play about Japan and China performed by men would not appeal to an audience, because the difference between Japan and China would be as inscrutable as the convention of a man playing a woman's role. But a play showing an exotic oriental Japan performed by a Japanese woman would be supremely legible and attractive to this audience.

The tour concentrated on cities with large populations of Japanese immigrants: San Francisco, Seattle, Portland, Tacoma. But, as it turned out, the Japanese immigrant population comprised only a small part of the audience in these performances, and hence various difficulties were connected with the perception of Japanese by (Anglo) Americans. According to their own testimony, in the beginning the troupe faced hostile managers who could not believe that "Japs" had anything worth calling dramatic art. For example, Kawakami Otojirō recounts the following words of frustration uttered by troupe member Maruyama on his deathbed at a Boston hospital:

> Ever since I came here, I have been taunted by our colleagues in the theater, who would ask me: Is there music in Japan? Is there theater in Japan? I kept being called "Jap" and was always looked down upon. This is my largest regret. It is your great responsibility to get rid of these taunts and ridicules.[2]

These taunts and ridicules came not only from disdainful Americans but also from Japanese residents. In Chicago, the Japanese consul proved to be the most hostile, as Sadayakko recalls:

> We went to the Japanese consulate, explained our problem, and asked for assistance. But the consul turned out to be a believer in Christianity, and refused to have anything to do with us, claiming that he hated theater. So we gave up on that issue and asked for assistance concerning our luggage: because of language problems, we had been unable to find out how to pick up our luggage. The consul, however, turned us away with: "I am no watch-dog for the luggage of actors," and refused to talk to us any further. A compatriot and yet so lacking in sympathy![3]

The troupe thus came close to starving in Chicago but were finally rescued through interventions by the Japanophile daughter of a theater manager. Sadayakko recounts the first performance in Chicago in vivid detail:

> Though we were finally able to rent the theater, they gave us nothing else: we had to use the backdrops we had brought from Japan, and for cherry blossoms, I had to cut up paper and others of the troupe would paste them on branches. What a circus! The program was to consist of just two plays, *Kojima Takanori* and *Dōjōji,* and when we finally opened, fortunately it was a huge box-office success. In *Kojima Takanori,* there is a fight scene: everyone attacks Takanori, everyone is thrown off, and everyone is supposed to attack him one more time. But the whole troupe had not eaten for the last three days:

「芸者と武士」（1902年パリ万国博覧会）
左端 音二郎、左から3人目 貞奴

5.1 *Geisha and the Knight* at the Paris World's Fair 1902 [*sic*]. Kawakami Otojirō as the samurai, far left; Sadayakko as the geisha, third from left. Courtesy of Waseda University's Tsubouchi Shōyō Memorial Theater Museum.

> when thrown on stage, no one had the strength to stand up again, so there was nothing to be done but to draw the curtain on the fallen men. Next was my *Dōjōji:* Because I was excited I was able to complete the dance and do it justice, but when I think back, I wonder how I managed to move even that much. This performance was a great popular success, and we earned a profit of about sixty dollars after expenses. Kawakami divided this evenly among the troupe members and said, "Now, go and eat a real Western meal for a change." Everyone said, "Thank you very much" and brought the money to a Western restaurant. When the food was finally brought to the table, however, we all just looked wordlessly at each other and cried.[4]

The courtesan-turned-madwoman of *Dōjōji* was one of the roles for which Sadayakko would become famous in the West.

In order to cash in on the popularity of this role, the Kawakami troupe stitched together the plot of *Dōjōji* and scenes from one other *kabuki* play, *Striking Swords* (Saya'ate). The result was the pseudo-*kabuki* smash-hit *The Geisha and the Knight* (Geisha to samurai). A March 1900 review of the performance in New York summarizes the plot of *The Geisha and the Knight* as follows:

> A beautiful geisha falls in love with a knight who is challenged by a jealous rival. They fight, but are separated by the geisha. Thereupon the lucky knight is claimed by his bride, whom he has neglected for the sake of the geisha, and is carried off. They flee into a sacred temple. The geisha tries to follow them, but is prevented by the monks. She dances to please them, and then slips into the temple. She soon returns with the unfortunate bride, and in a rage of jealousy tries to kill her, but is prevented by the knight, in whose arms she dies of a broken heart.[5]

The fight between the two "knights" is taken from the *kabuki* play *Saya'ate,* while the scene at the temple is taken from the dance play *Dōjōji.* Kawakami Sadayakko continued to receive great acclaim in the United States and Europe for her portrayal of the geisha gone mad with jealousy and rage, collapsing and expiring of a broken heart at the end.

A review of the troupe's performance in Boston is a good example of the way these pseudo-*kabuki* plays were perceived:

> The actors spoke in their native tongue, and they were accompanied by weird and monotonous instrumental music and strident chanting and singing. The chief characteristics of their art were its action and its vividness. There was apparently little or no attempt to appeal to the imagination, but the emotions were portrayed with bluntness and crudity.
>
> "The Geisha and the Knight" with us would be classed somewhere between a spectacle and a pantomime. The dialogue was limited, but the action was constant and vehement. The play opened with a fierce pitched battle. The next scene of the first act showed a second fight, in which the hero killed half a dozen of his foes with dexterity and dispatch. The second act brought forth an exciting duel, and the final curtain fell on another combat, with nearly everyone on stage in a more or less dilapidated condition. Yet, in the midst of all this extravagance, there was at times unquestioned power. Mr. Kawakami was ever dignified and impressive, and Mme. Yacco's death scene at the end of the play revealed tragic force.[6]

From New York, the Kawakami Troupe crossed to Europe, performing in London and later in Paris at the World Fair of 1900. Their repertoire consisted of more pseudo-*kabuki* plays such as *Zingoro, an Earnest Statue Maker, The Royalist, or Kojima Takanori, Kesa: The Wife's Sacrifice,* and, of course, the popular *The Geisha and the Knight.* The tour ended with the return of the troupe to Japan in January 1901. Three months later they were in Europe again, and returned a year later, after having performed in over 60 cities all over Europe, including London, Paris, Berlin, Vienna, Prague, Budapest, and cities in Russia, Italy, Spain, and Portugal.[7] Sadayakko was surrounded by adoring crowds everywhere she went.

BETTER THAN BERNHARDT: RESPONSES ABROAD

Touring the West and presenting herself in these pseudo-*kabuki* spectacles, Sadayakko was ineluctably caught within the structure of Orientalist vision.[8] The year 1900 was a moment when Japan still fitted unarguably into that part of the world the West regarded as its politically alien, culturally exotic, and discursively feminized other. And Sadayakko acted like the perfect embodiment of exotic and feminine Japan under the Orientalizing gaze of her audience. Such an interplay of gazing and flirting is apparent from the account of an interview conducted in Paris in 1900 and printed in an English-language pamphlet that was apparently published to coincide with the World's Fair.

> Sada Yacco enters clothed in a long black "kimono" her delicate and childish melancholy face lighting up with a smile. She has been ill. I ask her if she is better. "No better, cold! . . . cold!" she says in her caressing voice. We talk of the theater, of Paris, of London (which she adores) then we reach the subject on which she is to give me information i.e., "Love in Japan." "Different—so different!" she exclaims, "In this country men and women love each other freely; it is the custom. Japanese girls do not declare their love so frankly. Often they will die rather than to confess it.[. . .] Ah! to me, my friend, love in Japan is very noble, sublime and sacred."[9]

One can almost see the actress demurely fluttering her eyelids. Who represents whom in this scene? "Japanese girls" are represented by Sadayakko, who in turn is represented by the European interviewer and the frame of the publication. We do not know if Sadayakko spoke in French or in Japanese through an interpreter; we do not know to what extent the interviewer edited, or even fabricated, the words of the actress; we do not know to what extent Sadayakko was playfully enacting the role of the delicate "Japanese girl." What we *do* know is that the image presented to us on the pages of this booklet coincides neatly with the image of the oriental woman, popularized in Europe around the turn of the century through operas and musicals such as the operetta *Mikado* (1885)[10] and the opera *Madame Butterfly* (1904).[11]

The booklet contains a number of photographs and sketches, many of which capture the Japanese performers within a frame of exotic flowers. The text contains a plot summary of *The Geisha and the Knight;* a comparison of her death scene to that of Sarah Bernhardt in *Camille;* an explanation of the status of geisha, at which point Sadayakko is called in to explain "Love in

Japan"; and a biography of Sadayakko emphasizing her training in the performing arts, in which any hint of the fact that geisha engaged in prostitution is carefully avoided. There is further a history of Japanese theater explaining the exclusion of women from the stage in the Tokugawa period; a description of Otojirō's attempt to create "an Opera House on European plans" and its dismal failure due to the lack of understanding among Japanese people; a recap of the troupe's tour so far; and, as if in foreboding riposte to Kawakami Sadayakko's later vow to train "Sarah Bernhardts of Japan," the grand actress Sarah Bernhardt's reactions to Sadayakko's fame. This last section is worth quoting here in full:

> But Sarah? What did she think of it? Did she consider this Asiatic actress's death scene finer than her own? Oh! dear no, she spread her disapproval far and wide. Some time afterwards, I asked Madame Bernhardt what she really thought of the performance. Immediately came a storm of adjectives: "*Atroce! abominable! horribile!*—a pack of monkeys, my friend, a pack of monkeys!" This action of Bernhardt's against a fellow-artist was not met with favour by the French Press—"Never mind, exquisite little Japanese"—appeared in a well known French paper the next day—"it was hardly worth your while giving a *matinée* to be insulted. You are accused of dying like a monkey; go away, little Japanese, and come back in a year or so—before if you can—and you will find actresses trying to imitate you in every detail. Who will speak of monkeys then?"[12]

This pamphlet, with its gesture of sugary patronage of the Japanese actress, protecting her from the mean-spirited and racist attacks from her French rival, suggest the kind of eyes that gazed at Sadayakko in Europe. The list of people who were seduced by Sadayakko's charms and who sought to capture her in words and images begins to sound like a Who's Who of European culture at the turn of the century: Pablo Picasso, then nineteen years old, sketched her dancing. Auguste Rodin asked her to be a model for him, but she refused. Claude Debussy, Paul Klee, and Isadora Duncan praised her. "Yacco" dresses and "Yacco" perfume were marketed in France.

In her turn, Sadayakko, who had acted like a perfect creature of the Orientalist imagination, appropriated the costume, posture, and manners of the West when she returned to Japan in 1901. A newspaper article that described her arrival at Kobe harbor marveled how "Sadayakko looks like a Parisian lady":

> Sadayakko is wearing a new dress in Parisian fashion, and her hair, which used to be as black as crow's feathers and knotted in Takashimada or Ichōgaeshi style,[13] now appears golden as the color proudly worn by aristocratic ladies in those foreign countries. That hair is bound loosely in Parisian style, with a few strands curled around her luscious cheeks. Even the color of

5.2 Kawakami Sadayakko as a Western lady, and as a Japanese woman. *Engei gahō* (October 1908)

> her skin seems to have become milky white with a pale pink blush. And with her double eyelids on her bell-shaped eyes, she might indeed be mistaken as a Western lady [*seiyō fujin*].[14]

Thus, while she may have presented herself as the essence of the Orient to Western eyes, once back in Japan she presented herself as the perfect Western lady. And while she may have seduced the Western audience with her exotic dances, her compatriots at home looked at her askance, with more than a little ambivalence.

THE POLITICS OF VISION: RESPONSES IN JAPAN

When they saw or heard about the Orientalist pseudo-*kabuki* performances of the Kawakami troupe, Japanese men of culture and influence responded with ambivalence, if not anger. They considered it shameful for the entire nation to have their theater represented in this manner. A good example was the reaction of the painter Kubota Beisai, whose reviews of the troupe's Paris performances were serialized in the Japanese daily *Yomiuri Shimbun* in August and September of 1900. He objected to "the unprecedented plot that is a hodgepodge of *Striking Swords* and *Dōjōji* performed with off-the-wall costumes and unfathomable dialogue." He ridiculed the combat scenes, and about Sadayakko's performance he commented sarcastically that "according to the plot summary she is supposed to be a geisha, but she appears dressed like a high-class courtesan (*oiran*); this is strange but let us not ask such questions." He summed up the performance as "constantly noisy without unity; with dialogue too dull and monotonous" but remarked caustically that the Western audience seemed to love it anyway.[15]

The difference between responses to Kawakami by Westerners and those by Japanese attests to a complicated politics of vision: Who sees whom under what circumstances; what is visible and what remains invisible; who has control over what is exposed or concealed; who can gaze back and who decides what all these sights mean. And definitions of gender, theater, and nation are all involved in this serious play of hide and seek. Japanese government officials had allergic reactions against having the nation represented by the likes of geisha and actors (*geinin*), who were considered by the majority to be the equivalent of prostitutes and river-bed beggars. This allergy had been intensifying in the 1880s and 1890s, through the world's fairs and the *Nihonjin mura* or "Japanese Village" exhibitions.[16] Significantly, the first individuals to officially represent Japanese culture abroad had been performers of nonverbal art: in 1866 the first set of visas issued by the Japanese government had been given to two troupes of acrobats, under contract with an American and an Englishman respectively.[17] In 1885, the first Japanese Village opened in London, with performances of acrobatics, *sumō* wrestling, *kabuki* plays, and women dancing, as well as displays of houses, of craft making, and of daily life. The *Illustrated London News* of February 21, 1885 shows pictures of "A Street Corner" with lanterns and store signs; "A Place of Worship" with a woman in front of a Buddhist altar; "Screen Painting" with two men working; and "The Tea House" with geisha entertaining men in a house made of bamboo, wood, and paper. The article explains that the Japanese are fun-loving and diligent, their work is intricate, and their tea girls laugh into their sleeves. The tone of condescension was not lost upon Yano Fumio, a Japanese who visited the Village and reported that the whole project was deplorable, and that the Japanese were being perceived on the same level as "Hottentots, or inhabitants of Madagascar or Sudan."[18] He especially objected to the kinds of women, music, and dance displayed in the Village.[19] In later years, however, similar Japanese Villages opened in San Francisco, New York, Boston, Washington, and Sydney.

At first sight, the spread of the Japanese Villages seems to testify t popularity of Japanese culture in nations such as Britain, Germany, and the United States. However, the period leading up to the opening of the first Japanese Village in 1885 had also been a period during which Japan was trying to reform the unequal treaties with Western nations. This delicate political situation explains the skepticism of the Japanese government concerning the Japanese Villages and similar venues: At a time when it was crucial for Japan to prove its equal status with Western nations, what would be the effect of a public display in the Western metropolis of questionable Japanese individuals of dubious social status engaged in low-tech crafts and lowbrow forms of entertainment? There was every reason for the Japanese government to be cautious of this kind of publicity and scrutiny.

The controversy over the Japanese Village made it more difficult for Japanese performers to travel abroad in subsequent years. When the French government requested Japanese participation in the World's Fair of 1889, for example, plans of inviting a troupe of dancing girls from Japan fell through because of the humiliating memories of the Japanese Village. This, despite the French assurance that the girls would wear tights to cover any skin surface that might be visible from kimono openings, lodge in quarters in the countryside, commute by carriage to the Fair site, and refuse to attend banquets of any kind, all in order to avoid scandal.[20] The very idea of Japanese women performing under Western eyes raised the hackles of those men who would equate guarding Japanese women's chastity with protecting Japanese national sovereignty.

This brings us to the Paris World's Fair of 1900, the glamorous stage from which Sadayakko's fame reached as high as the Eiffel Tower. Here, Sadayakko stepped onto an Orientalist milieu, a stage that had been set up long before her arrival.

The world's fairs[21] were perfect examples of the penetration of the modernity of vision (*manazashi no kindai*) into social life through mass entertainment. The modernity of vision was organized gradually between the fifteenth and eighteenth centuries: It constituted the self as a subject of vision in polar opposition to the object of vision. This modern vision, equivalent of what historian Martin Jay calls the "scopic regime of modernity,"[22] enabled the conception of the world as transparent, abstract, and homogeneous space to be controlled and disciplined. As embodiments of the modernity of vision, world's fairs are ideological apparatuses that fashion imperialism, consumerism, and spectatorship. World's fairs were at once part of the propaganda apparatus of imperialism, showcases of advanced capitalism, and entertaining spectacles and diversions for the masses. For certain, the fairs and exhibitions displayed merchandise and taught the masses how to behave as consumers, but the dream of consumption and spectacular forms of entertainment also diverted the potentially revolutionary energy of the masses:

"The world's fairs transformed the revolting masses into consuming masses."[23] Most importantly for our argument, however, world's fairs performed a crucial function in the imperialist organization of people and their consciousness.

Already the first Great Exhibition of London in 1851 signaled the beginning of imperialist display. The famed Crystal Palace was a monstrous glass-made conservatory whose origins lay in the colonization of tropical regions.[24] More than merely housing rare tropical plants from the colonies, however, the Crystal Palace displayed evidence of Britain's imperial and industrial power in a homogeneous, transparent, and infinitely extendible tableau constructed of glass and steel.[25] At the Paris World's Fair of 1867, participating nations began to house their wares in their own pavilions, each one constructed to represent the typical architectural style of each nation: The Japanese pavilion was a tea-house where three geisha served tea to customers. At the World's Fair in the same city in 1889, the newly constructed Eiffel Tower provided a bird's-eye perspective of the whole fairground, a world in miniature seen from a distant and detached perspective.[26] A small railway connected the various pavilions, allowing fair-goers to "travel around the world." At the same fairgrounds, "primitive tribes" from Senegal, New Caledonia, French West Indies, and Java were displayed—a trend that culminated in the Chicago Fair of 1893. The display of human beings in Chicago's "White City" was arranged according to a conception of human evolution from primitive to civilized stages: the pavilions of the colonial powers at the center, the pavilions of semicivilized nations such as Japan a little further away from the center, the display of the "primitive tribes" on the outskirts.[27]

Within such an explicitly imperialist and colonialist schema of vision, Japan's position became ambivalent and twisted, caught in a kind of double-vision. Starting with the London Fair of 1862, Japan was exhibited under the scopic regime of the modern West.[28] Japan objectified itself under Western eyes, internalized what the West wanted to see, and reproduced this vision in the display of exotic *japonisme* arts and crafts. Yet at the same time, Japan longed to learn and appropriate the Western vision for itself, gazing at its own neighbors with imperial and colonial eyes.[29] Starting around its victory in the Russo-Japanese War in 1904, Japan began displaying "primitive tribes" in its own exhibitions: the Ainu in the north, the Okinawans in the south, Taiwanese, Koreans, and Manchurians.[30] By displaying minority people within its borders, as well as "different races" (*ijinshu*) beyond its borders, Japan thus advertised and represented the expansion of the empire through colonial acquisition.

The colonial expansion of Japan was inseparable from the politics of vision and the kind of evolutionary ordering of peoples that the world's fairs made possible and popular. In this context, Sadayakko's performance at the Paris World's Fair in 1900 struck a complicated chord. She was a potent reminder of how Japan was perceived by the West: exotic, delicate, quaint, and backward—definitely not modern and certainly not equal to the West in power. Not only was Sadayakko both geisha and popular performer (*geinin*), the plays in which she performed were bastardized versions of *kabuki.* And these played into all the stereotypes that modern Japanese people were presumably trying to overcome: barbaric men slashing each other with swords, disreputable women in brothels with untidy kimono and wild hair. The roles Sadayakko played were neither traditionally refined enough to satisfy proponents of *kabuki* as a Japanese national theater, nor properly modern enough to appease proponents of a newer, more Western kind of theater. Sadayakko's spectacle was read as the essence of the Orient by Europeans and as a shame on the nation by the Japanese. To certain Western eyes, she represented an image of Japan as beautiful, archaic, and fragile. To certain Japanese eyes, she was a reminder of an image that needed to be discarded if Japan was to look like a modern nation.

The disavowal of the Orientalized, feminized Japan went hand in hand with the "straightening" of theater. Theater needed to become not only a showcase demonstrating a modern, civilized, and masculine Japan; it also needed to become a school in which spectators would learn how to be subjects of such a nation. This was indeed the purpose of "straightening theater." In the years after her return to Japan in 1901, Sadayakko would participate in this demonstrative and pedagogical mission of theater in complex ways, to which we now turn.

PLAYS ABOUT TRAVEL AND WESTERNIZED PLAYERS: AROUND THE WORLD IN 80/70 DAYS

In 1910, ten years after her trip through the United States and Europe, Kawakami Sadayakko and her troupe performed another journey. This time, it was a journey on stage: a Japanese stage adaptation of a novel by Jules Verne, *Around the World in Eighty Days* (Le tour du monde en quatre-vingts jours). This play was meant for a Japanese audience, but it also incorporated elements from the troupe's world tour ten years earlier. This adaptation is in many ways paradigmatic of the kind of role Sadayakko played in changing definitions of women and theater at this crucial time in the formation of Japan as a modern nation-state and as a colonial empire. 1910 also happens to be the year of Japan's annexation of Korea, and thus a station on Japan's road to military aggression toward its Asian neighbors. Let us therefore take a closer look at the itinerary of *Around the World*, both the original novel and the Japanese play, and at the complicated negotiations that took place in the transfer from one country to another, one medium to another.

In the original novel, written and set in 1872, a British gentleman named Phileas Fogg bets that he can travel around the world in eighty days and proceeds to accomplish the feat with the help of his French servant. Fogg is a typically punctual and reserved British gent, while the ever-resourceful servant is aptly named Passepartout, i.e., "master-key," and personifies Gallic *esprit*. The two travelers employ various means of conveyance—carriages, steamships, railways, yachts, trading vessels, an elephant, and a wind-powered sledge, among others—all made available through Phileas Fogg's enormous cash reserve, carried around in Passepartout's suitcase. They face adventures galore on their journey around the world: In India they rescue a princess from the fate of *suttee* or widow-burning; in Japan the servant is lost and is later found performing in a theatrical troupe called the "Long Noses of the God Tingou"; in America the travelers are attacked by an angry Sioux tribe. Furthermore, they are being pursued by detective Fixx from Scotland Yard, who mistakenly believes the travelers to be fugitives who have committed bank robbery back in Great Britain.

On the surface, this novel seems to be about a mathematically calculated itinerary around the world, about the overcoming of various obstacles on the way, and about the importance of keeping track of one's hours and minutes on an eastward journey—by the end, the travelers have lost track of one whole day, which prepares the way for a spectacular happy end. How could this innocuous novel about world travel have anything to do with European colonialism? And how could the adaptation of this novel into a Japanese play have anything to do with the process by which Japan learned to be a colonial power?

Most interpretations of *Around the World in Eighty Days* have concentrated on the abstract structural image of circling the world.[31] Pierre Macherey declares "The works of Verne are nothing but a long meditation, or dream, on the straight line."[32] And what could be more abstract than a straight line circling the globe? Phileas Fogg is certainly the best representative of the scopic regime of modernity, a new kind of subject of vision, excluding and excluded from the object of vision. He travels around the world without wanting to become involved in it; he is the abstract traveler isolated from his surroundings. He declines to learn anything about the inhabitants of the land through which he journeys.[33] In fact, he does not even wish to see his surroundings, either. The title to chapter 14 puts it most succinctly: "Dans lequel Phileas Fogg descend toute l'admirable vallée du Gange sans même songer à la voir" (In which Phileas Fogg descends the whole length of the beautiful valley of the Ganges without ever thinking of seeing it). He is not even a pair of eyes circling the globe: He is no more than a *passport* circling the globe.[34] All he needs to do is to move through as much space in as little time as possible and to get his passport stamped as proof of his passage through certain checkpoints. The space through which he moves and the time it takes for him are homogeneous, abstract, and measurable space and time. Each mile, each minute, has the same value: More miles in fewer minutes is the ultimate value.[35]

Yet all this movement through time and space can only be grasped as abstract when the material conditions that make it possible have been sufficiently repressed. Traveling is never innocent or abstract; it affects the traveler as well as the environment through which he (in 1872 it was usually *he*)[36] travels. Moreover, traveling assumes certain preconditions that make the itinerary possible: among the most obvious are the means of transportation, such as railway and steamship lines, arrangements for exchange of money, services such as food and lodging, and, perhaps most fundamentally, the securing of safe passage through control of local populations. In other words, what makes the circling of the globe possible is the controlling of the globe by colonial powers: Great Britain, France, the United States, and, by 1910, the Japanese empire. The novel was published at a time "when travel was still exotic and romantic, yet essentially safe; an adventure, yet one available to anyone with enough courage and money."[37]

As succinctly summarized in the title used to designate the whole collection of his novels, *Voyages extraordinaires: Les mondes connus et inconnus* (Extraordinary voyages: Known and unknown worlds), Jules Verne depicted a universe in which the border between the known and unknown worlds was constantly moving.[38] It seems, however, that Verne himself had trouble recognizing that the majority of *les mondes inconnus* were in the process of moving out of the latter category into the category of *les mondes connus;* his novels "somewhat naively reflect the racist and ethnocentric prejudices which at that time provided convenient justification for colonial expansion and the pillaging of colonial territories."[39] In the latter half of the nineteenth century, Japan, too, was beginning to move from the unknown to the known side of the divide and was itself beginning to seek out and conquer unknown worlds. Yet there is little indication of this in Verne's novels. Although Verne described many geopolitical events and situations in his novels, he did not describe the immense changes going on in Japan during this time.[40]

In the 1872 trip depicted in *Around the World in Eighty Days,* for example, Japan appears as an ancient, unchanging, and inscrutable place. There is little suggestion of the recent political upheavals, the opening of Japan to the West after two and a half centuries of isolation, the change in government structure, or the various signs of modernization and Westernization. The area around the port of Yokohama is indeed described as "a thoroughly European quarter," but the farther away the travelers move from the port into the city, the further back they seem to regress in time. Depictions of temples and shrines are followed by a litany of exotic flowers and birds. The whole tableau was most likely taken from screen paintings available in France at the time; one scene is indeed explicitly compared to a screen painting:

> The Japanese quarter of Yokohama is called Benten, after the goddess of the sea, who is worshipped on neighboring islands. There Passepartout beheld beautiful fir and cedar groves, sacred gates of a singular architecture, bridges half-hid in the midst of bamboos and reeds, temples shaded by immense cedar trees, holy retreats where were sheltered Buddhist priests and disciples of Confucius, and interminable streets, where a perfect harvest of rose-tinted and red-cheeked children, *who looked as if they had been cut out of Japanese screens,* and who were playing in the midst of short-legged poodles and yellowish cats, might have been gathered.[41]

Interestingly, it is a theater performance that is the center of the travelers' adventures in Japan. And this performance is not that of a traditional *kabuki,* nor of *shimpa,* but of an acrobatic troupe about to depart for a tour of the United States. This reminds us that the first Japanese acrobatic troupe had reached the Lyceum in Paris in 1868. Thus the acrobatic troupe in Verne's novel is one of the signs of hybridity that emerge at the "contact zone" of the known and unknown worlds. It is not classical or modern theater, but a kind of hybrid performance that is thematized at the moment of contact.[42] The "Long Noses of the God Tingou" prove to Passepartout and the eyes of Westerners represented by him that "the Japanese are the first acrobats in the world."[43] At this point, Verne's depiction of Japan corresponds almost exactly to the kinds of images disseminated in the West through the Japanese Villages and world's fairs. As the Kawakami troupe stepped onto the stage at the Paris World's Fair of 1900, this was the kind of discursive setting into which their performance was inserted. And the Kawakamis' attempt to "straighten" theater found itself at a most complicated juncture.

What about the traveling woman in *Around the World?* The fundamental misogyny of Jules Verne has been pointed out by many.[44] The structure of the novel places emphasis on the rescue of an Indian princess from the funeral pyre, yet her characterization is sketchy at best. Mostly she is an abstract figure who serves the plot, leading Simone Vierne to equate her with *le jour fantôme,* the one extra day that the travelers gain by moving Eastward:

> Aouda in that sense is an image of the phantom day. She also stands in for money, since the voyage is calculated to end up without profit under a strict financial plan. She is part of that slight difference which distinguishes the day of departure from the day of arrival. This young woman . . . is the symbol of that which is most abstract in the novel.[45]

She is described as both exotic and yet almost "European" in both appearance and behavior. In the original novel, the Indian princess falls in love with her British rescuer and proposes to him at the end of the journey. Since the gentleman has won the bet but has spent his entire fortune in order to win it, the only gain he has made from his traveling is this woman, a souvenir rescued from the natives in the Indian colony. The novel ends thus with a romantic union with a charming and exotic woman: "Truly, would you not for less than that go around the world?"[46] Decades later, a fictional Japanese gentlemen would indeed go around the world for much less than that, as we will now see.

The Japanese version of *Around the World* is based on a translation of Verne's novel.[47] There is no published script for this Japanese version, and the scriptwriter is unknown. In the following analysis, I rely on a handwritten manuscript used by the Kawakami troupe, stored now in a collection at Waseda University's Theater Museum.

In the Japanese play, it is a Japanese gentleman who starts out from Osaka on a world tour accompanied by his Japanese servant. The Japanese journey around the world is shortened to *Around the World in Seventy Days.* (This can be explained by advances in transportation between 1872 and 1910, but it may also be a way of saying "We Japanese can do it faster than those Europeans!") The play opens with a scene in Osaka, proceeds to show scenes in San Francisco, London, a temple in India, Hong Kong, and Kobe harbor in Japan, and finally takes the audience back to Osaka.

On the most simple level, then, the adaptation is paradigmatic of the process of "twisted double vision": the process by which Japanese people, objects of the colonizing gaze in Jules Verne's time and spectacles for Orientalizing eyes at the time of Sadayakko's performances, themselves learned to become subjects of a colonial empire in 1910 and found themselves ready to gaze upon other people with colonizing and Orientalizing eyes. In *Imagined Communities,* Benedict Anderson outlines the same process, summarizing how Japan borrowed the European model of "official nationalism" and went on to imitate its imperialism.[48] This, then, is part of the process of "reproduction of imperialism," and the Kawakami performances can be seen as participating in the process.

However, *Around the World in Seventy Days* stages this general process of "imitating the Western model" in complicated and unpredictable ways. Indeed, it is the play's failure and/or refusal to imitate the Western model that leaves open the possibility for multiple identifications and multiple meanings. In the structure of the reproduction of imperialism, then, the Kawakamis produce a difference that disrupts the replication of the original.

In order to show this process at work, let us follow the itinerary of the Japanese world trip for a while. Act 1 scene 1 is set at a hotel in Osaka, where the Naniwa Club is meeting for a soirée. The talk of the Club centers on what it means to be a gentleman (*shinshi*): Most members have only recently become gentlemen through economic ventures and thus cannot boast of an aristocratic lineage. Hatsuta Jōji (the Japanese adaptation of the name Passepartout), a waiter who is also an acrobatic performer, argues that the epitome of the true gentleman is Fukuhara Takeo (the Japanese adaptation of Phileas Fogg). In contrast to all the nouveau-riche imitation gentlemen, Fukuhara is a true gentleman.

> Jōji: Friends of a feather flock together. They say, if you want to know about a person, look at his friends. His deeds are upright, his character is impeccable, the men with whom he keeps company are all of highly sophisticated tastes. He's not to be confused with the kind of gentleman who is only interested in beef, women, and gambling.
>
> (*Shiroko, Kuroko, Akako, Torako (wives of the pseudo-gentlemen) stand up and cheer.*)
>
> Jōji: On top of that, he is courageous; acts on his beliefs; does not say much; but once a word is spoken, he takes full responsibility. I would call that the way of the samurai [*bushidō*], the way of the gentleman.
>
> Hiraura: Ha, the way of the samurai!

Fukuhara enters, a debate ensues, and he ends up betting 30,000 yen that he can go around the world in 70 days. This opening scene lays out the theme of the play: Fukuhara Takeo's journey is motivated by his desire to prove he is a true gentleman and a modern-day samurai who will keep his word and his honor by accepting this challenge.[49]

This scene is also a clever interweaving of the original novel's chapters set in London's Reform Club and its chapters set at the Japanese acrobat show: Hatsuta Jōji, who becomes Fukuhara's servant, performs a series of dances using a long-nosed Tengu mask as part of the banquet entertainment. Thus the acrobatic antics, which are signs of Japan's quaint and exotic charm in the original novel, are restaged here in the context of a Western-style social occasion.

Just as the London of the original is replaced by the newly gentrified Osaka, the Japanese acrobatic show of the original is replaced by London theater. At the point at which the Japanese travelers arrive in London, which in the original novel was the starting point and destination of world travel, the center of civilization and all that makes traveling possible, the Japanese version performs something very strange. The script at this point simply indicates "Scene of Theater in London, English Capital. Here we present *Dōjōji.*" *Dōjōji* is the play that Sadayakko performed ten years earlier in London, as well as in other cities of the civilized world, as part of her pseudo-*kabuki* show entitled *The Geisha and the Knight.* In other words, by presenting the play within the play at this point, the performers are not merely repeating the experience of being looked at by Westerners, but are reversing and complicating the trajectory of looking. It is as if they are saying: "You Westerners may think you are the center of civilization, but for us you are just a stop on our world travel. We look at you as a convenient stage for our little song and dance. And you Japanese men of culture may think you can look down upon us, but look at those Westerners looking at us with open mouths." The earlier orientalist spectacle is here restaged and resignified to a more complex network of contexts and meanings, even as it is being reproduced.

The original novel ended happily with the hero's journey being rewarded by the native woman he rescued from the funeral pyre. In the Japanese play, things are more complicated. When the travelers see the *suttee* procession in India, they decide that they must rescue her from the barbaric natives:

> Fukuhara: It doesn't matter if it is a local custom: we, as Japanese men, cannot condone such an evil custom that goes against the laws of heaven. Jōji, can't we think of a way to somehow rescue this woman?
>
> Jōji: Of course there is! We must rescue her. Burning a human being alive—who's ever heard of such a barbaric thing? There's no way I'm leaving here without rescuing her (Act 4 scene 1).

But the Indian princess turns out to have been a Japanese lady abducted from her parents when she was seven years old, a long story in the tradition of convoluted *kabuki* plots. The relationship between the rescuer and the rescued in the Japanese version is figured as one of *giri* (duty) and *on* (obligation): The woman decides to repay her obligations to Fukuhara by becoming his lifelong companion and *hanashi aite*—literally translated as "conversation partner" but more like a "listening ear":

> Auta: I really don't care about what happens to me, but when I think of how the Master feels, I don't know how to console him.
>
> Oshimo: It's true; our Master is a bachelor, so there is no one to console him when he has suffered a great deal.
>
> Auta: I've been thinking: even a creature like me could perhaps console him by staying at his side and lending a sympathetic ear.
>
> Oshimo: If you could do that for even for a short time, how it would entertain him!
>
> Auta: No, I actually would like to stay my whole life. Even if I stay at his side for my whole life, I cannot repay my obligation to him. (Act 5 scene 3)

It may be that in the minds of the Kawakamis, the Indian princess has to be conceived as being really Japanese in order to convincingly conduct herself in this nonromantic manner, a manner possibly imagined by the Kawakamis to be typically, and even exclusively, Japanese.

Significantly, Fukuhara is the object of another "long-term obligation repayment plan," that of a widow whose father was rescued by Fukuhara's father a long time ago, during the pre-Meiji Restoration days. The widow helps Fukuhara win his bet by various means, including financial support and a last-minute scientific explanation of how he gained a day by traveling Eastward around the globe. Yet there is not even a hint of romance between widow Sakurai and Fukuhara:

> Sakurai: You see, I have the duty to serve you.
>
> Fukuhara: The duty to serve me? Why is that?
>
> Sakurai: My father, Sakurai Kyūma, was what they call a political rebel (*shishi*) during the restoration period; they say he dared a great deal for politics. A total of three times, he came close to losing his life to the shogun's forces, but each of those three times he was saved by your father, the present Count Fukuhara. Thus my father was able to accomplish his mission. You might say, your father is the guardian of our lives. It is only through his kindness that we are still alive today. Therefore, no matter how much I do, I am still far from repaying that obligation.
>
> Fukuhara: Ah, I've heard vaguely that such things happened at one time. Well, thanks to you, I'll be able to keep my honor and my word. (Act 1 scene 1)

A duty passed on from father to daughter, an obligation vaguely remembered from past eras, binds widow Sakurai to Fukuhara Takeo—romantic love is definitely not the operative code in this play. Instead, it is loyalty and filial piety, honor and duty, that carry the plot forward. In keeping with the speech given at McKinley's banquet in 1900, Kawakami presented the kind of play "that shows a hero who is loyal to his nation and obedient to his lord, who risks his life for the sake of filial piety [*kō*] and sacrifices his life for the sake of righteousness [*gi*]."[50] Heterosexual romance is pushed aside for the sake of homosocial honor.

A further complication occurs at the level of casting. Sadayakko does double duty in this play, not only restaging her traveling show *Dōjōji* as the *geisha* Hanako, but also wearing the trousers of the male protagonist of this travel play, the gentleman Fukuhara Takeo. This cross-gender casting has all kinds of consequences, and Sadayakko herself discussed some of them in an interview. She recounts the difficulty of making herself look tall enough: She had to wear platform shoes, but these add-ons were harder to conceal under a Western suit than they would have been under a kimono. She also encountered a dilemma with her voice: If she lowered it like a man, it would not project to the back rows, but if she tried to speak louder, it would come out squeaky.[51] Previously, in *kabuki,* neither being too tall nor having a gravely voice had prevented *onnagata* from impersonating women—but by this point, lack of height and deep voice was considered a liability for an actress trying to impersonate a man. Sadayakko's difficulty itself, then, was a manifestation of the new definition of gender grounded in the body. And yet, the very fact that Sadayakko was allowed to perform a male role suggests that the new definition was not yet stable—and in fact, it would never become absolutely stable.

Most intriguingly, Sadayakko says that one of the most awkward aspects of playing the role of Fukuhara was his love scene with the princess he rescues from the Indian funeral pyre. As explained by Sadayakko, it was not so much the lesbian implication of such a love scene but the fact that the princess was played by her niece Teiko that caused the awkwardness. But one could imagine Sadayakko, as well as the audience, finding love scenes between any two women to be slightly awkward. To assemble, on the same stage, women acting like men (Sadayakko as the Japanese hero), women acting like women (the niece as the Indian princess and other actresses as Japanese ladies), and men acting like men (everyone else, both Japanese and others), must have been more than a little confusing. Hence, making the Indian princess a Japanese in disguise and rendering her a mere "listening ear" might have been strategies to dilute the significance of her ethnic and gender difference. "We are all loyal Japanese bound by duty and obligation" might have been the antidote to the confusion of various kinds of differences and othernesses presented by this production.

The play, *Around the World in Seventy Days,* for whatever reason, contains little hetero romance. This refusal of the Japanese play to use the heterosexual romantic love plot to clinch the frantic traveling plot raises the question: What is the point of all the traveling? In the French novel, the traveling is motivated by the British gentleman's precise-as-a-pocketwatch personality and rewarded by the finding of a beautiful, exotic woman to bring home as a souvenir. In the Japanese play, on the other hand, the traveling is motivated by Fukuhara's need to prove he is a true gentleman, a true samurai, a true modern subject, and is rewarded by nothing more than the experience of traveling, staged more or less as a series of battles with local people. Almost every scene in every act contains at least one stage fight: The servant Hatsuta Jōji and the pseudo-gentlemen almost come to blows in act 1 scene 1; act 1 scene 2 begins with a fight between students (friends of Hatsuta Jōji, who is also a student-type character); act 2 ends with a brawl in San Francisco between rival campaigners in an election; act 4 involves the fight with the locals in India; act 5 and the whole play concludes with a reunion of Auta (the Japanese version of Aouda) with her father, but not before a couple of wild chases, a mob scene, and a threatened fistfight. Why all this fighting? Most likely, the reasons are the same as in the battle scenes of *Sino-Japanese War:* Brawls and fistfights repudiate the indirect action of choreographed movements, showing off the spontaneous eruption of physical movement prized in the straightening of theater.

There is, however, a further interpretation for the battle scenes of *Around the World in Seventy Days.* The hero's contentious journey, motivated by the need to prove his status as a modern subject of a growing colonial empire, visualizes, perhaps even more clearly than the original novel, what kinds of violence were needed to create the preconditions for safe and speedy world travel. And the hero's failure or refusal to replicate the heterosexual romance with a native woman might force us to remember, in contrast to the original novel, that romance is a trope that has often served to dress up and cover up precisely these kinds of violent encounters.

THE ULTIMATE POWER TRIP: DUMB TRAVEL

As a further twist in the doubling movement of objects and subjects of modern vision, Sadayakko performed the role of a *British actress* in a Japanese comedy by Masuda Tarōkaja, entitled *Dumb Travel* (Oshi ryokō). The plot was similar to that of *Around the World,* with two Japanese men, one a sophisticated cosmopolitan, the other a bumbling lovable fool, traveling from Japan to Europe. In the London scene, the "dumb" (because he can't speak English) Sōda Usuke is teased and seduced by actresses of the Empire Theater. They call him "soda whisky imported from Japan" and entice him to come to their performance of *Armed Peace* (Busōteki heiwa, though this is likely a translation from what was originally an English show), a spectacle in which they represent army officers from Britain, the United States, France, Germany, and Japan. In this play within a play, the actress Rose, portrayed by Sadayakko, plays the Japanese officer (or the Goddess of Peace in some newspaper accounts). The entire play ends with Sōda's "Nippon Banzai!"

Among the many extraordinary features of this play, first staged in 1908, is the fact that the London scene is performed almost entirely in English. The handwritten script (a revised version from 1926, also stored at Waseda's Theater Museum) shows the lines in English, with the pronunciation indicated in *katakana,* and the Japanese translation in parentheses.[52] In preparing for this production, Sadayakko and several fellow actresses underwent extensive training in the art of "acting like a Western woman acting like a man." Articles in *Engei gahō* document these efforts: learning how to wear shoes, how to walk with toes turned outward, how to hold the body straight, how to speak English.[53]

Dumb Travel, contrary to its title, is a testimony to the modern modes of travel that have become possible in the imagination, if not in reality, of a certain segment of the Japanese populace. In laughing at the bumbling Sōda Usuke, and in identifying with his suave cosmopolitan companion, spectators could soak in self-congratulatory sentiment: "We've come a long way." At the same time, spectators could marvel at the ability of actors and actresses to take on the role of English citizens on stage. This ability and effort to "become Western," legible in the rehearsals of actresses learning Western manners, and also suggested by Sadayakko's earlier adoption of Western clothes and hairstyle upon her return from the world tour, was still seen at this point as something remarkable and spectacular. This play is indicative of a transition period

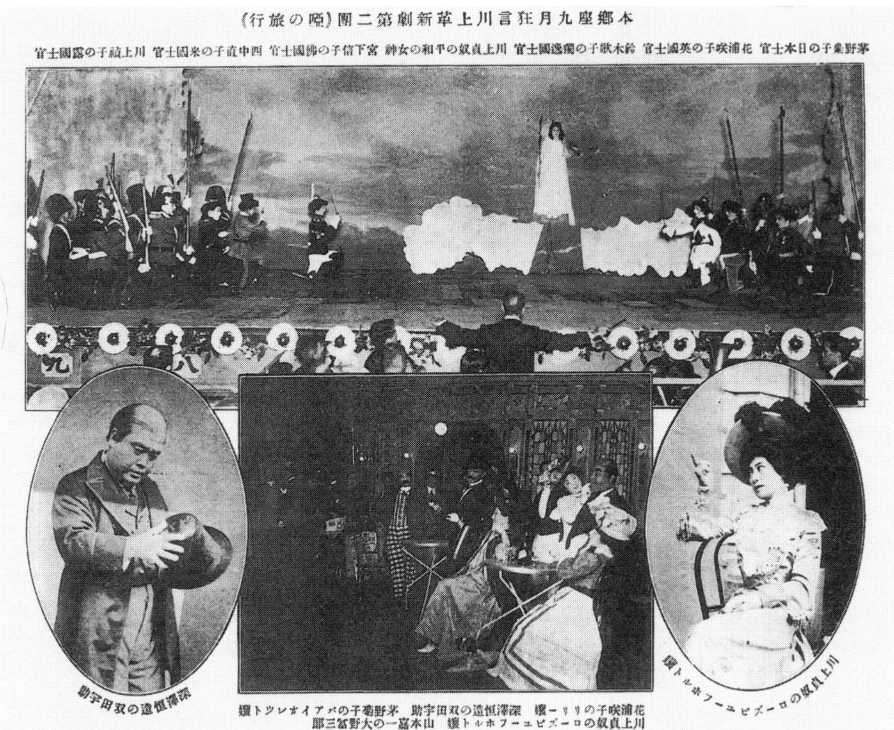

5.3 Kawakami troupe's performance of *Dumb Travel,* with Kawakami Sadayakko as an English actress, below right, and as the goddess of peace, above. *Engei gahō* (October 1908)

in the relationship of Japanese theater to Western material: Soon thereafter, in New Theater, it would become natural for Japanese actors to represent citizens of Western nations.

A JAPANESE GENERAL CONQUERS TAIWAN: OTHELLO AND NEW OTHELLO

Most of the roles performed by Sadayakko on stage and off attest to the mutual implication of the modern formations of woman and of theater. There was indeed a large area of overlap in the roles she played in the theater and outside it: She was a geisha, and she played a geisha (*The Geisha and the Knight*); she was a world traveler, and she played a world traveler (*Around the World in Seventy Days*); she was an actress, and she played an actress (*Dumb Travel*). It is for this reason that it seems to make little sense to separate her into "her life" and "her work," as is the convention of biography. Sadayakko was visible to various audiences both when she was performing on stage and when she was off stage, and that visibility becomes the basis of her embodying the process of wifeing and straightening.

Wifeing and straightening, or the modern formation of woman and theater, are dependent on each other: The consolidation of woman as properly belonging to the patriarchal family context, i.e., her wifeing, draws on the kinds of roles taught in the pedagogical institution called straight theater. At the same time, the replacement of *onnagata* by actresses to perform women's roles depends on modern definitions of gender. The roles performed by Sadayakko over the span of her career point to the processes of both wifeing and straightening, to their imbrication, and sometimes to their precariousness: singing, dancing, and crossdressing remained a significant part of Sadayakko's appeal.

Aside from the "travel plays" examined so far, there is another important set of plays performed by the Kawakami troupe. These might be called "colonial plays" since they deal even more explicitly with Japan's emerging imperial and colonial relations with its Asian neighbors. One subgenre of these "colonial plays" is constituted by those based on Shakespearean drama. During her career, Sadayakko performed in various versions of *Othello, The Merchant of Venice,* and *Hamlet.* The first Shakespearean performance of the Kawakami troupe turned out to be *The Merchant of Venice,* which took place in 1900 in Boston. The Kawakamis had just seen the performance of the play by the famous British actors Henry Irving and Ellen Terry, and they decided they could stage a Japanese version, featuring Sairoku (Shylock), a fisherman of Hokkaido, the northern island of Japan colonized during the Meiji era. They did not have the time to translate, or even understand, the words of the original; they simply imitated the gestures of Irving and Terry and mouthed gibberish to suit the action.[54] If this example of mimicry was the first in a line of gradually straightening Shakespeare productions, the various versions of *Othello* show the imbrication in the processes of straightening and wifeing.

Othello was one of the first plays advertised as a "straight play"(*seigeki*) by the Kawakamis. It was performed in 1903, shortly after the return of the Kawakami troupe from their second European tour. The production boasted the first appearance of Sadayakko as a professional actress in Japan, the first Western-style scenery, and was the first to keep the title of the original Western play. Yet the script was an adaptation rather than a translation, transposing the action from Venice and Cypress to Tokyo and Taiwan. Otojirō even conducted a research trip to Taiwan to better reproduce the scenery and customs of the place. Reactions from the critics, reported in newspaper articles as well as a special issue of *Kabuki* magazine, were generally favorable. But some critics voiced objections to the Japanization of the drama: They wished to see Shakespeare in the original. For example, one reviewer grumbled:

> If the Kawakamis truly intend to transmit the impressions of European theater [*ōshū engeki*] to our nation, why do they adapt [*hon'an*] the play and turn characters into present-day personages, of the kind that have saturated the stage already in the last five or six years, nay the last dozen years? I am not saying that it is unacceptable to transpose the setting to Taiwan, but I do believe that if they had set the costumes and the clothing proper to *Othello,* and had just taken the words and Japanized [*nihonka*] them alone, it would have better fulfilled their purpose. We have heard much about European theater in this nation, but none have yet made an appearance to our eyes.[55]

These objections suggest that at this point there existed already a trend away from adaptation towards translation.

The hero of the Japanese version is called not Othello but Muro Washirō. He is described as a "new commoner" (*shin heimin*), a term for former outcasts newly incorporated into the status of commoner under the Meiji government. He is a Japanese from the lowest caste who has been struggling to gain the status of a full-fledged national subject through his military conquests. While a "*shin heimin*" may be the closest thing corresponding to the "Moor" of Shakespeare's Venice, the designation of the Japanese Othello as a "*shin heimin*" produces its own associations and its own logic.[56] Lieutenant General Muro Washirō's success as a military man is the precondition for his being considered Japanese, and this logic is confirmed by the repeated discussion of how one should or should not behave "as a military person" (*gunjin to shite*). Muro Washirō is sent to Taiwan to quell the unrest on several islands: Natives have united with pirates from China, and certain foreign nations seem to be assisting the rebels. Muro Washirō promptly suppresses this potential revolution, is appointed governor of Taiwan, and begins stabilizing the populace by instilling feelings of loyalty to Japan in them. In this "colonial play," the relationship between Japan and other nations is a crucial background to the drama of Muro Washirō's effort to establish a masculine and militaristic subjectivity.

Tomone (the Japanese Desdemona), performed by Kawakami Sadayakko, is the woman who acts as a foil to the man and whose passion causes the masculine subject's downfall. Her marriage to her husband is called both an expression of "free love" (*jiyū ren'ai*) based on emotions rather than obligations, and an illicit, "wild union" (*yagō*), not sanctioned by her parents. She is a woman who betrayed her father in order to marry the man she loved; this is described as sufficient reason to suspect she will betray her husband, too. Othello is undone by his passion for a woman, and this is a most unmilitary and unmasculine behavior.

Yet the project of straightening embodied by *Othello* is open to question and even ridicule, as is shown by *New Othello,* a one-act parody of *Othello* first performed in 1906. The same characters act out the same drama of passion, jealousy,

5.4 Kawakami troupe's performance of *Othello,* with Kawakami Otojirō as Othello, center. *Engei gahō* (February 1910).

and revenge, but in a condensed manner, stripped of all the dignity of military rank and ceremony. There is no Iya Gōzō (Iago) in this play, since there is no need for him, the husband being predisposed to pathological jealousy without any help from a villain. All that is needed is for Katsu Yoshio (Cassio) to smoke by an open window: Muro Washirō interprets this to be a "wireless telegraph of love" (*ai no musen denshin*) and becomes furious. Tomone, again played by Sadayakko, responds to her husband's accusations by actually flirting with Katsu Yoshio, and a wild slapstick scene ensues, complete with multiple doorways and split-second entrances and exits. All ends happily when Muro Washirō apologizes for his behavior. By foregrounding the potential silliness of *Othello, New Othello* exposes the fragility of the male subject founded on militarism and paranoia. It is this kind of parodic element that contradicts and undermines the mission of straightening theater and that is therefore gradually marginalized from mainstream modern theater in Japan. Equally important is the fact that even in the serious and straight *Othello,* what attracted the attention of the audience was the elaborate scenery[57] and the dances of Sadayakko and other actresses in the banquet scene.[58]

Of the various Shakespearean adaptations by the Kawakami troupe, *Hamlet* is the one that comes closest to being a straight play. It is still an adaptation—

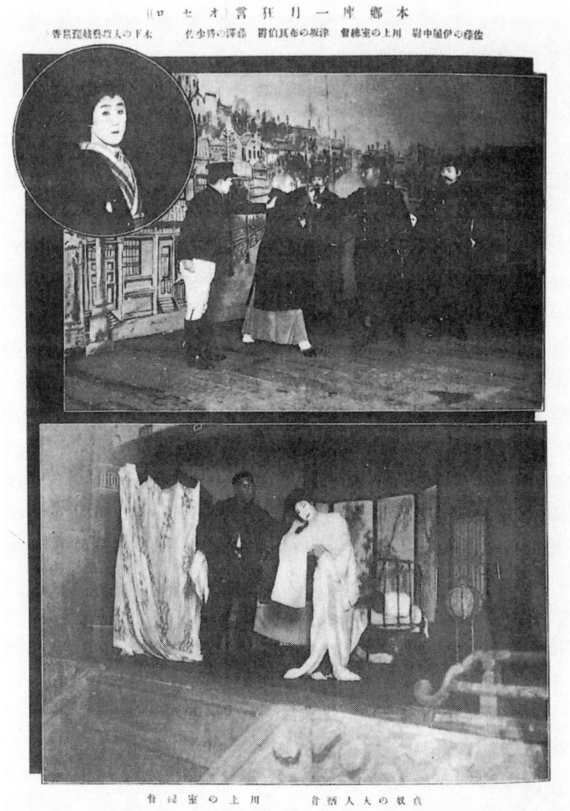

5.5 More scenes from *Othello,* with Kawakami Sadayakko as Lady Tomone. *Engei gahō* (February 1910).

Hamlet is Hamura Toshimaru, a young graduate of Kyoto University, and Ophelia is Horio Orie, a Japanese maiden, played by Sadayakko in the 1903 production. The story is set in modern Japan, but there is no sign of an engagement with other nations. Even Fortinbras who in the original invades the kingdom in order to restore order, is here Count Oritsu, a fellow Japanese rather than a foreign figure. The presentation of modern Japan as a self-contained universe in *Hamlet* is made possible by repressing Japan's relation to other nations. This would prepare the way for the presentation of a self-contained Western setting on a Japanese stage, without reference to the relationship between Japan and the West. This "translation" would indeed materialize in the Literary Society's production of *Hamlet.* A straight translation rather than adaptation, this production would feature Matsui Sumako as Ophelia, indicating the shifting of the spotlight from "straight theater," embodied in actress Kawakami Sadayakko, to "new theater," epitomized by actress Matsui Sumako.

A KOREAN PRINCE STUDIES IN KYOTO: ALT HEIDELBERG AND NEW NATION'S KING

Kawakami's straightening of theater pointed toward a relationship of Japan to other nations that could be figured as one of tutelage: Japan would learn from the West, become like the West, and would teach other Asian nations. This paradigm, however, raises the possibility that the student would some day equal, or even overcome, the teacher. For imperialist Japan in the 1910s, the prospect of overcoming the West as teacher was made increasingly visible and vocal, while the specter of an Asian colony becoming fully "educated" and independent was something that had to be suppressed carefully.

What happens to romance in this relationship between colonizer and colonized, teacher and student, is further complicated. *Around the World in Eighty Days* clearly represents the colonial relationship as both pedagogical and romantic: The Indian Aouda is educated by Europeans and so it seems only natural that she should escape her native land and fall in love with the European Phileas Fogg. In this paradigm, knowledge and power are distributed along gender lines: The colonizing male teaches, rescues, and thereby obtains the colonized female. In the Japanese version, *Around the World in Seventy Days,* the colonial dimension as well as the gender dimension are diluted by making the princess Japanese and noncolonial by birth, and by presenting her relationship to her rescuer (acted by a woman) through a language of obligation rather than a language of romantic love, hence reducing the importance of the gender difference between her and her rescuer.

What seems to be at work, then, is at least a partial effort to disavow Japan's masculine relationship toward its colonies. The status of heterosexual romance in representations of colonial relationships thus is a complex one, especially when it intersects with Japanese disavowal of its masculine role vis-à-vis its colonies. At the same time, there also existed an effort to contain the potential of the colony to become a full subject, and that goal was best accomplished by positing the colony as an eternal student.

In 1910, the year of Japan's colonial annexation of Korea, the Kawakami troupe performed a play that was first called *Korean King* (Chosen ō), and later changed to *New Nation's King* (Shin koku ō), due to state censorship.[59] Except for Kurata Yoshihiro, who offers a half-page description, historians of Japanese theater have ignored this play and the intriguing circumstances of its performance.[60] Yet this play, in which Kawakami Sadayakko performed the leading female role, is another paradigmatic play in the reproduction of imperialism: The main plot clearly illustrates the structure of colonial representation of the colonized, and yet at the same time, the play's romantic subplot works against the main plot, thereby threatening the stability of the structure of colonial representation.

In the last chapter of his study of Japanese colonization of Korea, *The Abacus and the Sword: The Japanese Penetration of Korea, 1895–1910,* Peter Duus makes an intriguing observation. Analyzing the various derogatory images of Koreans circulated by the Japanese in the years leading up to 1910, he concludes "The Korean might be lampooned or exoticized but was never romanticized" and that "it is interesting to note that the Japanese political and economic penetration of Korea produced no writers like Rudyard Kipling or H. Rider Haggard, who wove enticing tales of adventure in strange and unfamiliar lands, nor any fiction at all in which Koreans appeared as major characters."[61] The play *Korean King* does indeed include a Korean as a major character and does indeed romanticize him, which simply goes to show how the relationship of theatrical representation and imperial politics is a neglected field of study. Nonetheless, Duus's general thesis in this chapter is useful to explain some of the features of *Korean King.*

Duus's main thesis about how Japan represented Koreans in cultural practices can be summarized as follows. On the one hand, Japan represented Korea as being backward compared to Japanese modernity, since by doing so, Japan could justify its control of Korea: "By branding the Koreans as less 'civilized' than themselves, the Japanese could claim the right to demand that they alter their institutions and folkways or submit to Japanese political control."[62] As Duus points out, these are the same imperialist tactics used by European powers in India, Africa, and the like. But on the other hand—and this is where Japanese imperialism differed from Western imperialism—it was difficult for Japanese imperialists to represent Koreans as being totally different and distinct, because the two peoples had many things in common: "By stressing a common history and a common cultural heritage, the Japanese could cloak domination of the Koreans in the language of amalgamation, merger, and assimilation or suggest the 'naturalness' of annexation."[63] Thus, Japanese imperialists tried to have it both ways: They tried to justify the construction of a "joint community," since Japan and Korea were so similar, and yet keep the relationship asymmetrical and unequal, since Japan and Korea were so different. In the play *Korean King,* the theme of the similarity of Japan and Korea is suggested in the pedagogical relationship of teacher and student, while the difference of Japan and Korea is stressed in the romantic relationship between the male student and his girlfriend. But there are some unexpected twists.

This play is an adaptation of a five-act play, called *Alt Heidelberg,* by Wilhelm Meyer-Förster (1862–1934), first performed 1901.[64] *Alt Heidelberg* is a play about a prince from a small regional principality who is sent to Heidelberg University to study, where he promptly falls in love with a local waitress. Eventually, the prince must return home, in order to be crowned king and to marry a princess, but he vows to remember forever his good old student days in Heidelberg.

In *Korean King*, a Korean prince is sent to Japan to study at Kyoto University, where he falls in love with a Japanese waitress. The plot proceeds as follows: The play's opening act is set at the Korean court, with a description of how court life is stagnant and the officials corrupt. The next act is at an inn overlooking the Kamo River in Kyoto, where the prince and his tutor, a Japanese professor, have come to take up residence during the prince's period of study. There is much drinking of beer, shouting of student songs, and a general mood of celebration of academic and personal freedom. A Japanese waitress named Hana, the niece of the innkeeper, welcomes the prince, and they fall in love at first sight. The following acts describe their growing affection and the prince's enjoyment of student life, but suddenly he is recalled to the Korean court. His uncle the king has died, so now the prince must ascend the throne. He leaves with a heavy heart. In the last act, the Korean prince, about to be crowned king and about to wed a Korean princess, visits Kyoto for the last time and tearfully bids farewell to everyone, including the waitress, who is also about to wed a Japanese man.

The play seems on the surface to simply transpose the location of *Alt Heidelberg* from the court in Saxony to the court in Korea, and from Heidelberg University to Kyoto University. But what does this transposition mean? In the original play, Heidelberg University is the locus of the prince's enjoyment of a carefree life as a student, and later an object of his longing for the good old days. His tragic romance with the waitress serves to emphasize the mood of bittersweet nostalgia. In the Japanese adaptation, Kyoto University is represented specifically as the center of modern civilization, contrasted with the Korean court, which is represented as stifling and backward. The Japanese professor, for example, complains about the "moldy air" of the Korean court and about the "barbaric custom" of announcing the time by the beating of drums. The Korean officials are shown as perpetually yawning with boredom. These stereotypes are consonant with those described by Peter Duus, cited above. Moreover, the Japanese professor who educates the prince at Kyoto University is portrayed as a free thinker, having studied at Heidelberg University himself. So Japan, who has learned from Germany and mastered the art of acting modern, will now teach its pupil, Korea. This, too, conforms to the pattern described by Duus. As the Japanese professor proudly informs the Korean officials, "in Japan, especially in the literature departments of the universities, the fresh air of the West flows freely." The prince agrees, "once I enter that place of freedom, I will cast off the authority of the royal family, the authority of history."[65] Thus, whereas the German original stresses the theme of nostalgia and romance, the Japanese adaptation stresses the theme of Japan's educating and civilizing mission toward Korea.

The play, however, presents a problem for Japanese colonialism. By plugging Japan and Korea into the plot of a *Bildungsroman* and showing the process of educating a Korean king, the play raises the specter of a fully educated, mature, and independent Korea. The implied image of Korea as a sovereign masculine subject would be too dangerous in the volatile political context. This is surely one reason why this play had to be censored.

What, then, about the romance of the Korean King and the Japanese waitress? What happened to this subplot? In pursuing this question, one discovers other, gender-inflected patterns in the depictions of the Japanese-Korean relationship that are unaccounted for in the representational schema summarized by Duus. It is the figure of the waitress Hana, enacted by the actress Kawakami Sadayakko, that hints at the potential instability of the representation of the colonial relationship.

This play was one of the many plays performed by the Kawakami troupe in 1910 that dealt with Japanese colonialism. They had opened the year with their Taiwanese *Othello,* in June they performed their 70-day version of *Around the World* before opening their adaptation of *Alt Heidelberg* on October 1. The main plot of a provincial prince being educated in a university town perfectly matched the imperialist representation of the "civilizing" mission of the Japanese colonization of Korea. What is interesting, however, is that in the version performed in 1910 by the Kawakami troupe, the theme of romance between the prince and the waitress is censored and tempered. The manuscript has numerous markings in red ink, signs one can reasonably interpret to be related to government censorship.[66] At the time, all play-scripts had to be submitted to the police for approval prior to staging. Thus, the red markings can be read as changes made, if not by the censors themselves, then by the troupe members in anticipation of, or response to, the censorship.

The following changes were made in the script. First, the title was changed from *Korean King* to *New Nation's King*. Second, all references to Korea and to Korean locations were changed to the generic "New Nation." Third, the names of the Korean characters were changed to generic Sino-phonic names vaguely suggesting Asian-ness. Fourth, in a scene at the inn in which the Japanese students welcome the Korean prince, there are changes indicated in the stage directions for the music: The original instruction for playing the Japanese national anthem is changed to the playing of the Korean national anthem, which is corrected back to the Japanese national anthem, and then finally the whole music sequence is crossed out. Fifth, a significant number of speeches and stage directions are cut, especially those portraying the love affair. For example, a student's comment suggesting that "When the Korean Prince sees her, he will probably just turn into jelly like the rest of us" is summarily deleted. Similarly crossed out is one long speech, unfortunately rendered barely legible, in which the prince declares his love for the waitress in defiance of all social conventions.

How do we account for these changes? There were multiple reasons why this play was censored, with multiple factors working together. First, the play was topical, dealing with a contemporary political situation.[67] But that fact in itself was not sufficient reason for censorship. The Kawakami troupe, for example, performed very successful plays about Japanese victories in the Sino-Japanese War of 1894–95 and the Russo-Japanese War of 1904–05. They were so welcomed by the authorities, in fact, that they were invited to perform in front of the crown prince. Thus there had to be more than the fact that the play dealt with the contemporary political situation.

The censors neutralized the specific figure of the Korean King to the more abstract "New Nation's King." What did this mean? By deleting and diluting reference to a specific nation, the mission of Japan as the educator of *all* its colonial students is emphasized as the implied theme of the play. The specificity of the Korean political situation is lost; the play keeps stressing the theme of tutelage on an abstract ideological level. The message is that without granting any real sovereignty to these "new nations," Japan can elevate them through its own civilization. Benedict Anderson summarizes this process succinctly:

> [A]s the empire expanded after 1900, Japanification à la Macaulay[68] was self-consciously pursued as state policy. In the interwar years Koreans, Taiwanese and Manchurians, and, after the outbreak of the Pacific War, Burmese, Indonesians and Filipinos, were subjected to policies for which the European model was an established working practice. And just as in the British Empire, Japanified Koreans, Taiwanese or Burmese had their passages to the metropole absolutely barred. They might speak and read Japanese perfectly, but they would never preside over prefectures in Honshū, or even be posted outside their zones of origin.[69]

In the end, Korea is not allowed to be a full-grown nation, but must stay under Japanese tutelage.

But this explanation for the censorship is still insufficient because it fails to explain why specifically the romantic elements of the play were toned down.

The play foregrounded a love affair between a man and a woman of different social ranks. But that in itself was not sufficient reason for censorship. In fact many of the plays performed around this time dealt with love affairs between unequal lovers: usually a man of high social standing and a woman of low standing, a geisha, or courtesan, or prostitute. The reason *Korean King* had to be censored and had to be turned into *New Nation's King,* one may surmise, is that it dealt with the romantic theme in the context of Japan's colonial relationship with Korea, and the structure of the plot created dangerous and even seditious possibilities for interpretation.

Romance was a highly ambivalent trope in representations of Japanese imperialism. On the one hand, the rhetoric of romance could be used to sugarcoat Japan's domination of the colonies. This aspect is not discussed by Duus, although he does draw attention to the use of "family" as a metaphor to justify Japanese annexation of Korea, especially the metaphor of the older brother Japan guiding the younger brother Korea. But even a cursory look at popular cultural representations reveals that the metaphors of love, romance, and marriage were used in order to portray Japanese annexation of Korea in 1910 as if it were based on mutual consent, affection, and desire. For example, in 1910, the theater magazine *Engei gahō* published about a dozen poems on the theme "the annexation of Japan and Korea" (*nichi kan gōhō*). Significantly, these poems were solicited under the genre heading of "*jōka*" or "love poems." The following are a few examples:

> Tanin atsukai shita no wa kinō, kyō wa mutsumashi, Kara Nihon
> [Treating each other like strangers yesterday, today we're lovey-dovey Korea and Japan.]
> Tagai no kokoro ga yōyaku shirete, ureshiku hitotsu ni natta kuni
> [At last we know how we longed for each other in our hearts; happily we join as one nation.][70]

These poems clearly show how the rhetoric of romance could be used to euphemize and erase the violent nature of Japan's annexation of Korea. The poems are drenched in the vocabulary and syntax of romance; soppy sentiment is squeezed to the rhetorical limit to sugarcoat the colonial relationship. These representations, however, do not necessarily take the form of the male colonizer seducing the female colonized. That kind of aggressive masculinity is absent, replaced by a rhetoric of reciprocity, as well as the guise of public legitimation of the relationship, signified by phrases such as "honeymoon" and "combining the family register." These poems are appropriate shorthands for the staging of gendered colonialism taking place in 1910.

On the other hand, romance between the colonized and the colonizer could potentially threaten the hierarchical difference between the two peoples. Here, racism worked together with sexism. For example, scholars have pointed out some of the fundamental contradictions that existed in the 1910s to 1940s within Japanese colonial policies, specifically regarding intermarriage between Japanese and Koreans. On the one hand there were policies encouraging intermarriage, in order to assimilate Koreans into the Japanese empire. On the other hand, there were arguments discouraging intermarriage, most often made from a racist eugenics perspective.[71] Especially revealing, for example, is a document prepared by order of the Ministry of Health in 1943, which stated that "it is the general rule of domination that the male of the guiding or conquering race would take a female of the guided or conquered race as his wife," and which for that reason warned against intermarriage of Korean men with Japanese women.[72]

Romance between Korea and Japan was thus an ambivalent and troublesome trope. It could be used as a cover-up for Japanese domination of Korea, as it was used in the metaphor of the "marriage" of Japan and Korea in 1910, or it could signal trouble in the supposedly natural hierarchy of the Japanese race over the Korean race. Add to this the well-known fact that romantic love during this time in Japan was in itself regarded as socially subversive, and one has a very over-determined trope indeed.[73]

The language of romance was complexly entangled with the language of domination on the one hand and the language of defiance on the other. Any cultural representation of romance between colonizer and colonized in the Japanese empire was required to negotiate this ambivalence very carefully. Theatrical representations were likewise required to dance through this treacherous terrain, and actresses were deeply implicated in this process. The performance of *Korean King* must be understood within this context. The representation, even in fantasy form, of a love affair between a Korean prince and a Japanese maiden was too troubling, for too many reasons. The forbidden love was at least *doubly* forbidden: first on the level of the original plot of *Alt Heidelberg,* due to difference in status between the prince and the waitress, and second in the context of the Japanese adaptation, due to the difference in status between the Korean and the Japanese characters. Even without direct reference to Korea, an illicit, interclass, interracial relationship between the colonized and colonizer was too dangerous to present on stage. Thus the steamy brew of the antisocial, antihierarchical love between the prince and the waitress was diluted into a lukewarm puddle. The straightening of theater is thwarted here, too, but the digression wavers between subversive feeling, which has the potential to radically disrupt sociopolitical hierarchies, and sentimental melodrama, which recuperates affective energies back into the social order.[74]

The character of the waitress Hana, however, is in fact quite complex and requires a closer look. She is portrayed in act 2 as a modern girl, almost a New Woman, dressed in Western clothes and reciting a poem for the Korean prince in English (written out in *katakana* in the script). This no doubt capitalized on the Westernized and glamorous image of the actress performing the role, Kawakami Sadayakko, who was depicted in the Japanese popular press at the time as looking better in a Western dress than in a kimono and as being the center of social attention during the successful tours in the United States and Europe. Yet in subsequent acts in the play, the image of the waitress as glamorous actress starts to fade into a different image, resembling that of a geisha quietly longing for a man who will eventually leave her. This image, conventionally associated with *shimpa* melodrama heroines, is also supported by Kawakami Sadayakko's upbringing as a geisha. Finally, the marginalization of the romance plot in the play and the concomitant reduction of the significance of the leading woman's role is in keeping with the gender ideology of the day.

At least two more aspects of this complicated and troublesome production should be mentioned. Those aspects suggest that there was a contradiction between the logic of the play and the logic of the reproduction of imperialism, opening up the possibility of a resistant reading. The play offered problems for the audience's possible identification with the characters and problems for the audience's possible interpretation of what the play might end up meaning. Neither the Korean prince nor the Japanese waitress offered stable positions of identification for the ideal spectator of the play, that is, the educated Japanese males sitting in the audience. To argue this is not to ignore the presence of female spectators but to allow for the possibility that, as Laura Mulvey has suggested, built-in patterns of pleasure and identification impose masculinity as "point of view," regardless of the actual sex of the spectator.[75] To identify with the Korean prince, the spectator must cross national lines and resist the pull of the rest of the play to portray Koreans as different from Japanese. To identify with the Japanese waitress, the ideal spectator must cross gender lines and resist the pull of the rest of the play to posit her as the object of sexual desire.[76] The triumphant hero with whom the male Japanese subject of 1910 could have been expected to identify was neither the Korean prince nor the Japanese waitress, but the Japanese students and professors of Kyoto University, who presumably teach the Korean prince how to become a good Japanese student and thus a good subject of the Japanese empire. And becoming the "new nation's king" at this historical moment was entirely congruent with becoming a good subject of the Japanese empire. But this meant that the romance plot had to be marginalized.

Finally, an interpretive possibility that the audience might imagine, and that therefore had to be carefully policed, was that of the Korean prince as representing the promise of a would-be independent nation, freeing itself from the bonds of Japanese colonial tutelage. This possibility of a resistant reading had to be diluted. The plot of *Alt Heidelberg* offered a convenient ending that neatly foreclosed such a possible future for the prince, and the changes in the Japanese script further constricted possibilities for a resistant reading. The prince, now a generic figure not tied to a particular colonial territory, leaves the Japanese educational scene prematurely, but he will always be tied to Japan through melancholic nostalgia, an atmosphere accentuated in the Kawakami performance by, above all, sound effects at the end:

Hana: I'll never forget you. I'm allowed to remember you, aren't I?
Prince. Yes. I will never forget you either.
Hana: They talk about the springtime of one's life, you know, but I didn't know it would be so brief. . . . *(sinks into thought).*

(Shō, Chō, Ryū, enter)

Chō: Your Highness, the escort has arrived from the Kyoto Prefectural government.

Prince: Is it time already?
Chō: Yes. The night-train leaves at eight-thirty; you must leave soon.
Prince: All right. I will be with you in a moment.
(Shō, Chō, etc. leave)
Prince: Hana-chan, I have to go now. Take care of yourself. . . .
Hana: Oh, Your Highness. . . . You, too. . . .
(They stand as if struck by emotions; the sound of leaves falling in the autumn wind intensify the melancholy; the bell of the temple announces the impermanence of life, as the curtain descends.)

Thus the play ends in a sentimental tableau, the possibilities of romance as well as the possibilities for resistance diluted and dissolved into a general atmosphere of melancholic longing.

In short, in the process of adaptation and transformation, moving from *Alt Heidelberg* through *Korean King* to *New Nation's King* amounts to an oscillation of the focus of the play between romance and education, between the male-female relationship and the student-teacher relationship. While the colonial theme of "difference" between Koreans and Japanese is thematized in the romantic plot and the theme of "sameness" is thematized in the educational plot, what the play ultimately reveals is that education is predicated on "difference" between teacher and student, and that romance threatens the "difference" between colonizer and colonized. The romantic plot threatened to overthrow the educational plot, and thus it had to be censored, diluted, and controlled. All of the "colonial plays" performed by the Kawakami troupe revolve around the heroic figure of the modern masculine national and imperial subject, accompanied by his female sidekick. Romance is utilized as a plot device, but its subversive implications are always carefully controlled.

The actress Kawakami Sadayakko is implicated both in the modern formation of gender categories as well as in the process of the reproduction of imperialism. She was one of the first performers to prove that "women acting like women" were better than "men acting like women," thereby giving women a voice on the public stage. Yet she also thereby helped to consolidate the modern expressive and essentialist definition of gender as grounded in the physical body. She performed the role of the exotic geisha-girl while abroad, thereby confirming the schema of the Orientalized and feminized Japan objectified by the West. Once in Japan, she turned around to perform the role of the modern girl supporting the modern masculine Japanese national subject, thereby contributing to the reproduction of imperialism. And yet her acting in these roles was not without contradiction, suggesting, though arguably never fulfilling, possibilities for resisting that logic.

Geisha, actress, mistress, wife. *Dōjōji, The Geisha and the Knight, Around the World in Seventy Days, Dumb Travel, Othello, New Othello, Korean King,*

New Nation's King. The roles played by Kawakami Sadayakko on stage and off were varied, complex, and often contradictory. They attest to the imbricated processes of the modern formation of gender and of performance: woman's position within the family-state, and theater's function for colonial pedagogy. But they also attest to the multiple possibilities that were open to theater and to women in the late Meiji period, even as the definition of categories became more narrow and more strictly enforced. The wifeing and straightening of Sadayakko speak to us about these imbricated processes and possibilities.

PART III

Matsui Sumako

CHAPTER 6

A NEW WOMAN

WHO WAS MATSUI SUMAKO?

IN THE CHAPTERS ON KAWAKAMI SADAYAKKO, THE TERMS "wifeing" and "straightening" were coined to summarize the contentious and paradoxical process of the modern formation of woman and theater, respectively. In the case of Matsui Sumako, there is no need for neologisms, since two terms that were used in her time are ready at hand and as useful today as they were back then: "New Woman" (*atarashii onna*) and "New Theater" (*shingeki*). These terms will be used here to capture the continued and even more intensified process of the disciplining of womanhood and theater in the early Taishō period. The processes of the modern formations of woman and theater, first outlined in Part I and then traced through Kawakami Sadayakko in Part II, seem to converge and come to completion in the figure of Matsui Sumako, heroine of Part III.

Matsui Sumako is understood to be the "New Woman" of the "New Theater," the modern actress par excellence. Her body is placed on stage to serve as transparent medium for representing interiority. Yet her body is also opaque and threatening. It refuses to stay in the background and comes to signify in and of itself. This chapter will focus on Matsui Sumako as New Woman, looking both at others' representations of her and her self-representations. Both the theatricality of the New Woman and the sexuality of the actress will loom large as themes: While conventional theater history paints her as a sexually threatening femme fatale, her representation of herself as a New Woman reveals a feminist consciousness that cannot be discounted. Chapter 7 will trace Matsui Sumako's participation in New Theater, situating her in the context of ongoing debates about theater, sexuality, and commodification. Chapter 8 will examine a group of plays performed by Matsui Sumako and show how she negotiated the roles of femme fatale and feminist as a New Woman in the New Theater.

Despite the problems involved in any attempt to construct a biographical account of Matsui Sumako, it might be useful to present the main events of her life as building blocks for the various stories to follow. She was born Kobayashi Masako in 1886, the youngest of eight children in an area that is now Nagano prefecture. Her family was well-established in the region, but the death of her father created instability in the family's economic status. At the age of 16 she left home to live with her sister's family in Tokyo, helping out at the family cake shop and studying at a professional school for women to become a seamstress. Her first marriage was at the age of 21 to an innkeeper, but her husband divorced her after three months for "health reasons." Some scholars claim that her husband infected her with venereal disease, rendering her incapable of bearing children and therefore useless in the eyes of society.[1] One year later she married a history teacher, who was the first person to encourage her interests in the theater.

In 1909 she entered the Theater Institute of the Literary Society (Bungei Kyōkai Engeki Kenkyūjo), newly founded by Tsubouchi Shōyō, as one of its first group of students. As her acting studies became more time consuming, it became increasingly difficult for her to discharge the duties of a housewife, and she divorced for a second time in 1910.[2] The following year, she achieved her first stage success as Ophelia in *Hamlet* and started calling herself Matsui Sumako. Her performance of Nora in *A Doll House* in the same year established her as the first female star of the modern Japanese theater.

Around this time, Sumako became involved with Shimamura Hōgetsu (1871–1918). Shimamura Hōgetsu was 15 years her senior, a married man with three children, a well-known theater critic, an instructor at the Theater Institute, and director of *A Doll House*. Their affair soon became a scandal, and when Sumako was dismissed from the Institute, Shimamura Hōgetsu resigned as well, taking with him a number of its best students. Not only did he desert his own wife and children at this point, but he also gave up his position as one of Japan's most prominent literary critics in order to serve as Sumako's impresario.

Sumako, Shimamura Hōgetsu, and his disciples founded a new theater company called the Art Theater (Geijutsuza) and gained much commercial success due to Sumako's popularity. They toured as far as Taiwan, Korea, Manchuria, and Vladivostok. In 1918, however, Shimamura Hōgetsu died from influenza at the age of 47, and two months later, after performing the title role in *Carmen,* Sumako committed suicide.[3] She was 32 years old.

WHO IS THE NEW WOMAN?

The typical New Woman is represented in the Euro-American context as being young, middle class, single, well-educated, and financially independent, working outside the home to earn her living. She prefers a severe coiffure and rational dress; she smokes, drinks whisky, and rides bicycles. She demands freedom from the family and equality with men. She is first introduced in the 1890s, in magazines such as the *North American Review, Punch,* and *Yellowbook,* and is soon found in novels by Henry James and George Gissing and in plays by George Bernard Shaw and Henrik Ibsen.

The figure of the New Woman, an unmarried yet financially and emotionally independent woman, reflects the anxiety of an age in which women were not only demanding higher education and access to a wider scope of employment, but were becoming an increasingly vocal and visible political and sexual presence in society. The demand for suffrage, which began in England the 1860s, was becoming louder and rowdier in the 1890s: The suffragettes gathered in public places, marched en masse, and handcuffed themselves to the gates of the parliament. These spectacles were reported in Japanese news media in the 1910s, and thus entered the public imagination.[4]

By the 1890s, in some parts of Europe and the United States, young, reasonably well-educated women from the middle class were venturing into various professions previously closed to them. One of the professions was the theater. Because theater makes women vocal and visible in society, it was an attractive domain for women to move into. Yet it was also a troubling domain, since women's advance in it was predicated on their sexual attractiveness. There is thus a significant overlap between the image of the New Woman and that of the actress. We might characterize the image as a combination of the progressive, regressive, and transgressive.[5] Stepping onto the stage could potentially be a progressive step forward for women, or a regressive step backward, or a transgressive sidestep off the prescribed path. It could mean that women would become a professional presence in society, or that women would be regarded as sexual objects, or that women would turn themselves into sexual subjects and thus challenge male prerogative. These steps will be discussed in greater detail.

Despite the transgressive nature of the acting profession itself, the theater was a deeply conservative space at the end of the nineteenth century. Actresses became increasingly discontent with the conventional and even reactionary portraits of women in the plays of the time. The New Women roles created by playwrights such as Henrik Ibsen, George Bernard Shaw, and Oscar Wilde became ideal vehicles for some of the era's leading actresses who were looking for more challenging roles. Actresses such as Janet Achurch, Florence Farr, and Elizabeth Robins were instrumental in performing the figures of New Women on stage, premiering many of the plays of Ibsen in Britain, for example. These experimental productions were often played for matinee audiences, which tended to be predominantly female. Some actresses became managers as well, increasing their artistic and economic control over the production process.[6]

Not only did the New Woman have strong ties to the theater, both in the Western and the Japanese context, but she was in fact a fundamentally theatrical figure. The relationship between the New Woman and theatricality manifests itself in a certain kind of knowingness and complexity: The New Woman appears to us as a self-conscious presenter of her images, looking over her shoulder, adjusting her costume and her posture in response to the response of the audience. She reacts to the reactions of those who look at her, she picks up the script that attempts to circumscribe her and rewrites it in her own hand, performing differently.

Even if we shift our focus away from the purely theatrical realm, we see that the New Woman exhibits theatricality. It is not so easy to neatly separate real women and representations of her. For example, while the New Woman as demographic reality can be seen most demonstrably in the United States, here too we can see the process of women using the script given to them in their self-representations.[7] The first generation of New Women, while rejecting marriage and dedicating themselves to a public career, strove for a kind of respectability for the unmarried professional woman. The medical establishment, however, soon began looking at these New Women through the lens of sexology, which was rapidly developing at the time. Construing sexual disorder to be the symptom of social disorder, the medical establishment labeled these women as sexually deviant and prescribed cures and preventive measures in an effort to reassert social order. Partly in response to this reaction, the second generation of New Women, educated in the 1890s, often by the first generation of New Women, defined their own freedom in sexual terms. They rebelled against bourgeois morality and social conventions by wearing masculine clothes, cutting their hair short, smoking cigarettes, and sometimes consciously identifying themselves as lesbian. They insisted that women's assertion of "male" power and ambition was "natural." They insisted that it was gender distinction that was unnatural. Thus, these women defined themselves by taking up and twisting around the vocabulary of men who sought to define them.

Thus, in the United States, there seem to have been two distinct phases in the development of New Women, with the second phase a reaction against the first phase. In Japan, it seems the two generations overlapped in the 1910s. As soon as there was a small but visible contingent of women who received post-elementary education, who questioned the institution of marriage, and who strove for financial independence, they were depicted as socially deviant and sexually dangerous. The women thus labeled, however, immediately took on the label as a badge of honor, proudly proclaiming themselves to be "New Women."

In Japan, moreover, the New Woman was inextricably bound to theater. The term "New Woman" seems to have been introduced by theater reformer Tsubouchi Shōyō in his lecture of July 1911.[8] The following year, in a lecture entitled "Kinsei geki ni mietaru atarashii onna" (New Woman as seen in modern drama), he referred to Nora in Henrik Ibsen's *A Doll House,* Magda in Hermann Sudermann's *Heimat,* and Vivie in George Bernard Shaw's *Mrs. Warren's Profession* as examples of New Women. Tsubouchi Shōyō was of the opinion that the New Woman would sooner or later make her appearance in Japan. It is significant that for Tsubouchi Shōyō the model of the New Woman resided in modern European *drama.* In the following decade, the phenomenon of the New Woman would travel to Japan, via the plays and their performances, through the vehicle of actresses, themselves seen as New Women.

The feminist journal *Seitō* (Blue stockings), established in 1911, the same year as Matsui Sumako's debut, became the gathering place of women who sought to express themselves in new ways. The label "New Women" was given to the group soon after the journal's founding, when tabloid journalists gleefully reported that these women engaged in strikingly unfeminine behavior: They visited the brothels of Yoshiwara, they imbibed alcohol, and one of them, the painter Otake Kōkichi, dressed like a man. The group was immediately perceived and described as sexually and socially defiant and dangerous.[9]

What was meant as a mocking epithet, however, became a rallying cry. In 1913, feminist Hiratsuka Raichō wrote a manifesto that began with the lines "I am a New Woman. At least, I desire every day to be a truly New Woman, and I strive every day to become one."[10] This manifesto not only boldly reclaimed the sobriquet that had been thrown at women but recast "New Woman" as an ideal towards which one should aspire. One year later, the actress Matsui Sumako wrote a haiku to accompany a photograph of herself wrapped in a fashionable Western-style cape. Pointedly using the French word for the garment, the haiku declares a new identity for the wearer: "Wearing a *manteau,* I am a New Woman" (Manto kite / ware atarashiki / onna kana).[11] While Hiratsuka Raichō thus turns "New Woman" into a desirable ideal, Matsui Sumako turns it into a fashion statement. But this, too, is a bold gesture of appropriation. She associates the status of "New Woman" with taking on a piece of clothing, with wrapping herself up in a costume, with hiding the body rather than displaying it. She becomes a New Woman by wearing a manteau, not by stripping off veils or layers of a kimono, as one would expect of a sexual object.

The high visibility of the feminists tempts us to call them theatrical. They incorporate the viewpoint of the audience as part of constructing their own roles. Not content to let the world define them, they define themselves by using the script that is handed to them in a new way. Judith Butler delineates this mechanism of redeployment in *Excitable Speech:*

> Thus the injurious address may appear to fix or paralyze the one it hails, but it may also produce an unexpected and enabling response. If to be addressed is to be interpolated, then the offensive call runs the risk of inaugurating a subject in speech who comes to use language to counter the offensive call.[12]

Thus being branded "New Women" enabled some women to become subjects who could say: "Yes, I am a New Woman, and proud of it."

New Women are considered to have challenged the conventional definition of womanhood, that of the "good wife, wise mother."[13] New Women were critical of marriage as an institution and abhorred the idea that they should sacrifice themselves for husband, children, and the husband's parents. The paradox, however, is that the New Woman also *reinforced* the prevailing definition of womanhood as biological essence, rooted in the woman's body. To put it differently, New Woman is a sexual subject. There are several ambivalences contained in this formulation: She is a *sexual* subject as well as a sexual *subject*. First, she is a subject, but a necessarily *sexual* subject. This is to say that she is a subject who pursues her own sexual interests, that she is not merely a sexual object. This is the feminist face of the New Woman.[14] But she may therefore be a subject only in so far as she is *sexual*. Hence, she is seen most often as a sexual threat by men, as a femme fatale who schemes the man's downfall. Second, she is also a sexual *subject* in the sense that she is *subjected* to a power external to herself. Because of this dual structure of the subject as subjected, it is impossible to see the New Woman as completely in control of herself. Hence she is sometimes seen as a kind of puppet, empty of volition, compelled by her sexuality to act in irrational ways. This is the face of the New Woman as femme fatale, and the second ambivalence of the New Woman as sexual subject.

This can be seen in the various biographical representations of the actress Matsui Sumako. She fits the mold of the "New Woman": She was financially independent at the time of her debut as an actress, and she went on to have a successful career while rejecting the confines of a conventional family life. At the same time, however, the representations also attest to the fact that the definition of womanhood had shifted to focus even more narrowly on the body as a site of sexual differentiation and sexual threat.

WHO DID THEY THINK SHE WAS?: THE GOSSIPS AND OBITUARIES

The various accounts of Sumako's life and death present a remarkably consistent picture of the actress: There is an emphasis on her body and sexuality as the definitive essence of her personhood; the status of her relationship to her lover is the focus of intense scrutiny; her acting is described as a natural expression of her essence as a woman; and her achievements in the realm of theater are devalued as being merely natural, not artistic.[15] The first two trends attest to the formation of "New Woman" as a category resisting the patriarchal family structure yet resting on the definition of an essentialized womanhood; the last two trends attest to the formation of "New Theater" as the expression of interiority through a transparent medium. Sumako embodies the process of these formations as well as the contradictions inherent in them.

Before discussing these consistently negative representations of Matsui Sumako, however, I would like to complicate the picture in advance by listening to some women associated with the theater world, who through their appreciation present a different facet of the actress. It is not the case that opinions neatly line up by gender, with men attacking Sumako and women defending her. Nonetheless, perhaps it makes sense that those who shared similar experiences as "women in theater" would be subtler in their understanding of Sumako's situation. At the news of Sumako's death, many of the women working in and around the theater world reacted with sympathy. Theater critic Hasegawa Shigure admired Sumako's suicide;[16] critic Okada Yachiyo, on the other hand, wished that Sumako could have lived a little longer to continue her acting career.[17] The actress Hayashi Chitose combines these sentiments: When she first heard about the suicide she was impressed by Sumako's resoluteness, but then she wished Sumako had decided to live and keep working as an actress.[18] From their days together at the Literary Society, Hayashi remembered Sumako as a kind and gentle person, extremely studious and singleminded. Though she had heard negative rumors about Sumako, she chose not to believe them; "a nail that sticks out gets hammered," and she assumed this was the reason why Sumako was getting bad press. In this attitude Hayashi is the exception among people writing about Sumako: Most tend to simply repeat the malicious rumors that they have heard, replicating the effect of "hammering the nail that sticks out." Kamiyama Uraji, another actress who studied with Sumako at the Literary Society, also remembers Sumako fondly. She prefaces her remarks by saying that as a woman and as a fellow actress, "my sympathies for her are such that they could not be expressed in words."[19] She then goes on to describe Sumako's life during the years of training at the Literary Society: She would get up around 4 A.M. and finish working in the kitchen before leaving for dance lesson at 5:30 A.M. After half a day of practicing dancing, she would go to a sewing school several days a week, earning five yen per month for teaching sewing. From 6 P.M. she would attend classes at the Literary Society. Kamiyama reminisces that she and Sumako would share dinner dishes to save money, and that even in this busy routine, Sumako would find time to grow red and yellow flowers, as well as some vegetables, in her tiny garden.[20]

The emphasis on the process of daily training and rehearsal is unusual, since most accounts of Sumako's career tend to emphasize the sudden fame and the instant glamour that she achieved. The favorable views of Sumako from fellow actresses and women in the theater world serve to correct some of the biases of the conventional views of her.

One of the most noticeable features of contemporaneous accounts of Matsui Sumako is the emphasis on the body of the actress. Through description of her physique, metaphor, innuendo, or blunt statement, her physical sex and the sexual attraction of her acting is emphasized. The actress Mori Ritsuko, after confessing she hardly knew Sumako, describes the actress as an appropriate person to perform new theater due to her "sensuous expressions (*nikukanteki na hyōjō*), her voluptuous body (*hōman na nikutai*), and especially the well-developed muscles of her arms."[21] Mizushima Ryokusō elaborated that compared to the average Japanese woman, Sumako is well endowed: He also praises her straight arms, her high cheeks, and her eyes.[22] The arms and face attracted attention because they were exposed; the rest of the voluptuous body was covered up by costume and could only be deduced (except in the performance of *Salomé,* of course, which bared the body to the extreme).

Kawamura Karyō, a theater critic and practitioner who would later write an anecdotal biography of the actress, noted that Sumako's sensuality and sexuality is the kind that appeals to the "real senses" (*jikkan*).[23] As discussed in chapter 2, the appeal to "real senses" was at this time considered risqué and improper to theater, because it disturbs the attitude of detached observation and thus disrupts the proper relationship between the audience and the performer. Sumako was called "a highly sexual woman" (*hijō ni seiteki*),[24] "a woman of the flesh" (*niku no onna*),[25] and in the language used to describe her, we can detect much anxiety over the disruptive appeal of the female body. Murata Eiko, an actress who wrote of Sumako as a woman of the flesh and who repeated rumors that "Sumako died because she couldn't have sex anymore," entitled her essay "Dissecting Matsui Sumako." The language of dissection, of cutting apart the body to explore its secrets, reflects the infiltration of biological consciousness into everyday life in the Taishō period. It is this emphasis on biology that characterizes the definition of womanhood in the era of Sumako's life and death. The language of dissection also dovetails with the newly imported language of abnormal psychology. The special issues on Sumako of *Onna no sekai* and *Engei gahō* published in 1919 both contain articles that claim to "dissect" (*kaibō suru*) the motivations for Sumako's suicide.[26] That a postmortem examination of Sumako's psyche was considered proper and convincing is a sign of the times.[27] The first and primary motivation given for Sumako's suicide is her "perverse sexual desire" (*hentai seiyoku*) for Hōgetsu's corpse. She asked in her will that she be buried with Hōgetsu; from this, the psychological dissectors deduce that she must have been seized by an uncontrollable necrophiliac desire for Hōgetsu's dead body.

In a telling remark, one critic differentiated Sumako from the kinds of actresses that had preceded her, including Kawakami Sadayakko and actresses of the Teikoku Gekijō theater. Unlike the earlier actresses, who created "art/artifice" (*gei*) on stage, Sumako presented "the entity called woman" (*josei to iu mono*) as an "individual human being" (*ikko no ningen to shite*) on stage.[28] In other words, whereas other actresses were still seen as relying on the patterns and artifice developed by the *kabuki onnagata* to represent womanhood, Sumako was considered to naturally express her natural womanhood, her womanly essence. Instead of gender being regarded as an effect achieved as a result of successful performance, in these representations of Sumako, gender is regarded as that which originates and motivates performance.[29]

In so far as Sumako's gender—collapsed in this paradigm with her sex—was perceived to constitute the basis of her performance, it diminished the significance attributed to her performative skills. In fact, Sumako is described as a "child of nature" simply expressing what comes naturally to her.[30] Thus her art ends up being reduced to her nature:

> Sumako did well in presenting on stage women who are determined and desperate. Thinking about it now, I realize that it was her natural quality [*jishitsu*]. And the reason there was truth [*shinjitsu*] in her art is that she showed her raw nature [*kiji*].[31]

Words such as "*jishitsu,*" "*kiji,*" and just "*ji*" are often used to describe Sumako's natural qualities. Written with the character denoting "ground," the words have the connotation of something basic and intrinsic, before it has been adorned, cultivated, and modified. Since Sumako expressed her nature on stage, the line between stage and real life became blurred. The same natural characteristics—outspokenness, single-mindedness, sexual attractiveness—seemed to manifest themselves in her real life as well as in the roles she played on stage.[32] The fact that she tended to cry on stage when performing sad scenes was often mentioned: For fans it was a sign of her intense identification with her role on stage; for critics it was a sign of the lack of artistic control over her emotions.[33] For both, it was precisely the *lack* of artifice that characterized her art.

Later biographies build on the image of Matsui Sumako constructed by the early representations analyzed above. It is surprising that the most hostile portrait should come from Mori Reiko, a female novelist, writing about Sumako as part of a 12 volume collection of the lives of famous women in modern Japan. As in the case of Kawakami Sadayakko's biographies, narratives written with the explicit purpose of recovering women's history seem to compare the actress to an implicit masculinist standard and to arrive at a negative assessment. This standard values rational self-control and intellectual sophistication, a model dominant from the Enlightenment, and is used to castigate women for their irrationality, emotionality, and lack of self-reflection. The one exception is reserved for matters of the heart, romance, and affection, where rationality is to be replaced by selfless devotion. Anything less would make her too cold and calculating and not feminine enough.

In keeping with such a model of assessing actresses, Mori writes as follows about Sumako's relationship with Hōgetsu:

> Was it not the case that, rather than being in love with Hōgetsu, Sumako knew that she needed him for her own art, being utterly obsessed by the wish to be a great actress?
>
> Sumako was extremely assertive, but she was fundamentally emotional and not very intellectual. . . . She had almost no literary background at all, and seemed to have lacked the ability to read plays deeply and interpret them. Therefore, in preparing her roles, she must have blindly followed the instructions of the director, using physical craft to polish her roles: a doll's art. She was, however, highly gifted in aspects that required animalistic instinct, such as the timing of pauses between lines. The reason Hōgetsu became so attached to her must have been that Sumako became such a perfect puppet for Hōgetsu on stage.[34]

Mori's portrait of Sumako is paradigmatic in that it represents her as both manipulative *and* vacuous, as both the self-promoting star *and* as the director's puppet. Most biographers come up with this split image of Sumako. Though the two sides would seem to contradict each other, various critics and historians portray Sumako as both a femme fatale who manipulated Hōgetsu as lover and as a puppet manipulated by him as director. Osanai Kaoru, founder of the Free Theater (Jiyū Gekijō) and rival of Shimamura Hōgetsu, wrote after the latter's death and Sumako's ensuing suicide:

> Sumako was the wine bottle in which Mr. Hōgetsu could pour the wine which he had brewed. That wine has now dried up. There is no longer any *raison d'être* for the wine bottle, except to be stored away as an antique.[35]

Thus Sumako is described both as a dangerous seducer, and as an empty vessel into which Hōgetsu could pour his art. Historian Murakami Nobuhiko writes:

> [In Hōgetsu's mind,] Sumako was an irreplaceable actress, who faithfully realized his theatrical ideals—he could not let her go. On stage, she was a docile

> disciple, moving entirely according to his will; as wife and lover, however, she was utterly selfish and behaved according to her own whims, refusing to obey Hōgetsu, her master.[36]

The conflict between the two sides of Sumako's portrait is discursively reconciled by those who write about her: She may have been selfish at home but selfless on stage, she may have been seductive precisely because she was empty.

What these various stories about Sumako manage to erase is any sense of Sumako's agency. For example, even when Sumako's self-centeredness is emphasized in the biographies, it is understood that this "self" is not to be taken seriously. Mori writes: "She may have had a strong ego, but it was the ego of a spoiled child, and not the truly strong ego of an autonomous human being."[37] In another instance, Sumako's eagerness and perseverance in rehearsal is reread as a sign of her slavish devotion to Hōgetsu.[38] Again, Sumako is denied agency in her own actions. One wonders where this last image—Sumako as Hōgetsu's puppet—originated, since there is at least one account that claims Hōgetsu to have been utterly inadequate as a director and that Sumako became "increasingly idiosyncratic in her style."[39] These representations reveal a great deal of anxiety over the body of the actress and its potential to elude control. The anxiety is also evident in several biographies that replicate the sensationalistic tone of the journalists of Sumako's own time. Matsumoto Kappei, for example, manages to write a history of the modern Japanese theater that panders to prurient interests by indiscriminately quoting gossip that pandered to prurient interests in Sumako's lifetime. He cites no less than three separate episodes about Sumako's bad manners and devotes several chapters to Sumako's questionable relation to the substantial fortune Hōgetsu left at his death. This is surely one way in which the myth of Sumako keeps being reproduced.[40]

One of the best ways to write a story that emphasizes agency in Matsui Sumako is to concentrate on her relationship with feminism in Japan. The notion of "Hōgetsu's puppet" acquires a new meaning when we consider the fact that it was Sumako's performance of Ibsen's *A Doll House* in 1911 that caused the "Woman Question" to receive wide recognition in Japan. This confluence in Japan of the beginning of a self-conscious feminism and the beginning of modern theater is highly significant. Members of *Seitō,* a feminist literary journal that was founded in the same year, were immediately branded as "Japanese Noras," who, like the heroine in *A Doll House* would abandon their home, husband, and children in search of their true selves.

It would seem logical that Matsui Sumako, who had left her second husband to find her true vocation as an actress, would be considered one of the "Japanese Noras." Yet once again, biographers of Sumako manage to shift the limelight away from her:

> In a foreign country called Norway, Nora had to leave her home and family. In our country Japan, however, it was Shimamura Hōgetsu, family head and university professor, who had to leave his home. . . . And it was by depending on Hōgetsu that Matsui Sumako was able to continue her acting career.[41]

Thus, agency is shifted from the woman to the man: The man achieves modern subject-hood, while the woman remains merely his instrument, his excuse for breaking free from the feudal fetters.[42]

The very same process is at work in a fictional dialogue, published in 1915, in which a man sympathetic to Sumako and a man critical of her engage in a discussion of the relationship between Sumako and Hōgetsu. At one point, one of the men suggests an analogy of their relationship with that of Monna Vanna, the heroine of Maurice Maeterlinck's play of the same name. Monna Vanna deserts her husband Guido for his enemy, General Princivalle, and this act has been customarily interpreted as the triumph of love over death. Lest we think that Sumako is equated with the free-loving heroine Monna Vanna, however, the other man chimes in with the correct interpretation: "You mean, Mr. Hōgetsu as Monna Vanna, Mrs. Hōgetsu as Guido, and Sumako as Princivalle, right?"[43] In this extraordinary gender-bending analogy, Hōgetsu becomes the heroine of a love triangle, deserting his female husband and running off into the arms of the enemy, General Sumako! Once again, the focus of the heroic action is shifted from the woman to the man, and the woman is relegated to the role of seducer.

Ultimately, the figure of Sumako persists as a myth, ungraspable except through the various representations of her. She also constitutes a peculiarly potent epistemological trap, one that ensnares those attempting to understand her. Kurawaka Umejirō's attempt to distinguish the real Sumako from the misunderstandings and myths surrounding her only reveal the shakiness of the distinction. His account of Sumako flip-flops endlessly—she was not a humble person, but she was not arrogant either; she was arrogant without knowing arrogance—before he finally gives up the attempt to understand her all together:

> Recently, I think I have been able to gain a true understanding of her. But I might yet be wrong. It may be that it's actually only society that really understands Sumako. Or it may be that it's only the late Professor Shimamura who understood Sumako.[44]

A reading of Matsui Sumako as a feminist must necessarily work through the figures she represented on stage. This will be the task of chapters 7 and 8, which will examine the roles the actress performed during her career. Before looking at Sumako on stage, however, we turn to a very different kind of text:

Matsui Sumako's autobiographical writings. Let us see how her own words might counter other people's relentless insistence on her mindless body.

WHO DOES SHE THINK SHE IS?: HER MEMOIRS AND ESSAYS

Peony Brush (Botanbake) is Sumako's memoir.[45] It is a small book, about postcard size, with 230 pages, including more or less fictionalized autobiographical sketches, essays, and photographs. Two photographs show Sumako dressed in traditional *kimono,* and each of these is accompanied by a *waka,* a classical Japanese verse of 31 syllables, presumably composed by the actress herself. The verses are traditional in both form and content, describing delicate natural phenomena:

> Ura ura to / tatsu kagerō ni / hana moete /
> hakage kagayaku / beni tsubaki kana
> [In the heat waves rising dimly / the flowers burn / the leaves shimmer / of the red camellia.]
> Iro moyuru / wakaba no kage no sasayaki ni /
> soto otozureru hatsunatsu no kaze
> [To the whispering shadows / of young leaves burning with color / a gentle visit / by the winds of early summer.]

The repeated metaphor of "burning" adds a dash of passion to the otherwise tame description of nature. This visual and textual representation of the actress as a "traditional" Japanese woman is drastically reversed by the last photograph in the book: It shows Sumako dressed in a long cape and is accompanied by a haiku, a more recent and terse form of only 17 syllables. The message is compact and clear: "Wearing a *manteau,* I am a New Woman" (Manto kite / ware atarashiki / Onna kana).

These two sets of images, almost stereotypical representations of the "traditional" and the "new" woman, frame a further set of images: 19 photographs of Matsui Sumako in various roles she played in her short but spectacular career, accompanied this time by the names of the plays and the heroines, and the lines that correspond to the photographed scenes. These include the mad scene of Ophelia in Shakespeare's *Hamlet,* Nora's entrance in Ibsen's *A Doll House*, and the dance of the veils in Wilde's *Salomé*. These images raise the inevitable question: Who is this woman who looks "premodern" in some moments, modern in others, Japanese in some respects, Westernized in all others? Is she perhaps acting at all moments, playing roles in all the photographs, including the three that are supposed to show who

6.1 Matsui Sumako dressed in kimono. Courtesy of Waseda University's Tsubouchi Shōyō Memorial Theater Museum.

she "really" was, without the theatrical costumes?[46] Even before reading the main text, a reader's desire to grasp the "real" nature of the actress is thwarted by this careful layout of competing roles.

Although it is arguably the one text that comes closest to expressing Matsui Sumako's "real" feelings, *Peony Brush* has been mostly dismissed by critics and historians. The reason given for this is telling: Rumor has it that the book was ghostwritten by her director and lover, Shimamura Hōgetsu. In his afterword to the reprinted edition of *Peony Brush,* the critic Matsumoto Kappei cites a line from the journal *Onna no sekai* (Women's world): "That thing called *Peony Brush* is also entirely the result of Mr. Hōgetsu's efforts."[47] Although Matsumoto claims to be critical of those who question Sumako's authorship, he nonetheless perpetuates their logic: While Sumako's authorship cannot be ascertained, each successive citation of the rumor of Hōgetsu's

6.2 Matsui Sumako in *manteau*. From *Peony Brush*.

ghostwriting serves to justify the book's dismissal. Mori Reiko, for example, considers *Peony Brush* to be on the whole a work marred by narcissism and sentimentalism, "despite Hōgetsu's extensive help in writing it."[48]

There is, however, at least one part of the text of *Peony Brush* whose authorship is never doubted by anyone: the "Introduction" or "In Place of a Preface" (Jo ni kaete) penned by the alleged ghostwriter Shimamura Hōgetsu himself. This short essay is a passionate defense of Matsui Sumako, and the figure of the actress that emerges from it is worth examining in detail.

Hōgetsu begins by listing the external and internal characteristics required of actors (*haiyū*). External characteristics include strong voice, balanced physique, attractive facial features, and powerful facial expressions. The more important *internal* characteristics are psychological ones, which Hōgetsu elaborates as follows:

> Someone who is easily distracted cannot become an actor. Someone who hesitates cannot be an actor. An actor must be someone who surges forward in a straight line on the road ahead. Otherwise it will not work. For example, if an actor were to think of something else while saying the lines on stage, the thoughts and feelings within the lines would be interrupted. This is why you might find an actor sometimes forgetting the lines, or allowing a lapse in the gestures. (i)

The way to prevent these gaps and to sustain concentration is to "maintain the given thought and feeling in a pure state, and proceed without relaxation or hesitation"(ii). This, however, can cause one to be perceived as stubborn, irrational, emotional, thoughtless, and selfish(iii). In sustaining this pure state, one often neglects the subtle maneuvers required to get along in society, the various techniques "of layering the heart two or three times, of creating a front and a back side in conversations, of smoothly chiming in with others"(iii).

In Hōgetsu's explanation, acting on stage must strive toward singleminded interior purity, while social life off stage is understood to be duplicitous, reactive, and manipulative. The binary of front versus back (*omote/ura*) or public statements versus true feelings (*tatemae/honne*) has been a familiar mantra of scholars characterizing Japanese social interactions. What catches our attention here, however, is the idea that theater performers should transcend this binary and achieve a truthful and interior state that combines thoughts (logos) and feelings (pathos). They should then project this interior state, with no hesitation, no distraction, in a straight line extending in front of them. This idea of theater as the expression of a truthful interiority is radically new and characteristic of the kind of performances staged by Shimamura Hōgetsu and Matsui Sumako. The next chapter will discuss this idea of the New Theater in greater detail.

Hōgetsu goes on to say that it is because Matsui Sumako has learned to sustain these internal psychological characteristics that she comes into conflict with conventional society:

> The stage renders your nerves ever more delicate and disadvantageous for social maneuvering. In other words, the more deeply you enter into art, the more difficult it becomes for you to get along with society. You are a tragic woman who bears the same destiny as many a vulnerable artist in history. (iii-iv)

This might explain why Matsui Sumako receives criticism from both inside and outside her troupe. A good actress is bound to receive bad press. Recognizing that fact, Hōgetsu calls Sumako's commitment to her art in the face of criticism "heroic" (*hiroikku*).

Hōgetsu's defense of the actress in the second half of the essay involves a complex manipulation of three sets of binary oppositions: femininity versus masculinity; nature versus artifice; and Japanese essence versus Western-style training and acting. The complexity of Hōgetsu's argument suggests how actresses were situated within the discursive context of the modernization and Westernization of Japanese theater, as well as the discursive context of the rise of feminism.

First, Hōgetsu claims that Sumako's art is a natural outgrowth of the straightforwardness (*gōchokusei*) and expansiveness (*rikichōsei*) of her soul. But since straightforwardness and expansiveness are "masculine" characteristics, they must be balanced with "feminine" subtlety (*enkyokusei*), which Sumako achieves through her craft (v). We are faced with a strange paradox: Her masculine soul or "nature" (*shizen*) is contrasted to her feminine craft or "artifice" (*gikō*). The odd alignment of genders is compounded by the ambiguity over the status of nature versus artifice. Which is dominant in Matsui Sumako, nature or art, masculine or feminine? According to the modern formation of theater, true art must come directly from nature and not from artifice or craft. Yet according to the modern formation of gender, true femininity must also be defined by nature, not by artifice or craft. Hōgetsu tries to resolve this logical paradox through a marvelously ambiguous sentence: "Thus nature always stands on artifice" (shikashite shizen wa tsune ni gikō no ue ni tatte iru). Does this mean nature is superior to artifice? Or that nature is supported by the basis of artifice? Does Sumako's masculine nature stand triumphant over her feminine artifice? Or is her masculine nature anchored firmly by her feminine artifice?

Having suggested Matsui Sumako's fundamentally masculine characteristics, however, Hōgetsu must now defend Sumako against those who accuse her of having become too masculine:

> When we talk about masculinity, we of course refer merely to the masculine colors which appear on the surface of femininity. In no way would these masculine colors threaten to erase the colors of Japanese femininity with which your nature is endowed. (v)

So now Hōgetsu has reassured readers that Sumako's masculinity is a superficial one and that her natural femininity is fundamental. But had he not one paragraph ago declared that Sumako's "soul" was naturally masculine, and her femininity was artificial? Here, the vocabulary of colors (*shikisai*) may well be strategic, since it can blur the distinction between something that is a naturally given characteristic and something that is added on. Later in the essay Hōgetsu shifts the terms slightly to those of painting: "An outline sketched [*sobyō*] by masculine expansiveness, and contoured by the shading [*kage o tsuketa*] of feminine subtlety: that is her art" (vi). From the carefully mixed palette of Hōgetsu's words, Sumako emerges thus as a layered portrait of many colors and dimensions.

We should also note the stress on "Japanese" femininity in the above sentence. Hōgetsu insists that Matsui Sumako remains naturally Japanese despite her training in Western theater. Hōgetsu goes on to describe how Sumako trained herself from being an initially frail and typically reticent Japanese woman to an actress speaking and moving in a Western manner:

> When you first rehearsed your role as Nora in *A Doll House,* you could not even maintain a straight line with your stretched-out arm for any length of time. It took a long period of training for you to turn it into a beautiful straight line. Similarly, it must have taken many months to change your voice from a strained twittering, and to stop your lips from pursing shyly when laughing. (v-vi)

These passages align femininity with Japanese nature and masculinity with training in the Western style of acting, which reshapes that nature. Sumako here is no longer the artist expressing her "masculine nature" but an artist whose feminine nature is unquestioned, though subject to modification. Her "feminine" and "Japanese" "nature" may be reformed by theatrical training, but it is in no danger of being erased. As Hōgetsu reassures the reader, "the softness of Japanese femininity still remains in you" (vi).

This tortured aligning and realigning of femininity and masculinity, internal nature and theatrical technique, and Japanese essence and Western influence point to the complexity of the discursive positions in which actresses were situated. Trained to become expressive and assertive enough to perform plays by Shakespeare and Ibsen, actresses risked being perceived as Westernized and masculinized: Whence the necessity of defensive emphasis on their feminine and Japanese essence. But the same passage also highlights the training and disciplining of a body, which enables a woman to stand tall and speak up, going beyond the boundaries of what is defined as womanly comportment.

The 17 essays that follow Hōgetsu's introduction display various other facets of Matsui Sumako and add complexity and depth to our portrait of her as a New Woman. Despite the problems of authorship of these essays, not to mention the problems of autobiographical self-representation, we should consider these texts carefully, interpreting them and analyzing them along with biographical representations of her by others. Six of the essays in *Peony Brush* can be read as fictionalized reminiscences about Sumako's childhood and pre-acting days, eight as descriptions of her experiences as an actress, and three as her "feminist" reflections.[49]

The first group of texts presents young girls who clearly exhibit signs of early interest in the theater. These girls, variously named, depicted through first or third person narration, are surely modeled on Sumako herself. These texts cannot be read as straightforward "records" of Sumako's life, however.

They are carefully crafted vignettes that may be read for their thematic concerns and their performative gestures. These texts are meant to tell the reader something about the actress. They are like the photographs that Sumako presents in the other pages of the memoir, or like the different costumes she wears in those photographs, showing off different facets of what she is capable of performing and what she would like the audience to see.

In "Female Butterfly" (Mechō) a young girl, about 12 years old, enjoys the excitement of dressing up in order to perform the role of the "butterfly girl," whose function is to pour the ritual sake at wedding ceremonies (22–28). The text enunciates a clear connection between the girl's sexuality and theatricality, between heightened sensations of the body and theatrical deployment of the body. The text opens with the girl, named Katsumi, being teased and tickled by her two female friends.

> The two girls grab her by both of her sleeves, and rattling the sliding door, throw Katsumi down by the knees of the boy. The two continue tickling her viciously. Katsumi turns red up to her ears, at the thought of fooling around like puppies so close to an unfamiliar boy. Gasping "please stop—" she struggles with all her might to get up on her feet. But the more she struggles, the more she is pushed towards the boy. He moves his knees away little by little. His face is kept turned away. (19–20)

After this childish yet nonetheless erotic escapade, Katsumi's mother prepares the girl for her performance at the wedding ceremony. Accompanied by much excitement and fidgeting, her hair is washed, her face is covered in white foundation, and her body is robed in an elaborate kimono with a red and gold sash.

The ceremony in which the two pour sake from matching decanters is described as a moment of first contact between Katsumi and the young boy.

> Katsumi gets up on her knees gracefully, so unlike her usual tomboyish manner. She turns towards Ichirō and tries to put together the mouth of her decanter to the decanter held out by Ichirō. Their hands tremble, and the two mouths fail to meet. Twice the mistake is repeated. On the third try, she boldly bends her body forward from the knees, and clicks the decanters together. At that moment, Ichirō's short-cut hair gently pricks Katsumi's forehead, and his sweaty warm scent touches her face. Standing up and sashaying away, kicking the hem of her kimono, she feels the soft cotton fabric cling sensuously around her legs. Katsumi feels like she is in a dream. (27)

This performance marks a transition in the girl's development: "Katsumi, whom everyone recognized and indulged as a tomboy, started turning into a sensible and graceful maiden from about this time" (30). When she sees the boy again, he is wearing a junior high school uniform, and the two greet each other quietly.

So far, both girl and boy have matured according to a normal pattern of gendered development. The last few pages of the text, however, reveal that both eventually veer off the normal course laid out for them. It is suggested that Katsumi becomes an independent woman, perhaps returns to being a tomboy. Shrugging off suggestions that she marry someone in the village and settle down, she goes off to Tokyo, just like Matsui Sumako did, at the age of 16. The boy, on the other hand, turns into a juvenile delinquent, steals money from the family, impregnates a maid, also escapes to Tokyo, and is not heard from again.

This text can be read as an updated Taishō version of the Meiji classic by Higuchi Ichiyō "Child's Play" (Takekurabe).[50] The similarities are striking: Both involve young children at the dawn of adolescence, at first innocently at play, but coming to feel attracted to one another. They reluctantly separate when adulthood approaches with separate destinies for each gender. The differences are equally telling of the times: In "Child's Play," the boy is headed toward higher education, while the girl is destined to become a geisha. In "Female Butterfly," on the other hand, the boy has become a delinquent, superfluous in the Taishō economy, while the girl is headed to Tokyo and, it is suggested, to a career as an actress.

That the boy in "Female Butterfly" is portrayed as a passive performer who "moved about just as instructed, always keeping quiet" (23) but who then becomes a delinquent seducer, seems to be a comment on the bifurcated portrait of Sumako as puppet and as femme fatale. If the displacement of male anxiety about female sexual subjectivity was embodied by the New Woman, then this text seems to throw the anxiety back to men: The figure of the inscrutable boy reminds us that men were the ones with economic resources and mobility, and that men seducing women was a much greater social problem than women seducing men.

That Matsui Sumako was a conscientious and eager student of the craft of acting is also reflected in several texts of the memoir. The "Shop Keeper" (Mise no hito) is perhaps the most intriguing, because it shows an early scene of practicing elocution, which was to become part of the acting student's curriculum of the Literary Society. Hisae, the young female protagonist, has just started working at her brother-in-law's cake shop and must learn how to say "thank you" to the customers. At first, she is hesitant: Her voice sounds amateurish (*shirōto jimite*), as if struck by stage fright, unable to make the scene her own (*ita ni tsukanai*) (7). Eager to improve her skills, she observes and analyzes her brother-in-law's elocution:

> Yukichi's "arigatō" is directed towards the back of the customer, the "ari" is low and thick, produced from the pit of the stomach, loud and strong, the "ga" of "gatō" slightly blurred, the "tō" slightly lifted, light and soft, almost

> snuffed out. It is a dignified elocution, with the weight that befits a master of the shop. (10)

She notes the difference of tone when the shop clerks pronounce the same "arigatō"—the word sounds distorted in their delivery, but is nonetheless suitable to the context:

> It sounds like "a'eentsoo." Even when she tries to listen very closely, it still sounds like that. And of the "a'eentsoo," the "een" sounds fairly clear, but the "ntsoo" is extremely low, and almost inaudible. It sounds vigorous, but also just business-like. It is quite different in character from her brother's master-like elocution. And yet, it matches the scene [*ita niwa tsuite iru*]; it suits the shop. Now that she knows clearly how to pronounce it, Hisae wants to try it out on each client that comes in, yet she is always too hesitant to say it in time. It would be a shame not to try it at least once, she thinks, since she went to the trouble of studying it. (11–12)

When Hisae finally pulls off an appropriate and yet spontaneous-sounding "*arigatō*" on her own, she feels that she has become a professional (*kurōto*), that she has performed a role (*hitoyaku sumashite*) and conveyed a message (*nen ga todoita*) (13).

This text is itself a performance whose message is that Matsui Sumako took every opportunity to observe human behavior even before she became an actress; that when she performs a role, she researches it, creates sketches from real life, and takes the stage as a professional; that her acting, far from being an impulsive and natural outpouring of emotions, is a studied craft. It also reminds us that daily life is not so far from performance either, that in our mundane exchanges with one another, we are acting as well. We may pronounce our thank-yous differently depending on our own particular role in a particular scene. The exchange in a shop, in particular, contains many elements of theatrical performance: a public space in which participants have definite roles, a script that is more or less set in advance, a particular tone and pace for speaking, and a successful elocution tied to the transaction of money.

Unlike the case of Kawakami Sadayakko, Matsui Sumako's motivations for becoming an actress are not often discussed by critics. Insight into this question can be gained by looking at another reminiscence text, "Young Tears" (Osanai namida). It is written in the third person, but the protagonist is clearly modeled on Matsui Sumako herself.

> People often asked her "Why did you want to be an actress?" She always answered "Because I liked it, that's all." But was that really all? Was that really all that made her dare so much?
>
> Indeed, there must have been many more complicated feelings involved.

> Of course, there were various reasons: in creating a new theater, we could not maintain something as unnatural as men acting as women; or since conventional actors lacked psychological interpretation [*kokoro no kaishaku*] and were of low repute [*jinkaku ga hikui*], they needed new actresses to make up for that lack. But these were all intellectual reasons that she thought of, or learned about, after the fact. She thinks that the motivation that moved her feelings in the beginning were quite different. (37–38)

The real reason she wanted to become an actress was that after the death of her father, and especially after the breakup of her first marriage, her actual life had become so empty that she wanted to live a more fulfilling life on stage.

> She found real life [*jissai no seikatsu*] tedious, and wanted to lead a life on stage that would be more intense than reality. She wanted to elevate her tedious and withered life by making it into art. In other words, rather than to go on living with an empty heart from which all energy has been drained, she wanted to pour her body and soul into this art, to become so engrossed in it that she would forget everything else, and to go on living with it as her consolation. (38)

Already, the complexity of pinning down human motivation is dramatized by these opening remarks. The first paragraph debunks the image of simple and naive fondness for the theater—"Because I liked it"—that is, the public image that Matsui Sumako projected. The following paragraph lists more complex intellectual motivations—the desire for reforms in the theater—of the kind that male theater practitioners around her were voicing. Finally, she rejects all of the above to put forward an emotional motivation as the most fundamental one. Yet the wording of this explanation catches our attention. The complex, somewhat jumbled, metaphor of pouring one's body and soul (*mi mo tamashii mo*) into acting in order to fill an empty heart (*kokoro*), complicates the portrait of Sumako as an empty vessel into which *the director* poured his art, as well as the portrait of a Sumako whose acting was merely the spontaneous expression of her nature. The wording implies a conscious decision to make acting the center of one's life, and to train one's body and soul for the sake of art. At the same time, it leaves the agency of the actress somewhat vague: Can one choose "to lead a life on stage that would be more intense than reality" or "to become so engrossed in it that she would forget everything else"? Or are these lines meant to describe what eventually happened to the actress, justifying her troubled personal life, or deflecting attention away from it, by commanding the reader to look at her stage performance, not her life offstage?

On the one hand, the decision to start acting begins to sound in this text like a defensive response to psychological trauma, especially the abandonment by men: her father, her first husband. On the other hand, what the death of the father and the separation from the first husband signify above all is the plunging of the woman into a socially ambiguous and economically perilous state. The part of the text that describes this period has a vague and dreamlike quality to it, corresponding to the ambiguity in the woman's social standing. The narrator is hospitalized and even attempts suicide. For a single woman, there is literally no space to live in but that on the stage.

> Once she started acting on stage, she had the desire to perform roles that she could identify with [*jibun to dōka shita yō na*], and thus to appeal to wider society. Among the various roles she was given to perform, there were some that perfectly matched her feelings at the time. It is at times like that, after she weeps and weeps exhaustively on stage, that she feels at least slightly relieved. After the play is over, from the moment she takes off the costume in the dressing room to the moment she is back home and falls asleep, she thinks of the lines in the play at every opportunity and immediately the tears come to her eyes. (44)

It seems that the stage allowed Matsui Sumako to work through her traumas and release her emotions. On another level, this text can be read as an advertisement for the kind of deep identification with characters that New Theater was promoting. Whereas crying in the *noh* theater would be symbolized by a gesture of slowly bringing up a cupped palm to the eyes (*shiori*), and crying in *kabuki* would consist of an extended and virtuosic aria of wailing, crying in New Theater must come spontaneously from the inside of the actor. Matsui Sumako is here tied to the artlessness of a woman bursting into tears on stage, tears motivated by her interior emotions, which are identified with those of the heroines she is portraying.

In "My Hometown" (Watashi no kokyō) the first-person narrator reminisces about the village amateur theatricals: The leading female role was performed by a handsome man who charmed men and women alike—until he opened his mouth (98).

> No sooner had he spoken his first line, than the audience burst out laughing. The voice was unmistakably that of a man; it destroyed the effect of the beautiful posture and face. Everyone in the village kept talking about this incident. (99)

Tamura Toshiko had commented about the *onnagata*'s voice in the actress debates: An *onnagata* may look like a beautiful woman, but the voice gives away his true gender.

The text contains a contrasting instance of crossgender performance: At the end, the narrator finds an old set of samurai clothes. She puts on a hat and acts like a samurai. The family has experienced decline, and these implements are the last vestiges of their former status. Sandwiched by these two crossgender performances, both of which are associated with the past, the narrator's relationship to her parents is portrayed in warm tones. She visits the grave of her father and thinks of the role of Magda in Hermann Sudermann's *Heimat.* Much like the heroine of the play, she has come home after achieving success as a performer. She has faced opposition from those around her, but unlike Magda, she feels her father would have supported her:

> And I . . . I have attempted to become, of all things, an actress, and have caused a furor among relatives and acquaintances.
>
> I wonder what Father might think, sleeping underground. Would he look down upon me as an unhappy woman, like Schwartze looks down on Magda? Or would he sympathize with me? Wondering thus, I gaze at his grave.
>
> My dear father is a deeply affectionate man, and he knows my feelings well. And since I have paddled out this far on my journey, he would surely pray that I would arrive at my destination, no matter how I am tossed by the rough waves. Staring at the tip of my toes, before I knew it, I had walked back to the gate of my house. (104–5)

At home her mother takes out the *shamisen* and encourages her to dance, while accompanying her on the instrument and in song. They repeat the dance five times, correcting each other. Thus the text can be construed as a series of performative gestures to show how Matsui Sumako has maintained her parents' support in pursuing an acting career and how she is fulfilling her filial duties. The text tells us in essence that Sumako may be a prima donna and a New Woman, but she is a better daughter than Magda. We will hear much more about Magda in chapter 8.

One of the most interesting essays dealing with Sumako's acting days is "Summer in Kyoto" (Kyō no natsu), which depicts the actress as a kind of *flaneur.* The *flaneur* is a fin-de-siècle conception of the writer as walker, a sophisticated observer who roams the city in a leisurely way.[51] The *flaneur* is generally conceptualized to be male, and the female is generally excluded from the position: She is regarded as part of the spectacle to be enjoyed: the shop assistants, waitresses, and of course, the streetwalkers.[52] Here, however, four actresses and their director, presumably Shimamura Hōgetsu, walk about the streets of Kyoto on a summer night.

The actress who walks the streets of Kyoto at night is either progressive, regressive, or transgressive. She is either taking steps forward into a realm of movement hitherto only open to men; or she is following the footsteps of streetwalkers, with whom actresses kept being associated; or she is sidestepping these conceptualizations and creating space for new kinds of movements.

Regressing is the first move shown. Our female walkers see Kyoto's famous brand of geisha, the *maiko,* with their sleeves blowing in the wind, their voices meltingly soft. The former women are looking at the latter women, the actresses are subjects while the geisha are objects, but the text connects the two groups of women: The same evening wind blows through the unwound hair of the actresses. They have just finished performing Hermann Sudermann's *Heimat* and are enjoying their leisure time, just as the geisha are enjoying the cool breeze in their casual attire.

Progressing is fantasized but impeded. The women realize that they are not allowed to roam freely like the male actors. The male actors tell them about the pleasures of spending a night on the famous stage of Kiyomizu Temple, which hangs out over a cliff:

> We remembered how two days ago, we climbed, also accompanied by the Professor, to the stage at Kiyomizu Temple situated high up on the cliff, and looked down. . . . How I wanted to go there! The urge was almost irresistible. Yet we were bound by the word "woman," and to spend a night on the stage of Kiyomizu Temple would have been a major incident.
>
> Although we were supposed to be used to being on one stage or another, when it came to this one stage, it didn't seem like our director would grant us permission so easily. (113–115)

Although the actresses had made much progress, this particular stage was still off-limits to them.

Finally, there occurs a certain kind of transgressing. Our New Woman sees a group of students in front of a book shop. They are admiring what is described as a displayed "picture card" (*ehagaki*) of the "Magda play," most likely a photograph of Sumako dressed in the costume of Magda, the heroine of Sudermann's *Heimat*. Without noticing that the actress is standing behind them, the students engage in gossip about her:

> "Oh yes, they say this actress M. who's performing Magda is quite extraordinary. They say she's an exceedingly prim woman."
>
> "Did you know that she's the daughter of a banker in Yokohama? Her father was strongly opposed to this in the beginning. That's why she had enormous difficulties studying, but they say that now, because of her recent success, he has relented and lets her do what she wants. . . . They say that as soon as she became famous as Nora, the Baron of——got his hands on her. That woman's finished!" (116–117)

Sumako finds the whole situation hilarious, although she feels sorry for the innocent Baron. The anonymity of a busy city street is combined here with the recognizability of photography, which made the images of performers such as Matsui Sumako more memorable and accessible. Thus "Summer in Kyoto" captures a new moment in the history of theater: the copresence of anonymity and recognizability, the actress as both circulating *flaneur* and circulated photograph. Yet there is a fascinating gap between the photograph and the *flaneur,* the Sumako who is captured in the picture and the Sumako who roams the streets unrecognized. This gap seems to stand for the New Woman's ambiguous status. She is sexualized, but she is a subject. She is fixed as an image, yet her body evades capture.

The three essays on feminist topics are perhaps the most surprising in *Peony Brush* because they display a facet of Sumako's character that is hardly mentioned at all in the biographies. These essays make the strongest case for Sumako's agency—her ability to think, judge, and act—which is erased in the biographies. One essay, "Nora and Magda" will be discussed further in chapter 8, in the context of Sumako's performance of feminist roles on stage. Another essay, "Recent Complaints" (Saikin no fuhei), deals with Sumako's own difficulties as a woman in a man's world. The complaint centers on the double standard of society that praises self-assertiveness in men but chastises it in women such as Sumako: "In other words, they expect women to be much more saintly than men. Isn't it strange that men are allowed things that women are not, although we are all human beings?" (168). Sumako also complains about her colleagues in the theater:

> Many people say that ever since the days of the Literary Society, my personality has caused problems. Do they mean to say that the people I have problems with are all saints and I am the sole villain? Isn't society strange? I have performed Nora, I have performed Magda, that's all, but those who once were my superiors now feel that I have become the center of the organization, and say they are irritated by that. What am I supposed to do? And hasn't that person spread rumors that make me look guilty, as if I had started all the problems? I thought I should keep quiet because I am a woman and because I am younger—but before I knew it, everyone in the world came to believe *his* version of what happened! (170–171)

Thus Sumako defends herself against those who criticize her as a self-centered star who antagonizes her colleagues, by arguing that her fellow actors are at least as responsible for the quarrels as herself and that it is the double standard of society that imposes the guilt on her alone. There is obviously much self-justification and self-righteousness in this essay, but if one decides to cite accusations against her in her biography, as so many do,[53] one should at least take a look at a text that might be read as Sumako's self-defense.

Another essay, simply titled "Reflections" (Kansō) is the most forceful in its feminist tone. The whole text takes the form of Sumako's answer to the question "When do you feel proud to be an actress?" Sumako replies:

> As an actress, I feel more humiliation than pride. I feel persecuted. Must a woman always flirt and curry favor with others? Must she always silently

> obey the commands of others? These have long been considered the customs and virtues of women in Japan. This has contributed immeasurably to the degradation of our work and our art. (158)

The actress is in a more difficult situation than other artists, since she must work with other people: She cannot work in isolation like poets or painters do (169–170). Sumako wonders in despair: "When will we have a Sarah Bernhardt of the Japanese theater?" (163).

Sumako's concluding remarks to "Reflections" are significant: The only time she feels proud to be an actress is when she is able to surpass the *onnagata.* She writes:

> Pride as an actress—I could almost say I have never felt such a thing. In the West, actresses existed from early on and were allowed to perform in plays, no matter how complex and women-centered these plays might be. Women portrayed in Japanese plays, on the other hand, were all performed by male actors called *onnagata,* who used conventionalized gestures. Since these gestures were on the whole in accordance with the Japanese tradition that valorizes lack of expression, there were few plays in which the individuality of women was emphasized. This is why after many years of practice, even male actors were able to carry off these roles admirably. Not only did they carry off, they *owned* these roles. But in Western theater, there are many plays that center on the woman, and portray various individual personalities. In order to perform these roles, an *onnagata* must first break out of the Japanese gestures that he has absorbed through many years of practice. And as soon as he has overcome these patterns after much struggle, his masculine nature becomes all too apparent. Whenever we see that, we are filled with happiness. . . . (164–165)

We thus end up with a portrait of Matsui Sumako that is quite complicated and different from the conventional picture of her as Hōgetsu's puppet: the first modern actress, the first woman to prove that women could be better portrayed by women than by men, the quintessential and self-proclaimed "New Woman." Against the conventional historiographical and biographical narratives that would depict Matsui Sumako as a mindless body or a self-centered child, I have attempted in this chapter to construct a feminist reading of the actress that emphasizes her agency, her acting, and her words. The next chapter will emphasize her position in the gradual formation of the "New Theater" and will examine its imbrication with "New Woman."

CHAPTER 7

A NEW THEATER

NEW THEATER AS THEATER OF LOGOS

JUST AS ACTRESS KAWAKAMI SADAYAKKO'S PRESENCE enabled the project of straightening theater, actress Matsui Sumako's presence animated the project of bringing theater into a new era. This was the era of New Theater, a bundle of practices and ideas that correspond to a well-established movement in Japanese theater history: the *shingeki*. At first, *shingeki* was merely a descriptive phrase employed to distinguish new theatrical experiments from *kabuki* (the latter now being labeled the *old* theater, or *kyūgeki*). *Shingeki* gradually came to refer to a specific cluster of troupes that emerged in the early twentieth century, including Osanai Kaoru's Free Theater (Jiyū Gekijō), Tsubouchi Shōyō's Literary Society (Bungei Kyōkai), Shimamura Hōgetsu's Art Theater (Geijutsuza), and a host of small troupes that came and went, but some of which survive to the present day. Today, the term also refers to the legacy of those troupes: the few existing *groups of actors* who trace their artistic lineage to those troupes, the kinds of Japanese and Western *plays* most often performed by those troupes, and, most importantly for our purposes, a set of *assumptions* about what theater is and ought to be.

By using the term New Theater, I wish to highlight this set of *assumptions* that characterized the performances of Matsui Sumako and her colleagues in the early twentieth century. In the 1900s and 1910s, a few fundamental terms of debate about theater were hammered into place: theater's relation to society, to Japanese nationhood, and to the West; theater's dilemma between artistic integrity and commercial success; theater's imbrication with gender and sexuality. My premise is that many of these assumptions are still operative today. This chapter will not provide an exhaustive account of the history of this genre, since several reliable surveys of "who said and did what when" exist, at least in the Japanese language.[1] The purpose here is rather to point out what was significant and *new* about New Theater, and especially what was new and noteworthy about the women acting in it. It is my contention that, New Theater was a set of interlocking practices based on the Western model of the "theater of logos," but with several significant departures from the model. The presence of the actress Matsui Sumako was crucial for both those aspects of New Theater that followed the "theater of logos" model as well as those aspects that departed from it, namely the aspects relating to gender and sexuality.

It is important to note that New Theater was not a mere continuation of the project of straightening theater. It involved a different group of people, coming from different social strata and trained in different pursuits: New Theater practitioners were mostly former students and professors at highly prestigious universities, *not* apprentices in popular entertainment or street politics, as were many of the straighteners of theater such as the Kawakamis. One estimate holds that 80 percent of New Theater audience members were also students.[2] Due to the difference in social positioning and educational background, New Theater practitioners and spectators had a more reverent attitude toward playwrights as intellectuals and toward play scripts as texts to be read carefully,[3] a more dismissive attitude towards money and popular success,[4] and a degree of identification with Western ideas and Western practices that was not found in earlier genres.

If one had to choose three major advocates of New Theater, one would face few objections choosing Tsubouchi Shōyō, founder of the Literary Society, Shimamura Hōgetsu, founder of the Art Theater, and Osanai Kaoru, founder of both the Free Theater and the Tsukiji Small Theater. In relation to Matsui Sumako, Tsubouchi was her initial boss, Shimamura her teacher and later lover, and Osanai her lifelong critic. Interestingly, all three participated in sets of debates or disagreements, and paired up and against each other concerning the status of the play, the actor, and the audience. This, then, will become the organizing framework for our discussion of New Theater and its faithfulness to and departure from the theater of logos.

In *Writing and Difference,* Jacques Derrida summarizes what he calls the "theater of logos" as containing the following elements. First, there is the godlike "author-creator who, absent and from afar, is armed with a text and keeps watch over, assembles, regulates the time or the meaning of representation, letting this latter *represent* him as concerns what is called the content of his thoughts, his intentions, his ideas." Next, the author-creator's thoughts, intentions, and ideas are represented by "[i]nterpretive slaves who faithfully execute the providential designs of the 'master.'" Such an interpretive slave "only transcribes and makes available for reading a text whose nature is itself necessarily representative," that is, a text that imitates and reproduces the real. Finally, there is the "passive, seated public, a public of spectators, of consumers, of 'enjoyers'" who attend a text-like production "offered to their voyeuristic scrutiny."[5]

The "theater of logos" constituted the mainstream of modern Western theater since the late nineteenth century, and New Theater sought to faithfully imitate it. While certain elements of the "theater of logos" can be found in premodern Japanese theater, especially in the plays of Chikamatsu Monzaemon, as will be discussed later, it was the combination of all elements and their claim to hegemony that characterized the theater of modern Japan. Hence, New Theater would require a faithful representation of the author-creator's intentions, interpretive slaves whose function would be to transcribe the texts, and a passive public of spectators and connoisseurs who would consume and read these texts. New Theater would require these in the name of the universal. It was not so much that the advocates and practitioners of New Theater believed in the inherent superiority of modern Western (European, Russian, and, to a lesser extent, American) theater, but that they thought it representative of the universal ideals: the true, the good, and the beautiful.[6] And, because these advocates of New Theater took the modern West to be universal, they earnestly and enthusiastically attempted to import into Japan those modern dramas as well as those accompanying ideologies and staging conventions as intact as possible—as intact as the necessities of translation and production allowed, and as intact as state censorship permitted.[7]

Although many New Theater practitioners saw themselves as intensely involved in building a national theater and contributing to the buildup of the Japanese nation-state, just like the Kawakamis had seen the project of straightening theater as a national project, nonetheless (or perhaps therefore) New Theater was heavily censored by the state. New Theater practitioners found that both the category of woman and the category of theater became narrower in the 1900s and 1910s, following the establishment of many of the institutions of the nation-state in the 1890s. There were less permeable borders and more strict patrolling by the state.

Two major aspects of social change affected the positioning of theater and its relationship with the Japanese nation-state during this time. First, the Japanese victory in two international wars, the Sino-Japanese War (1894–1895) and Russo-Japanese War (1904–1905), intensified nationalist sentiment, since the victories appeared to prove that Japan was capable not only of dominating its Asian neighbors but of standing up to the Western powers as well. It was a period of rising nationalist rhetoric that specifically extolled the characteristics of a Japan that is non-Sinic and non-Western. Against the Japanism of the state and conservative ideologues, the idea of "the West" could be used as a critical element and as a challenge to the status quo. "Westernizing," in this context, meant different things than it had in preceding years. Whereas in the early Meiji years, to Westernize was to follow the government's lead in reforming society, now, in the context of increasing nationalism, to Westernize came to have a potentially critical valence. Whether it was as an allegiance to things Western *because* they were Western, or to things Western because they *seemed universal,* or to things *universal which turned out to be Western,* it could be used strategically to oppose the state-sponsored glorification of Japan.

Second, in the aftermath of the Russo-Japanese War, a serious postwar depression bred social agitation, lending steam to a variety of social movements of socialist, communist, and anarchist persuasions. The culmination of the social protest was the 1910–1911 High Treason Incident, in which several hundred anarchist activists and intellectuals were arrested, and 12 of them were quickly convicted and executed on the basis of trumped-up charges of plotting to assassinate the emperor. At this time of increasing social unrest, the state tightened its grip on culture in order to maintain ideological control. Censorship, although certainly not the only mechanism by which the state sought to control cultural and intellectual life, was nonetheless one of the most visible and was a highly effective means of curbing antistate expression. During this time, books and magazines were routinely banned when they were considered to contain material injurious to public morals. Scripts for the theater were under even stricter surveillance: They had to be submitted for approval to the Metropolitan Police Board at least one week before the performance, only approved scripts could be staged, and no deviations from the approved script were allowed. During the performance run, at least two seats were to be set aside for police observers, and if the actual performance veered in the slightest from the approved script, the production could be shut down on the spot.[8]

This system of censorship was potentially devastating to the *sōshi shibai* (political theater) of the early Meiji period, out of which milieu Kawakami's troupe had emerged triumphantly in 1894 at the outbreak of the Sino-Japanese War. The political theater of the time relied heavily on ad lib exchanges rather than on written scripts, and hence could not easily be approved for performance. The police routinely disrupted these political improvisations, dispersing the audience by force, just as it did with political speeches (*enzetsu*). More will be said about the ideological significance placed on the written script and its faithful reproduction in the context of New Theater performances, but it is interesting to note that these were in consonance with state censorship procedures.

Around 1905, the end of the Russo-Japanese War, the Japanese government began to take seriously the effect of literature and theater on youth, especially on students, and therefore began to squelch expressions of romantic love, considered corruptive of young students. Shortly thereafter, it began cracking down on expressions of socialist and revolutionary ideas as well.[9] Unlike earlier in the Meiji period, when theater was the target of reform because it was too old-fashioned, now the theater was to be placed under surveillance for its dangerously *new* ideas.[10]

In 1910, the year of the annexation of Korea and the censored performance of *Korean King* by the Kawakami troupe, the theater censorship laws were revised: The new rules expressly forbid actors from mingling with the spectators during the performance and forbid spectators from entering the backstage area during performance. This legal segregation of actor from spectator formalized what had been debated for some time in the theater reform movements. Yet the concern about separating actor from spectator also reflected a more immediate concern about demarcating and maintaining proper categories of bodies: Populations had to be controlled by preventing them from mingling and erupting in unpredictable ways. It is not a coincidence that this was the year of the High Treason Incident, a moment when the concept of the "masses" (*minshū*) was crystallizing along with a strengthening collective demand for suffrage, democracy, and economic justice. Increasingly faced with the threat of an uncontrollable mass of bodies, the ruling powers desperately attempted to police crowds by physically and metaphorically roping off speakers from addressees.[11]

The law was specifically responding to rumors of actors having love affairs with women of the aristocratic class. But it was also symbolic of the state's desire to separate the lowest of the land from the highest, the incendiary speaker from the impressionable addressee, the titillated spectator from the seductive spectacle. The state's regulation of bodies, which Foucault calls "the art of distributions,"[12] was epitomized by the theater censorship laws. By eliminating, as Foucault would phrase it, "the effects of imprecise distributions, the uncontrolled disappearance of individuals, their diffuse circulation, their unusable and dangerous coagulation," the theater aided the state in its procedures of "knowing, mastering, and using" individual bodies.[13]

The theater complied by turning the addresser into attractive spectacles, the addressee into passive spectators. Censorship was an inescapable factor that structured New Theater's relationship to state and society, yet we would miss the complexity of the picture if we were to forget the imbrications of state censorship with the self-censorship of theater practitioners themselves and with the apparatus of disciplining and policing such as education, journalism, and literary criticism. Even in those instances where New Theater appears to have clearly challenged the social and political status quo, we might look carefully for what made such challenges possible and visible, and what choices and compromises had to be made in the process. We will come closer to understanding New Theater if we see that it was not only a vehicle for subversive expression potentially threatening to the state but at the same time a disciplining mechanism potentially mobilized for the state, molding actors and spectators, and channeling the energies of the people, especially those of educated students and intellectuals, away from collective political mobilization and toward individual and private reflection.

This is because theater practitioners who did critique the status quo found themselves advocating personal freedom rather than political rights. This retreat from the political to the personal is often cited as the characteristic failure of modern Japanese literature of this period: Even socially conscious Naturalist writers such as Shimazaki Tōson and Tayama Katai appeared to be turning away from grappling with the political and social issues of the day, focusing instead on depicting their own private and inner worlds.[14] Following the 1910 suppression of social and political dissent, in what poet Ishikawa Takuboku called "the suffocating conditions of our era" (jidai heisoku no genjō), New Theater was pressured to do the same: finding private answers to social questions, personal solutions to political problems, and individual satisfaction instead of collective struggle.

Yet at the same time, it cannot be denied that the turn from the public to the personal allowed something that was of major significance for the development of feminism. This was the questioning of the dynamics within that which had previously been the unquestioned black box of the personal and private realms: relationships between family members, between children and parents, between women and men, and between self and society. Gaps were being pried open between the acting self and the assigned role, between the woman and the good wife and wise mother. The New Woman had been a manifestation of the opening of this rift, and Matsui Sumako as New Woman emerged precisely in this opening.

Moreover, while the definitions of the categories of woman and theater became narrower and more strictly enforced by the state, resistance to these definitions also grew. In this context, the concept of "nature" in the modern definitions of gender and performance comes to have several contrary meanings. The emphasis on what is "natural" in defining womanhood and theater could theoretically and practically result in the questioning of state control over these realms. In other words, the argument that something was "natural" could be used to protest repressive institutions and laws, much in the same way as certain forms of gay activism today deploy the argument that homosexuality is "natural" in order to protest against discriminatory laws. Indeed, the essentialist and expressivist definition of gender became a strong basis for modern feminism.

The argument that the essence of woman was grounded in her physical and physiological nature, for example, could be used to argue for the liberation of that nature and to open up discussion about sexuality, pregnancy, abortion, motherhood, and prostitution. On the basis of a definition of womanhood grounded in the body, feminists were able to engage in debates concerning the meaning of women's sexuality—often coded as a discussion of "chastity" (*teisō*)—or the need for government support for mothers (*bosei hogo*).[15] The definition of womanhood may have become narrower from the time of Kawakami Sadayakko to that of Matsui Sumako: The normalization of monogamous heterosexual marriage not only marginalized certain options for women—to be unmarried or unattached or attached outside the system of legal marriage—but it also prescribed the proper modes of behavior within the wifed role. Yet this narrower definition also made possible the emergence of a self-conscious feminism in Japan: If all women had something in common by being women, there was something to be gained for women by talking with each other. The proud "I am a New Woman" declarations by Matsui Sumako and Hiratsuka Raichō are made possible by such women talking with each other and by the redeployment of definitions of womanhood. We must, then, look at both sides of the coin in considering the significance of the modern definition of woman.

In the realm of theater, as well, an emphasis on "natural" expression could and would be used in critiquing the Confucian morality of the old theater and in calling for a modern, "natural" theater. The inculcation of Confucian morality by nationalist reformers of culture, summarized in the phrase "promoting good and punishing evil" (*kanzen chōaku*), had been the focus of theater reform debates in the early Meiji years; even in the efforts to straighten theater by the Kawakami troupe, there were repeated gestures to emphasize morality (*giri*) over feeling (*ninjō*). The New Theater advocates, straining against the straightjacket of this old morality, used "nature" as a rhetorical device, crying for greater political, social, and cultural freedom in the name of nature. The theater of the West was seen as an appropriate way to introduce "natural" theater to Japan, because its conventions were antithetical to those of the old Japanese theater. The issue is *not* whether Western theater was indeed more natural than old Japanese theater, since what is seen as natural is always produced through conventions. What is important is that at this point in history, Japanese theater practitioners deemed it important for Japanese actors to perform modern Western (mostly European and Russian) plays, and that by doing so, they were chastising the unnaturalness of both theatrical and social conventions. They saw these unnatural conventions as residues of old Japan that stifled and suffocated them at every turn. It is therefore crucial to understand the two sides of the coin in the modern definition of theater as well: On the one hand, it is a narrowing of heterogeneous possibilities, of the "polysemic and radial"[16] textual and theatrical strategies found in earlier forms of theater; yet on the other hand, the importation of Western plays that dealt with social problems allowed advocates of New Theater to deploy the category of the "natural" to protest the "unnatural" social conventions around them, including those conventions that deeply affected the status of women.

The complicated stance toward the Japanese state and society in New Theater is further complicated by its stance toward the rest of the world. In contrast to the Kawakami troupe, which often explicitly thematized Japan's relation to other nations in their performances, the New Theater rarely foregrounded international relations. Yet in New Theater, it is assumed that Japanese theater should be like that of the advanced Western nations. And it is assumed that Japanese actors can act like Westerners in British, German, Russian, and Scandinavian settings created on the Japanese stage. Westernization, in other words, is not thematized, but simply assumed as a basis of New Theater's performances.

As a corollary, New Theater does not thematize the expansion of the Japanese empire, but simply treats the empire as a given.[17] Unlike Kawakami's theater, it does not discuss how Koreans or Chinese are like or unlike Japanese, but simply assumes that the Japanese empire exists. Behind New Theater's nonchalance regarding Japan's position in Asia lies the assumption that since Japan is closest to becoming a member of the elite group of civilized nations, if not already a member by virtue of its victory in the Russo-Japanese War, it should naturally lead other Asian nations. As far as New Theater is concerned, this state of affairs does not even need to be remarked upon: Asia is undistinguished as a theme in New Theater. Theater historian Ōzasa Yoshio points out that while playwrights become self-conscious and critical in the postwar period vis-à-vis colonialism, the New Theater produced until the end of the war was characterized by "obtuseness about colonial mentality" (shokuminchi shugi teki na shikō ni kansuru mushinkei sa). Even when colonial situations were depicted, they were not thematized as special problems.[18]

The new attitude toward Japan's position in the world goes hand in hand with a new attitude about "originals." As Westernization fades from foregrounded theme to backdrop, freewheeling adaptation (*hon'an*) gives way to straight translation (*hon'yaku*). The connecting thread is a new, or heightened, respect for the original: a sense that the original Western text must be taken seriously, treated with reverence, transplanted carefully to Japanese soil, with as little disturbance as possible. Whereas Westernization in the early years of Meiji was characterized by a pragmatic attitude of borrowing whatever seemed useful from the sources and adapting it to the Japanese environment, even when the result was a haphazard mishmash, Westernization in the late Meiji and early Taishō years was both more careful and more wholehearted. Whereas in the 1870s and 1880s, Western institutions were imported because they were useful and functioned better, in the 1900s and 1910s, Western ideas were imported because they were thought to be universal and to make you a better person.[19] Whereas straightening theater meant borrowing useful plots from Western plays and adapting them into Japanese theater; New Theater meant making Japanese theater as Western as possible.[20]

Even in Kawakami Sadayakko's performances and in the series of scripts stored in the Kawakami archive, it is possible to see how in the course of straightening theater, loose adaptations and subversive parodies were gradually replaced by more faithful and "straight" translations. Matsui Sumako's performances further malleated and polished the conventions of theatrical translation and staging until the interlocking assumptions of New Theater had been hammered into place: that the script is of prime importance; that a Western text is universal and therefore should be relevant in Japan; that a translation of a Western text should be faithful to the original; that the translation should be faithful, yet nonetheless sound natural on stage; that the acting of the play should be natural, too, and not draw attention to itself; that the audience should be attentive and listen to the words; that the audience should thus enter into communion with the Western playwright's ideas and intentions. Thus New Theater might thus be summarized as a theater in which the purpose is to create equations between a series of terms: the West and Japan, the original text and the translation, the script and the staging, the performance and the audience's response. The less information lost or added on the way from one end of the transfer to the other, the better. And because of this ideology of transference, the materiality of the intervening steps is underplayed.

The experience of attending a New Theater performance, then, becomes something equivalent to the reading of a text as well. The staging itself becomes a transparent medium through which the audience can read the original intentions of the European playwright. The audience is also reading the interiority of the performers, which is supposed to coincide with that of the playwright. Transparency, or the repressing, disavowing, and repudiating of materiality, supposedly produces a pure communion of the interiorities of playwright, performer, and audience.

The process of straightening theater was the process of installing straight gender, i.e., the definition of gender that represses, disavows, and/or repudiates its performativity. New Theater begins with this definition as a premise—the process and the contentiousness of straightening is already of the past, it is forgotten, repressed, disavowed, repudiated. It is a situation that critic Karatani Kōjin calls "inversion" or the hiding of the "origins." The hiding is completed when it begins to look like there was something always already there, something that was hidden and distorted in the premodern period but that can now be expressed honestly and straightforwardly in the modern period.[21] And what is now expected to be expressed in a straight and pure manner, through the performances of Matsui Sumako and her colleagues in New Theater, is nothing other than the natural essence of gender and theatrical performance.[22]

ACTORS AS INTERPRETIVE SLAVES: THE OSANAI-TSUBOUCHI DEBATE

This is where New Theater begins to diverge from what Derrida calls the "theater of logos," the dominant mode of Western theater. Neither Derrida, nor

Antonin Artaud, on whose ideas Derrida is basing his argument, deal with the dimensions of gender and sexuality pertaining to theater. Yet in New Theater, gender and sexuality are of crucial importance.

New Theater was a theater of logos, but it was also a theater of purity, in its installation of a new relationship between play and actor, actor and audience. New Theater is characterized by an intense desire to maintain purity and a marked anxiety about the potential for impurity. New Theater idealizes pure, uncommodified, natural interiority, and it this pure interior essence that is supposed to be expressed freely in the New Theater, with the actors as straight translators or enslaved interpreters of the author-creator's intentions, and the spectators as passive readers of the text. The resulting communion, a pure reading experience, is supposed to be innocent of commercial or sexual transactions. One account describes how, for the audience of that time, to go to a performance was equivalent to reading a play, no more, no less:

> This was because, to put it in an extreme way, it was sufficient for actors of modern theater [*shingeki yakusha*] at that time to take the burden of reading plays off the shoulders of theater-goers and to do this work in their place. Even when the actors' expressions were clumsy and inadequate, the theater-goers would supplement and fill in the gaps with their own personal imaginations, and would perceive the performance as if tracing the printed words on stage. There would even be students alternating between looking at the stage and looking up the text of the play in the original language.[23]

The experience of going to the theater had changed drastically from *kabuki*. What had been an experience of "participating" in a communal event, with elements of ritual and social intercourse—negotiations with the tea houses and restaurants, interaction with the other theatergoers, visits backstage, and possible transactions, sexual and otherwise, with the performers after the show—became an experience of just "looking" and tracing the printed words on stage. This constricting of the polymorphous sensuality of theatergoing and the emphasis on the purity of the reading experience is what characterizes New Theater.[24]

This emphasis on purity is of course a double-edged sword. New Theater is able to use the ideal of the uncommodified, natural, and pure in order to critique the social status quo as commodified, unnatural, and impure. Yet this critique is won at the expense of abjecting certain bodies as fundamentally impure. Mastui Sumako, for instance, was abjected as precisely this kind of impure figure: She was both commodified and sexual, and doubly vilified because of what was perceived as her commodified sexuality.

In order to discuss New Theater's emphasis on purity, we need to take a brief look at a playwright from premodern Japan, whose work was the object of intense study and experimentation by New Theater. This playwright is Chikamatsu Monzaemon (1653–1724), hailed in the Meiji period as the William Shakespeare of Japan. By investigating this playwright and the reasons for his resurgence in the modern period, some light might be cast on the relationship between theater, sexuality, and commodification.

What are we to make of the fact that the Japanese Shakespeare is most acclaimed for writing about the buying and selling of women in the so-called *kuruwa* or "pleasure quarters" of the Tokugawa period?[25] There have been many attempts to comprehend this kind of trafficking in women: linking it to the sacred prostitution of shamanesses; valorizing it as the equivalent of European madams running their refined and cultured salons; praising it as the celebration of robust sexuality that did not yet suffer from the repression of the Meiji period; castigating it as the clearest sign of Tokugawa oppression of women; and analyzing it as the government's method of social control.[26] Above all, one could argue, the pleasure quarters were arenas of performance and commerce. The courtesan's job was much like that of an actress, and also much like that of a merchant. The commodity being sold and bought here was precisely a performance, a "sex act" with the emphasis on "act" rather than on "sex."[27]

Yet as soon as performance becomes a commodity, there arises a desire to buy that which is not a performance, but the real thing: real emotions, unfeigned affections, true love, signified by terms such as "truth" (*makoto*) and "feelings" (*nasake*). A striking indication of this paradox is the development of ritualized techniques that the seller of the commodity employed in order to assure the buyer he was getting the real thing. For example, the erotic guidebook *The Great Mirror of the Erotic Way* (Shikidō ōkagami) of 1688 lists six methods for the courtesan to show her *shinjū* or "true feelings" to her client: 1) peeling off one's nail to give to the client; 2) exchanging letters swearing love, often signed with blood; 3) cutting off one's hair to give to the client; 4) tattooing the name of the client in one's arm; 5) cutting off a finger to give to the client; 6) plunging a dagger in one's arm or thigh.[28] But as these ritual techniques of proving "realness" become more drastic as well as more refined, the more intensified becomes the desire to obtain that which is not mere technique.

The problem with this desire is that its fulfillment can never be proven on the level of reality. One can never know what someone else is truly feeling. As long as one is confronted by someone else's otherness as an Other, as a person separate from oneself, one can never be fully convinced of that other person's sincerity, and one's desire can never be fulfilled.[29] This, in fact, is the very definition of the Other. The true feelings of the seller cannot be proven by the seller, and the buyer has no final reassurance that he got the real thing. The realness can only be guaranteed by framing the relationship as fantasy. It is only in fantasy, in fiction, and, in our case, in a play, that a relationship can be shown to be based on real emotions. The relationship is real because the narrator says it is real; because the relationship is *framed* in such a way; because, in the case of Chikamatsu's plays, the relationship most often ends with a double suicide, and the narrator announces that the seller and buyer were bound by true feelings, a fact that, he implies, was proven by their final acts.

While this structure of acts, of the real, and of fantasy are part of a general structure of sociality,[30] the theatrical framing of the real reaches a highpoint in Chikamatsu's plays. This is not due to Chikamatsu's peculiar genius, but it is due to his timing. Chikamatsu wrote for the puppet theater, his reason being that *kabuki* actors recklessly changed the playwright's words in order to curry favor with the audience, but puppets could not do so.[31] Chanters in the puppet theater dared not tinker with the playwright's words, since puppeteers needed to coordinate their movements with the chanters, an arduous task that did not leave room for improvisation. In the background of this choice by Chikamatsu lies also the fact that the commodification of *kabuki,* the selling of performance that could be bought by anyone with money,[32] bred a desire for uncommodified performance. In writing for puppets, Chikamatsu could ideologically reject the audience-directness of the actors, who were also often prostitutes themselves, although practically, of course, the puppet theater was a commodified performance as well. But Chikamatsu was the first "author" in the modern sense;[33] he expected his plays to be staged faithfully as he had written them.[34] His plays for puppets are the embodiment of the newly created desire for the uncommodified real and the newly privileged ideological rejection of commodified performance.

In the Meiji period, Chikamatsu was picked up by those searching for a new cultural practice: pure art, pure theater, purged of commodified performance and commodified sexuality. As the antidote to *kabuki* and as the apotheosis of "real emotions," Chikamatsu's plays became literally "training grounds" for straightening theater in the 1890s and 1900s.[35] Chikamatsu's plays were read as being not about the traffic of women and commodified performance, but as being about the true love of women and pure dramatic art. This is why he was equated with Shakespeare, who was also read at this point as representing pure emotions and pure art. For example, Ii Yōhō, at one point a member of the Kawakami troupe, started staging "study performances" of Chikamatsu plays in 1902, which attempted to cleave as close to the original text as possible while still following basic *kabuki* conventions, while Hanabusa Ryūgai, also in a performance in 1902, attempted to "fundamentally depart from musical theater [*gakugeki*], eliminate the narrator [*chobo*], abolish dance-like gestures, and perform in the manner of Straight Theater [*seigeki-teki*]."[36] Hanabusa accused Ii Yōhō's performances of being too *kabuki*-like, but in the sense of respecting the original text, Ii's performance was also modern and an important step in the direction of New Theater, no less than Hanabusa's experiments at straightening.[37]

This fault line opened up by Chikamatsu was maximized by New Theater in the 1900s and 1910s. Tsubouchi Shōyō had been publishing his studies of Chikamatsu's plays since the 1890s and had formed a Chikamatsu Study Group (*kenkyūkai*). By 1907 a number of the Study Group's members were publishing papers and performance reviews. Director Shimamura Hōgetsu also started out by studying Chikamatsu.[38] His notion of romantic love, in which two people sacrifice all for each other, seems to derive from a modern reading of Chikamatsu. Even the manner of his death and that of his lover, Matsui Sumako, suggests the model of double suicide.

It is intriguing that the puppet metaphor comes up again and again in the context of New Theater, and especially in the context of actress Matsui Sumako's life on stage and off: She performed a doll who breaks free of the strings binding her and turns into a feminist (Ibsen's *A Doll House),* yet she was also repeatedly ridiculed as being the soulless puppet of her director. At the same time, that very director, Shimamura Hōgetsu, was also likened to both the doll who leaves the house and the puppet who is manipulated by a malicious femme fatale.

The foregrounded split between the body of enunciation and enunciated that characterized Chikamatsu's puppet theater, and that Roland Barthes memorialized as "a total spectacle, but divided,"[39] made the puppet play as written text possible. Theater of logos began with Chikamatsu in Japan, and the original "interpretive slave" was indeed a puppet. The limits of the theater of logos, however, become apparent when the obedient puppet begins to have a life of her own.[40]

Among other things, then, the Japanese Shakespeare attests that commodification breeds desire for the uncommodified. This is the lesson of recent critical analysis of sexuality as well. Sociologist Katō Shūichi, for example, argues that we must *not* think of the relationship between commodified sexuality and uncommodified sexuality as being one of a linear temporal transition from one to the other, or that the uncommodified sexuality is the original, natural, unalienated, pure form of sexuality that is then distorted, corrupted, alienated by capitalism and patriarchy. Katō argues that the idea of "sexuality" (*sei*) itself originated simultaneously with its "commodification":

> "[S]exuality" was born as a phenomenon particular to modern capitalist-patriarchal society, and was by its nature a "commodity" from the very beginning. At the same time, the concept of an uncommodified, original sexuality was born, as the negation and reflection of commodified sexuality.[41]

The binary opposition of prostitution and monogamy, pleasure quarter and home, sex worker and housewife come into being in the same manner. The latter terms—monogamy, home, and housewife—are formed as the negation of the former terms—prostitution, pleasure quarter, and sex worker—which are then understood to be the corrupted, fallen counterpart of the latter terms.

The same structure with regard to commodification and negation of commodification holds true in the realm of art. In the European context, scholar Rachel Bowlby has shown that the idea of "art for art's sake" came into being as an ideology at the same time that art was becoming thoroughly imbricated with industry and commerce, through mass publishing, mechanical reproduction, and the development of advertisement.[42] Pierre Bourdieu summarizes the relation between art and commodity neatly when he characterizes the artistic field as a semi-autonomous field "which is constituted in the nineteenth century by taking the reverse of economic law as its fundamental law."[43] Just as the notion of an unalienated, uncommodified labor comes into being as the negation of commodified labor, as uncommodified pure sexuality comes as a negation of commodified sexuality, and as uncommodified "real" comes as a negation of commodified "performance," the notion of an uncommodified "pure" art (romantic genius, art for art's sake) was created as a negation of commodified art.

In this context, it is entirely understandable that New Theater would engage in heated discussion about art, sexuality, and commodification. The ideology of New Theater as uncommodified pure art was first introduced in the debate over the status of actors between Osanai Kaoru, founder of the Free Theater, and Tsubouchi Shōyō, founder of the Literary Society. As we saw in chapter 1, the status of the performers had changed radically in the Meiji period, from that of river-bed beggars (*kawara kojiki*) to that of professional artists. As the designation of actor changed from fixed social status to chosen profession, a new line of distinction emerged among actors: professionals versus amateurs. The difference between the amateur and the professional is conceptualized as a matter of training and remuneration,[44] whereas the difference between the actor and the nonactor in the premodern era had been of prescribed hereditary status, of being inside versus outside the law.[45]

The "amateur versus professional" debate between Osanai Kaoru and Tsubouchi Shōyō came at a moment when both *kabuki* as well as *shimpa*—after the Kawakami attempts at straightening had met only limited success—are increasingly perceived as old and decadent theater, intensifying the call for a new kind of actor for a new kind of theater. This led to a debate about whether one should rely on actors trained in the older traditions, or train new actors from scratch. At stake is the procurement of "interpretive slaves" required by the theater of logos. Which would yield more obedient interpreters serving the New Theater?

Osanai Kaoru had founded the Free Theater with *kabuki* actor Ichikawa Sadanji in 1908. In asking *kabuki* actors to perform modern European plays in the Free Theater, Osanai declared that he was turning professionals (*kabuki* actors) into amateurs (modern theater actors).[46]

> I would like to fully support actors—those who are actors by profession. I would like to guide the *professional actor* [in English] in the right path. I think that even among the current actors, there are one in a thousand or one in two thousand who are serious and true artists. It is cruel to dismiss the whole by looking only at the scarcity of numbers. My wish is to pick up the one in a thousand or two thousand among professional actors who has a serious brain and heart, regardless of the immaturity or maturity of his art, regardless of the beauty or ugliness of his physique, and thus to create an organization for experimental performances [*shien*], which may be few in number but serious in purpose.[47]

Osanai therefore decided to use *kabuki* actors, already trained professionals, for his theater productions. Osanai saw the rival Literary Society as turning amateurs, i.e., those with no experience in acting, into professionals, i.e., modern theater actors. He contrasted the two projects in clear terms, though he did not see them as engaged in incompatible tasks:

> The critical tasks of the theater world today are "to make amateurs into actors [*yakusha*]" on the one hand, and on the other hand, "to make actors into amateurs." Professor T [Tsubouchi Shōyō] and Mr. SH [Shimamura Hōgetsu] seem to be aspiring for the first project. We intend to commit ourselves to the second project.[48]

Osanai's counterpart, Tsubouchi Shōyō, accepted that characterization to a certain extent. He also found it "quite reasonable that Mr. Osanai would find hope in professional actors [*kurōto no haiyū*]." Yet Tsubouchi Shōyō feared that using professionals would be ultimately impossible, because they would not be able to fulfill the three conditions he demanded of his actors: first, a thorough understanding of the playwright's intentions combined with the willingness to serve the playwright's demands; second, a willingness to rehearse extensively enough to realize the intentions of the playwright; and third, the theater manager's willingness to let the actor devote such time to rehearsals. In his experience, none of the three conditions had ever been met. Professional actors, no matter how serious in spirit, would not or could not spare the time to rehearse more than once or twice. *Kabuki* actors did not see the need for extensive rehearsals for "serving the playwright's demands," since their rehearsals consisted mostly of verbally agreeing on the movement of persons on stage. One *kabuki* actor responded to the New Theater's emphasis on rehearsals with sarcasm and puzzlement: "If I put my mind to it, it won't take me more than three days to memorize even the thickest of scripts. And yet you tell me I'd have to rehearse for thirty or forty days? What on earth am I supposed to rehearse?"[49] New theater therefore turned to amateurs who could be made into "interpretive slaves" willing to rehearse 30 or 40 days. The issue of rehearsal, and what on earth it was that they were supposed to rehearse, will come up again in the discussion of Shimamura Hōgetsu and his theater.

On both sides of the amateur-professional debate, however, there is the implicit recognition that the conceptualization of the actors has fundamentally changed, from that of outcast social status to a profession that one can choose to enter. The difference between amateur and professional is simply a matter of training and of remuneration, not a matter of fixed social status. This had several implications.

First, women, by definition, were "amateurs" since they were not trained in *kabuki* technique. Turning amateurs (women) into professionals (actresses) was the slogan of the Literary Society, which successfully employed actresses in its performances. On the other hand, turning professionals (*kabuki* actors, including *onnagata*) into amateurs (actors of modern theater, including actors of women's roles) was the method of the Free Theater, led by Osanai Kaoru.

Second, amateur status, defined by lack of training and remuneration, was a precarious and elusive one. Here, we might also mention the short-lived but significant phenomenon of amateur theater performances by intellectuals and literati (*bunshigeki*). Such literati theatricals started in 1905, involved mostly theater critics writing for newspapers in the Tokyo area, and continued until about 1908. They were the forerunners of the New Theater in that they were performed by amateurs without the profit motive, but they also lacked any training in New Theater techniques, as well as any innovative or critical attitude toward old theater techniques. As a result, most performances ended up as mere imitations of professional actors, a copying of specific *kabuki* actors' gestures and speech patterns. These, then, were amateurs imitating professionals, rather than amateurs espousing a principle of "amateurism" and making that new principle the basis of their profession.[50]

In contrast, the major concern of New Theater was to get rid of precisely the old professional ways and to train amateur women and men to become actors and actresses in the new ways. How to cease sounding and moving like *kabuki* actors and like *specific kabuki* actors, and how to purge the citation of preexisting vocal and physical patterns were major concerns for New Theater. This mission required a new school.[51]

In 1909, Tsubouchi founded the Theater Institute of the Literary Society (Bungei Kyōkai Engeki Kenkyūjo). The first class consisted of 21 students, 4 of them female, including the student later known as Matsui Sumako. It was the first coeducational theater school in Japan. The modern and ambitious curriculum included lectures in the theory of art, history of Japanese theater, Shakespearean theater, and modern drama, as well as practical exercises in English conversation, elocution, sketching, and singing. Tsubouchi Shōyō taught *The Merchant of Venice* in the original language as part of his lectures on Shakespearean theater, while Shimamura Hōgetsu taught *A Doll House* in English translation, as a model of "modern realistic drama."

In March 1910, the students of the Theater Institute gave a private trial performance of *Hamlet*. Matsui Sumako was Ophelia. This was different from the 1907 performance by the members of the Literary Society, because it used trained actresses for the first time. The students also performed *Hamlet* in 1911 at the recently opened Imperial Theater (Teikoku Gekijō). Critics declared that "Ophelia's song of madness . . . could never be as effective if it were performed by the conventional *onnagata* of *kabuki*."[52] At this point, the Theater Institute decided that the remaining 15 "students" would be paid 100 yen per year: They became professional (*kurōto*) actors. A contract was signed with the Shōchiku Company, founded in 1902 and by this time moving toward monopolizing the management of theater, and *Hamlet* was performed in Osaka as well.

In 1911, the newly professional actors of the Literary Society performed *A Doll House* at the Imperial Theater, in response to heavy courting by the management of that theater. Through the success of this performance, Matsui Sumako became the undisputed star of the Literary Society. The commercial success of *A Doll House* was a shock to Tsubouchi Shōyō for several reasons: With only two years of training, amateur students of theater had acquired value as professionals, and their performances had come to circulate as commodities, attracting large audiences. The exchange value of the commodity seemed quite divorced from the use value, that is, the actual level of the performers' artistic accomplishment. They were also achieving success in a kind of play that was quite different from his own ideals of national theater, as will be discussed later. What might have bothered Tsubouchi the most, however, was that it was an *actress* who was attracting all the attention.

If the actress was the object of fascination for the public, it was the object of intense surveillance and discipline for the school teachers. The Theater Institute of the Literary Society had been extremely strict about the sexual conduct of its students. For example, one of the rules of the Institute stated: "When male and female students wish to rehearse together, whether inside or outside the school building, they must first notify the office and receive instructions from the teacher."[53] These may have been necessary gestures in an environment where actresses were still being confused with geisha and prostitutes. Of the 81 students who had entered the Institute by the third year, 21 were expelled due to "misconduct." The last one to be expelled for this reason was none other than Matsui Sumako, and this lead to the dissolution of the Institute itself.

New Theater thus sought to distinguish its actresses from sexually commodified women, which included, according to their criteria, the actresses of the less pure branches, including, for example, the Imperial Actress School

(Teikoku Joyū Yōseijo) founded by Kawakami Sadayakko. The women from this school were often confused with geisha and expected to perform the same kinds of services at private functions. One actress recalls:

> When we had time, we would be invited to the mansions of the so-called bourgeois class: we would not perform plays, but display our other talents [i.e., dancing, playing music]. The payment received allowed us some financial luxury. We would be instructed to gather on such days in our most elaborate coiffeur [*bunkin takashimada*] and our longest-sleeved kimono [*furisode*]. . . . One day, there was a party at a notable's residence, and once we were finished with our performance, we were told to serve sake to the guests. Ms. Mori [one of the first and most famous students of the school] gathered us together, and we immediately left the mansion in protest. I remember Ms. Mori saying something to the effect that we are not geisha, and that we must clarify the nature of our profession [*shigoto*].[54]

And a staff member of the Literary Society also recalls how in contrast to the students of the rival Tokyo Actors' School (Tokyo Haiyū Gakkō), who were fond of fashionable kimono and silk scarves and preferred to make a detour through the pleasure quarters on the way to the school, the students of the Literary Society were dressed in plain cloths and walked the straight and narrow path: "Professor Tsubouchi instructed the young students who expected to enter the acting profession to avoid being actor-like [*yakusha rashii to iu koto*] as much as possible. He strictly disciplined those who would even think of dressing fashionably or adopting airs . . . the students looked intentionally uncouth, as if to embody the intentions of Professor Tsubouchi."[55] Matsui Sumako is described in the same passage as wearing a stained kimono of cheap silk, a narrow sash, and no socks, looking more like a "female student" (*onna shosei*) than an actress.

What we have here is a competition in a "purer than thou" structure, which is another instance of différance at work: There was no such thing as a purely pure actress, since by definition a professional actress was commodified merchandise, but New Theater tried to assert the purity of their women by contrasting them against "less pure" women. Decades later, the management of the all-female Takarazuka theater would encapsulate this structure in their motto, "Purely, Righteously, Beautifully" (*kiyoku, tadashiku, utsukushiku*), all the while exploiting the sexual allure of the performers.[56]

In the debate between Tsubouchi and Osanai, the status of amateur is defined as negation of the professional, as a person lacking in professional acting experience, as someone who is not commodified. The same vocabulary of amateur (*shirōto*) versus professional (*kurōto*) was used during this time to categorize women in relation to sexual commodification: The *kurōto* was a sex-worker, a woman doing business by exchanging sexuality as a commodity;

the *shirōto* was the non-sex worker, the chaste (*katagi no*) woman defined by her position within the bourgeois family as negation of the sex-worker.[57] It was crucial that the actress be a *shirōto* in both senses of the term, a negation of the commodified body at both levels.

Matsui Sumako was an amateur trained in the Theater Institute from scratch. An often-repeated anecdote reveals the degree of her "amateurism," specifically her lack of schooling in foreign languages. An actor from the Tokyo Actor's School who was asked to teach English to her recalls how Sumako would place two copies of *A Merchant of Venice* side by side on the desk and would annotate one with the readings in syllabics, the other with the Japanese translation. Since she did not know even the alphabet, each word had to be taught in many laborious steps: identifying the letters "i" and "t"; inscribing the syllabics and learning the pronunciation; inscribing the translation and learning the meaning of "it." Sumako would annotate every single instance of "it" and "is" and everything else, carefully inscribing the pronunciations and meanings with a finely sharpened pencil. The teacher recalls "I imagine she must be the only one who started without knowing the ABCs and went straight to reading Shakespeare in the original."[58] The female *kabuki* impersonator (*onna yakusha*) Ichikawa Kumehachi also agreed that it would make more sense to train amateurs to become actresses, since it is hard to straighten a bent branch, but easier to shape it from the bud.[59] She herself was a bent branch, trained in the *kabuki* tradition, but she had high hopes for the young actresses who would come into the theater with a fresh mind and an eagerness for learning.

Osanai Kaoru, on the other hand, claimed to be turning professionals into amateurs, which was like trying to force a bent branch back into being a bud and then straightening it out. Yet Osanai was also a teacher at the Tokyo Actor's School, turning amateurs into professionals. Moreover, influenced by Gordon Craig's idea of the actors as "Über-Marionette," Osanai sought to turn his actors into puppets (*ningyō*) in service to the play.[60] This desire, more than any other, shows that Osanai, too, was seeking a malleable amateur to be molded into a professional according to his own ideals. He wrote in 1909:

> The script is the puppeteer [*ningyō tsukai*]. The actor is the puppet. The task of the actor is to become the puppet of the script. . . . A puppet has no "self" [*jiga*]. A puppet moves according to the will of the puppeteer. The actor will be able to truly become a person inside the drama only by becoming the puppet of the script.[61]

Surely, such a puppet was not likely to come from the ranks of professional actors, but from the ranks of amateurs willing to put up with becoming interpretive slaves.[62]

In the debate with Osanai Kaoru, then, Tsubouchi Shōyō's position of training amateurs to be professionals won in the end. The latter's victory meant that women, as amateurs, could be trained as actresses. But it also meant that actresses would be tainted and seen as professionals. In this context, Tsubouchi Shōyō's unease about the sudden success of the actresses of the Literary Society makes logical sense. It has to do with anxiety about the instability of the boundary between the amateur and the professional, and about the ease with which a woman and an artist can cross over from the status of the amateur to the status of professional. The overnight success of the actress evokes the memory of the initiation rite (*mizuage*) of the prostitute—in a single night's encounter, an amateur woman can be purchased and become a professional woman. Likewise, an amateur artist can become a professional by being "bought" by more and more customers—and this is exactly what was happening in the Literary Society.

While New Theater pretended to desexualize theater and presented itself as scandalized by sexual liaisons among theater practitioners and those around them, it also commodified the sexuality of its performers, especially of its actresses. The kinds of roles performed by Matsui Sumako are also evidence of the commodification of sexuality in New Theater, as the next chapter will show. The New Theater could not afford to ignore the sexual appeal of the actress, since, like in the Kawakami troupe's productions, the actress was bringing in the bucks. In her insightful study of the all-female Takarazuka Revue, Jennifer Robertson points out how "the exotic and ambivalently erotic allure of the Revue is manipulated strategically by the management on the condition that the Takarasiennes remain objects of fans' desires without any reciprocating sexual agency of their own."[63] Similarly, New Theater attempted to manipulate strategically the sexual allure of the actress while carefully proscribing her sexual agency.

FAITHFULNESS TO THE ORIGINAL: THE TSUBOUCHI-SHIMAMURA DEBATE

The ideological emphasis on purity in New Theater was also embodied in its various practices. Theater of logos required faithful representation of the "author-creator," and this required new conventions of speech and action, going further than the repudiation of indirect speech and action—that is to say, song and dance—in the process of the Kawakami troupe's straightening of theater. This, too, had significant implications for the actress.

Perhaps the most drastic example of New Theater's drive to be Western, as well as its reverence to the original text, was the proposal to present European drama in the original language. Linguist Ueda Kazutoshi proposed in 1907 that such a radical measure would be necessary to reform Japanese theater:

> Let us build a theater building in the purely Western style. Then, let us invite famous actors and musicians from each country. . . . Regardless of whether people understand them or not, and certainly regardless of the material cost, let us invite them here to perform in a grand manner. A few intellectuals might discern the contrast with Japanese theater, and our theater world might be inspired through this breath of fresh air.[64]

Earlier that year, Shakespeare's *Julius Caesar* had been performed in English by a Japanese cast. The performance was mostly a disaster, since the actors had barely memorized the lines, yet the intention had been the same as those of Ueda Kazutoshi. These attempts formed the extreme edge of the move towards Westernization of Japanese theater.

A more realistic strategy, which came to dominate New Theater, was to stage Japanese translations of European plays. But what was required was a very specific type of translation. While loose adaptations and subversive parodies had been the norm for the Kawakami troupe, in New Theater one does not find a Hamlet set in Kyoto or a comedy version of Othello. Everything has been straightened; theater is a serious matter.

Moreover, New Theater demands two kinds of allegiances from the translation: allegiance to the original text, and allegiance to the naturalness of the text as spoken on stage. Not surprisingly, the two allegiances are often at odds with each other. Yet the ideology of New Theater does not recognize there to be a contradiction since it believes that it should be possible to translate European texts faithfully into Japanese and to transcribe the resulting text faithfully onto the stage. If European texts embody universal ideas of culture, and if Japan is becoming a cultured nation, why should Japanese theater not be able to represent universality on stage? The only hindrance to such a staging of universality would be conceived as Japanese particularity, and this in turn is understood to be Japanese backwardness: peculiarities of Japanese language and physique, timeworn habits of the mind and the body. But according to New Theater, these are vestiges of the old Japan, which are to be overcome through education, training, and technique. New forms of discipline will scrub away old habits until we end up with a Japan that is like the universal West in every respect.[65]

It is precisely in this process that Japanese language and Japanese physique are discovered as qualities particular and peculiar to Japan. It is the drag against a full identification with the West, the impossibility of a perfect passing as Western, that come to be understood to be Japanese qualities. And to a certain extent, it is these Japanese peculiarities, now understood to be Japanese *essences,* that are later made to serve as the basis of postmodern performance genres such as *butō* and underground theater. Contemporary theater trainer and director Suzuki Tadashi recognizes this process when he points out the following: "Modern Japanese actors have gone to tremendous pains, throwing themselves into the effort of imitation, yet they have never achieved an appropriate likeness. So the failure has been attributed, quite bluntly, to the physiological: their arms and legs are too short."[66] A similar process has been sighted at work in *butō,* the postmodern dance genre, where the *butō* practitioner Hijikata Tatsumi has claimed to have created a style of movement suitable to Japanese body structure, very different from the movements of ballet or modern dance.[67]

The difference between the Japanese body and the Western body, however, is also a relation of différance. There is no such thing as a pure Japanese body or a pure Western body. It is only in comparison to another body that one can make a comment such as "hers is a more Japanese body" or "this movement is less suitable for a Japanese body." And incessant comparisons are made in the context of turn-of-the-century Japanese theater: Was Sadayakko more Japanese than Sumako? Who was taller? Who had longer legs? Rounder eyes? Larger breasts?

Hence, the ideology of the theater of logos, the ideology of faithfulness to the origins, extends from translation to the staging of the Western original: the closer the translation to the original, the better; but in addition, the closer the staging is to the translated text, the better. The closer a stage set for Ibsen evokes a Scandinavian living room, the better; the longer the legs of the actor impersonating a Russian gentleman, the better. And, of course, the more voluptuous the breasts of the actress impersonating a German diva, the better. Actors and actresses must not only dress like Westerners but move like them and talk like them. They shall no longer address each other as "Washirō" and "Hamura" and "Orie," but as "Othello" and "Hamlet" and "Ophelia." And it must seem natural for Japanese actors and actresses to address each other that way.

The language of New Theater tried to adhere to the principle of *genbun itchi* (unification of speech and writing), adopting a colloquial style of dialogue that was perceived to be a natural representation of everyday speech.[68] And in acting, the New Theater touted the practice of *shasei* (sketching from life), the imitation of bodily gestures of people in their daily lives. Yet both *genbun itchi* and *shasei* involved irresolvable contradictions, suggested in part by a conflict between the stance of Tsubouchi Shōyō and the stance of Shimamura Hōgetsu.

In practice, the demands of *genbun itchi* and the demands of translating modern European drama often contradicted each other. The result of translating European drama was often a verbose and flowery style of dialogue that was probably not found anywhere outside of the theater. Faithfulness to the original text of the European author-creator and faithfulness to Japanese everyday speech could not easily be reconciled. Yet the ideology of New Theater demanded exactly that reconciliation. Learning to speak these "natural" lines also took some unnatural exertion of energy and a strict disciplining of the voice. For example, one of theater reformer Tsubouchi Shōyō's pet projects was the practice of "elocution," of loudly declaiming theatrical lines in a way that would express their inner meanings, a technique he had learned from an American teacher.[69] Tsubouchi Shōyō had convened an Elocution Study Group (Rōdoku Kenkyūkai) at Waseda University, in which he taught students to declaim various texts, and this Elocution Study Group later became the core of the Literary Society's Theater Institute.[70] For Tsubouchi Shōyō, elocution was more about extracting the full dramatic sonority out of a text, *any* text, than about the production of specifically Western and modern drama. For him, *kabuki* scripts and Shakespearean plays seemed as good as any text to train Japanese actors in the art of elocution. Tsubouchi and the other, younger members of his group would soon find themselves in disagreement over this point.

The workshop performance in 1907 of Shakespeare's *Hamlet* by the Literary Society is a good illustration of the difficulty of achieving the unification of writing and speech, of maintaining faithfulness to the original in translation and staging. The performance came two years before the founding of the Theater Institute of the Literary Society and involved mostly students and intellectuals affiliated with Waseda University. This was a milestone event: the first time in Japan that *Hamlet* was performed in straight translation rather than in adaptation, the first time that Hamlet was called "Hamlet" and Ophelia was called "Ophelia." Unlike the Kawakami troupe's "Hamura Toshimaru as a Kyoto University student" version, Tsubouchi Shōyō, the translator of the text, was careful to preserve the setting of the original and to keep all the speeches as well.[71] This caused some theatergoers to criticize the production for excessive faithfulness to the original. One objected to the line spoken by Laertes upon seeing Ophelia's drowned corpse: "Too much of water hast thou, poor Ophelia, / And therefore I forbid my tears" (*Hamlet* 4.7). Noting that the translation should consider the mentality of the average audience member rather than slavishly follow the original, this critic chided "To come up with a bad joke like this at a moment of crisis struck me as an excess of cleverness."[72] Gertrude's description of Ophelia's death came under attack as well: "What an unreasonably flowery and long-winded speech this is. In the case of a speech such as this, is it really necessary to stick to translating the original as closely as possible?"[73]

Shakespeare was not the best text for New Theater precisely because its format in blank verse and its verbal pyrotechnics made it impossible to translate into natural-sounding Japanese. Tsubouchi Shōyō was rather fond of Shakespeare and not only produced the first full Japanese translation of a Shakespearean play (*Julius Caesar* in 1883), but eventually went on to translate all of the bard's plays, finishing in 1928. It made sense, then, that Matsui Sumako's public debut, taking place in May 1911 at the newly built Teikoku

Gekijō, would be as Ophelia in Shakespeare's *Hamlet,* translated by Tsubouchi Shōyō. It was a performance for which she received considerable praise, but the production also manifested some of the same problems as in 1907.

Tsubouchi Shōyō's ultimate goal in involving himself with New Theater, however, had been to create a new genre that would be worthy of being called Japan's "national theater" (*kokugeki*), and what he envisioned seems to have been some kind of amalgam of Shakespeare, *kabuki,* and grand opera.[74] Song and dance were never distant from his concerns. He went as far as building a new dance stage in the grounds of his own residence and wrote a number of dance plays and musical plays, some of which were also performed by Matsui Sumako while she was a student at the Theater Institute. Tsubouchi's obsession with dance and the discrepancy between him and the aims of the younger members of New Theater is suggested by his refusal to have nails mar his dance stage's beautiful cypress floor—this would make it impossible to construct any elaborate sets on the stage, and would derail the New Theater's dramatic performances.[75] Tsubouchi Shōyō had also been against the abolition of the narrator and the incidental music that accompanied the actors in *kabuki* and puppet theater performances. In his opinion, the narrator (*chobo*) should be reformed, not abolished. He did not fundamentally disagree with the format of the *kabuki* theater, and even his translations of Shakespeare were, in a way, the "combination of Shakespearean bones with *kabuki* flesh and blood."[76]

Tsubouchi Shōyō's students and colleagues, however, had a different view. Straight theater had already abjected song and dance—Shakespeare, *kabuki,* and opera were to their eyes all equally old-fashioned. The attempt to stage Shakespeare faithfully only accentuated its distance from present-day Japanese concerns. The object of imitation and importation could not be just any Western drama; it had to be *modern* Western drama, since it was the modern West that Japan was trying to emulate. In contrast to Tsubouchi Shōyō, Shimamura Hōgetsu and other younger members of the Literary Society wanted New Theater to be entirely modeled on Western theater, especially modern European theater. Osanai Kaoru, another New Theater practitioner, shared this view. When he established the Tsukiji Small Theater in 1924, Osanai pledged that for the first several years, the troupe would only perform Western plays in translation.[77]

Beyond Tsubouchi's ill-fated obsession with Shakespeare, however, his concern for elocution lived on as a principle of New Theater, and elocution also became a technique taught at the Literary Society. It took a great deal of training for actors and actresses to learn how to speak in a way that sounded natural. Moreover, elocution (*rōdoku*) as a technique literally meant that students had to "read aloud": that they would have to read the script carefully, then recite it in a manner that would bring out its inner meaning. This emphasis on reading and reciting signaled an important change in the status of the play script, a change that was happening simultaneously in Western theater as well.[78] As theater historian Gay Gibson Cima reminds us, in theater before the age of Henrik Ibsen, "the script was viewed not as something fixed and immutable but as a kind of template for performance," and therefore "the actor, undaunted by the playwright's words, felt free to alter them."[79]

Here it might be useful to glance again at Jacques Derrida's notion of "theater of logos" and the idea that opposes it: Antonin Artaud's call for a "theater of cruelty." Artaud points out something akin to one of the major principles of New Theater when he attacks the "theatrical superstition of the text and the dictatorship of the writer."[80] Derrida connects this point to the practice of reading the text: "*dictation:* at once citations or recitations and orders" that are taken by the performers, and "*diction* which made theater into an exercise of reading." Artaud decries the fact that for "certain theatrical amateurs this means that a play read affords just as definite and as great a satisfaction as the same play performed."[81]

Such an emphasis on the reading and reciting of the play was quite foreign to the world of *kabuki,* as well as the world of premodern Western theater, where the norm was a combination of rote memorization of the crucial speeches and improvisation of the noncrucial dialogue. An actor would know little more than his own lines; the larger structure of the play would not necessarily be transparent to him.[82] For a *kabuki* performer, as well for a Western performer of drama before Ibsen, reading the entire play carefully for the purpose of interpretation would have seemed a strange idea indeed.

This is why it was so radical of Shimamura Hōgetsu to insist on the perfect memorization of the lines, going so far as to include the following item in his "Rules for Rehearsals": "The Art Theater's rehearsals should always begin with the perfect memorization and recitation of the lines." In a 1918 article dedicated to the issue, he explained why he objected to the lack of discipline of the *kabuki* actors:

> In old theater, you will often find old theater actors who have not been able to memorize his lines, and you will find on opening day that a stagehand crouches behind the actor on stage, and supplies almost every single word and sentence as a prompter. And this often does not stop in the first day or two. In worst cases, the entire run of fifteen or twenty days requires the presence of the prompter. Even then, an actor might not be able to say his lines perfectly, and may substitute some convenient ad-lib nonsense. Strictly speaking, these are acts of contempt against the audience, and a hateful crime against art.[83]

Whereas *kabuki* actors often do not bother memorizing the lines at all, in *shimpa* or straight theater, according to Shimamura Hōgetsu, "an actor may memorize only the main points; and as for the details of the exact words, an actor might just freely make them up on the spot."[84] For New Theater, both of these practices are unacceptable: "the artistry of an actor begins with the extremely mechanical work of memorizing every single word and sentence."[85] Not memorizing the lines perfectly would have consequences for the kind of direct expression New Theater is trying to create.

> A performance in which the lines are not memorized would not only hinder the structure of the performance, but would also change its flavor completely. This is what we ought to fear the most. Why should this be so? It is because of the nature of human language. Between a word and another word, a sentence and another sentence, and between one person's lines and another, there is an extremely subtle linkage [*myakuraku*]. It is this linkage that defines the expression of the soul [*tamashii no hatsugen*], changing it into various shapes. To not memorize lines would be to destroy, or at least to alter, this linkage. Therein lurks the crime of the stage, and the deceit of the actor.[86]

Only a fully memorized and elocuted script could convey the sense of an expression coming naturally from inside the actor's "soul" or interiority. The full memorization of the script was the technical precondition for the fantasy of "direct speech."

Yet there emerges a paradox about memorization, direct speech, performance, and gender. Matsui Sumako was noted for her perfect memorization, not only of her lines, but of all her gestures and facial expressions as well. As her biographer noted, "there was no variation from the previous performance; it was exactly the same."[87] This observer, like many others, suggests this to be an indication of Sumako's lack of subjectivity—she is an empty vessel, possessed and filled only by her director and lover's genius, embodying his will, his intentions, night after night, with no room for variation, improvisation, and hence no room for her own thought, speech, and action. She was his puppet, his Über-Marionette. These comments on Sumako's acting style are written in a strange mixture of tones: a touch of approval, a touch of condescension, a touch of fascination, a touch of abhorrence:

> Great actors of old would say things like: "you can't call yourself a real actor if your performance on opening night differs from your performance on closing night; trial and error is something you do while rehearsing and once the show starts and you let in spectators and take their money, you don't have an excuse for performing differently today from yesterday." This should indeed be the ideal, but reality is usually far from this dream. But Sumako's Nora, performed with all her will, seems to have realized and embodied the anecdotes of those great old actors.[88]

How could anyone become so perfect a puppet? And is a perfect puppet a perfect performer? And this is precisely the paradox of direct and indirect speech and action. The complete memorization and internalization of "lines" and "patterns" that are required for "natural" acting here end up yielding the impression of an automaton repeating the same sentences and same gestures over and over again, totally subverting the impression of improvisational spontaneity and variation associated with direct expression. The strangeness of this paradox, which derives from the paradox of direct speech and action, is explained away by male critics by referring to the puppet's gender. If it is assumed that it is natural for a female to be lacking in subjectivity, then that can be used to explain away the paradox of Matsui Sumako, who was both super-puppet and super-star. As a woman, an actress can be entirely spontaneous or entirely controlled—either way she is less than man; she is either too wild and undisciplined or too mechanical and inhuman.

The same effort to construct the appearance of natural and direct expression of interior and anterior essence had to be made for bodily movements, that is, the fantasy of "direct action." In 1907, shortly after returning from travels in Europe, where he saw Sarah Bernhardt's rehearsals, playwright Matsui Shōyō (no relation to actress Matsui Sumako) proposed a new acting technique that "goes further than the photograph which merely copies the outlines, further than the painting which only depicts the impressions of that moment, but is a technique that combines human emotions with the physical movements which express these emotions, animating the body of the actor."[89] Matsui's proposal, based on the ideas of François Delsarte (1811–1871), regarded the body as a transparent medium for the expression of inner emotions: "the body, after it has been emptied of the ego until there is no self [*onore o munashū suru made ni jiga o nuki saritaru*], will be flexible, able to bend and twist freely, and an appropriate dwelling place for the emotions."[90] By removing bad habits from the body, "we may return it to its original form, given by nature, able to express one's inner emotions with utmost freedom, sensitivity, and liveliness."[91]

One of the subjects taught at the Literary Society that sought to put these ideas into practice was called "sketching" (*shasei*): The students were required to observe people in their daily lives and copy their bodily gestures in class. As Matsui Sumako described it in an interview:

> For example, male students would be asked to become a fishmonger, a barber, or a rickshaw puller; female students would be asked to be a hairdresser, a girl from downtown, or a geisha. We would observe these people closely, and present our studies in class, receiving criticism from our teacher. He would correct us, saying "try it this way, rather than that way," and we would further refine our acting.[92]

It was the *genbun itchi* of movement that was sought in these classes. Matsui Sumako confessed that this "sketching" was more difficult than "dancing," since "in dance, the pattern is entirely pre-determined, and thus no matter how complicated the moves are, all you have to do is to memorize what the teacher shows you."[93] Sketching was a way of training actors to imitate real-life gestures, not preset choreography. It was drawing art from nature, not from other art.

Yet this was not an easy lesson for New Theater to inculcate in its performers. As late as 1926, Osanai Kaoru would have to repeatedly admonish his troupe members: "don't dance, but move; don't sing, but talk."[94] And moreover, note how "dancing" and the imitation of preset patterns creeps back into the training process the moment the teacher corrects the student. Instead of saying "no, observe more closely," the teacher says "try it this way" and shows a gesture to be imitated by the student. This gesture then becomes the new pattern to be cited, and eventually the basis of what came to be known as the New Theater's own acting style: "The custom of playing foreign plays and reciting dialogue in the often unnatural rhythm of translated Japanese became a part of the accepted acting style."[95]

New Theater expected actors and actresses to read the play script carefully, to memorize the lines perfectly, identify themselves with the characters entirely, and to bring them to life faithfully. Unlike in *kabuki,* or in premodern Western theater, there is no room for blatantly showing off virtuosic skills.[96] There is no knowing wink of the actor to the audience, no shouting of the actor's name by the approving audience member. This means that the audience is not meant to acknowledge the presence of the actor as actor either, but to pretend that they are transparent mediums, through which the intentions of the playwright can be read.[97] The suppression of the materiality of the medium, exemplified by the practices of *genbun itchi* and *shasei,* are part of the mechanism of the theater of logos that allows the faithful representation of the author-creator's intentions.[98]

The materiality of the body of the actress, however, along with the visual and aural pleasures of song and dance, keeps disrupting the purity of the reading experience. Matsui Sumako, transparent or opaque, performed both the kind of play advocated by Tsubouchi Shōyō and the kind promoted by Shimamura: Her public debut performance included both the dance play *Hachikatsugi hime,* composed by Tsubouchi Shōyō, and two acts of Henrik Ibsen's *A Doll House.* But it was for the latter that she became famous. Although earlier she had also appeared in the Literary Society's workshop productions of *Hamlet,* it was neither as "Orie" nor as "Ophelia" but as "Nora" that Matsui Sumako burst into the limelight of Japanese theater history. This meant that the struggle between Tsubouchi Shōyō, the advocate of song and dance, and Shimamura Hōgetsu, the advocate of modern Western drama, was decisively won by the latter, and that Western drama became the mainline of New Theater. This also meant that Western ideas about women and about feminism entered Japan via New Theater. As seen in the previous chapter, in

Japan, "New Woman" was a theatrical figure first and foremost. And the following chapter will show that the New Woman on stage was a troubling figure, both a feminist and a femme fatale.

SPECTATORS AS CONSUMERS: THE SHIMAMURA-OSANAI DEBATE

In the context of New Theater, the repudiation of the commodified means that the performers will see their production not as commodities to be consumed by the spectator but as something else: as pure love, pure art, not sold and bought but offered as a gift and accepted because it is good. This situates the New Theater in a nuanced position vis-à-vis the theater of logos, since in the theater of logos, the audience is conceived as being at once passive and voyeuristic, a consumer and enjoyer, who is nonetheless satisfied with scrutinizing a text-like production.[99] How did New Theater talk about its audience, and the relation between the audience and the performers? In a heated exchange instigated by the commercial success of productions starring the actress Matsui Sumako, Shimamura Hōgetsu and Osanai Kaoru debated this topic by relating it to the conflict between art and commerce. For a fledgling theater form with neither the broad audience base of *kabuki* nor any support from the state, the question of financial stability was an urgent one. Because New Theater defined itself in terms of anticommodification, however, it found itself in a position where it had to resolve the dilemma of making art while making a living.

Shimamura Hōgetsu argued for a dual road of art and profit: to use profitable, commercialized productions to finance the more artistic, experimental productions.

> Our naive imagination [*kūsōsei*] attempts to gain both self-satisfaction and financial reward by combining project [*jigyō*] and profession [*shokugyō*]; our impatient practicality [*genjitsusei*] will discard this contradiction and will attempt to run towards either the extreme of paralyzing the self by sticking with the profession, or starving the self by sticking to the project. This is where our tough experience instructs us, or our clever compromise [*dakyōsei*] dashes in, pointing us towards the dual road. Today to engage in the project, tomorrow in the profession, to grasp financial reward on the left hand, and develop and create the self with the right hand. There is no other way but this dual principle to live truly in this contemporary age. . . . Who can refuse this dual road? Here is the standpoint of the Geijutsuza theater. With the right hand we will perform plays that will harmonize with the profession, and with the left hand we will perform plays that will transcend the profession. Thus we will create with our own power the path we will follow. Moreover, we cannot but recognize that happiness exists even within this sad reality.[100]

In another essay, Shimamura Hōgetsu declared that even if he had to put up with 100 productions that play up to the masses (*minshū*), versus only one production that ignored the audience but aimed only at what seemed artistically valuable, he would consider it a right balance between the two roads.

Osanai, on the other hand, argued in favor of art for art's sake, presenting himself as uncompromising, uncorrupted by commercialism.

> Of course, theater costs money. Money is theater's condition. Even I know as much. Yet I also believe that honest work will yield sufficient funds necessary for an honest way of life. You may laugh it off as a dream, but I cannot believe otherwise. Of course, before reaching that state, one may have to live by licking salt. One may be reduced to drinking just water. Yet in the end, one will be able to eat bread like other people. In the end, this shall happen. If you cannot believe that, it would be better to give up your art at the outset. It would be better to give up art, and concentrate on making money. That would be more honest. That would be much more serious. A dual road, which is like "giving alms while stealing" shall never become a unified road.[101]

In making this argument, Osanai obscured the fact that he was obtaining funding from *kabuki* performances and wealthy patrons. This has led to charges of hypocrisy against Osanai, but one could also point out that it is precisely those with secure financial grounding who can best exemplify the spirit of amateurism, artistic purity, and freedom from commodification.[102] It remains indisputable that for both Osanai Kaoru and for Shimamura Hōgetsu, the realm of "art" is conceptualized as ideally independent from commercialism.

New Theater comes into being by repudiating the commodification of earlier forms of theater and by positing the realm of pure art, separate from commodification and opposed to it in principle. The reversal of the values of the economic field, which characterize the artistic field[103] such as the New Theater, is revealed also in anecdotes about Shimamura Hōgetsu's aversion and lack of experience with financial matters. He would, for example, insist that ticket-sales from every "sold-out" performance should remain the same, even when a greater numbers of spectators would pay extra to squeeze into a sold-out performance and stand in the back of the auditorium.[104]

It is significant that as Shimamura Hōgetsu became more savvy about money matters, as he became more commodified, the eyes looking on him became more critical. The men around him began seeing him as both contaminated by economic concerns and corrupted by the dangerous sexuality of a woman, Matsui Sumako. "The great Professor Shimamura, whom I had worshipped like a God, seemed to become closer and closer to being just another man [*zokujin*]" wrote a close associate.[105] The term "*zokujin*" suggests both a layman fallen from religious purity, and a philistine fallen from the high throne of art for art's sake. As Shimamura Hōgetsu the director was more commodified and Shimamura Hōgetsu the man was more attached to Matsui Sumako (and the two movements went hand in hand), he was perceived to have lost his purity: Artistically and sexually, he had sold out.

The ideological victory of Osanai's position of art for art's sake meant that New Theater repudiated commercial success. It also laid the groundwork for New Theater's association with the left. But it eventually created a rift between New Theater and both proletarian theater and popular theater. It is beyond the scope of this book to discuss the developments in popular theater and those in leftist proletarian theater, and the later maneuverings of the New Theater to avoid both camps. Suffice it to say that in repudiating popular success, New Theater severed any possibility of alliance with popular theater, and in holding on to the ideal of art for art's sake, many practitioners of New Theater ended up isolating themselves from the overt political activism of the proletarian theater, as well as from its increasingly violent confrontation with state repression.[106]

Aside from the consequences for theater, some of the consequences for women included the denigration of sexually commodified prostitutes and of the sexually dangerous femme fatale. However, as the next chapter will show, the New Theater's abjection of commodification and sexuality, as well as its emphasis on the transparency of expression, that is, its deemphasis of the materiality of the signifier, is always incomplete. New Theater is constantly threatened by what it tries to cast out.

In the process of straightening theater and in the debates surrounding New Theater, then, certain shared assumptions emerge. First, the realm of *kabuki* and the pleasure quarters, which had always been seen as contiguous, are together chastised as being the realm of commodified art and commodified sexuality. Second, the realm of modern theater and the home are constructed separately as the realm of the *negation* of commodified art and sexuality, as the realm of pure art (theater), and pure sexuality (home) respectively. Third, at the same time, the men in *kabuki* and the women in the pleasure quarters are labeled, for better or worse, as professionals with both artistic and sexual experience, while the actress and the housewife are labeled as amateurs with artistic and sexual inexperience. Fourth, the language of professional and amateur nonetheless implies a division that can be crossed over, through the accumulation of experience, by being sold and bought more often, by more people.

The actress stands at the nexus of these various debates. The theater of logos had demanded actors to be interpretive slaves, productions to be transparent translations of the original text, and spectators to be passive consumers. The New Theater had responded by training amateur women to be professional—but ideally not too professional—actresses, by instituting performance practices to suppress the materiality of the signifier—especially the sexuality of the actress—and by insisting on the uncommodified purity of the performance—all the while relying on the popularity of the actress to pay the bills.

It should be clear by this point that there might have been at least three different but interlocking strands to the argument in favor of introducing actresses to the Japanese stage: the straightening theater strand, which saw *onnagata* as unnatural and actress as natural and therefore desirable; the New Theater strand, which saw that women were central in Western plays and Western theater and hence regarded women as required on the Japanese stage as well; and finally the backlash against both the straight and the new, exemplified by later developments in *shimpa,* some forms of New Theater, and in Takarazuka, which saw women as having sexual appeal for the audience and sought to make the best use of it. For all these reasons, the actress was brought onto the Japanese stage.

CHAPTER 8

FEMINISTS AND FEMMES FATALES

THE FEMINIST AND THE FEMME FATALE

THE PRECEDING CHAPTERS SHOWED MATSUI SUMAKO as a New Woman, a sexual subject par excellence. When performed on stage, however, the New Woman takes on various hues: The primary colors that make up the full palette are that of the outspoken and rational feminist on one end and the seductive and irrational femme fatale on the other end, with many gradations in between. During her short but brilliant career, Matsui Sumako performed a number of roles that might be called feminist, but also a number of roles that could be labeled femme fatale. How are we to understand an actress who acted both as a feminist and as a femme fatale? And what is the relationship of both figures to the definition of womanhood as grounded in the body? And are the feminist and femme fatale figures as distant from each other as they might seem at first glance?

The femme fatale is an emblematic figure of modernity.[1] As the male's body is alienated by and submitted to industrialization and urbanization, the woman comes to inhere even more closely to the body in a compensatory gesture. The femme fatale is a figure embodying the fears and anxieties prompted by this shift in the understanding of sexual difference, in which the woman is made to stand for the body in opposition to the man, who is standing for the mind.[2] The power of the femme fatale is therefore peculiar and ambivalent: Her power is not based on conscious will, but her body itself is given agency independently of consciousness; she is not the subject of power, but she is the carrier of power; intention is evacuated from her, yet she is regarded as willful and powerful. This connects to one side of the ambivalence of the New Woman as sexual subject—she is threatening because she is sexual, and yet she is not in control of herself because she is subjected to sexuality.

It is this very paradox that situates the femme fatale in relation to feminism. Feminist film scholar Mary Ann Doane reminds us that because the femme fatale "seems to confound power, subjectivity, and agency with the very lack of these attributes, her relevance to feminist discourses is critical."[3] On the surface, the femme fatale and the feminist might seem to be antithetical to each other. Yet a feminism that only acknowledges intellectual awareness and willful action and that disregards the physical presence and disruptive sexuality symbolized by the femme fatale will be an impoverished one. Not only that, a feminism that repudiates the ambivalence embodied by the femme fatale will be a fatally flawed one as well. The negative portrayals of both Kawakami Sadayakko and Matsui Sumako by women biographers in so-called "women's history" texts are examples of the destructive effects of a narrow definition of feminism: They show the costs of repudiating the kind of ambivalence that the femme fatale embodies by her very presence and provokes through her various gestures.[4]

In this chapter, the focus will be on a trio of roles performed by Matsui Sumako: the wife and mother Nora in Henrik Ibsen's *A Doll House,* the opera singer Magda in Hermann Sudermann's *Heimat,* and the mountain sprite Rautendelein in Gerhart Hauptmann's *Die Versunkene Glocke* (The sunken bell). The next chapter will contrast Matsui Sumako's performance of Oscar Wilde's *Salomé* with the performance of the same role by Kawakami Sadayakko. While conventional drama history would paint Nora as a burgeoning feminist, Magda a fallen woman, Rautendelein an ingenue fairy, and Salomé as a genuine femme fatale, Matsui Sumako's performances and my readings suggest more complex portraits that combine aspects of the feminist and the femme fatale: These characters were both feminist figures who caused controversy by raising the question of women's social awakening *and* femme fatale figures who shocked and seduced the audience.[5] And the actress who embodied these characters was both feminist and femme fatale as well.

LEAVING HOME: A DOLL HOUSE

The 1911 premiere of *A Doll House*[6] is one event for which Matsui Sumako's name gains admittance into the standard history texts. This event is situated at the confluence of many processes. It marked a decisive step for New Theater itself: The successful performance proved that modern European plays could be translated and imported onto the Japanese stage with impressive results. It was also the first time that a woman trained in New Theater's acting techniques performed to a large audience, and hence it signaled the birth of the modern actress and a step forward for women in Japan. Moreover, the thematic content of *A Doll House* and the responses of Japanese feminists to the play sparked debate about the "Woman Question" (*fujin mondai*). While there were also interpretations of the play that neutralized the gender issue, reading it, for example, as a statement about individual freedom versus family responsibility, the play hit the most resonant chord in raising the question of woman's role in society. And self-identified feminists certainly responded in loud voices, though not necessarily always in unison.

That *A Doll House* is a modern feminist play and that its performance was epoch-making from the perspective of women's liberation seem to go without saying.[7] Nora is the wife of the banker Torvald Helmer. At the beginning of the play, she presents herself as a carefree, macaroon-nibbling mother of three children preparing for Christmas festivities. As the play progresses, however, it is revealed that in the preceding year, Nora had borrowed money with a falsified signature in order to send her husband to a curative journey to Italy. Bank clerk Krogstad, about to be fired for his shady dealings, threatens to reveal Nora's forgery to her husband. Nora makes a frantic attempt to distract her husband from Krogstad's letter announcing this fact, and dances the famous Tarantella dance. In the end, however, the husband discovers the truth and is dismayed. Nora realizes from his manner that she can no longer continue to live in this doll house, and after a forceful declaration of independence, leaves the house at the end of the play. In one of the most celebrated dramatic exits, the house door bangs shut after Nora walks out, and this sonic metaphor echoed throughout the world for many decades.

Nora is trapped in conventional expectations of female roles and manages to escape from this trap at a high cost. Although it has become customary to regard Nora's departure from her home as a feminist triumph, other interpretations can and have been put forward. For one thing, Nora's future remains uncertain at the end of the play, and this unresolved ending allows room for divergent interpretations.[8] Furthermore, the play raises, but does not solve, the question of motherhood as woman's "natural" duty. Nora abandons her children in order to fulfill her duty to herself, an action that cannot help but provoke strong reactions. To schematize crudely, feminist interpretations have considered the characters in this play to be motivated more by social factors than by purely psychological ones, and the characters' experiences to be more paradigmatic than unique. Feminists in various periods and various locales have drawn connections between the play and the status of women in their own societies and have also welcomed rather than criticized the heroine's attempts to break free from social expectations.[9] Not all Japanese feminists, however, interpreted this play in an easily distinguishable feminist mode.

Although *A Doll House* has now become almost synonymous with feminist problem play, it seems that this was not necessarily the intention of the playwright.[10] Nonetheless, it is clear that Ibsen was at least aware of the difficulties facing women in modern society and was sympathetic to their plight. His "Notes for a Modern Tragedy" (1878) could be a description of the problems faced by

Nora: "A woman cannot be herself in modern society. It is an exclusively male society, with laws made by men and with prosecutors and judges who assess feminine conduct from a masculine standpoint."[11] Whatever Ibsen's own intentions, the characters he created began to walk on their own, especially once they crossed national borders into Britain and Germany, and onward to Japan.

In certain ways, Germany was a relay station on the way to Japan. Germany was one of the first countries with a large readership to accept Ibsen,[12] and it was based on its popularity there, as well as in Britain, that the play was introduced to Japan. The early reception of *A Doll House* in Germany was skewed by an alternate ending provided for the first performance of the play in 1880, and this had consequences for the play's reception in Japan. While the original ending left the future of Nora uncertain, offering both the unmistakable sound of her departure and the hope for eventual reconciliation, the alternative ending showed Helmer persuading Nora to stay by appealing to her motherly feelings. This ending was provided by the playwright himself to accommodate the sensibilities of German audiences and influenced the reception of the play: Until the 1890s, when the feminist interpretation took over, *A Doll House* was seen in Germany as a sentimental drama of intrigue and reconciliation.

Rolf Fjelde's English translation of the original ending reads as follows:

> Nora: (*picking up the overnight bag).* Ah, Torvald—it would take the greatest miracle of all—
>
> Helmer: Tell me the greatest miracle!
>
> Nora: You and I both would have to transform ourselves to the point that— Oh, Torvald, I've stopped believing in miracles.
>
> Helmer: But I'll believe. Tell me! Transform ourselves to the point that—?
>
> Nora: That our living together could be a true marriage. (*She goes out down the hall.*)
>
> Helmer: *(sinks down on a chair by the door, face buried in his hands).* Nora! Nora! (*Looking about and rising.*) Empty. She is gone. (*A sudden hope leaps in him.*) The greatest miracle—?
>
> (*From below, the sound of a door slamming shut.*)

The alternate ending was as follows (in my translation):

> Nora:—that our living together could be a true marriage. Farewell. (*Is about to leave.*)
>
> Helmer: Well, then, go! (*Grabs her by the arm).* But first you ought to see your children for the last time!
>
> Nora: Let me go. I won't see them! I can't do that!
>
> Helmer: (*Drags her towards the door on the left).* You must see them! (*Opens the door and says quietly*) See, there they sleep peacefully and without care. Tomorrow, when they wake up and call after their mother, they'll find themselves—motherless.

Nora: (*trembling*) Motherless—!
Helmer: Just like you were once.
Nora: Motherless! (*Fights inwardly, lets the overnight bag fall, and says*) O, I sin against myself, but I cannot abandon them. (*Sinks half down in front of the doorway.*)
Helmer: (*Joyously, but quietly*) Nora! (*The curtain falls.*)[13]

This was the version used when *A Doll House* was first translated into Japanese by Shimamura Hōgetsu.[14]

Several characteristics of the women's movement in Germany influenced the reception of Ibsen there, and possibly also influenced the reception of *A Doll House* in Japan as well. Greater political restrictiveness in Germany meant that "the moderate feminists were very moderate, the radical ones—when they did find themselves—very radical."[15] Female suffrage, for example, was not demanded until 1902, in comparison to Britain, where the suffrage movement had started in 1867. Another conservative characteristic of the German feminist movement was its emphasis on "motherliness" (*Mütterlichkeit*), despite the fact that the leaders of the movement were often trained teachers who had given up the option of motherhood. There was a strong tradition regarding women as destined for motherhood due to their physical and psychic constitution, and the women's movement sought to preserve this "natural" feminine quality and to extend its gentle influence to society as a whole.[16] This emphasis on motherhood, along with the various problems it caused for feminist logic, was also shared by the women's movement in Japan.

Shimamura Hōgetsu, a Waseda University professor recently returned from studies in Germany, first mentioned Ibsen in "Torawaretaru bungei" (Imprisoned literature), an essay published in the January 1906 (Meiji 39) issue of the journal *Waseda bungaku*. This essay declared Ibsen to be the father of the "modern problem play" (*kinsei mondai geki*). In November of the same year, in the same journal, he translated *A Doll House* from a popular German edition. This version contained the altered ending: Nora is persuaded by her husband and decides to stay at home. Hōgetsu then revised his Japanese translation by referring to William Archer's English translation, and used the revised translation as the script for the performance at the Literary Society. The revised translation was published in *Waseda bungaku*, January 1910 (Meiji 43), so readers had a chance to "study and prepare" *(yoshū)* for the performance. It is significant that most of the plays performed by Matsui Sumako, both at the Literary Society and later at the Geijutsuza theater, were first published in magazines as translated texts. It was part of the new mode of experiencing theater as the reading of texts, which corresponds to Derrida's theater of logos. It is also significant that Hōgetsu was familiar with the "German ending" of the play: It may well have influenced his interpretation of the character of Nora and his choices as the director of the production. In 1911, he wrote an article in the journal *Kabuki* that shows the range of interpretations that were present in his mind:

> If one were to perform this play in the United States, it might be interesting to pursue an interpretation of her character that would be much stronger and would almost transcend the distinction between men and women. However for Japanese people in the present day . . . this would cause the majority to find Nora repulsive. If Nora arouses antipathy at that moment, the effect of that play as a whole would be damaged. Although cheap sympathy is not what is required, we cannot afford to arouse antipathy at that moment. Even after having toned it down to the current mild level, there seemed to be those among the numerous spectators who reacted negatively.[17]

Hence, Hōgetsu chose an interpretation that would use the original ending yet would still hold the audience's sympathies—a milder, gentler Nora, exuding feminine sensitivity and sadness about her decision to leave her husband and children.[18]

The performance took place in September of 1911, at the private theater of the Literary Society. Matsui Sumako took the role of Nora, and two instructors took the roles of Torvald Helmer and Nils Krogstad. Another actress-in-training performed the role of Mrs. Linde, but the roles of the nurse and the maid had to be assigned to male actor-students, since there were not enough actresses. This performance was surprisingly successful, though due to the constraints of time, only acts 1 and 3 were presented.[19] Between acts 1 and 3, the director stepped in front of the curtains to explain the plot of act 2, but the audience was still left with the impression that Nora's transformation from the childish wife of act 1 to the resolute feminist in act 3 was rather too sudden and surprising. This undoubtedly influenced the reactions to the play. Some spectators might also have been familiar with the alternate ending, which shows the heroine's decision to stay at home out of motherly love, and these spectators might have been quite shocked by the heroine's resolute departure concluding the staged version. Or it may simply be the case that the complexity of Nora's character, the resolve and resourcefulness that she keeps carefully hidden underneath her frivolous surface in act 1, also remained hidden to the spectators, who were too dazzled by the mere presence of an actress on stage. Despite director Hōgetsu's efforts to subdue the character of Nora, she nonetheless managed to surprise, shock, and scandalize the audience.

Three dance plays by Tsubouchi Shōyō were also presented as part of the same day's program—which explains the time constraint. This program symbolized two different views on theater that were present within the Literary Society from the beginning and that were soon to rip the institution apart.

Shimamura Hōgetsu's belief that the modern Japanese theater should faithfully represent modern European spoken drama squared off with Tsubouchi Shōyō's desire to create a Japanese national theater on the basis of *kabuki*'s music and dance.

Matsui Sumako's own reminiscences in *Peony Brush* vividly describe the process of staging this drama. She describes the development of her interest in this play through studies at the Literary Society.[20] Significantly, she learned the play as a *foreign* text, in English translation, before thinking of it as something that she herself would one day perform.

> The first time I learned about the play called *A Doll House* was the day of the first lecture of "Modern Drama" taught by Professor Shimamura at the Literary Society.
>
> At that time, I had barely begun studying foreign languages; therefore, far from appreciating the play as a play, I had to concentrate on deciphering the English sentences. Moreover, since we studied the play in small segments and for only two hours once a week, not much remained in my head, although we must have heard much about Nora's character from the Professor. Therefore, I did not even think about what type of person would be good as Nora, what kind of person would achieve success performing that role. The following year, however, Professor Shimamura published a translation of the entire play in the January issue of *Waseda bungaku:* This is when I realized what a great role Nora is, and also what a difficult role. And I thought that if I studied for another ten years, I might be able to rehearse the role, clumsy though it might be. And thereafter I would sometimes secretly glance at the play. But since I was afraid that others would sneer—"What are you reading Nora for? You think you can perform her?"—I did not dare rehearse that role in public.[21]

Thus the actress-in-training encounters the play first as a set of *foreign* sentences, then as a *translated* text, and finally as a great role that she secretly aspires to *rehearse* one day. Rumors about a planned production of the play, and descriptions of other students rehearsing the play are followed by the announcement that auditions would be held for a September production.

> Professors Shimamura and Nakamura sat at the back of the room, while Ms. Hirota and I cowered close together in a far corner, though it was a hot day, and started reading. At the dialogue scene between Nora and Krogstad, Professor Tōgi did such a fine job of impersonating the arrogant moneylender that I became really incensed: I leaned forward as I read my lines, and the room fell quiet. Even the whispering of the other people ceased for a while. When the first act was finally over, Professor Nakamura announced "That scene with Krogstad was indeed dramatic" and laughed, while he lightly fluttered his hand, with a cigarette held between two fingers, towards that serious, bearded face.[22]

Intense rehearsals followed, lasting for three months. This was a major difference from traditional theater practices and underscored the seriousness of the New Theater.

> By the time the private theater was constructed, we were rehearsing every other day, from eight o'clock to eleven o'clock in the morning, while it was still cool. How many times was I told to "play in the spirit of a young girl"! By this point, I no longer had time to think about whether Nora was good or bad in becoming self-aware and deserting her beloved husband and children. I only thought about what I would do on stage.[23]

Thus, having moved from foreign text to translated text, and then having studied a literary interpretation of the role, the actress now is engrossed in how to express the role. There is even a hint that the expression is beginning to lean in the direction of citing patterns again. The actress is intensely and almost exclusively concerned about "what [she] would do on stage." In contradiction to the ideology of the theater of logos and the avowed principles of the Literary Society Institute, the acting of New Theater contained the kernels for the development and citation of patterns and mannerisms from the beginning. This was perhaps inevitable given the ultimate impossibility of completely direct speech and action. Yet the paradox is that Matsui Sumako's acting continued to be described in the language of nature and instinct, rather than in the language of craft and training.

Matsui Sumako begins the account of the final stage rehearsal for the previews (*shien*) with a description of her feelings of anxiety.[24]

> September 21, Meiji 44.
>
> The rehearsals of *Nora* have been going on for three months already: The three-day previews finally start tomorrow. Today is the day of stage rehearsal, doubling as a day of final review. . . .
>
> After breakfast I want to go to the Literary Society, but it's still a little too early. So I open the "Tales of European Theater" that I started perusing yesterday, and begin reading again, wanting to visualize the patterns of [famous Russian actress Alla] Nazimova's *A Doll House* performance in my mind. Upon reading a few lines, the comparisons between her staging and mine begin bubbling up, and I can't read any further: I imagine myself acting this way and that way, resigned that I will never reach her level of performance because I lack the power. The image of Professor Shimamura, his face propped up on one hand, utterly absorbed in directing the play, rises in front of my eyes. And the image of Professor Nakamura, who is always holding a cigarette in one hand and twirling his beard with the other hand. Scenes from the play run through my mind: the scene of confrontation, when I stand still, and the sweat pours down my back.

> No matter how hard I try to calm down, I can't stop thinking of today's performance. I am so nervous that I can't even read a book. This must stop, I think, and find myself listening vacantly to the sound of vehicles passing by on the street outside. Ah well; I dress casually and depart for the Literary Society.[25]

Again, the "patterns of Nazimova" catches our attention, as an instance of the contradiction of New Theater ideology. After the intense rehearsal process, the actual performance is somewhat of an anticlimax.

> At four o'clock, the first act opens.
>
> The opening bell stops ringing, I sing *Tra, la, trala, la,* and step onto the stage: until that moment, my feelings have been that of indescribable anxiety.
>
> The costume change after the third act—changing from the doll's dance costume to the normal dress costume—goes smoothly: I receive help from both Ms. Linden and the costume designer, so I just manage to change in time.
>
> Finally I finish acting Nora. Without any time to think about success or failure, I must start preparing for the minister's role in the next play, *Hachi katsugi.*[26]
>
> The talkative hairdresser keeps imitating Nora's line "I'm taking off the doll's costume" while pulling the strings of my brown wig. Then Professors Shimamura and Nakamura and a few others walk in, and tell me, "For some reason, today you did not perform as well as in rehearsals; you might have been too nervous."
>
> I had known that from the beginning, but hadn't been able to do anything about it. This lark is now dispirited more than ever.
>
> We finish performing *Hachi katsugi* also without incident, and the curtains open one more time for photographing.
>
> Almost everyone has gone home, and only a few spectators remain. I search the auditorium for my nieces, whose presence I had forgotten till then due to my concentration on stage. Looking down from the stage, I immediately recognize the familiar faces. The two seem ill at ease, as if half-way ready to go home, standing in the shadow of a pillar and looking in this direction.[27]

One of the striking features of Matsui Sumako's account of the day is that she places the performance in the context of daily life: riding the train to and from the theater, preparing for bed after the show is over, cooking breakfast the next morning. The glamorous actress returns to a young woman who thoroughly enjoys entertaining her two nieces.

> Relieved at being among family, I ask Sumi to help me take all of my futons from the closet:
>
> "Now, we have to somehow arrange these, so that the three of us can sleep on it. How shall we arrange it?"
>
> The entirety of my futon collection consists of two triple-width futons, a quilt, a nightgown, and a blanket. There is not much we can do: We put the

> two futons together, with one person sleeping in the middle where the two futons meet. "You've got to bear a little pain" we joke. Then, having decided that Sumi would have the quilt, and that Kimi and myself would share the blanket—pulling at it from both sides—we go on to hang up the mosquito net. Since we only have one pillow, I wind up my everyday sash, wrap it in a cloth, and further wrap it in a towel. Thus supplied with enough pillows, we are finally ready to go to bed.[28]

Yet the next morning, a servant comes to pick up the nieces before they even have had a chance to eat breakfast. Sumako realizes that her profession as an actress is still frowned upon by her relatives.

> I think while cooking eggs in clam sauce: Why was he ordered to come and pick them up so early? What harm is there in letting the girls stay for an extra two or three hours—I wouldn't try to persuade them to become actresses! Even my own sister, whom I regard almost as my mother, treats me differently. Maybe I am too sensitive, but I cannot help being a little bit resentful.[29]

While this essay ends thus on a tone of melancholy, it also hints at Sumako's satisfaction with her career. At an earlier point in this essay, she comments on the tragic life of a former teacher of hers: The woman had married and come to Tokyo, but had become ill and had to return to her parental household. She died soon thereafter.[30] In contrast, Sumako, whose divorce from her first husband was also attributed to illness, has forged a successful career for herself.

Because of the success of the previews, the Literary Society was asked to perform the same play on the stage of the Teikoku Gekijō theater. This was a major step forward for the institution, which had until then conceived of itself more as a school than a professional theater company. This surprisingly fast ascent exacerbated tensions within the institution and led to new debates with those outside as well. The performances took place in November of the same year and contained all three acts. Nora was to become one of Matsui Sumako's most popular roles.

In an interview, Sumako reflects on "What gave me the most trouble on stage."[31] Costume problems come to her mind first: Her hair was supposed to unravel during her Tarantella dance in act 2, but it never seemed to do so on cue; she also had trouble putting on and taking off the *manteau* in act 3. She further recalls that in act 3, when Nora turns away from her husband, refusing all help and contact from him, a spectator sitting in one of the front rows exclaimed "Surprise, surprise" (*odoroita ne*). The actress wryly remarks that *she,* too, was surprised. She goes on to comment that indeed many spectators seemed to be surprised at Nora becoming "a self-aware, strong, and cool woman." But, she wonders, "Why weren't they surprised at Helmer's

8.1 Matsui Sumako in the Tarantella dance scene from *A Doll House*. *Engei gahō* (October 1911). In the insert on the upper right, she is dressed in a *manteau*, ready to leave the house.

equally sudden change?" She answers that "this has been our custom: Even with a husband like Helmer, a woman had to grin and bear it, sacrificing herself for her man—that's been considered woman's virtue."[32] When that woman became self-aware and independent, the audience was startled, noted the actress. In addition, there might have been two more reasons for the surprise, as already noted: First, even with act 2 restored, the transformation of the heroine might have seemed under-rehearsed and too abrupt; and second, the dissemination of the conciliatory ending through Shimamura's translation might have left the audience under-prepared for the confrontational ending. This may explain why spectators were so shocked when Nora banged the door shut behind her.

The critics, however, gave Matsui Sumako rave reviews in general. Ihara Seisei'en was drawn in by the transformation of the heroine and described it in organic metaphors that emphasized the naturalness of the acting:

> At first the waters are still but gradually ripples arise, and transform into a myriad of different states; and during that whole time not a single lax moment,

> but great tautness in the facial expressions and dialogues. The audience is entirely drawn to this heroine.[33]

Kawamura Karyō declared Matsui Sumako to be the first true actress in Japan:

> I was deeply moved and delighted to hear, for the first time, natural lines [*shizen na serifu*] spoken by an actress born in Japan. . . . For the first time in my life, I saw a modern play that filled me with a sort of gentle and sad and inexplicable feeling. It was due to Madame Sumako's powers that I even cried a few tears at the part where she solemnly thanks her husband for his kindness so far in her life.[34]

In another article he declared:

> Ever since my youth, I have seen many excellent performances, but I have never been more astounded than by the Nora in *A Doll House* performed by the Literary Society. How enormous the power of an actress that we now see on the Japanese stage, how great the presence of an actress! I was utterly dumbfounded.[35]

The performances of *A Doll House* at the newly built, up-to-date, and supremely fashionable Teikoku Gekijō theater attracted a great deal of public attention: The response of the feminist women writing for the journal *Seitō* is one example. The November 1911 issue of this magazine included a bibliography of writings on *A Doll House,* preparing the readers for a special issue on that play, published in January of the following year. The reactions to *A Doll House* published in the January issue turned out to be quite diverse. Some of the members had seen the plays, others had only read it in translation; the members were resolutely divided in their judgment of the heroine's behavior.[36]

What all of them have in common, however, is a certain way of reading the play and of experiencing the performance as though they were the reading the play. This is a New Theater mode of experiencing theater as though one were reading the intentions of the playwright. All the women also express their responses in a particular style of writing. It is that of *genbun itchi,* the mode of writing that creates the impression that the text is a faithful and spontaneous expression of interior feelings and intentions. What the texts in *Seitō* show might thus be called a mode of *genbun itchi* of both writing and reading, of both text and theatrical performance.

Yet there are also moments when this mode breaks down or opens up other possibilities for communication and pleasure between women. It is striking that many of the women writing in response to *A Doll House* treat the heroine of the play like a "real woman," like a friend or acquaintance whose feelings and actions can be praised or chastised. At least one woman extends this way of relating to "real woman" to the actress, praising Matsui Sumako as a feminist role model. This mode of relating to theater is rather different from the New Theater mode of reading theater as a text, as well as from the premodern mode of theater as an extension of the pleasure quarters. The latter was what New Theater was trying to overcome: the client-professional mode in which the audience is sensually titillated (*jikkan*) and perceives itself as having potential access to the performer as sexual commodity. New Theater attempted to install a new mode according to which the audience arrives at a pure communion with the intentions of the playwright, with the performance as a transparent medium. Yet in the responses of feminists to Nora and Matsui Sumako, there is an excess in the circuit from audience to the figure on stage—they love her, hate her, or are utterly torn about her.[37]

Katō Midori,[38] a working mother and writer, comments with a touch of envy: "As somebody's wife she wouldn't be able to study freely, and so she must become single to look into a lot of things . . . what an admirable attitude."[39] Since Katō lives in Osaka she has not yet seen the Literary Society's performance of *A Doll House* starring Matsui Sumako. Yet on the basis of Tsubouchi Shōyō's introductory lecture,[40] she can imagine what kind of an impact the play must have had on Scandinavian society:

> The tens of thousands of women who have seen the play till now must have all put themselves in Nora's shoes and reflected on their own position. There must certainly have been women who awakened together with Nora. There might have been homes, founded on lies, that fell apart in marital strife, just because the couple had seen this play. Needless to say, this play exerted an extraordinary influence on society.[41]

Katō's essay also contains a careful analysis of Nora's character. Pointing out how Nora seems to change drastically from the "unaware" (*mujikaku*) state in act 1 to a "self-aware" (*jikaku*) state at the end of the play, Katō concludes that even at the beginning, Nora could not have been entirely foolish, but merely pretended to be so to please her husband. There was a seed of self-awareness hidden in her interior, which gradually came out in successive moments of the play.[42] This description of an interior self that gradually manifests itself outward echoes both the formation of woman as defined by an internal biological essence manifesting itself outward and the formation of theater as defined by an expression of interiority through a transparent medium. Human development, acting technique, and gender ontology here come together in the image of gradual awakening.

Ueno Yōko[43] and Ueda Kimiko,[44] on the other hand, expressed ambivalent feelings. Their responses betray traces of the "good wife, wise mother" ideology prevalent at that time. Ueno's is the longest essay on the topic, taking up almost 50 pages of *Seitō*.[45] In general she is in support of Nora, recognizing her plight to have parallels in the lives of all women. Yet when it comes to her decision to leave her family, Ueno's argument becomes more convoluted. On the one hand, Ueno is critical of the family ideology of "good wife, wise mother," since there are many women who remain single by choice or by force of circumstance. Yet Ueno's rhetoric for women's advancement depends on the fundamental assumptions of "wifeing," as discussed in the chapter on Kawakami Sadayakko. Ueno blames Nora's stubbornness in not listening to Helmer's pleas when he finally lets go of his pride and gives in to her.[46] She accuses Nora of selfishness, of thinking "that she can sacrifice everyone else in order to attain her own individual goal."[47] Such a childish, self-centered view will be impossible to uphold in society, Ueno insists. As an alternative, Ueno exhorts women who recognizes social injustice to struggle to improve themselves as a human beings and raise themselves up to become ideal wives to their husbands.

> Women must gain their own perspectives and nurture their abilities, so that they can become good conversation partners [*hanashi aite*] to men, good consulting partners [*sōdan aite*] to them, and even their right hand in managing their lives [*shosei jō no kataude*]. When this happens, man would treat woman with proper respect; woman on the other hand would encourage, console, and respect man, without resentment but with her characteristic submissiveness [*shiorashiku*], standing with the self-awareness and pride of being his high-minded helper and partner in life.[48]

The language of women's equality with men slides at this point into the language of wifeing. The "rewifeing" of women, or the reincorporation of the awakened and improved woman back into the family structure, is a common theme on stage and a common concern in society at large. And it was especially powerfully at work in the reception of disturbing plays such as *A Doll House* in Japan.

Ueda Kimiko's response to Nora was more emotional, though no less complex:

> The sad cry of Nora is the cry of all Scandinavian women; nay, it is the sad complaint of all the women in the world. Sacrifice is beauty. A sacrifice made to a loved one for his interest is beautiful. Yet the harmony of all beauty is destroyed when that sacrifice is taken for granted, and nothing is given in return.[49]

This statement implies that when the sacrifice *is* appreciated, it is worth the effort. Like her fellow contributors to *Seitō,* Ueda points out Helmer's selfishness in thinking only of his own honor and advancement. If only he had been more appreciative! Ueda's sentimental response, however, is set within an intriguingly theatrical framework—perhaps reflecting Ueda's own interest in playwriting. At several points in her essay, Ueda calls the reader's attention to Nora's own playacting within the play: pretending to be the childish wife in act 1, and dancing the Tarantella to distract her husband in act 2. The gap opened up between external appearance and the internal truth presumed to lie behind it, the gap that lies at the dramatic as well as the theatrical level of this play, is echoed in the rhetorical framework that ends the essay. After a visionary declaration for the pursuit of "women's true happiness," the writer concludes, "There are times when my daily efforts for this end seem silly and sad to me. Yet a moment later, I regain my senses, and then I go on to grieve endlessly for that earlier feeling of silliness and grief" (132). The gesture of melancholy should perhaps be read as a rhetorical strategy to negotiate a speaking position that is not reducible to either pro- or anti-Nora. Neither endorsing nor condemning Nora's final decision, the writer is able to voice strong feminist sentences and to then quickly escape criticism by sighing and withdrawing backstage.

Despite these differences in the members' attitudes toward Nora, the *Seitō* group was branded as the "Japanese Nora Training Institute." The message of *A Doll House* elicited strong responses, and "Noraism" became a term describing the self-centered behavior of the emancipated woman, or of the "*atarashii onna*" (new woman). Any expression of sympathy toward Nora was regarded as a challenge to the "good wife, wise mother" ideology. Since the members of *Seitō* had decided to devote an entire issue to the play, they were accused of Noraism by association, regardless of the actual position taken by individual members.

Of those whose contributions appeared in *Seitō,* Hiratsuka Raichō was the only one who was entirely critical of Nora. Ironically enough, she was the woman most often called "the Japanese Nora." Raichō's criticism of Nora can be summarized as follows: First, she takes Nora's apparent childishness and impulsiveness in the first two acts at face value, rather than as a disguise; second, she views Nora's sudden awakening at the end of the play with skepticism; and finally, she suggests that Nora must move beyond self-centered emancipation and find her "true self," by which Raichō means something like Buddhist enlightenment. The essay starts with an insult: "Dear Nora, as a Japanese woman I find it almost impossible to believe that a woman as impulsive and blind as you should be a mother of three children, rather than a girl of fourteen or fifteen years."[50] It ends with nothing less than a death sentence: "if you cannot arrive [at the true self], if you cannot embody this miracle, ask for a pistol, ask for poison. Farewell."[51]

Raichō had read the play in translation while in college and had been impressed by the heroine's revolt against the ideology of "good wife, wise mother." The 1911 production of *A Doll House,* however, was a disappointment for her:

> Sumako's acting was reputed to have much fire and vitality, but I remained somehow unimpressed, and the stage failed to absorb me to the end. The portrayal of Nora's innocence was fair enough, but the emotional progress of her awakening was not accompanied by any expression surging up from the inside; in the end what stood out was the strangely hysterical acting; it looked like a trivial fight between husband and wife—there was nothing to touch the heart.[52]

The reform of Japanese theater had produced new expectations on the part of the audience: Whereas the traditional theater had focused on the spectacular and the external, for New Theater the expression of psychic interiority was paramount. Matsui Sumako's performance was judged according to this new definition of theater. The impression of this unsatisfactory performance seems to have influenced Raichō's views of *A Doll House* itself:

> Dear Nora, the sound of the door that you slammed was indeed impressive. Once you stepped outside, however, there was complete darkness. You didn't know east from west. Your steps are so precarious. So precarious I feel like I need to escort you.[53]

Hiratsuka Raichō's response to the play was indicative of the ambivalent reactions to the play even among feminist women in Japan. Nonetheless, the mode of Raichō's response was enabled by the New Theater's mode of experiencing theater, and it was because of this mode that the performance of a feminist role by an actress could elicit such strong reactions.

In marked contrast to Hiratsuka Raichō's cool response was Otake Kōkichi's passionate ovation. Otake reports that she has seen the play twice in Osaka and thought that *A Doll House* would be most appropriate for educating women. She notes that there were indeed many women's groups (*fujin dantai*) in the audience as well. Upon interviewing these groups, however, she found that the reactions of these groups were highly conservative and critical of Nora:

> One after the other, they all said:
>
> "Nora didn't have to be so extreme, abandoning her husband and her three pretty children, and leaving her home like that. As long as she became aware of her own position and of her environment, there was no need for her to leave the house. She could have continued to live with Helmer and her children. She should have patiently corrected bad habits and educated herself. . . . There was no need for her to become angry like that, to think like that."
>
> That's precisely what's wrong with Japanese women today![54]

Otake is encouraged, however, when she interviews the actress Matsui Sumako. With elation she reports to the readers:

> I also met Ms. Matsui. I would like to announce to you something that ought to make you most happy, and that we ought to celebrate together: Here is a woman who uses her being a woman as a climbing rope, who grounds her art in the strength of being a woman, and attempts thence to build up the richness of her artistry and the natural skill that overflows from the essence of being a woman [*onna jishin no naiyō kara afure deru shizen gikō*]. . . .
>
> I cannot help but think that Ms. Matsui is attempting to ground herself on her sex of being a woman [*jishin no onna da to iu sei*].
>
> Ms. Matsui is not imprisoned in the pattern of being an actress. I would not equate her with what society calls an actress. I see her as a true artist. . . .
>
> I cannot help but be impressed that a woman would start from her own sex [*jiko no sei*] and venture on this journey.[55]

Otake's emphasis on starting from the sex (*sei*) of the woman, of the actress grounding her art on being female, is striking, but not surprising. For Otake, the actress embodied the new formation of woman and theater, in which womanhood was the starting point of performance, not the other way around.

Otake's was the most positive reading of the play and of its performance.[56] Partly due to her high-spirited actions and exuberant writing, of which this report on *A Doll House* is an early indication, *Seitō* soon gained notoriety as a gathering of women who espoused radical ideas, who drank cocktails in bars, and who visited the pleasure quarters in Yoshiwara. The New Women of *Seitō* encroached on what was supposed to be male territory and self-consciously performed men's roles, even while insisting on being women and acting like women.

Matsui Sumako's performance as Nora in *A Doll House* heralded the beginning of New Theater, in which the performance was perceived to be a transparent medium expressing inner meanings. At the same time, however, it also announced the arrival of a feminist voice on stage who called upon women in the audience to awaken and assert their independence. This call, and the response, were different from the premodern mode of experiencing theater as part of a complex social intercourse, but they were also out of alignment with New Theater's mode of understanding theatrical experience as the reading of a text, or as the experience of pure communion between the playwright's intentions and the reader's mind. The presence of a feminist figure on stage made possible a new type of feminist expression on the part of the audience; this was made possible by New Theater but also broke its bounds. Theater was no longer for the entertainment or edification of men of leisure: Here was theater that had the potential to awaken and agitate women.

THE POINT OF NO RETURN: *HEIMAT*

While Nora in *A Doll House* is the best known example of the feminist role, Magda in *Heimat* (The home) shows this relationship even more clearly. The extent of the power and threat exerted by the image of a feminist on stage is revealed by the controversy surrounding this play. The play was censored in Japan because it was perceived to be injurious to public morals: It was feared that the performance of the play would incite the audience to rebel against patriarchal authority. The censors sought to return the subversive New Woman into the fold of the family, and thus to restore order both in the realm of gender and the realm of performance. The state disciplined. The director acquiesced. The critics hissed. The actress, however, had her own opinions on the matter. Let us now look at this play and its performance in Japan more closely.

Hermann Sudermann's *Heimat* (1893) is a play that portrays a woman called Magda, daughter of an old-fashioned and stubborn army lieutenant colonel. Magda has left her home in defiance of her father's wishes to marry the local pastor and has become a "fallen woman" in Berlin. But now she returns home as a successful opera singer, 12 years after her initial departure. At first she intends only a short visit, but her sister and the pastor manage to engineer a temporary reconciliation between father and daughter: On the condition that her past remains unquestioned, Magda agrees to stay at her parents' home for the time being. Enter Doctor von Keller, a government official. He is Magda's ex-lover from her Berlin days, the man who seduced, then abandoned her. Magda had given birth to Keller's child and had become a singer to support the child's upbringing. Now that Magda is famous, Keller asks for Magda's hand, thinking she would be a political asset to him. Magda is about to agree for the sake of her child, when he tells her that the child must be given up for adoption, since it was born out of wedlock. This is too much for Magda, and she commands Keller to leave the house. The father brandishes a pistol to threaten his daughter into accepting this marriage, but she is unyielding. At the climax of this confrontation the father collapses from a stroke, and Magda realizes that she should never have come home.

The play was performed by some of the leading actresses of the age, most notably Sarah Bernhardt, Eleonora Duse, and Stella Campbell.[57] It was extremely popular in Europe until World War II, after which Sudermann's reputation declined. It is regarded as a naturalist play that combines a concern with social problems with the French tradition of the well-made play: unity of time, place, and action.[58]

The tightness of the construction of Sudermann's plays was often noted and criticized by his contemporaries as being too mechanical.[59] In *Heimat,* however, it seems to underline the theme of the play: woman's sense of confinement in the home. All four acts take place within the span of 24 hours, within a single scenery set: that of the drawing room of Magda's father's house. Significantly, we never see the heroine outside the drawing room, although we hear the other characters describe her great success on the operatic stage as Maddalena dall'Orto (1.9.268), the crowd that gathers outside her hotel (1, 7, 263), and her appearance at the ball on the arms of the Oberpräsident (1.9.267–268). The confinement of space dictated by the principles of the well-made play highlights Magda's dilemma.[60] She wishes to make peace with her home, but she has become too free and expansive to be happy within its strictures:

> Magda: I've felt it, since the first minute I've been back here: Paternal authority stretches its net to capture me again—the yoke stands ready, and I'm supposed to crawl into it (2.9.290).[61]

Both in language and staging, then, the play emphasizes the confinement a woman feels in the home, legitimizing her earlier decision to leave it and her defiance at the end.

The plot of *Heimat* can be seen as a continuation of the plot of *A Doll House:* Magda's story is the story of what might happen to a woman after she leaves the doll house, achieves independence and success in the world, then tries to go back home. Whereas *A Doll House* stages the question of women's liberation through the figure of a woman *leaving the home, Heimat* stages the same problem through the figure of a woman *returning home,* only to find the home inhospitable and impossibly confining.

The theme of women's struggle between career and home is delineated most clearly when Magda must choose one or the other. Keller demands that Magda give up her stage career and use her social and musical skills to further *his* political career:

> Keller: That you'll have to give up the stage and the concert hall—well, that just goes without saying.
> Magda: So—it goes without saying?
> Keller: But of course. You don't understand the situation. . . . I have the greatest respect for your triumphs up to this point, but—(*delicately*) the highest prize after which womanly vanity may strive is only given out in salons, you know.
> Magda: (*to herself*). My God, what am I doing, it's all madness.
> Keller: What did you say?
> Magda: (*shakes her head*)
> Keller: And one more thing: you see, a woman, an ideal woman, as she is pictured in modern times, is supposed to be the companion, the faithful, self-sacrificing helper of her husband. . . . I imagine for example how you would, through your personal dignity and the magic of your song, conquer my enemies. . . . (4.10.340–341)

Magda at first mumbles that this is madness, then is momentarily reduced to silence at this threat to her career. Before she has a chance to counter this threat, another threat arises, this time to her motherhood, and this is what causes her to change her mind.

At its most conservative end, the play holds up the ideal of motherhood as surpassing even artistic and personal freedom. This is indicated by Magda's reply to her father's question about what she holds to be sacred.

> Schwartze: Tell me, my daughter, every person holds something to be sacred. What do you inwardly regard as being sacred in this world?
> Magda: My art!
> Schwartze: No, that is not enough. It has to be more sacred.
> Magda: My child.
> Schwartze: Good. Your child. . . . (4.7.343–344).

Magda is willing to marry Keller, her ex-lover, because she believes this would provide a happy home for her child as well as satisfy her father's wishes for preserving her reputation. Yet when Keller demands that Magda give up their child in order to preserve *his* reputation, Magda is outraged and storms off. Through this action, she reveals herself to be a "good mother":

> Magda: You forget, darling, that the child, for whom this union is to be made, will keep the narrow-minded people away from us.
> Keller: Yes—that—. I must admit, dearest Magda, it will be painful for you, but this child must of course stay a deep secret between us. No one must suspect—
> Magda: (*shocked and incredulous*). What, what are you saying?
> Keller: We would be—ruined—in every respect! No, no, that is absurd to even think about! . . . But-uh, we could go on a short trip every year, wherever we would have the child brought up.—One would write some made-up name in the visitor book; that would not be noticed in a foreign country, and is (*thoughtfully*) probably not illegal. . . . And when we are fifty years old and the other legal conditions are fulfilled—(*smiling*) that could be taken care of, couldn't it?—then we could adopt the child under some kind of pretext—don't you agree?
> Magda: (*explodes into a shrill laughter, then folds her hands and stares in front of her*). My Sweet Child! My Little One! Mio bambino! *Mio povero-bam*—! You—I am supposed—to—hahahahaha—Out, out! (*Tries to open the door*). Out! (4.10.324).

The final straw for Magda's forbearance is this threat that her child will be taken away, the threat to her motherhood.

The emphasis on motherhood in *Heimat* is not particularly surprising given the context of the nineteenth-century ideology of women's biologically determined roles, even within the German bourgeois feminist movement.[62] Yet the structure of the drama does not indicate that Magda chooses motherhood over all else. Instead, the dilemma of Magda is seen to lie in her desire to have it all, to combine the roles of successful artist, loving mother, respectable wife, and dutiful daughter. The last role is made impossible when her father dies, but Magda herself, unlike the "fallen women" figures of the time,[63] is not punished by death. No judgment is made in her favor, but one could argue that none is made against her, either.

As Shimamura Hōgetsu pointed out, this ambivalence makes various performative interpretations possible. He was aware of the various performances of *Heimat* by famous actresses in the West and pointed out their different interpretations:

> According to European critics, Sarah Bernhardt's Magda is said to have stood straight at center stage in the final scene, displaying the glory of the new world and presenting an interpretation that sees the prospect of the new morality in Magda's victory. Mrs. Campbell, on the other hand, is said to have collapsed tearfully, showing remorse and suggesting that Magda's world was doomed to failure. . . . In our production . . . we showed that the three worlds, of Magda, of the Schwartze family, and of the pastor, remained in conflict, each unable to compromise, with much difficulty ahead for the new morality.[64]

The triangulation between the interpretation of Magda as a defiant feminist, as a remorseful daughter, and as caught in the middle of an irresolvable conflict is an exact parallel to the director's earlier triangulation between the interpretation of Nora as a strong feminist appropriate for a performance in the United States, the German interpretation of her as a remorseful mother, and the toned down interpretation the director chose for the performance in Japan. By positing the extremes of radical and conservative interpretations, Shimamura Hōgetsu attempted to position himself as the moderate mediator. It was a precarious position that would open the production to critique by both the radicals and the conservatives.

When the play was performed in Japan, the actress Matsui Sumako became identified with the role of Magda, and the combined actress-singer became a figure who provoked and answered the "Woman Question" and the "Actress Question." First, by translating the word "Sängerin" (singer) of the original as "*opera joyū*" (literally "opera actress"), Hōgetsu's translation strengthened the association between the character Magda and the actress performing it.[65] The focus on the heroine was further intensified by changing the title of the play to *Magda*.[66] Matsui Sumako herself was transgressing family morals, by divorcing her husband and by becoming involved with a married man. She had decided to forge a career rather than nurture a family. She thus provoked the "Woman

Question" concerning woman's proper role in society. Yet it was also Matsui Sumako who, according to critical and popular opinion, answered the "Actress Question" once and for all in the affirmative: Yes, women were capable of performing on stage, and they were more persuasive than *onnagata,* the traditional male impersonators of female roles.

Hōgetsu used the English translation by Charles E. A. Winslow,[67] but he also consulted the earlier (1909) Japanese translation in which the play is appropriately retitled *Shin fujin* (New Woman). Hōgetsu's own translation was published in *Waseda bungaku* (March and April 1912).[68] The performance took place in May of 1912 at the Yūrakuza theater. Matsui Sumako took the role of Magda; instructors of the Literary Society played the roles of Magda's father and of her ex-lover; the roles of Magda's sister, step-mother, and aunt were performed by actresses-in-training at the Literary Society; other female roles were taken by male actors, due to the dearth of qualified actresses.

In an interview of the major performers concerning preparations for their respective roles, Matsui Sumako commented on the difficulties of playing the role of a cosmopolitan European lady. Her comments draw our attention to the efforts and material preparations necessary for a Japanese woman to act like a Western woman—or, to be more precise, like a German New Woman who has lived as an opera diva in France and Italy, among other places. This effort is usually invisible from the perspective of the spectator who assumes a natural and transparent relationship between the signifier (Japanese woman's body) and the signified (the Western woman). But the material production of this relationship is evident when we pay close attention to the actress as signifier.

> This role had a more complex character than that of Nora, which I performed before, and was therefore difficult. Yet as I become more and more accustomed to the stage, things do get easier in some ways.
>
> As for make-up, I tried to make it very different from Nora's make-up; I tried to make Magda look stronger. In Act III, I exit after cursing Keller, then enter again at the end: in the second entrance, I tried to make my face look a bit pale.
>
> As for hair style and costume, I received advice from Ms. Kate. Ms. Kate is a lady who teaches English at Waseda. My character enters for the first time in Act II, wearing a gown [*shakō fuku*] decorated with medals. In my first entrance in Act III, I wear a loose nightgown; in the second entrance I wear a travel dress under a manteau. In Act IV, I take off the manteau, revealing the same travel dress.
>
> I wear the same wig in all three acts, but in Act II, I fasten some flowers to my hair.
>
> I use Italian words at one point on stage, but I didn't learn those from an Italian. Professor Shimamura taught them to me. But there are places where foreign words are used in the original, which I deliberately omitted. In Act IV,

> there is a line, "*Mio bambino! Mio povero bam—*" but we thought that using foreign words at that emotionally charged moment would undermine the tension. So I say the line in Japanese instead. I also omit the line in Act II "I can't find the words," which is supposed to be in French.[69]

The emphasis on preparation and rehearsal counters the myth that Sumako's acting was just a natural outpouring of her personality or of her feminine essence. It was a carefully produced construction that was nonetheless meant to be read as natural and direct expression.[70]

Two photographs of Sumako in the role of Magda are included in *Peony Brush,* the memoir of the actress. In both she is wearing an elaborate gown of velvet-like material, with heavy brocade borders. She is turned slightly away from the camera, her head subtly twisted back in the other direction. Several medals decorate her upper body, and the long trailing hem is arranged in front of her feet. Her arms are exposed from the elbows down to her hands, which hang in a relaxed position by her side. The only difference between the two photos is that in the first one she is wearing a cape over her dress, as if to show she has just arrived (or is about to depart). The cape, or manteau, was a metonymic garment signifying the ability and desire of women to leave the house and roam the wider world. It reminds us again that the actress wrote the haiku: "Wearing a *manteau,* I am a New Woman."

The response from theater critics was overwhelmingly positive. Following the success of Matsui Sumako's performance as Nora, her portrayal of Magda sealed her reputation as the actress who could perform women's roles in New Theater. Kusuyama Masao even praised the performance as being better than the original play:

> *Magda* surpasses the translated text, and in a certain sense it even surpasses the original text [*gensaku*]. The delicate human sensitivity, the color and atmosphere of subtle spirits touching each other—the performance expresses more than what is contained in the original text. This is not a simple art. It is Sumako's intrinsic power, Sumako's complex personality, that is expressed on stage to an extent that surpasses the original text.[71]

This response is significant because it shows two assumptions: first, the assumption that the approximation to the original text is the standard measure of a performance's success, though exceeded here; second, the assumption that what is expressed in the performance is the personality of the actress. The first assumption installs the idea of an originary master text, to which any Japanese translation, and any Japanese staging using such a translation, must adhere to closely. The response of theater critics to the performance of *Heimat* points to the straight line that is drawn from original to translation to staging. This

8.2 Matsui Sumako as Magda. Courtesy of Waseda University's Tsubouchi Shōyō Memorial Theater Museum.

is also assumed by Ikuta Chōkō, who evaluates Hōgetsu's translation from the standpoint of its faithfulness to the original text and praises the actors for being faithful to the text.[72]

The second assumption, that of a straight line drawn from the interiority of the actress to the performance, is also new. At this point, a certain slippage occurs between this assumption and the assumption that what is expressed in the performance is the personality of the dramatic characters: The character of Magda is equated with the actress portraying her, and the body of the actress becomes the transparent medium through which this blended personality is expressed. The resulting assumption, that what is expressed in the performance is the interiority of the character through the transparent actress's body, is evident in Kawajiri Seitan's praise for "Sumako's mental ability to interpret the original text, and to embody the role through every facial expression, every

8.3 Matsui Sumako as Magda with *manteau*. From *Peony Brush*.

movement of the hands and feet."[73] Sumako's makeup was commended as natural looking, "as if it wasn't made up at all."[74] Her acting is best when she looks like she is not acting at all; thus by a subtraction of the materiality of the medium, she is equated with her role.

The same critic also mentions the episode of a *kabuki* actor amazed by Sumako's performance in *A Doll House:* "[W]hen he first heard of the characterization of Nora, he doubted such a complex character could be presented in full on stage." Kawajiri cites this as evidence that *kabuki* actors are not capable of representing complex and subtle personalities and emotions, in contrast to new actresses like Matsui Sumako. Playwright and critic Ihara Seisei'en also praised the actress for portraying the complexity of the role:

> Sumako's Magda is more sophisticated than her Nora, and the acting is of a grander scale. She embodies the fashionable actress, and smoothly combines

> the two contradictory aspects of cursing the burdens of obligation and morality on the one hand, yet expressing warm emotions towards her father and sister on the other hand.[75]

The novelist Masamune Hakuchō also found the acting compelling, especially in comparison to "feeble new actress-plays and clichéd old-plays."[76] Thus through the performance of the feminist figure of Magda, Matsui Sumako sealed her triumph as a New Woman in New Theater.

What were the reactions of the New Women of *Seitō* to this performance? As in the case of reactions to *A Doll House,* the feminists were not unambiguous in their approval of Magda. Hasegawa Shigure thought Matsui Sumako had improved upon her performance of Nora: "composure and dignity have been added to her acting, and her physical appearance seems to have improved along with her art."[77] She also considered Magda's feelings of being torn between old and new thinking to be less radical than Nora's total rejection of old thinking. For this reason, more Japanese women might identify with Magda than with Nora.

Hiratsuka Raichō, on the other hand, was almost entirely critical of Magda. Her assessment of the heroine of *Heimat* is similar in tone to her dismissal of Nora in *A Doll House.*[78] Although she saw the Literary Society's staging, she professed to prefer writing about Magda as read in textual form. The staging almost turned her sympathy for Magda to dislike, she says, but she ascribes this reaction to her dislike of crowds and of the theater in general. As a text, however, *Heimat* does not strike her as a very deep problem play either: Magda's act of leaving the house 12 years ago was impulsive and thoughtless, unlike Nora's act of resolution. Magda's compromising attitude is also criticized by Hiratsuka: "I cannot overlook her conciliatory attitude towards her home and her father, her spirit of lukewarm harmony and compromise."[79] As in the case of *A Doll House,* Hiratsuka worries about what would happen to the heroine after the end of the play, and concludes pessimistically, "Thinking of Magda, my heart sinks into darkness again."[80]

On the other hand, Otake Kōkichi is as enthusiastic for Sumako's Magda as she was for her Nora:

> There is no one who deploys her body as faithfully, as seriously. . . . Impressed, I gazed at every little thing she did. Technique, art, life, work, taking all these together, I want to praise her. And I want to pray that she will not be defeated and diminished amongst the many ambitious people who surround her, but that she will grow ever greater.[81]

Nonetheless, Otake professes that she prefers Ibsen's play over Sudermann's, since the latter seemed to have too many extraneous characters.

Two other women responded to *Heimat*. Kiuchi Tei saw the stage version first, then read the play "highly excited and almost dragged into it; it seemed as if the play was reading me, instead of my reading the play."[82] Naganuma Chie,[83] on the other hand, did not find the play to be presenting a particularly new perspective: Even Magda seemed still too feminine and self-deprecating. "Magda needs to spit more intense and brilliant fires and flames; she needs to pursue her selfhood more fully."[84]

These feminist reactions to *Heimat* and Sumako's portrayal of the role of Magda do not present one coherent opinion but suggest the kind of excitement and discussion the performance provoked. They also show how the reception of this play was inseparable from the reception of Ibsen's *A Doll House*. Taken together, these plays raised the question of women's status in the home and in society, and the convincing performance of Matsui Sumako was crucial in conveying the feminist message of women's need for independence from the home.

What is most striking about the Japanese performance of *Heimat* is the kind of social and political controversy it provoked. Immediately after the initial run in Tokyo, the police announced that all further performances would be banned. The Japanese authorities could not condone the attack against family values that they thought the play represented. Magda's behavior was considered to be "clearly contrary to the code of filial piety [*kōdō*] delineated in the Imperial Rescript on Education, and absolutely inadmissible in the family."[85] In the debate over this issue, male artists and intellectuals frequently choose to see the play as representing the struggles of an artist, rather than the struggles of a New Woman. Thus they would interpret the controversy surrounding the play in terms of their own struggles for freedom from social constraints.[86]

In a quote cited by an anonymous review article entitled "Maguda mondai no kiroku" (Records of the Magda question) in *Waseda bungaku*, a representative of the police censors explained why the play was allowed to be performed at first and later banned:

> There were three reasons why we allowed the public staging of Sudermann's *Heimat*. First, we allowed it because the play is a translation from a foreign language, and not something familiar that came from the mind of a Japanese. Second, we allowed it because it was to be performed by the artists of the Literary Society, who are seeking to reform the theater and to improve the tastes of the national subjects. Thus, third, the audience would also be people with high minds, with intelligence, good taste, and highly developed critical faculties [*hihansei*]; they would never degenerate into hasty agreement and blind action.
>
> The reason we have decided to prohibit any further performances is . . . that the structure of the play is contrary to traditional Japanese ethical

> thought, and is incompatible with national morality. . . . In short, we fear what would happen if this play were to be performed in the future in front of people who lack critical faculties, and what direction such a result would take.[87]

Thus it is clear that the authorities feared what would happen if a sophisticated audience's detached attitude toward the performance would be replaced by a less critical one: A blind enthusiasm for the ideas espoused in the play would pose a danger to the state-sanctioned morality of obedience to one's parents and loyalty to one's superiors. Portrayal of a rebellious young woman would be sufficient to arouse rebellious thoughts in the hearts of the audience watching the play. The government censors saw theater as potentially more dangerous than the printed novel: Reading, or a certain mode of experiencing theater as reading, is associated with critical distance and a critical audience, whereas a different mode of experiencing theater, one based on "hasty agreement and blind action" is associated with emotional immediacy and disruption of the social order. A calm reader, here, is also an obedient and orderly subject of the nation state. An audience that is moved easily by theater is also an audience that can be moved to rebellion.

Faced with the threat of a ban, the director Shimamura Hōgetsu had to compromise and alter the text in order to suit "the teachings of loyalty and filial piety which are the basis of Japanese national morality."[88] The most dramatic alteration concerned the ending of the play. The original ambiguity, the suspension of judgment in the conflict between the old and new moralities, had to be resolved in favor of the status quo. The original play ends with the father collapsing from a stroke. Magda expresses her anguish but is still unrepentant:

> Magda: (*jumping up and raising her hands in despair*). Ah, I should never have come back!
> Pastor: (*makes a gesture to order silence*).
> Magda: (*misunderstanding this gesture*). You chase me away already? . . . I have driven him to his death—am I not allowed to bury him?
> Pastor: (*simply and peacefully*). Nobody will hinder you from praying at his coffin!
>
> (*Curtain*) (4.13.348).

This ending left judgment suspended and allowed the performers and members of the audience to make up their own minds about who was justified and who was to blame. Yet this potential for varied readings had to be closed down for the purposes of the Japanese performance. This is what Hōgetsu added after the last line of the original play:

Magda: Ah, father, father! (*Collapses weeping in front of his body.*)
Pastor: (*Quietly looking at her*) Magda.
Magda: (*Looks up as if noticing him for the first time.*)
Pastor: Look at this. This is the result brought about by a woman who has become independent and free. . . . With no spirit of sacrifice, only that of independence and freedom. . . . Just like beasts—isn't this what you said of society yourself? God has only words of love and sacrifice. Magda, you say you love your child; why then do you refuse to appreciate your father's love and caring for you? If your child were to become like you are now, what would become of you?
Magda: Ah, I know. Say no more. I cannot bear any more.
Pastor: If so, Magda, return once more to filial love. Return to human love. You say you are an independent, free woman, but don't you see that you suffer from conflicting anguish deep in your heart? You are lonely, aren't you? You are starved for love, aren't you? True freedom can only be found in the garden of love.
Magda: Ah . . . please . . . no more. . . .
Pastor: Look upon your father, who gave his life for love. What will happen to this family now? What will happen to your mother and sister? Will the Colonel's soul be able to rest in peace?
Magda: Ah! (*A look of terror.*)
Pastor: Do not let your father die in vain. . . .
Magda: (*Suffering from guilty conscience:*) It is all my fault. I shall follow your instructions.
Pastor: Thank you. Then, let us ask for God's forgiveness together. And let us pray for the Colonel.
Magda: (*Prays silently.*)
(*The curtain descends slowly.*)[89]

This and other textual alterations[90] severely diluted whatever socially subversive potential might have existed in the play, thus appeasing the Japanese authorities.

Hōgetsu's excuse for giving in to the censors was precisely the open nature of the ending, and his conciliatory posture places him on the side of the pastor, who "mediates between the world of Schwartze and the world of Magda."[91] We are also reminded of the alternate, conciliatory ending to *A Doll House,* which Hōgetsu had translated a few years earlier. The director also argued that the ideology of a play is less important than the opportunity it presents to an actress like Matsui Sumako to prove herself.[92] This attitude of appeasement, however, was severely criticized by many intellectuals. Komiya Toyotaka wrote in *Shin shōsetsu* that the Literary Society betrayed its principles in altering the script;[93] *Miyako Shimbun* editorialized that rather than performing the altered version for the sake of profit, it would have been better for the Literary Society to have forfeited commercial success by not performing the play at all.[94] Ishibashi Tanzan interpreted this incident as an example of the government trying to control the thoughts of the people and bemoaned the lack of passion among the literati: "Why don't they rise up and fight the government?" he demanded.[95] All these critics felt that something had been irretrievably lost by altering the ending of the play.[96]

Interestingly, the actress Matsui Sumako published her own views on the controversy, suggesting the possibility of a feminist reappropriation. In an essay titled "Nora and Magda," she compares Nora of Ibsen's *A Doll House* to Magda of Sudermann's *Heimat.*[97] The former leaves home in order to find herself, while the latter's devotion to her child is stressed over her career. Thus, on a superficial level, the latter may appear to represent a more conservative position than the former. But this is not so, says Sumako. "Magda has been fighting against the rough winds of the world and has already achieved her independence; her self-awareness is much stronger than that of Nora at her departure from home."[98] When Magda returns to her child, it is as a woman who is fully aware of her own worth, while Nora, at the end of the play, has barely begun her process of learning.

The essay replies to two related controversies that surrounded the performance of these plays in Japan. Much of the debate that *A Doll House* ignited centered around the question of whether or not Nora was justified in leaving her children. Sumako declares her sympathy for the heroine's decision, since it is impossible for Nora to gain independence and self-awareness if she were to continue acting as the doll wife in the doll house. The other controversy concerned the censorship of *Heimat.* Sumako's reply to this controversy was that Magda does not lose anything by returning home: She has already achieved independence and self-awareness, and her choice is made from a position of strength rather than from one of despair. This argument is still used today within feminist movements to defend women who decide to stay home with their children.

While the reduction of the social problem of women's freedom to the level of personal consciousness has its problems, one cannot help but be struck by Sumako's interpretation, especially in the light of the more centrist position her director and lover proposed. What seems to have made a strong impression on the audience is the image of a woman performing on stage in the role of a woman who has made a career for herself in performing. This message came across in spite of the forced changes that were meant to contain any threat that these performing women might present to the social order. Matsui Sumako performed the role of a feminist calling for female members of the audience to awaken and to gain independence by leaving the house. The censors recognized this, as did theater critics and feminist spectators. The former saw this performance as a threat; the latter hailed it as a form of New Theater made possible by a New Woman.

ARTISTIC HEIGHTS AND SEDUCTIVE DEPTHS: THE SUNKEN BELL

Hermann Sudermann's *Heimat* and Gerhart Hauptmann's *The Sunken Bell* (Die versunkene Glocke) are almost mirror images of each other. Whereas the former deals with the problem of the female artist, placing her in the confinement of the home, the latter portrays a male artist as he roams about the mountains and valleys.[99] The former's language of oppressive confinement is in contrast to the latter's language of expansiveness and change. *The Sunken Bell* centers on Heinrich, a bellmaker with artistic ambitions who must decide between the freedom of the mountains and the domesticity of the village. At the same time, he is torn between Rautendelein, the seductive mountain nymph, and his faithful but conventional wife in the village.[100]

As the curtain opens, the first figure we see on stage is Rautendelein, who flirts with supernatural creatures such as a water sprite and a wood sprite but who in the end brushes off their advances. Heinrich arrives on stage and collapses: The most recent bell he forged has toppled into a mountain lake, an act perpetrated by supernatural creatures who dislike the Christian sounds of the bell ringing in the mountains. Rautendelein attends to Heinrich and they fall in love. The villagers come to take Heinrich back home, and Rautendelein decides to go down to the village to stay with him. The next act takes place inside Heinrich's house in the village. As his wife Magda looks on anxiously, Heinrich is brought back from the mountain, but he is very ill. Rautendelein arrives, disguised as a village maiden, and uses magic to restore Heinrich to health. His wife is puzzled but joyous. In act 3, we are back on the mountain, at a new workshop erected by Heinrich. Here, assisted by mountain dwarfs, Heinrich is forging his grand creation: a pagan bell in honor of the sun goddess. The priest arrives and tries to bring the bellmaker back to Christianity and the life of the village, but he is chased away by Heinrich. In the following act, villagers attack the workshop and set fire to it, whereupon Rautendelein bargains with Nickelmann, the water sprite, to save Heinrich. With the help of the water sprite, Heinrich puts out the fire and defeats the villagers. Finally, his two children come trudging up the slope, carrying a jug containing the tears of their mother, Magda, who has died from grief—she has been buried in the same lake where the sunken bell lies. Heinrich shouts that he can hear the bell ringing and madly dashes down the mountain. In the fifth and final act, Rautendelein has married Nickelmann to fulfill her part of the bargain. Heinrich climbs up the mountain one last time to see her, they embrace, and the bell-maker dies.

The Sunken Bell, called a "Mischung von romantischem Singsang und bombastischem Klingklang" (mixture of romantic sing-song and bombastic ring-ding),[101] is composed mostly in verse form, with colorful dialects distinguishing various human and superhuman characters: Heinrich speaks the lofty language of the artist, Magda the plain patois of the village woman, Rautendelein the delicate rhymes appropriate for a nymph. The staging emphasizes the grand scale of movement between mountain and village, stressing in particular the sense of height. Location changes and weather changes are supplemented by verbal imagery of vertical movement: climbing up to great heights, falling back into the abyss.[102] This is in stark contrast to *Heimat,* which stresses the narrowness of the home through its language and its staging.

Yet the play actually has many elements in common with naturalist works, and the continuity becomes especially clear in the light of the Japanese reception of the play.[103] The theme, articulated in Hauptmann's naturalist plays, is the struggle of the male intellectual-artist between various forces, embodied by women, that attract and repel him.[104] This play, like the straight plays performed by Kawakami Sadayakko, portrays women as foils to the struggle of men attempting to establish themselves as subjects. This is in contrast to certain other plays performed by Matsui Sumako, such as *A Doll House* and *Heimat,* which center on a woman's struggle. Whereas Sumako performs the role of the feminist fighter in the woman-centered plays, in the woman-as-foil plays she performs the role of the seductive femme fatale. Yet these two roles are not as antipodal as they might seem at first glance.

The most common critical interpretation of *The Sunken Bell* has been the biographical one. Hauptmann himself was confronting self-doubts about his artistic career,[105] and was also experiencing great trouble with his marriage.[106] According to the biographical interpretation, Heinrich's artistic struggle represents that of Hauptmann himself, Magda represents the playwright's own wife, and Rautendelein represents the playwright's childlike mistress, an aspiring actress.[107]

The identification of theater practitioners with dramatic characters continued in the context of the play's production in Japan. It has been often pointed out that Shimamura Hōgetsu faced troubles similar to those of both Heinrich and Hauptmann as the husband of one woman and the lover of another.[108] His decision to produce *The Sunken Bell* in 1918 was based on a number of considerations, but the desire to stage the conflict of the bellmaker Heinrich as his own is often seen as central. The conflict was not merely that between a bourgeois wife and a free-spirited lover; it was, for Hōgetsu, also that between different principles of artistic production. The director was struggling to find a balance between making art and making a living, a dilemma faced by most theater directors in the modern era. Eventually he was to decide on a "two dimensional road" (*nigen no michi*): bringing in profit through popular commercial productions in order to finance the more experimental, "artistic" productions. Yet, as discussed in the previous chapter, he was sharply criticized for this compromise,[109] and *The Sunken Bell* can be seen as part of Hōgetsu's continuing engagement with the problem. He saw the play as representing the conflict between the "ideal to create" (*tsukuran to suru kokoro*) and the common forces of society, citing this as the major reason for staging it.[110] And yet, the performance was the first in a series under contract with Shōchiku, a major production company, a circumstance that further complicated the question of artistic versus commercial consideration.[111]

If Hōgetsu was Heinrich, Sumako was Rautendelein. In her interpretation of the role, we can see another aspect of *The Sunken Bell* that is often overlooked. The Japanese critics considered the role of a fairy-tale maiden to be unsuited to the sensuous appeal of this actress, who had performed the role of Sudermann's prima donna so well. While Ihara Seisei'en thought of her as "competently expressing the naive, vivacious, and active girl,"[112] Oka Kitarō found her "too fleshy."[113] An anonymous reviewer for the *Tokyo Asahi Shimbun* found her hips too wide and her strides too heavy for a mountain nymph.[114]

A closer look at the text reveals, however, that Rautendelein is indeed more of a fin-de-siècle femme fatale than an innocent elf. She is described in the text as being "half child, half maiden" *(halb Kind, halb Jungfrau)*, an alluringly ambiguous stage in life. She first appears combing her long hair in the fashion of Lorelei (1.761). She then engages in a narcissistic dialogue with her own reflection in the well water (1.761–762):

> Rautendelein: (*Combs her hair quietly for a moment or two. Then, leaning over the well, she calls down.*) Hey! Nickelmann! He doesn't hear me. I'll sing to myself, then.
> Where do I come from? Wither shall I go?
> Tell me—I long to know!
> Did I grow as the birds of the woodland gay?
> Am I a fay?
> . . .
> (*Dialoguing with her reflection in the well*)
> Well, good day to you, my sweet maid of the well!
> What's your name? Rautendelein? Indeed! I see—
> You say you're the prettiest of all girls. But look at me.
> For I, not you, Rautendelein should be.[115]

Images of women combing their hair and gazing at themselves in the mirror were pervasive in fin-de-siècle European culture and often suggested "fantasies of feminine evil" arising out of the anxiety caused by female self-sufficiency.[116] Though Heinrich insists on calling her "child" (*Kind*), Rautendelein is very much a sexual being who evokes sexual desire in almost all male creatures that look upon her, including the water sprite and the wood sprite (1.764; 791). She is described in sexual terms by these supernatural creatures:

> Nickelmann: Hot days are followed by still hotter nights.
> Rautendelein: Maybe. Cold water is your element:

So go back where you came from, and cool yourself down.
(*Waldschrat laughs. Nickelmann sinks silently down into his trough and disappears.*)
Waldschrat: (*still laughing.*) Ods bobs!
Rautendelein: My garter's twisted at the knee!
It cuts me.
Waldschrat: If you want, I'll loosen it for you.
Rautendelein: Wouldn't you like that! No. Go away!
You bring ill smells with you, and oh, the gnats!
Why, they are swarming round you now, in clouds.
Waldschrat: I love them better than the butterflies
That swoon with dusty wings about your face,
Now writhing on your lips—now in your hair,
Or clinging to your hips and breasts at night.
Rautendelein: (*laughing.*) There! That will do. Enough! (3.816–817).[117]

On stage, Rautendelein shows herself to be a singer (1.762) as well as a dancer (1.785–786).[118] She performs the role of femme fatale perfectly. Rautendelein's devotion to the male protagonist and her ultimate sacrifice for him neutralize her sensuous threat, but the complaint of the Japanese critics suggest that Rautendelein's femme fatale side was realized all too well in Matsui Sumako's performance.[119]

Sumako recorded the songs composed for this production. She thus became the first actress whose voice became a commodity for mass consumption, through the newly developed technologies for mechanical reproduction of sound. Her voice has been described as high and clear, if somewhat lacking in subtle phrasing. Matsui Sumako herself is said to have liked the role of this supernatural femme fatale a great deal, perhaps because it allowed her to explore subtler expressions of the femme fatale's sexuality.[120] In an article written immediately after Sumako's death, Kusuyama Masao, translator of *The Sunken Bell*, remembered how the actress "particularly liked Rautendelein, a role in which she could sing and dance, and dart back and forth between reality and illusion."[121]

Was Rautendelein also a feminist? The answer will be left hanging until the next chapter, in which the femme fatale as sexual object is seen from another angle, as sexual subject and hence as a figure with a potentially crucial feminist dimension.

Matsui Sumako's career was defined by her position in New Theater. She was supposed to be the embodiment of a new kind of performer who could become the transparent vehicle for the transmission of logos. Yet her body was opaque and troubling, and her presence on stage provoked more complicated responses than a pure communion of minds. She acted as both feminist and femme fatale, awakening, seducing, and disturbing the audience.

Moreover, Matsui Sumako remained attached to the appeal of song and dance, and today she may be remembered in Japan as much for "Katúsha's Song," which she performed on stage in a theatrical adaptation of Leo Tolstoy's *Resurrection* and also recorded, as for her portrayal of the feminist heroine Nora. She performed in adaptations from opera, such as Georges Bizet's *Carmen* (itself based on the novella by Prosper Mérimée) and new music was composed by Nakayama Shimpei for her to sing in this version.[122] Shimamura Hōgetsu also wanted her to sing and dance, going so far as to build a dance stage for her.[123] The actress also appeared in a number of joint-productions with *shimpa* actors, mostly as a way to help finance her own struggling theater company, and gained popularity for performing temptresses in these melodramas.[124] Song, dance, melodrama, and the appeal of the sexuality of the performer were precisely what New Theater had been trying unsuccessfully to purge from the stage.[125]

Like Kawakami Sadayakko, Matsui Sumako led a life that became the focus of scandal while she was alive and the subject of much speculation after her death. Like Kawakami Sadayakko, she pursued a career the narrative of which is often eclipsed by the narrative of her relationship to her "leading man." The processes of the "wifeing" of women and the "straightening" of theater shaped the reception of Matsui Sumako as well as that of Kawakami Sadayakko. But Matsui Sumako went further, even as the definitions of woman and theater evolved. Matsui Sumako took over where Kawakami Sadayakko left off, finally convincing skeptics that actresses were necessary and superior to *onnagata*. As a New Woman in a New Theater, she presented a challenge to the status quo, both in theater and in society, though this challenge came at a high price.

EPILOGUE

REVEALING THE REAL BODY

IN 1914, TWO COMPETING PRODUCTIONS OF OSCAR WILDE'S *Salomé* appeared on the stage in Japan. One featured Kawakami Sadayakko, recently widowed, who was trying to revitalize her career by performing a role that was quite different from both the Orientalized geisha she had performed in the West and the modern traveler she had performed in Japan.[1] The other production starred Matsui Sumako, the actress who had premiered the role in Tokyo one year earlier and who was currently at the peak of her career.[2] The play *Salomé* itself became extremely popular in Japan and was presented to the public by various actresses in no fewer than 27 separate productions between the premiere in 1913 and the end of the Taishō era a dozen years later.

The years leading up to this competition of Salomé had seen various debates for and against actresses. What these debates revealed was an emerging understanding of gender as defined by the physical body. Eventually the arguments in favor of actresses won over those against actresses, yet the victory was an ambivalent one: It confirmed the definition of womanhood as an essence naturally grounded in a woman's body, a definition that would also justify the reduction of woman to nothing but her body. *Salomé* marks a moment in Japanese history when the alignment between gender, sex, sexuality, and performance thus registered a recognizable shift: from gender defined as theatrical achievement, to gender defined as grounded in the visible body and as basis for theatrical expression. There is a shift from gender as the endpoint of acting to gender as the beginning of acting. The title role of Salomé epitomized the new definition of womanhood as rooted in the physical body and of woman's body as the basis for acting. The "competition" between Kawakami Sadayakko and Matsui Sumako in 1914 and the latter's victory over the former signaled the final triumph of the newer alignment.

If we examine the early history of how Oscar Wilde's *Salomé* was received in Japan, we can see how the play was first introduced as an example of highbrow

European literature before becoming a script for performance. And if we trace the history of what happened to *Salomé* after early Taishō, we see how the figure was gradually reduced to a mere pretext for the spectacular unveiling of the female body. The initial reception of *Salomé* as literary text is significant because it shows the establishment of a new alignment of script and performance. New Theater introduced the idea that a theatrical performance should faithfully reproduce and represent the script, with the script itself now revered as a form of literature. The later "degradation" of *Salomé* into a pretext for pornographic spectacle exposes the limits of New Theater and the return of the sexuality that had been driven off into the wings.

Input the keyword "Salomé" and launch a search on the Internet—you will be confronted, after various pages about Oscar Wilde and several other representations of Salomé from the history of literature and art, with a host of pornographic pages. What accounts for this connection of Salomé and spectacular sexuality? Based on the Book of Matthew 14:8 as well as some apocryphal texts, the story of Salomé tells of King Herod's stepdaughter, who becomes enamored of Jokanaan, or John the Baptist. When he spurns her, she seeks revenge. She succeeds and is given the head of the Baptist on a platter. But seeing her caress and kiss the head, King Herod is seized with terror and orders her executed as well. Whereas Rautendelein in *The Sunken Bell* is a role whose femme fatale aspect is rather carefully disguised beneath a fairy-tale surface, Oscar Wilde's *Salomé* presents a heroine who is the quintessential femme fatale.[3] Even before she enters the stage, the sexual allure of Salomé is evoked through the Young Syrian Captain's incessant declaration of "How beautiful is the Princess Salomé tonight!" (319). That Salomé is not only beautiful but dangerous is suggested by the Page, who keeps warning the Young Syrian Captain that "You must not look at her. . . . Something terrible may happen" (321). What distinguishes Salomé from the typical femme fatale is that she does not remain an object of sexual desire for men but declares her own sexual desire for a man. The language she uses to describe Jokanaan objectifies his body: "Thy mouth is like a band of scarlet on a tower of ivory. It is like a pomegranate cut with a knife of ivory. . . . Let me kiss thy mouth" (328). In her study of femme fatale figures in European fin-de-siècle theater, Gail Finney finds that Salomé's seductive praises of Jokanaan share much with the traditional male depiction of female anatomy and reaches the conclusion that Salomé is a masked depiction of one man's prohibited longing for another.[4]

In terms of the textuality of the play, there may thus be a question of whether Salomé is truly a femme fatale or a man in drag; in terms of its staging in Japan, however, there is no question that Salomé was a role whose performance was inconceivable for a male performer of female roles. When Richard Strauss set Oscar Wilde's play to music in 1905 to create the opera *Salomé*, the dramatic and musical climax became the "Dance of the Seven Veils,"

9.1 Kawakami Sadayakko as Salomé. Courtesy of Waseda University's Tsubouchi Shōyō Memorial Theater Museum.

in which the heroine performs what amounts to a striptease: Salomé slowly removes seven layers of veils while dancing in order to seduce her stepfather and make him execute Jokanaan. Because of the nature of this scene, *Salomé* is a play that would be extremely difficult, if not impossible, for a *kabuki onnagata* to perform. The whole point of the scene, and hence of the play, is to strip down the woman to her bare body, or as close to it as the censors allow. And it is indeed this scene that becomes the archetype of striptease in Japan and a pretext for pornographic materials.[5]

Comparing the two performances of Kawakami Sadayakko and Matsui Sumako, critic Osanai Kaoru wrote that Kawakami Sadayakko's performance produced in him only "feelings of disappointment and exhaustion and pity" and that it "revealed her age": "[H]er flesh was too desiccated; her blood was too dry," lacking the all-important element of sensuality. In contrast, "Matsui

9.2 Matsui Sumako as Salomé. Courtesy of Waseda University's Tsubouchi Shōyō Memorial Theater Museum.

Sumako's Salomé was quite voluptuous physically, though rather superficial and impoverished spiritually."[6]

The dancing of Kawakami was criticized by Osanai Kaoru as looking too Japanese, due to her training in Japanese dance and the lack of heft to her hips. This is another indication that *kabuki*-style gestures could not convey the overt sensuality required for the role. Matsui Sumako's dance, on the other hand, was choreographed by Giovanni Vittorio Rosi, an Italian director, and emphasized her well-endowed body. In a review in *Engei gahō*, Honma Hisao praised her "extremely able portrayal of the egoistic, aggressive, and selfish aspects of the woman called Salomé"[7] and elsewhere proclaimed that "Sumako's *Salomé* dominated all others."[8]

Photographs and drawings of the two performances suggest that this contrast was also present in the costumes. A photograph of Kawakami Sa-

9.3 Magician Shōkyokusai Tenkatsu as Salomé. Courtesy of Waseda University's Tsubouchi Shōyō Memorial Theater Museum.

dayakko's performance shows the actress in a long-sleeved dress of heavy brocade, which Osanai aptly described as "a peculiar Elizabethan robe of silver," covering her body from neck to toe. Osanai complained that so much of her body was covered in cloth that she looked like a bandaged patient. He objected in particular to the covering of the feet: He reminded the reader that in the stage design by Charles Ricketts, the floor was black so that Salomé's white bare feet would stand out. Covering Salomé's bare feet constituted a grave insult to the play.[9] This stage photograph of Kawakami Sadayakko's performance is interesting also because it places the woman in a subservient position vis-à-vis the man: Jokanaan, portrayed by Inoue Masao, has emerged from the well and stands rigid in the upper right corner of the picture. His arms are crossed in defiance, his face turned directly to the audience. Kawakami Sadayakko's Salomé, on the other hand, is situated in the lower left, her body and face turned upward at Jokanaan, arms raised as if in supplication or fear: not a very threatening figure.

In comparison, Matsui Sumako's costume revealed both of her arms up to the shoulders, as well as her bare feet. The dress was fastened at one shoulder in toga-fashion, and during the "Dance of the Seven Veils" it would come off to reveal most of her torso. Different photos show her in different stages of undress. Although in this photograph she gazes up at the erect figure of Jokanaan in a pose similar to that of Kawakami Sadayakko, one might notice that in the case of Matsui Sumako there is less vertical distance between the man and the woman.

The tide was turning against Kawakami Sadayakko's style of acting. Her Salomé was too heavily inflected with the tradition of the geisha imitating the *onnagata*; a woman acting like a male performer of female roles was not convincing in this particular role. As a woman acting like a man acting like a woman, Sadayakko embodied the kind of theatricality of gender that was in the process of being marginalized, disavowed, and foreclosed. In contrast, the audience was being won over by Matsui Sumako's new acting style of accentuating the sensuality of her woman's body. Sumako, in other words, was the embodiment of the new alignment of sex, gender, and performance.

From Sadayakko to Sumako, more and more body parts were revealed. And as this progresses, the gaze of the spectator changes as well. There is less and less of a zone of invisibility and tolerance, as the critical gaze removes layers of veils from the surface of the woman's body and then begins to penetrate into her interior. The gaze scrutinizes her motives as well as her actions, psychoanalyzing her behavior off stage as well as on stage. Sumako is pursued even into her grave, as journals publish articles after her 1919 suicide, speculating knowingly about her "abnormal psychology," which supposedly motivated her to follow her director and lover, Shimamura Hōgetsu, who had died shortly before. They toss about "medical" terminology such as hysteria and necrophilia.[10] This may be a kind of making the invisible visible—the defining feature of modern visual discipline—in one of its least palatable forms.

Yet while there is a move toward progressive revelation of more and more body parts and progressive disclosure of the interior of the body, a different kind of movement is happening on the margins, a set of moves that are disturbing to some, delightful to others, and destabilizing to all. For example, in 1915, the female magician Shōkyokusai Tenkatsu staged a performance of *Salomé*. This production featured an even more revealing costume for the heroine, but also wine goblets and veils appearing out of thin air, and Jokanaan's decapitated head talking aloud. The audience is distracted by the various objects appearing and disappearing on stage, and their gaze is deflected from the surface as well as the interior of the body of the actress. This performance, then, is both a continuation of the enterprise of modern theater and a destabilizing of the enterprise.[11]

Another actress, Shimoyama Kyōko, performed *Salomé* in 1915 in the context of a satire, as a play within a play about a lecherous director and a voluptuous actress. The director is backstage, leaning forward against the stage-set and leering at the actress dancing as Salomé on stage. At the climactic moment, the stage-set collapses and the director is thoroughly humiliated. This play was meant to poke fun at Shimoyama's rivals, the actress Matsui Sumako and her director Shimamura Hōgetsu, and *Salomé* is used to highlight and ridicule the illicit romance between them.[12] These comic and parodic representations suggest that something not unlike the "camp" elements of Oscar Wilde's own style accompanied and destabilized the surface seriousness of staging *Salomé* as part of the very serious movement to straighten, modernize, and westernize Japanese theater. Shimoyama's performance can even be read as a kind of metatheater: It stages the staging of *Salomé* and exposes to the audience's view, through a complex set of relays, their own voyeuristic gaze that structures the spectacle they are watching. It might well have acted as a critique of the structure of the visuality of sexuality and visual pleasure all together.

One year after winning the "competition," Matsui Sumako repeated her performance of *Salomé*, and the review of this revival production is accompanied by what can only be described as a "comic strip" version of *Salomé*: Caricatures of the main events in the play are presented in the upper margins, full of visual and verbal puns.[13] Salomé is transfixed, literally, by the melodious sound of Jokanaan's voice. At one point, King Herod is torn, literally, between feeling hot and cold. At another point, he is drowned, literally, in alcohol, his body trapped in a wine goblet. The comic strip version seems to serve as parodic commentary on the play, suggesting, perhaps, that we should not be taking this play all too seriously. The authority of the literary text is here taken down several pegs, first through the reduction to a telegraphic synopsis, second through the playful intertwining of visual puns, and finally through the marginalized placement of the cartoon at the edge of the page.

These parodic destabilizations notwithstanding, in premiering this role, Matsui Sumako laid the ground on which all following actresses were to tread. Her performance was noted for the sensuality of her body and announced the era of a new kind of theater and a new kind of woman: Henceforth, a woman was defined by her physicality, and that became the basis for her theatrical performance. Mizutani Yaeko, an actress of the generation following Matsui Sumako, summarizes the meaning of this role for actresses:

> The most important scene in *Salomé* is the place where she strips one veil after the other to show off the beauty of her body. Although my body is not that attractive, I performed this scene, thinking of it as being part of my training.[14]

The display of the body became the testing and training ground for actresses in the years following 1914. It was by showing their bodies that women proved they were better than *onnagata* in performing the role of women.

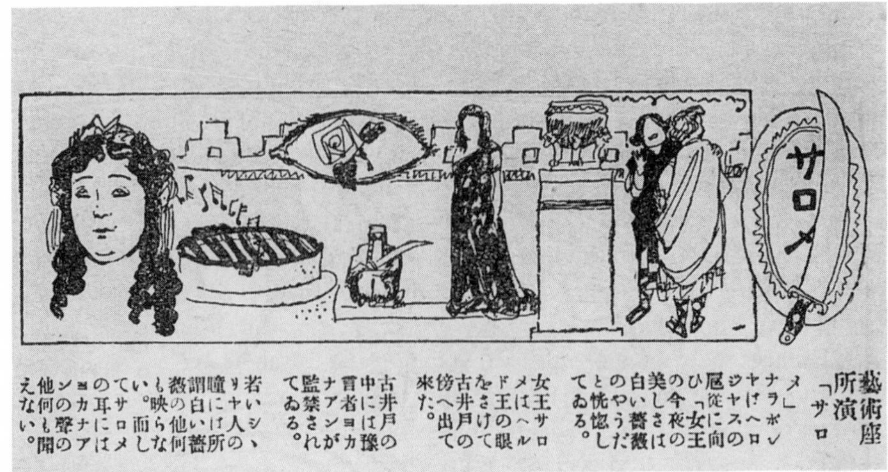

9.4 Comic strip of *Salomé. Engei gahō* (June 1915).

The display of the female body, however, did not signal an uncomplicated triumph for women. To focus on the theatrical disclosure of the female body leads easily to the commodification of woman's sexuality. The "Dance of the Seven Veils" in *Salomé* gradually became a pretext for a striptease. Actor Tanaka Eizō recalls the performance of the play in the 1920s in popular musicals and revues:

> The reason *Salomé* was so popular had something to do with the allure of the semi-nude body. This was an era when it was not possible to gawk at shapely legs in revues and when strip-shows were still unheard of—therefore being allowed to stare to one's heart's content at the body of an actress who dances for nearly an hour on stage clothed in nothing but brassier and loincloth must have been profoundly attractive to the audience at the time.[15]

By the late 1920s, geisha in Tokyo had developed a routine in which they would strip off seven layers of kimono sashes while singing "Give me Jokanaan's head."[16] *Salomé* had indeed become a pretext for stripteases and a showcase for commodified female sexuality.

Salomé, then, stands as the emblem of this time. She is the figure who could only be represented by a "real woman" on stage and therefore justified the emergence of the actress into the public sphere. Yet she is also the figure who reduced the performer representing her to a bare body, an object of the voyeuristic gaze.

We could end the story here, draw the curtains, turn off the lights. Yet, is it sufficient to have only *seen* Salomé, to have paid attention to just the visual aspects of her performance on stage?

We cannot forget that theater is a genre that makes full use of both visual and linguistic modes of communication. In theater, two semiotic modes of communication overlap: One is the linguistic mode in which the speaker/sender of the message is active and the listener/receiver of the message is passive; the other is the voyeuristic mode, according to which the viewer/receiver of the message is active and the viewed/sender of the message is passive.[17] Historically, in the linguistic mode it has been the male who speaks and the female who listens; in the voyeuristic mode it has been the female who is viewed and the male who views. This is what feminist criticism of literature and art has pointed out and sought to remedy.

Of course feminism has also emphasized the kind of activity that goes on the female side of the two modes of communication, the side that has been presumed to be passive: the active listening or reading that shapes the linguistic mode, the active showing or "to-be-looked-at-ness" that shapes the voyeuristic mode.

In theater, the genre that combines the two modes, the performer speaks and is also the one being seen, while the spectator is a listener who is also the one who looks. An actress, then, is both active and passive in multiple ways: She is seen (passive) but is also the one who shows (active). She is the one who speaks (active), but her words are presumed to be just a repetition of the words of the playwright (passive). And yet, here too, another layer of activity is revealed: It is in repetition that there is always the possibility of repeating with a difference. It is precisely such a possibility of "repetition with difference" that Judith Butler calls agency.[18]

Seen from one direction, Salomé is a woman who is forced to disrobe and display her naked body—she is precisely a fetishized object of the voyeuristic gaze. Yet considered from another angle, that same Salomé is a New Woman who speaks and moves in new and different ways, and the actress who performs her is also trained to speak and move in new ways that challenge the status quo. And these new and different ways of speaking and moving might be precisely the kinds of things that would be invisible if we only focus our attention on visuality, and precisely the kinds of things that a feminist analysis of theater cannot afford to leave out.

Let us then for a moment return to actress Mizutani Yaeko's comments about *Salomé*: "The most important scene in Salomé is the place where she strips one veil after the other to show off the beauty of her body. Although my body is not that attractive, I performed this scene, thinking of it as being part of my training." It is easy to take this quote and condemn the voyeuristic objectification of the woman's body, which is still pervasive in ways that are important for us to notice and combat. And yet, as we listen to the words of this actress, do they not also convey the development of a certain kind of awareness of the body that may not have existed before, and can we not see this kind of bodily awareness as something more than merely internalized voyeurism? Mizutani goes on to say, "At that time, I did not pick and choose my roles. I grappled with everything that was given to me, and my mind was utterly devoted to trying to incorporate [mi ni tsukeru] everything."[19] These words tell a complicated story of elusive yet persistent agency: the agency of disciplining one's mind and one's body in order to act differently, to become something other than oneself. In other words, when we regard Salomé only through the model of voyeurism, something falls out of the picture—the agency of the actress, the ability to create difference.

Salomé is about as unconstrained in expressing her own appetites as any female figure before or since. As soon as she appears on stage she pronounces "I will not stay" and goes on to enunciate verb after verb of desire, will, and demand: "I desire to speak with him;" "I will kiss thy mouth;" and, finally, "I demand the head of Jokanaan." Her words are so "unfeminine," in fact, that some have interpreted them as the veiled expression of Oscar Wilde's desire, that is, the expression of male desire for another man. Yet does not a woman, an actress, who repeats such "manly" and "unfeminine" words acquire a way of speaking that was hitherto foreign to her?

Let us also listen to Matsui Sumako herself, the words from a memoir she published shortly after performing Salomé. Here, too, we might be able to hear a new kind of voice and a new mode of speaking:

> When it comes to the art of expressing the spirit of my role on stage, I move on the basis of my own beliefs, despite my being a woman. There are many situations when I feel superior to at least some of the male actors. Yet when I try to proceed according to my own beliefs, they oppose my actions, saying "How presumptuous, she's only a woman," or "It's silly to follow a woman's

> opinion." For example, in preparing for our upcoming performance of *Salomé*, we have received instructions from Mr. Rosi. I understand clearly the psychology that should accompany those physical movements taught us by Mr. Rosi. And as long as it does not conflict with the opinion of our teachers, I eagerly immerse myself in the attempt to act out and embody this psychology, using my art in which I believe. The problem is when some person is unable to understand Mr. Rosi's psychology. That person comes up with his own interpretation and tries to force me to follow it. And when I show my displeasure, or refuse to follow, he immediately treats me as presumptuous. Even thinking about it, my eyes fill with tears of frustration. And even as I try to dry my tears, his quick eyes find me, and he damns me as "a coward who uses woman's tears." What in the world gives men the right to say such selfish things? What in the world have women done to be persecuted thus by men? They say even worms have souls; as long as women have souls, we will not tolerate being humiliated and persecuted forever. An artist with a mind less tenacious than mine would have given up her art without hesitation. She would have gone to seek solace somewhere else. But I have given up my parents and my sisters to pursue this art. My art is my one and only treasure, attained in exchange for everything in the world. I would rather die than give up this art. Therefore, I must continue to fight against this torment, and must ever continue being pulled along this path of art.[20]

A heartfelt outpouring of anguish caused by sexism? Or a carefully crafted feminist manifesto? Perhaps it was not even written by Matsui Sumako herself: It is whispered that her director, Shimamura Hōgetsu, was the ghostwriter of her memoirs. The assumption is that no woman, and certainly no mere actress, could articulate her grievances in such a manner. An actress, it is believed, merely mouths and intones the words written by others. She is not the originator of words, just a repeater.

Yet, aside from the question of who was at the origins of these words, should we not also consider the question of what changes are brought about by the repeating of such words? Should we not seriously consider how the speaking of certain words affects the speaker? Should we not seriously consider the possibility that by repeating, a woman learns a new way of speaking? Even when the words are put into her mouth by another, by a playwright in a foreign country, by her director, by her lover, or by any other man around her?

And we must also think about the kind of movement of the body acquired by the actress who performs a role such as Salomé. How does the acting out of a woman who insists on her own desire affect the body of the actress? Even when the acting is merely on stage? Does it not ripple outward and change her relationship with her choreographer, her director, her fellow actors, and her audience? How can the body move differently when it is no longer encased in a long kimono? Even as the same body is being offered to the voyeuristic gaze of the spectators? Does it not acquire an increased range of mobility, a new set of muscles, greater freedoms and powers? As the arms are released from long and heavy sleeves, against what could they now be raised in protest and in self-defense? As the legs emerge from underneath the layers of kimono, in what new directions could they now stride forth?

Actresses such as Mizutani Yaeko, Matsui Sumako, and Kawakami Sadayakko are usually not considered feminist, because their acts are judged to be physical rather than intellectual, emotional rather than rational, geared toward a selfish goal of standing isolated in the limelight rather than a communal goal of the improvement of women's lives. But we need to remember that feminism is not just about words and ideas, and that the body for feminism is not merely a transparent medium for the expression of words and ideas. Feminism is about finding one's voice, raising one's voice, and training the vocal chords to make speeches. It is about standing up, raising arms, marching, sitting in, and training the body to do new things. It is to be seen, but it is also to show. It is about a growing awareness of one's own mind and body—and about a kind of training of the mind and body that was perhaps previously only available to women who were also commodified sexually.

The figure of Salomé is a perfect symbol for the ambivalence inherent in all of the above. She is a femme fatale whose sexual threat is contained through her execution at the end of the play. Yet she is also a New Woman, perhaps even a protofeminist, who speaks and dances her sexual desire. And the actresses who performed the role of Salomé were equally complex figures who cannot be contained within facile categorizations.

Actresses in Japan stood at the confluence of multiple processes and responded to them in complex ways. Compared to *onnagata* and to geisha, they strove to differentiate themselves by insisting on their natural femininity and on their artistic purity free from commodificaton. Subjected to the ideology of wifeing, they resisted being confined into the role of good wife and wise mother. Castigated as subversive New Women, they took on that label as a title of honor. They participated in the straightening of theater, the imagining of the nation, and the reproduction of empire. And most paradoxically, they embodied the essentialist and expressive definition of gender and, by doing so, performed a new understanding of what it means to act like a woman in modern Japan.

NOTES

CHAPTER 1

1. A clarification of terminology: In this book, I use "actress" rather than "female actor" because of the complex cultural connotations that the term "actress" carried at the turn of the century in English-language theater. "*Joyū*" carries similar connotations in the Japanese context. Although I believe "actor" ought to be a gender-neutral term when applied to individuals today, historically it makes more sense to call Kawakami Sadayakko and Matsui Sumako "actresses" rather than "actors." I use "performer" to translate the Japanese term "*haiyū*." "*Haiyū*" is an ungendered term that subsumes "*dan'yū*" (male actor) and "*joyū*" (female actor, which I usually translate as "actress").
2. See for example the first line of the editor's "Introduction" in Laurence Senelick, ed., *Gender in Performance: The Presentation of Difference in the Performing Arts* (Hanover, N.H.: University Press of New England, 1992), ix-xx.
3. Ibid., ix.
4. Texts on the theatricality/performativity of gender include essays in Sue-Ellen Case, ed., *Performing Feminisms: Feminist Critical Theory and Theatre* (Baltimore, Md.: Johns Hopkins University Press, 1990); Marjorie Garber, *Vested Interests: Cross-Dressing and Cultural Anxiety* (New York: Routledge, 1992). Judith Butler's work is of course central to the debate. See her "Gender Trouble, Feminist Theory, and Psychoanalytic Discourse," in *Feminism/Postmodernism,* ed. Linda Nicholson (New York: Routledge, 1990), 324–40; "Performative Acts and Gender Constitution: An Essay in Phenomenology and Feminist Theory," in *Performing Feminisms: Feminist Critical Theory and Theatre,* ed. Sue-Ellen Case (Baltimore, Md.: Johns Hopkins University Press, 1990), 270–82; *Gender Trouble: Feminism and the Subversion of Identity* (New York: Routledge, 1990); *Bodies that Matter: On the Discursive Limits of Sex* (New York: Routledge, 1993).
5. In considering the sociological concept of "sex role," R. W. Connell suggests that the dramaturgical metaphor of "role" is "apt for situations where (a) there are well-defined scripts to perform, (b) there are clear audiences to perform to, and (c) the stakes are not too high (so it is feasible that some kind of performing is the main social activity going on)." Thus he concludes that the metaphor

of "sex role" is inappropriate for most social contexts, except in specific situations like ballroom dancing. R. W. Connell, *Masculinities* (Berkeley: University of California Press, 1995), 26.

6. Butler, *Bodies that Matter,* x.
7. Ibid., 12.
8. Butler, *Gender Trouble,* 146–47.
9. Butler, *Bodies that Matter,* 12.
10. The double meaning of "acting" is summarized by Naoki Sakai: "on the one hand, to act is to behave, to initiate a movement of the body; on the other hand, it is to disguise, to hide the inner self, to imitate and take the role of another." See Naoki Sakai, *Voices of the Past: The Status of Language in Eighteenth-Century Japanese Discourse* (Ithaca, N.Y.: Cornell University Press, 1992), 301.
11. Butler, *Bodies that Matter,* 12–13.
12. For a more nuanced account of the history of *kabuki* performed by women (*onna kabuki*), by young men (*wakashu kabuki*), and by adult men (*yarō kabuki*), see Maki Morinaga, "The Gender of Onnagata as the Imitating Imitated: Its Historicity, Performativity, and Involvement in the Circulation of Femininity," *positions: east asia cultures critique* (forthcoming).
13. See Morinaga, "The Gender of Onnagata," for a description of the circulation of femininity as a set of signs. See also Cecilia Segawa Seigle, *Yoshiwara: The Glittering World of the Japanese Courtesan* (Honolulu: University of Hawaii Press, 1993).
14. Italics in excerpt are in the original. William Elliot Griffis, vol. 2 of *The Mikado's Empire,* 2 vols., 11th ed. (New York: Harper, 1906), 515.
15. Suematsu Kenchō's *Engeki kairyō iken* (Views on theater reform), 1886, quoted in Komiya Toyotaka, ed., *Japanese Music and Drama in the Meiji Era,* trans. Edward G. Seidensticker and Donald Keene, vol. 3 of *Japanese Culture in the Meiji Era,* 14 vols. (Tokyo: Ōbunsha, 1956), 217. Suematsu was the chairman of the Engeki Kairyōkai and a prominent politician. *Engeki kairyō iken* was the transcription of a speech made by him in October of 1886. The full text of was published in one newspaper, detailed summaries were given in two others, and the full text was reprinted in three issues of the journal *Bijutsu shimpō* before appearing in book form in November of the same year. This suggests the high level of general public interest in theater reform. The group's call for modern theater buildings was to eventually culminate in the opening of Japan's "imperial theater," the Teikoku Gekijō, in 1911. This theater, which was not a state-run institution but an enterprise sponsored by prominent industrial as well as political figures, symbolizes the oblique relations that would bind theater and the state in modern Japan. See Mine Takashi, *Teikoku Gekijō kaimaku* (The opening of the Teikoku Gekijō) Chūkō Shinsho, no. 1334 (Tokyo: Chūō Kōronsha, 1996).
16. Ōzasa Yoshio, *Nihon gendai engeki shi* (History of Japanese contemporary theater), 6 vols. to date (Tokyo: Hakusuisha, 1985–1999), 1:15–28. This meant that while the social status of performers rose substantially, the performers were also incorporated into the state. Homogenization and incorporation were the principles at work, as in the case of the physical space and performance time for theater, described later.

17. Ōzasa, *Nihon,* 1:32. See Karatani Kōjin, *Origins of Modern Japanese Literature,* trans. Brett de Bary, et al. (Durham, N.C.: Duke University Press, 1993), 56–57, for discussion of the significance of the *kabuki* actor Ichikawa Danjūrō appearing without makeup or wig at this performance.
18. See, for example, Fukuzawa Yukichi's account in his *Fukuō jiden,* translated as *The Autobiography of Fukuzawa Yukichi,* trans. Eiichi Kiyooka (Lanham, Md.: Madison Books, 1992), 104–23.
19. See Lorraine Helms, "Playing the Woman's Part: Feminist Criticism and Shakespearean Performance," in *Performing Feminisms: Feminist Critical Theory and Theatre,* ed. Sue-Ellen Case (Baltimore, Md.: John Hopkins University Press, 1990), 196–206; Phyllis Rackin, "Androgyny, Mimesis, and the Marriage of the Boy Heroine on the English Renaissance Stage," *PMLA* 102, no. 1 (1987): 29–41; Juliet Dusinberre, *Shakespeare and the Nature of Women* (New York: Macmillan, 1975); Lisa Jardine, *Still Harping on Daughters: Women and Drama in the Age of Shakespeare* (Brighton, Great Britain: Harvester, 1983); Linda Woodbridge, *Women and the English Renaissance: Literature and the Nature of Womankind, 1540–1620* (Urbana: University of Illinois Press, 1984); Joan Kelly, "Did Women Have a Renaissance" in *Becoming Visible: Women in European History,* ed. Renate Bridenthal and Claudia Koonz (Boston: Houghton, 1977), 137–63.
20. I use "male performers of female roles" rather than the more familiar "female impersonator" for the sake of clarity. I realize that by doing so I may be reinscribing the binary opposition between the male and the female, the impersonating body, and the role performed by that body.
21. Elizabeth Howe, *The First English Actress: Women and Drama 1660–1700* (Cambridge: Cambridge University Press, 1992), xi.
22. John Stokes, Michael R. Booth, and Susan Bassnett, *Bernhardt, Terry, Duse: The Actress in Her Time* (Cambridge: Cambridge University Press, 1988).
23. Examples of feminist critique of theater include: Gayle Austin, *Feminist Theories for Dramatic Criticism* (Ann Arbor: University of Michigan Press, 1990); Sue-Ellen Case, *Feminism and Theatre* (New York: Methuen, 1988); Gay Gibson Cima, *Performing Women: Female Characters, Male Playwrights, and the Modern Stage* (Ithaca, N.Y.: Cornell University Press, 1993); Tracy C. Davis, "Questions for a Feminist Methodology in Theatre History," *Interpreting the Theatrical Past: Essays in the Historiography of Performance,* ed. Thomas Postlewait and Bruce A. McConachie (Iowa City: University of Iowa Press, 1989), 59–81; Jill Dolan, *The Feminist Spectator as Critic* (Ann Arbor, Mich.: UMI Research Press, 1988); Lesley Ferris, *Acting Women: Images of Women in Theatre* (New York: New York University Press, 1989); Gail Finney, *Women in Modern Drama: Freud, Feminism, and European Theater at the Turn of the Century* (Ithaca, N.Y.: Cornell University Press); J. Ellen Gainor, *Shaw's Daughters: Dramatic and Narrative Constructions of Gender* (Ann Arbor: University of Michigan Press, 1991); Lynda Hart, ed., *Making a Spectacle: Feminist Essays on Contemporary Women's Theatre* (Ann Arbor: University of Michigan Press, 1989).
24. Loren Kruger, *The National Stage: Theatre and Cultural Legitimation in England, France, and America* (Chicago: University of Chicago Press, 1992).

25. For example, James Fujii, *Complicit Fictions: The Subject in the Modern Japanese Prose Narrative* (Berkeley: University of California Press, 1992); David Pollack, *Reading Against Culture: Ideology and Narrative in the Japanese Novel* (Ithaca, N.Y.: Cornell University Press, 1992); Mary N. Layoun, *Travels of a Genre: The Modern Novel and Ideology* (Princeton: Princeton University Press, 1990).
26. Important English-language work in modern Japanese theater includes: David Goodman, *Japanese Drama and Culture in the 1960s: The Return of the Gods* (London: M. E. Sharpe, 1988); Brian Powell, *Japan's Modern Theatre: A Century of Change and Continuity* (New York: St. Martin's Press, 2001); J. Thomas Rimer, *Toward a Modern Japanese Theatre: Kishida Kunio* (Princeton: Princeton University Press, 1974); Ted Takaya, *Modern Japanese Drama: An Anthology* (New York: Columbia University Press, 1979).
27. Nonetheless, this was an important and beautiful exhibit. For the exhibit catalogue, see Samuel Leiter, ed., *Japanese Theater in the World* (New York: Japan Society, 1997).
28. Representative recent anthologies include Egusa Mitsuko and Seki Reiko eds., *Onna ga yomu Nihon kindai bungaku: feminizumu hihyō no kokoromi* (Women reading modern Japanese literature: Experiments in feminist criticism) (Tokyo: Shin'yōsha, 1992); Egusa Mitsuko and Seki Reiko, eds., *Dansei sakka o yomu: feminizumu hihyō no seijuku e* (Reading male writers: Towards the maturation of feminist criticism) (Tokyo: Shin'yōsha, 1994); Paul Gordon Schalow and Janet A. Walker, eds., *The Woman's Hand: Gender and Theory in Japanese Women's Writing* (Stanford: Stanford University Press, 1996).
29. For example, Donald Shively, "The Social Environment of Tokugawa Kabuki," in James R. Brandon, William P. Malm, and Donald H. Shively, *Studies in Kabuki: Its Acting, Music, and Historical Context* (Honolulu: University of Hawaii Press, 1978), 1–61. Other significant analyses of sexuality in the Tokugawa period can be found in Gary P. Leupp, *Male Colors: The Construction of Homosexuality in Tokugawa Japan* (Berkeley: University of California Press, 1995); and Gregory M. Pflugfelder, *Cartographies of Desire: Male-Male Sexuality in Japanese Discourse, 1600–1950* (Berkeley: University of California Press, 1999).
30. Jennifer Robertson's work on the all-female Takarazuka is crucial in this area. See especially *Takarazuka: Sexual Politics and Popular Culture in Modern Japan* (Berkeley: University of California Press, 1998). See also my review in *Journal of Japanese Studies,* 25, no. 2 (1999): 473–478. See also Kawasaki Kenko, *Takarazuka: shōhi shakai no supekutakuru* (Takarazuka: Spectacle of consumer society) (Tokyo: Kōdansha, 1999).
31. See Ayako Kano, "Towards a Critique of Transhistorical Femininity," in *Gendering Modern Japanese History,* ed. Kathleen Uno and Barbara Molony (Cambridge, Mass.: Council on East Asian Studies Publications, Harvard University, forthcoming) for a full discussion of this issue.
32. It should go without saying that the categories of "Japan" and the "West" need similar historicization, though they will receive less attention than the category of "woman." Naoki Sakai's writing is suggestive in this regard. See for example, "Nashonariti to bo(koku)go no seiji," in *Nashonariti no datsukōchiku,* ed. Sakai Naoki, Brett de Bary, and Iyotani Toshio (Tokyo: Kashiwa Shobō, 1996), 9–53.

33. Muta Kazue, *Senryaku to shite no kazoku: kindai Nihon no kokumin kokka keisei to josei* (Family as strategy: Women and the formation of the modern Japanese nation-state) (Tokyo: Shin'yōsha, 1996); Ōgoshi Aiko, *Kindai Nihon no jendā: gendai Nihon no shisōteki kadai o tou* (Modern Japanese gender: Interrogating the philosophical task of contemporary Japan) (Tokyo: San'ichi Shobō, 1997); Ueno Chizuko, *Nashonarizumu to jendā* (Engendering nationalism) (Tokyo: Seidosha, 1998).
34. Important recent analyses include: "Chapter 3: Performing Empire" in Robertson's *Takarazuka;* Ueno, *Nashonarizumu to jendā;* Wakakuwa Midori, *Sensō ga tsukuru josei zō: dainiji sekai taisen ka no Nihon josei dōin no shikaku teki puropaganda* (Images of women created by war: Visual propaganda for the mobilization of Japanese women under World War Two) (Tokyo: Chikuma Shobō, 1995); Louise Young, *Japan's Total Empire: Manchuria and the Culture of Wartime Imperialism* (Berkeley: University of California Press, 1998). See also Molony and Uno, eds., *Gendering Modern Japanese History.* On Japanese imperialism in general, see also W. G. Beasley, *Japanese Imperialism, 1894–1945* (Oxford: Clarendon Press, 1987); Peter Duus, Ramon H. Myers, and Mark R. Peattie, eds., *The Japanese Informal Empire in China, 1895–1937* (Princeton: Princeton University Press, 1989); Peter Duus, Ramon H. Myers, and Mark R. Peattie, eds., *The Japanese Wartime Empire, 1931–1945* (Princeton: Princeton University Press, 1996).

CHAPTER 2

1. Muta Kazue, *Senryaku to shite no kazoku: kindai Nihon no kokumin kokka keisei to josei* (Family as strategy: Women and the formation of the modern Japanese nation-state) (Tokyo: Shin'yōsha, 1996), 181–2.
2. For an alternate view, see Gregory M. Pflugfelder, *Cartographies of Desire: Male-Male Sexuality in Japanese Discourse, 1600–1950* (Berkeley: University of California Press, 1999).
3. Minaguchi Biyō, "Onnagata to joyū" (Onnagata and actresses), *Engei gahō* (October 1909): 76–80. Minaguchi Biyō was a member of the first class of what was to become Waseda University's literature department and a member of Tsubouchi Shōyō's study group for elocution (Rōdoku Kenkyūkai).
4. Minaguchi, "Onnagata," 76. In the Japanese, there is no distinction of plural or singular for "woman" or "man."
5. Such efforts are described in the secret treatises on the *onnagata*'s art, for example, in the famous "Ayamegusa," but were also known to the general public: "One who performs a woman on *stage* [*butaijō no onnagata*] was supposed to maintain womanly behavior even in daily life" according to Iizuka Tomoichirō, *Kabuki gairon* (Overview of kabuki) (Tokyo: Hakubunkan, 1928), 280–81. For "Ayamegusa," see Charles J. Dunn and Torigoe Bunzō, ed. and trans., *The Actors' Analects (Yakusha Rongo)* (New York: Columbia University Press, 1969), 49–66.
6. Tamura Toshiko, "Ne hanashi" ("Ne" story), *Engei gahō* (January 1912): 144–146; quote from 144.

7. Ibid., 146.
8. Ibid.
9. Ibid.
10. Hasegawa Shigure (1879–1941) is one of the few women writing for and about the theater at this time. She wrote *kabuki* plays in the traditional style, as well as modern plays such as *Aru hi no gogo* (One afternoon). Later, she became a biographer, writing a series of biographical sketches called *Bijin den* (Tales of beauties), including those of Kawakami Sadayakko and Matsui Sumako. She also founded the magazine *Nyonin geijutsu* (Woman's art), which published plays by Enchi Fumiko and others, as well as essays and short stories.
11. Hasegawa Shigure, "Kyūgeki wa onnagata" (Old plays are for *onnagata*), *Engei gahō* (January 1912): 50–52; quote from 52.
12. Ibid., 50.
13. Ibid., 52.
14. Minaguchi, "Onnagata," 77.
15. Kojima Koshū, "Geki no ikan ni yoru" (Depends on the kind of play), *Engei gahō* (January 1912): 147–51. Kojima admits that the soft voices and manners of Japanese women are due to their upbringing, and his position, as the title suggests, is that of seeing the actress as appropriate for certain kinds of plays. The question is whether or not such kinds of plays are the best for a Japanese audience. See also the discussion of the "eclectic" position below.
16. The Yūrakuza theater, built in 1908, is mentioned as an example of such a theater.
17. Mayama Seika, "Onnagata wa nagaki kenkyū no kekka" (*Onnagata* is the result of long study), *Engei gahō* (January 1912): 52–53.
18. Nakayama Hakuhō, "Joyū wa fuhitsuyō" (Actresses are unnecessary), *Engei gahō* (January 1912): 146–147.
19. Kojima, "Geki," 148.
20. This novelist had caused a major scandal several years earlier (1908) by attempting a double suicide with Hiratsuka Aki, a woman who was later to take on the name of Raichō and found the feminist literary magazine *Seitō* (Blue stockings). After the failed suicide attempt, Morita wrote a serialized novel about the incident, called *Baien* (Smoke) (1909), using Hiratsuka's letters to him. For an interesting analysis of this novel, see Egusa Mitsuko, "Watashi no shintai, watashi no kotoba: *Baien, Futon* no shūhen" (My body, my words: On *Smoke* and *The Quilt*), *Kindai 1*, vol. 5 of *Nihon bungaku shi o yomu* (Reading Japanese literary history), Yūseido Henshūbu ed., 6 vols. (Tokyo: Yūseido, 1990), 177–208.
21. Morita Sōhei, "Joshi wa oshiu bekarazu" (Women should not be taught), *Engei gahō* (January 1912): 48–50; quote from 49.
22. I am not arguing that these terms are all equivalent. But they seem to be occupying the same position in these debates, by being set against the art, artifice, and the stylized acting of *onnagata*.
23. Minaguchi, "Onnagata," 76.
24. Yanagawa Shun'yō, "Joyū wa ooi ni yūbō" (There is much hope for actresses), *Engei gahō* (January 1912): 45–48; quote from 45.
25. Ibid., 46.

26. Kema Namboku, "Joyū to onnagata no kachi" (The values of actresses and *onnagata*), *Engei gahō* (March 1912): 95.
27. The complex histories of the increasingly strict legal sanctions against theatrical sexuality (first banning women, then young men, from the stage), of the various fashions successively developed in response to these sanctions (forelocks, shaved foreheads, purple headcloths, wigs), and of the sexual fascination each of these "survival tactics" inspired in turn seem to best illustrate Judith Butler's point that "the law is not only that which represses sexuality, but a prohibition that generates sexuality or, at least, compels its directionality." Judith Butler, *Bodies that Matter: On the Discursive Limits of Sex* (New York: Routledge, 1993), 95. For a discussion of the social context of *kabuki* theater, see Donald H. Shively, "The Social Environment of Tokugawa Kabuki," in *Studies in Kabuki: Its Acting, Music, and Historical Context,* James R. Brandon, William P. Malm, and Donald H. Shively, eds. (Honolulu: University Press of Hawaii, 1978), 1–61.
28. Kema, "Joyū," 95.
29. Unthinkable, that is, except in the context of discussing the tradition of *onnagata* as "sexual perversion." This is a theme that becomes the dominant paradigm in the 1910s. See Furukawa Makoto, "Dōseiaisha no shakai shi"(The social history of homosexuals) in *Wakaritai anata no tame no shakaigaku nyūmon* (An introduction to sociology for those of you who want to know) (Tokyo: Takarajimasha, 1993), 218–222.
30. Nakayama, "Joyū," 147.
31. A women-only theater was actually to be realized soon after, in the form of the Takarazuka Revue. For a comprehensive and illuminating discussion of Takarazuka, see Jennifer Robertson's book *Takarazuka: Sexual Politics and Popular Culture in Modern Japan* (Berkeley: University of California Press, 1998) as well as her articles: "Gender-Bending in Paradise: Doing 'Female' and 'Male' in Japan," *Genders* 5 (July 89): 50–69; "The 'Magic If': Conflicting Performances of Gender in the Takarazuka Revue of Japan," in Laurence Senelick ed., *Gender in Performance: The Presentation of Difference in the Performing Arts* (Hanover, N.H.: University Press of New England, 1992), 46–67. In my view, the founding of the all-female Takarazuka as well as the persistent popularity of the all-male *kabuki* do not contradict with the formation of the modern essentialist and expressive definitions of gender. Any view of Japan as a utopia of polymorphously performative gender must be carefully qualified in light of the fundamentally conservative gender ideology of the Takarazuka management, as well as the state support responsible for the survival of the all-male *kabuki* theater as "Japanese national theater" sanitized and stripped of all hints of homosexuality.
32. Uchida Roan, "Joyū mondai" (Actress question), *Kabuki* (November 1908): 32. Uchida compares actresses to geisha and implies that in Europe actresses are the equivalent of geisha.
33. Kuwano Tōka, *Joyū ron* (On actresses) (Tokyo: Sampōdō Shoten, 1913).
34. Ibid., 124.
35. Ibid., 142–43.
36. Minaguchi, "Onnagata," 78.

37. Ibid., 78–80.
38. Kojima, "Geki," 149.
39. Ibid., 150.
40. Ibid.
41. The following section is much indebted to Morinaga Maki, "The Gender of *Onnagata* as the Imitating Imitated: Its Historicity, Performativity, and Involvement in the Circulation of Femininity" *positions: east asia cultures critique* (forthcoming).
42. Jennifer Robertson, "The Shingaku Woman: Straight from the Heart," in *Recreating Japanese Women, 1600–1945,* ed. Gail Bernstein (Berkeley: University of California Press, 1991), 88–107; quote from 90. For information about the lives of women in pre-modern Japan see also parts of Robert J. Smith and Ella Lury Wiswell, *The Women of* Suye Mura (Chicago: University of Chicago Press, 1982); Richard Varner, "The Organized Peasant: The *Wakamonogumi* in the Edo Period," *Monumenta Nipponica* 32, no. 4 (Winter 1977): 459–83; Anne Walthall, "Devoted Wives/ Unruly Women: Invisible Presence in the History of Japanese Social Protest," *Signs* 20, no. 1 (Autumn 1994): 106–36.
43. See Ueno Chizuko, "Kaisetsu" in *Fūzoku, sei* (Folk customs and sexuality), ed. Ogi Shinzō, Kumakura Isao, and Ueno Chizuko, vol. 23 of *Nihon kindai shisō taikei* (Collected Japanese modern thought), 23+1 vols. (Tokyo: Iwanami Shoten, 1990), 505–50.
44. Ibid., 519–21.
45. Rather than that of "equal rights between men and women" (*danjo dōken*).
46. Ibid., 547.
47. For a good summary, see Judith Butler, *Gender Trouble,* 106–11. "The conclusion here is not that valid and demonstrable claims cannot be made about sex-determination, but rather that cultural assumptions regarding the relative status of men and women and the binary relation of gender itself frame and focus the research into sex-determination" (109).
48. Kameda Atsuko, "Shūzoku ni miru josei kan: sekushizumu no shintō to shūzoku no hen'yō" (Views of women in folk customs: The permeation of sexism and the transformation of folk customs), *Josei no imēji* (Women's images), vol. 1 of *Kōza joseigaku* (Lectures in women's studies), ed. Joseigaku Kenkyūkai (Women's studies study group), 4 vols. (Tokyo: Keisō Shobō, 1984), 162–83; quote from 180–81.
49. Gail Bernstein, "Introduction," *Recreating Japanese Women, 1600–1945,* ed. Gail Bernstein (Berkeley: University of California Press, 1991), 1–14; quote from 6–9. Sharon H. Nolte and Sally Ann Hastings "The Meiji State's Policy Toward Women, 1890–1910," in Bernstein, *Recreating,* 151–74. Sharon Sievers, *Flowers in Salt: The Beginnings of Feminist Consciousness in Modern Japan* (Stanford: Stanford University Press, 1983), 10–25.
50. One exception to this rule were *kabuki* actors and women wearing *hakama* trousers, a fashion taken up by female students (*jogakusei*). See Article 62 of a law passed in 1873, quoted in Ogi, Kumakura, and Ueno, eds., *Fūzoku, sei,* 12.
51. Vera Mackie, *Creating Socialist Women in Japan: Gender, Labour and Activism, 1900–1937* (Cambridge: Cambridge University Press, 1997), 31–41.

52. Tachi Kaoru, "Ryōsai kenbo" (Good wife, wise mother), in *Josei no imēji* (Women's images), vol. 1 of *Kōza joseigaku* (Lectures in women's studies), ed. Joseigaku Kenkyūkai (Women's studies study group), 4 vols. (Tokyo: Keisō Shobō, 1984), 184–209; quote from 192.
53. Ōwaki Masako, "Hōritsu ni okeru josei kan" (Views of women in law), *Josei no Imēji* (Women's images), vol. 1 of *Kōza joseigaku* (Lectures in women's studies), ed. Joseigaku Kenkyūkai (Women's studies study group), 4 vols. (Tokyo: Keisō Shobō, 1984), 102–128. The "Public meeting regulations" (Shūkai jōrei) of 1880, which were passed to suppress the movement for popular rights, had barred the following categories of people from attending political lectures: military personnel, policemen, teachers and students of public and private schools, and apprentices in agriculture or the arts. The 1890 revisions to the regulations added the category of "women" (*joshi*) to these groups.
54. Furukawa Makoto, "Dōseiaisha no shakai shi," 218–22. See also Pflugfelder, *Cartographies,* 23–96.
55. Jennifer Robertson, "The Shingaku Woman," 90.
56. Saeki Junko, "Hanasaku Edo no bishōnen: ai no zankoku bigaku" (Blooming Edo's beautiful boys: The cruel aesthetics of love), in *Edo no shinjitsu: dare mo idomanakatta kinsei Nihon no wakarikata* (Edo's truth: An unprecedented way of understanding early modern Japan), (Tokyo: JICC, 1991), 218–32; quote from 223–25.
57. See Iwamoto Kenji, "Sekkin to hedatari: Close-up no shisō" (Nearness and distance: The ideology of the close-up), *Nihon eiga no tanjō* (The birth of Japanese cinema), vol. 1 of *Kōza Nihon eiga* (Lectures on Japanese cinema), 7 vols. (Tokyo: Iwanami Shoten, 1985), 250–259. Iwamoto says that around 1914 the lack of close-ups in Japanese cinema began to be criticized in Japanese cinema journals, along with the unnaturalness of using *onnagata.* See also Satō Tadao, "Nihon eiga no seiritsu shita dodai" (The foundation for Japanese cinema), in *Nihon Eiga no tanjō* (The birth of Japanese cinema), vol. 1 of *Kōza Nihon eiga* (Lectures on Japanese cinema) (Tokyo: Iwanami Shoten, 1985), 2–52.
58. Ōzasa Yoshio, *Nihon gendai engeki shi* (History of Japanese contemporary theater) 6 vols. to date (Tokyo: Hakusuisha, 1985–1999), 1:61.
59. Hagii Kōzō, *Shimpa no gei* (The art of shimpa) (Tokyo: Tōkyō Shoseki, 1984), 184. Ichikawa Kumehachi later became an instructor at Kawakami Sadayakko's Actress Training Institute and seems to have taught mostly *kabuki*-style dancing. See Matsumoto Shinko, *Meiji engeki ron shi* (A history of Meiji theater discussions) (Tokyo: Engeki Shuppansha, 1980), 943–44. On the Actress Training Institute, see chapter 4. Also see Angela Kimi Coaldrake, *Women's* Gidayū *and the Japanese Theatre Tradition* (London: Routledge, 1997) for a fascinating discussion of female performers of musical storytelling (*gidayū*).
60. One exception is the "Actress Tournament" (Joyū taikai) of 1905, in which Ichikawa Kumehachi, Chitose Beiha, and other female performers appeared in *kabuki*-style vignettes and dances. Matsumoto Shinko, *Meiji,* 927.
61. Ōzasa, *Nihon,* 1:61; Matsumoto Shinko, *Meiji,* 927.
62. By the Edo period, "*shibai*" had come to signify performance facilities that had some degree of permanence. The *Kōjien* dictionary lists the following meanings

for "*shibai,*" tracing the etymology of the term: 1) to be on the lawn, or the lawn itself; 2) seating on the lawn for performances; 3) short for "*shibai goya*" or performance shed; 4) performances, especially "*engeki*" or dramatic enactments; 5) acting, pretending.

63. "*Engeki*" is written with the characters for "extending, developing, enacting" and "drama." It seems to be a relatively new term. In canonical theater history books, the first instance of "*engeki*" as a proper noun is usually the "Engeki Kairyōkai" or the Theater Reform Society, established in 1886.
64. There is the problem of terminology that reflects a deeper problem about conceptualization of the past and present as well as the question of where modernity begins. To see the *kabuki* theater as "old" or "traditional" is to already situate one's view in the "new" or "modern" theater. A different camera angle would view the *kabuki* as an "early modern" (*kinsei*) form of theater, locating the origins of modernity in pre-1868 Japan.
65. Enami Shigeyuki and Mitsuhashi Toshiaki, *"Modan toshi kaidoku" dokuhon: arui wa kindai no "chikaku" o ōdan suru "chishiki/kenryoku" no keifugaku* (A reader to "decode the modern city:" Or, a genealogy of knowledge/power traversing the "senses" of the modern) (Tokyo: JICC, 1988).
66. Moriya Takeshi, "Geinōshi ni okeru kinsei teki naru mono" (What is early modern in performance history) *Kinsei* (Early modern period), vol. 4 of *Nihon bungaku shinshi* (A new history of Japanese literature), ed. Matsuda Osamu, 6 vols. (Tokyo: Shibundō, 1990), 169–92.
67. Moriya, "Geinōshi," 177.
68. Ibid., 178.
69. The presence of the population of spectators and art students is read by Moriya as signs of a mass society. He therefore places the beginning of Japanese mass society in the Genroku period—late seventeenth to early eighteenth centuries. The "masses" (*taishū*) consist mostly of small-scale merchants living in towns, with small families and a few employees, valuing hard work and thrift but also finding enough leisure to enjoy cruising the pleasure quarters. We might note how this picture of the "masses" is usually gendered entirely as male. The development of such a mass society is based on conditions such as the prosperity of the townspeople due to the rise of the urban economy in the early Edo period, the expansion of leisure time due to urban working conditions, and the rise of intellectual standards due to general education and publishing. According to Moriya, this participation of the masses in culture differentiates early modern Japan from medieval Japan.
70. The state's effort to reform theater culminated in, and to a certain extent subsided with, the 1911 opening of the Teikoku Gekijō, the unofficial "imperial theater." See Mine Takashi, *Teikoku Gekijō kaimaku* (The opening of the Imperial Theater) (Tokyo: Chūō Kōronsha, 1996). It is interesting to note that as far as theater reform was concerned, commercial considerations were secondary to political considerations about national prestige: Teikoku Gekijō was not a moneymaking venture, and the executives serving on its board were barely paid a salary. See Mine, *Teikoku,* 305.

CHAPTER 3

1. Her given name was "Sada," her name as a geisha was "Yakko." While in the United States, she combined the two names to create the stage name "Sadayakko," which is sometimes spelled "Sada Yacco" in English-language newspapers. To prevent confusion, I will refer to her as "Sadayakko" throughout this book.
2. The list of accounts examined for this chapter include the following:

1) Standard theater history texts: Ihara Toshio, *Meiji engeki shi* (History of Meiji theater) [1933] (Tokyo: Hōō Shuppan, 1975); Akiba Tarō, *Nihon shingeki shi* (History of Japanese new theater) [1955], 2 vols. (Tokyo: Risōsha, 1971); Kawatake Shigetoshi, *Nihon engeki zenshi* (Complete history of Japanese theater) (Tokyo: Iwanami Shoten, 1959); Ōzasa Yoshio, *Nihon gendai engeki shi* (History of Japanese contemporary theater), 6 vols. to date (Tokyo: Hakusuisha, 1985–1999), vol. 1 *Meiji, Taishō.*
2) Newspaper articles: articles from *Yorozu Chōhō, Miyako Shimbun, Yomiuri Shimbun, Chūō Shimbun, Jiyū no Tomoshibi, Niroku Shimpō, Chōya Shimbun, Hōchi Shimbun, Jiji Shimpō, Kokumin Shimbun, Mainichi Shimbun, Osaka Mainichi Shimbun, Tokyo Asahi Shimbun, Osaka Asahi Shimbun, Tokyo Nichinichi Shimbun, Kabuki Shimpō,* collected in Shirakawa Nobuo, ed., *Kawakami Otojirō, Sadayakko: shimbun ni miru jimbutsu zō* (Kawakami Otojirō, Sadayakko: Their personalities as seen in newspapers) (Tokyo: Yūshōdō, 1985).
3) Contemporaneous critiques: Hasegawa Shigure, "Madamu Sadayakko" (Madame Sadayakko), in *Shinpen: kindai bijin den* (New edition: Legends of modern beauties), ed. Sugimoto Sonoko (1936; Tokyo: Iwanami Shoten, 1985), 49–99. First published in *Fujin gahō* (Ladies illustrated journal) (March 1920); various articles in *Engei gahō.*
4) Later impressionistic reminiscences: Ozaki Hirotsugu, "Kawakami Sadayakko," *Joyū no keizu* (Genealogy of actresses) (Tokyo: Asahi Shimbunsha, 1964), 1–70; Toita Kōji, "Kawakami Sadayakko," *Monogatari kindai Nihon joyū shi* (An anecdotal history of modern Japanese actresses) (Tokyo: Chūō Kōronsha, 1980), 20–37; Satake Shingo, *Sadayakko: Honoo no Shogai* (Sadayakko: A life in flames) (Tokyo: Kōfūsha, 1984).
5) Academic studies: Yoko Chiba, "Sada Yacco and Kawakami: Performers of *Japonisme,*" *Modern Drama* 35, no. 1 (March 1992): 35–53; Jonah Salz, "Intercultural Pioneers: Otojirō Kawakami and Sada Yakko," *The Journal of Intercultural Studies* 20 (1993): 25–74; Mihara Aya, "*Geisha to samurai:* ikoku de umareta 'Dōjōji'"(Geisha and the Knight: A "Dōjōji" born in a foreign land), *Gekkan geinō* 35, no. 4 (April 1993): 26–30.
6) Women's history: Yamaguchi Reiko, *Joyū Sadayakko* (The actress Sadayakko) (Tokyo: Shinchōsha, 1982); Marukawa Kayoko, "Saishō o patoron to shita meigi kara ichiyaku kokusai joyū ichigō e" (From famed geisha patronized by prime minister in a single leap to the first international actress), in *Meiji ni kaika shita saien tachi* (Talented women blossoming in Meiji), vol. 2 of *Jinbutsu kindai*

josei shi: onna no isshō (Individuals in modern women's history: Women's lives), ed. Setouchi Harumi, 8 vols. (Tokyo: Kōdansha, 1980), 2:19–62; Sugimoto Sonoko, "Bunmei kaika ki no maboroshi no staa: Kawakami Sadayakko" (The unsung star of the civilization and enlightenment period: Kawakami Sadayakko), in *Ranse no shomin* (The populace in an age of strife), vol. 10 of *Meiji no gunzō* (Group portrait of Meiji), ed. Ozaki Hideki, 10 vols. (Tokyo: San'ichi Shobō, 1969), 41–59.

7) Fictions: Akashi Tetsuya, *Geinō chōhen shōsetsu: Kawakami Otojirō* (A grand novel about the performing arts: Kawakami Otojirō) (Tokyo: Sankyō Shoin, 1943); Ezaki Atsushi, *Jitsuroku Kawakami Sadayakko: sekai o kaketa honoo no onna* (The true records of Kawakami Sadayakko: A fiery woman who spanned the world) (Tokyo: Shin Jimbutsu Ōraisha, 1985); Fukuda Yoshiyuki, "Oppekepe" (Oppekepe), *Shingeki* (New Theater) 11, no. 1 (serial no. 128) (January 1964): 56–124; Sugimoto Sonoko, *Madamu Sadayakko* (Madame Sadayakko) (Tokyo: Shūeisha, 1980).

3. Kawatake Shigetoshi, *Nihon engeki zenshi,* 1009.
4. Ibid., 1004.
5. Ozaki, *Joyū no keizu,* 1–15.
6. Toita, *Monogatari kindai Nihon joyū shi,* 20–37.
7. On the ideology of "good wife, wise mother," see for example Koyama Shizuko, *Ryōsai kenbo to iu kihan* (The norm of good wife wise mother) (Tokyo: Keisō Shobō, 1991); Kathleen S. Uno, "The Origins of 'Good Wife, Wise Mother' in Modern Japan," in Erich Pauer and Regine Mathias, ed., *Japanische Frauengeschichte(n)* (Marburg: Förderverein Marburger Japan Reihe, 1995). See also various articles in Gail Lee Bernstein, ed., *Recreating Japanese Women, 1600–1945* (Berkeley: University of California Press, 1991).
8. Sharon H. Nolte and Sally Ann Hastings, "The Meiji State's Policy Toward Women," in Berstein, ed., *Recreating Japanese Women 1600–1945,* 151–70.
9. See for example, Anne Allison, *Permitted and Prohibited Desires: Mothers, Comics, and Censorship in Japan* (Boulder, Colo.: Westview Press, 1996).
10. Vera Mackie, *Creating Socialist Women in Japan: Gender, Labour and Activism, 1900–1937* (Cambridge: Cambridge University Press, 1997), 43.
11. Ibid., 48–49.
12. Yamaguchi Reiko, *Joyū Sadayakko* (The actress Sadayakko) (Tokyo: Shinchōsha, 1982). This is to date the most reliable and thorough account of Sadayakko's life.
13. Both the origins of geisha and their history to the present day are entangled with the history of organized sex work. Various sources locate the origin of the term "geisha" and the concept in the early to mid-eighteenth century, in the milieu of the pleasure quarters set up by the government. Originally the term was used for both male and female entertainers, specifically to refer to those trained in the performing arts such as playing *shamisen* and singing. In Yoshiwara, the most famed pleasure quarter, the geisha prided themselves on being distinct from prostitutes and not readily or routinely selling sexual services, yet across the river in Fukagawa, geisha and prostitutes were virtually indistinguishable. See Kishii Yoshie, *Onna geisha no jidai* (The eras of the female geisha) (Tokyo:

Seiabō, 1972), 3–8; Cecilia Segawa Seigle, *Yoshiwara: The Glittering World of the Japanese Courtesan* (Honolulu: University of Hawaii Press, 1993). Geisha continued to exist in the Meiji and Taishō periods, ostensibly selling their skills in art and entertainment rather than their sexual services. At least one scholar believes that geisha defined themselves against prostitutes, and that with the banning of public prostitution in 1957, the concept of the geisha as nonprostituting entertainer came to an end as well. See Kishii, *Onna geisha,* 434.

14. Murakami Nobuhiko, vol. 4 of *Meiji josei shi* (History of Meiji women), 4 vols. (Tokyo: Rironsha, 1972), 17–18.
15. Yamaguchi, *Joyū Sadayakko,* 25.
16. See Marukawa, "Saishō o patoron to shita meigi," 19–62. See also Sugimoto, "Bunmei kaika." See the difference from Sugimoto's later interpretation, below.
17. Marukawa, "Saishō o patoron to shita meigi," 27.
18. Kawakami Sadayakko, "Meika shinsō roku" (Records of the true nature of master artists), *Engei gahō* (October 1908): 80–94; quote from 80. This was supposed to be the first half of a two-part interview, but the second half was never published. The interview was recorded on September 20, 1908; the interviewer was Kawajiri Seitan.
19. Ibid., 80.
20. In an age when only the richest 4 percent of the adult male population had voting rights, Kawakami Otojirō's popularity with the masses did not translate into political success. His two campaigns were total failures. Yamaguchi, *Joyū Sadayakko,* 65–6. If he were alive today, Otojirō would surely have won a seat to the national diet.
21. For an overview, see Kano Ayako, "Nihon feminizumu ronsōshi 1: bosei to sekushuariti" (Japanese feminist debates 1: Motherhood and sexuality), in *Wādomappu feminizumu* (Wordmap feminism), Ehara Yumiko and Kanai Yoshiko, eds. (Tokyo: Shin'yōsha, 1997), 196–221.
22. Sugimoto, *Madamu Sadayakko,* 198.
23. At least since the end of the Russo-Japanese War, which produced a sizable number of widows, the various problems faced by women who had lost their husbands had become a topic of general social concern.
24. Ezaki, *Jitsuroku Kawakami Sadayakko.*
25. Kawakami Sadayakko, "Joyū rekihō roku" (Records of visits with great actresses), *Engei gahō* (February 1911): 40–46; quote from 43. Shibusawa Ei'ichi was an important politician and entrepreneur of the Meiji period. See *The Autobiography of Shibusawa Eiichi: From Peasant to Entrepreneur,* translated, with an introduction and notes, by Teruko Craig (Tokyo: University of Tokyo Press, 1994).
26. Kawakami Sadayakko, "Meika shinsō roku," 88.
27. Marukawa, "Saishō o patoron to shita meigi," 60.
28. Kawakami Sadayakko, "Otto ni wakarete nochi" (After my husband's departure), *Engei gahō* (November 1912): 169–172; quote from 171–72.
29. *Tokyo Mainichi Shimbun,* 4 October 1916, quoted in Yamaguchi, *Joyū Sadayakko,* 205.
30. *Miyako Shimbun,* 2 October 1920, quoted in Yamaguchi, *Joyū Sadayakko,* 205.

31. "Sadayakko o ika ni shobun subeki ka" (How should we dispose of Sadayakko?), *Shin engei* 1, no. 1 (March 1916): 59.
32. *Shin engei* 1, no. 3 (May 1916): 131–134.
33. Ibid., 132.
34. Ibid., 132.
35. Ibid., 131.
36. Shirakawa, ed., *Kawakami Otojirō, Sadayakko.*
37. Kawakami Otojirō and Kawakami Sadayakko, *Kawakami Otojirō, Sadayakko manyū ki* (Records of the wanderings of Kawakami Otojirō and Sadayakko), reprinted in Fujimori Eiichi, ed., *Autorō* (Outlaw), vol. 6 of *Dokyumento Nihonjin* (Documentaries of Japanese), 10 vols. (Tokyo: Gakugei Shorin, 1968), 6: 6–68.
38. Ibid., 29.
39. This series has been reprinted in Fujii Sōtetsu, ed., *Jiden Otojirō, Sadayakko* (Autobiography: Otojirō, Sadayakko) (Tokyo: San'ichi Shobō, 1984).
40. I will deal with this issue further in Part III.
41. Sugimoto, "Bunmei kaika," 42.
42. Ibid., 42–43.
43. Ibid., 43.
44. Ibid., 59.
45. Marukawa, "Saishō o patoron to shita meigi," 19–62.
46. Ibid., 62.

CHAPTER 4

1. Benito Ortolani describes *shimpa* as "the first to develop outside the *kabuki* world after the Meiji Restoration as an attempt to modernize and westernize Japan's drama. The name began to appear in the newspapers starting from the very first years of our century to distinguish the drama of the 'new school' from that of the 'old school' (*kyūha*), that is, of *kabuki.*" Benito Ortolani, *The Japanese Theatre: From Shamanistic Ritual to Contemporary Pluralism,* rev. ed. (Princeton: Princeton University Press, 1995), 233.
2. That dominant mode is what Artaud attacks as the theater of repetition and Derrida later calls the theater of logos. The meaning of these terms will be clarified later in chapter 7 in which the discussion will focus on Japanese theater's dialogue with the dominant mode.
3. Ortolani, *The Japanese Theatre,* 164.
4. Ibid., 167.
5. Asai Ryōi, *Edo meishoki* (1662), in *Zoku zoku gunsho ruijū* (Tokyo: Kokusho Kankōkai, 1906), 8: 757–758. Translated in Donald Shively, "The Social Environment of Tokugawa Kabuki," in *Studies in Kabuki: Its Acting, Music, and Historical Context,* ed. James R. Brandon, William P. Malm, and Donald H. Shively (Honolulu: University of Hawaii Press, 1978), 1–61; quote from 10.
6. Gary P. Leupp, *Male Colors: The Construction of Homosexuality in Tokugawa Japan* (Berkeley: University of California Press, 1995), 3.

7. Biddy Martin, *Femininity Played Straight: The Significance of Being Lesbian* (New York: Routledge, 1996), 73.
8. Shively, "The Social Environment," 5.
9. Iizuka Tomoichirō, *Kabuki gairon* (Overview of kabuki) (Tokyo: Hakubunkan, 1928), 282.
10. Ibid., 287.
11. Martin, *Femininity Played Straight,* 73.
12. I have been able to microfilm about a dozen of them to date, thanks to research funds provided by Cornell University and the University of Pennsylvania.
13. The *Yomiuri Shimbun* of the same date reports the same story with the same tone: "old actors lack spirit and decorum" and so forth. These and other quotes from newspapers are collected in Shirakawa Nobuo, ed. *Kawakami Otojirō, Sadayakko: shimbun ni miru jimbutsu zō* (Tokyo: Yūshōdō, 1985).
14. New commoners, or *shinheimin,* was the term used by the government to designate those who were formerly of the "non-human" caste. Actors, both old-school and new-school, were seen as closely linked to this caste.
15. Also translatable as "effeminate" or "flaccid"; I have here chosen to resist the temptation of the more gendered translations.
16. Published in *Miyako Shimbun,* 19 August 1894, rpt. in Shirakawa, *Kawakami,* 160.
17. Matsumoto Shinko, *Meiji engeki ron shi* (A history of Meiji theater discussions) (Tokyo: Engeki Shuppansha, 1980), 182–85.
18. Similarly Orientalized representations of the Chinese can be found in Kobayashi Kiyochika's satirical prints about the Sino-Japanese War, in the collection of the University of Pennsylvania Museum. Also see Frank Chance, "Images of Victory: Woodblock Prints from the Sino-Japanese War," paper presented at the Mid-Atlantic Regional Conference of the Association for Asian Studies, Towson State University, October 1995.
19. See, for example, Marjorie Garber's discussion of crossdressing, passing, and espionage in the essay "Phantoms of the Opera: Actor, Diplomat, Transvestite, Spy." Garber, *Vested Interests: Cross-Dressing and Cultural Anxiety* (New York: Routledge, 1992), 234–66.
20. Kawatake Shigetoshi, *Nihon engeki senshi,* (The complete history of Japanese theater) (Tokyo: Iwanami Shoten, 1959), 855–57.
21. "Haiyū ni odori wa iranu" (Actors don't need to dance), *Jiji Shimpō,* 30 January 1903; rpt. in Shirakawa, *Kawakami,* 375.
22. "Drama" and "dance" are written with *kanji* characters usually read as "*engeki*" and "*butō.*" In this article, however, the characters are glossed in *katakana* as "do-ra-ma," "da-n-su."
23. "Shimpa engeki no hensen" (Changes in new-school theater) *Tokyo Nichinichi Shimbun,* 1 January 1904; quoted in Kurata, *Kindai geki no akebono* (The dawn of modern drama) Mainichi Sensho, no. 4 (Tokyo: Mainichi Shimbunsha, 1981), 185–187.
24. Judith Lynne Hanna, *To Dance is Human: A Theory of Nonverbal Communication* (Chicago: University of Chicago Press, 1987), 19.

25. Pointing out that any kind of writing is both verbal and visual, and any kind of oral utterance is both verbal and gestural, Naoki Sakai asks, "How is one to differentiate, then, the text of bodily movement from a visual or verbal text? Or how is one not to differentiate them? . . . Characteristics that may appear to adhere to the features of one kind of text could well be viewed as another kind of text. And it is only insofar as one categorization of the text is opposed to a different one that it can possibly be qualified as a specific kind of text." Naoki Sakai, *Voices of the Past: The Status of Language in Eighteenth-Century Japanese Discourse* (Ithaca, N.Y.: Cornell University Press, 1992), 137–38.
26. Immanuel Kant, *Critique of Judgment,* trans. J. H. Bernard (New York: Hafner, 1951), 45–73.
27. Sakai, *Voices of the Past,* 169.
28. "Performative" is used here not strictly in the theatrical sense but in the sense of speech-act theory.
29. Note that Naoki Sakai defines song as located on the border between verbal and nonverbal behavior, and between direct and indirect speech. He also sees it as a kind of technology of the subject. See his "'Jō' to 'kanshō': seiai no jōcho to kyōkan to shutai-teki gijutsu o megutte" ("Feeling" and "sentiment": On sexual affections, common feeling, and subjective technology), in vol. 2 of *Jendā no Nihonshi,* ed. Wakita Haruko and Susan B. Hanley, 2 vols. (Tokyo: Tokyo University Press, 1995), 2: 137–177.
30. The irony, of course, is that the military uses much music and dance, for instance in its choreographed formations, its fighting songs, and its marching bands. There are aspects of the military that are about straightness, but there are also aspects that are entirely unstraight. The Kawakami troupe ended up focusing on both aspects of the military body: It was both choreographed and able to break free from choreography. Thanks to Joe Murphy for reminding me of the complexity of the military.
31. These critiques and the replies from the performers of *The Transfer of Edo Castle* were published in a series of articles entitled "Gekikai no sakki" (Murderous tension in the theater world) in *Miyako Shimbun,* 10 July to 25 July 1903; rpt. in Shirakawa, *Kawakami,* 394–403.
32. Gotō Chūgai, "Shin mugen geki o okosu no yō naki ka" (Is there not a need to establish a new theater of dreams and fantasy?) *Shin shōsetsu* (March 1905), quoted in Matsumoto Shinko, *Meiji Engeki,* 462.
33. For an insightful discussion of melodrama in the context of Japanese performance and cinema, see Joseph A. Murphy, "Approaching Japanese Melodrama," *East-West Film Journal* 7, no. 2 (July 1993): 1–38.
34. Sakai, *Voices of the Past,* 150.
35. This lack of differentiation also had to do with a lack of concern for enunciation. Enunciation is the act of producing an oral or written product, contrasted to the resulting product, which is called the enunciated. The definitions are circular: An act of enunciation is that which produces an enunciated; any enunciated exists only because of a foregoing enunciation. Enunciation is a fleeting process, since it is an act that can never be repeated in an identical manner. As a listener or reader, one can never seize hold of an act of enunciation but can only deal with

the traces of the enunciation. For a concise definition of enunciation versus enunciated, see Robert Stam, et al., *New Vocabularies in Film Semiotics: Structuralism, Post-Structuralism and Beyond* (London: Routledge, 1992), 105–7.

36. Roland Barthes, *Image, Music, Text,* trans. Stephen Heath (New York: The Noonday Press, 1988), 175.
37. Ibid., 177. Barthes goes on to point out that "Bunraku evidently excludes improvization, doubtless aware that the return to spontaneity is the return to all those stereotypes which go to make up our 'inner depths.' Here we have, as Brecht saw in connection with the oriental actor whose lesson he wished to receive and propagate on this point too, the reign of the *quotation,* the pinch of writing, the fragment of code, none of the promoters of the action being able to take responsibility in his own person for what he is never alone in writing." Barthes, *Image,* 177–78.
38. Sakai, *Voices of the Past,* 164. While narration (indirect speech) comes into its own in the form of the modern novel, dialogue (direct speech) is consolidated into drama. Noguchi Takehiko traces this process, focusing on "invention" of the third person viewpoint (*sanninshō),* which he connects with the process of phonocentrification and vernacularization associated with the language reform of the modern period. The corollary of the separation of the third person narrator in prose narrative (*shōsetsu*) seems to me to be the separation of dialogue (*serifu*) in theater from the narration (*katari*). See Noguchi Takehiko, *Sanninshō no hakken made* (Until the discovery of the third person) (Tokyo: Chikuma Shobō, 1994).
39. Sakai, *Voices of the Past,* 206.
40. Antonin Artaud writes "No one in Europe knows how to scream any more, and particularly actors in trance no longer know how to cry out. Since they do nothing but talk and have forgotten they ever had a body in the theater, they have naturally also forgotten the use of their windpipes." Artaud, *The Theater and Its Double,* trans. Mary Caroline Richards (New York: Grove Press, 1958), 141.
41. Sakai, *Voices of the Past,* 301.
42. A spasm that is uncontrolled may be unmediated, but it is on the borderline of being an "action" and may be closer to "unaction." Similarly, an unmediated cry or grunt may be close to direct, but it is on the border of speech and unspeech. "Everything that acts is a cruelty. It is upon this idea of extreme action, pushed beyond all limits, that theater must be rebuilt." Artaud, *The Theater,* 85. This extreme action might be direct action, though what Artaud had in mind for his "Theater of Cruelty" in fact borrows heavily from Balinese and Japanese "indirect" theater actions.
43. See Jacques Derrida, *Margins of Philosophy,* trans. Alan Bass (Chicago: University of Chicago Press, 1982), 3–27.
44. Sakai, *Voices of the Past,* 171.
45. Joan Riviere, "Womanliness as a Masquerade," in *Formations of Fantasy,* ed. Victor Burgin, James Donald, and Cora Kaplan (London: Methuen, 1986), 35–44; quote from 38.
46. Luce Irigaray, *This Sex Which Is Not One,* trans. Catherine Porter and Carolyn Burke (Ithaca, N.Y.: Cornell University Press, 1985), 76.

47. Luce Irigaray, *The Irigaray Reader,* ed. Margaret Whitford (Oxford: Basil Blackwell, 1991), 8.
48. Elizabeth Wright, ed., *Feminism and Psychoanalysis: A Critical Dictionary* (Oxford: Basil Blackwell, 1992), 243.
49. Judith Butler, *Gender Trouble: Feminism and the Subversion of Identity* (New York: Routledge, 1990), 141.
50. Ibid., 140, 141.
51. *Jiji Shimpō,* 10 June 1908; quoted in Matsumoto Shinko, *Meiji Engeki,* 924.
52. In the Edo period (1600–1868), the general populace was divided into four ranks: warriors, farmers, artisans, and merchants. Merchants were considered the lowest of the four, though their economic power increased in the later years of the period. The Meiji government abolished these ranks, and many former merchants rose to positions of power. Shibusawa Ei'ichi was born to a prosperous agricultural family but rose to political and social power through his financial acumen. *Around the World in Seventy Days* depicts the phenomenon of the "instant-gentleman" (*niwaka shinshi*), whose social status was gained through economic enterprise, as distinguished from the old aristocracy, whose status depends on blood lineage.
53. Reported in *Jiji Shimpō,* 16 September 1908; rpt. in Shirakawa, *Kawakami,* 466–467.
54. Published in *Yorozu Chōhō,* 7 August 1908; rpt. in Shirakawa, *Kawakami,* 460–461.
55. *Miyako Shimbun,* 17 September 1908; rpt. in Shirakawa, *Kawakami,* 467.
56. *Yamato Shimbun,* 16 September 1908; quoted in Kurata, *Kindai geki,* 224.
57. Ōzasa Yoshio, *Nihon gendai engeki shi,* 6 vols. to date (Tokyo: Hakusuisha, 1985–1999), 1:27.
58. See Mine Takashi, *Teikoku Gekijō kaimaku* (The opening of the Imperial Theater), Chūkō Shinsho, no. 1134 (Tokyo: Chūō Kōronsha, 1996), 221–35.
59. Kawakami Otojirō, *Jiden Otojirō, Sadayakko* (Autobiography: Otojirō, Sadayakko), ed. Fujii Sōtetsu (Tokyo: San'ichi Shobō, 1984), 84–85.
60. Kurata, *Kindai geki,* 166.
61. Ōzasa, 1: 68–69.
62. For a discussion of *giri* and *ninjō,* see Sakai, "'Jō' to 'kanshō.'"
63. Serialized first in *Chūō Shimbun,* 6 January to 6 March 1901. Reprinted as *Jiden Otojirō Sadayakko;* quote from 174–75. Also see Kawakami Otojirō "Sekaiteki engeki o okosu no hitsuyō" (The need to found a world-class theater), *Tokyo Asahi Shimbun,* 13–19 October 1902. In this article, he argued for the establishment of actors' schools and the reform of plays to suit modern morality, critiqued his former political plays for lack of aesthetic consideration, and pleaded for the improvement of the social status of actors and the building of national theaters.
64. Ogasawara Kyōko, *Toshi to gekijō: chū kinsei no chinkon, yuraku, kenryoku* (Cities and theaters: Soul-quelling, play, and power in from the middle ages to the early modern period), Heibonsha Sensho, no. 14 (Tokyo: Heibonsha, 1992).
65. Enami Shigeyuki and Mitsuhashi Toshiaki, *Modan toshi kaidoku dokuhon: arui wa kindai no chikaku o ōdan suru chishiki/kenryoku no keifugaku* (A reader to

decode the modern city: Or, a genealogy of knowledge/power traversing the senses of the modern), Bessatsu Takarajima, no. 75 (Tokyo: JICC, 1988), 92.

66. Enami and Mitsuhashi point out that the Moritaza relocated to a place that had been the Shin Shimabara pleasure quarters: There is still some reference to the theater district as a place outside the norms and laws of ordinary society (*ikai, akusho*). None of the changes discussed below happened overnight or in a smooth progression. It was a contentious, if fairly rapid, process with many contradictions and "regressions."
67. Shively, "Social Environment," 11.
68. Iizuka, *Kabuki gairon,* 57.
69. Enami and Mitsuhashi, *Modan toshi,* 98–99; Ōzasa, *Nihon,* 1:30–31.
70. According to Ōzasa, the Kabukiza was built in Western-style on the outside, Japanese-style on the inside. When the purely Western style Teikoku Gekijō theater was built in 1911, the Kabukiza was renovated in purely Japanese style. From this architectural genealogy alone, we can sense the "traditionalization" of *kabuki* as Japanese national theater.
71. The Yurakuza was smaller than the traditional theaters, had chair seating on the first floor, and forbid eating except in the dining area. See Kawatake, *Nihon engeki zenshi,* 894–895.
72. "Teikoku" means "empire." Together with the Teikoku Joyū Yōseijo (Imperial actress training institute) established in 1908 and Teikoku Gekijō (Imperial theater) built in 1911, the names reflect the rise of general empire consciousness in late Meiji Japan.
73. Kurata, *Kindai geki,* 249–50.
74. *Osaka Mainichi Shimbun,* 8 June 1910; *Osaka Asahi Shimbun,* 10 June 1910; rpt. in Shirakawa, *Kawakami,* 482–483.
75. It was soon superseded in those criteria by the Imperial Theater (Teikoku Gekijō), which opened in February 1911. It had the support of major industrialists and was equipped with total chair seating, a smoking room, a powder room, a promenade, a roof garden, etc. It extended the management system Kawakami introduced by abolishing tea houses and selling tickets directly to spectators. See Mine Takashi, *Teikoku Gekijō kaimaku* (The opening of the Imperial Theater), Chūkō Shinsho, no. 1334 (Tokyo: Chūō Kōronsha, 1996); Kawatake Shigetoshi, *Nihon engeki zenshi,* 896–899; Kurata Yoshihiro *Kindai geki no akebono,* 219–221.
76. Enami and Mitsuhashi, *Modan toshi,* 92–6.
77. Hatoyama Kazuo, "Engeki kairyō" (Theater reform), *Engei gahō* (January 1907): 69–71; quote from 70. Hatoyama also proposes reforms of theater buildings and prohibiting eating and smoking. Similar proposals for reform are made by Ishikawa Mikiaki, editor of the newspaper *Jiji Shimpō.* See his "Yonkajō no yōkyū" (Four demands), *Engei gahō* (May 1907): 1–3. His demands are 1) shortening the time of performance; 2) abolishing the tea house (*chaya*) that acts as an expensive middleman between audience and performer; 3) eliminating the partitions of seating; and 4) prohibiting eating and drinking. Many of these proposals were in the process of being implemented by the Kawakami troupe.
78. These principles were published in *Miyako Shimbun,* 15 October 1903; rpt. in Shirakawa, *Kawakami,* 413.

79. "Engeki kairyō no dai ippō" (The first step of theater reform), *Hōchi Shimbun,* 31 October 1903, rpt. in Shirakawa, *Kawakami,* 413–417.
80. *Yomiuri Shimbun,* 18 January, 1904; rpt. in Shirakawa, *Kawakami,* 423–425.
81. *Yomiuri Shimbun,* 17 June, 1905; rpt. in Shirakawa, *Kawakami,* 458.
82. Michel Foucault, *Discipline and Punish: The Birth of the Prison,* trans. Alan Sheridan, 2nd ed. (New York: Vintage, 1995), 163–66.
83. Eve Sedgwick, *Between Men: English Literature and Male Homosocial Desire* (New York: Columbia University Press, 1985), 1.
84. Naoki Sakai, *Translation and Subjectivity: On "Japan" and Cultural Nationalism* (Minneapolis: University of Minnesota Press, 1997), 216 n. 26.
85. Mainstream *shimpa* develops its own curious aesthetic based on the coexistence of *onnagata and* actresses. On *shimpa* aesthetic, see Hagii Kōzō, *Shimpa no gei* (The art of shimpa) (Tokyo: Tokyo Shoseki, 1984).
86. Homosexual acts as part of the samurai culture may have been more hegemonic and even *normative* than antihegemonic and transgressive. See Leupp, *Male Colors,* 3. They also preceded the installation of the straight/queer opposition in modernity.
87. Sakai defines "intertextuality" as "the regime of possible channels between verbal and nonverbal texts" that changes from one discursive space to another. Sakai, *Voices of the Past,* 13. My understanding of "intertextuality" and "framing" in relation to gender and sexuality comes from Joseph Murphy's incisive comments on an earlier draft of this chapter.
88. This sentimentality (*kanshō*) is not private, but communal; it sublates singularity into generality. It is used to create a community that transcends political difference and is opposed to real feeling (*jō*), which can disrupt such a community. *Jō* is what cannot be captured in representation, the otherness of the Other. Naoki Sakai, *Translation and Subjectivity,* 213–214. Sentiment (*kanshō*) on the other hand, is what is imagined, erroneously, to be most private, and therefore is the best means for ideology to work by being internalized. Sakai Naoki, "'Jō' to 'kanshō,'" 145–46. For a discussion of sentimentality in the context of the popular vocal art of "*naniwabushi,*" see Hyōdō Hiromi, *"Koe" no kokumin kokka: Nihon* ("Voice" and nation-state: Japan) (Tokyo: NHK Books, 2000).
89. Jennifer Robertson points out a related, though more complicated, strategy for reproducing imperialism that operated in the performances of the all-female Takarazuka Revue: Just as there was a process of assimilation (*dōka*) in performance, which involved "the production of the external markers of a character through technical expertise (*kata*), as well as the dialogical creation of a character's inner life, in order to animate the role," there was a process of assimilation in Japanese colonial policy: "Asian peoples were pressed to become Japanese in outward appearance and behavior, and in Japan, foreign institutions and artifacts were rendered indigenous by their infusion with an ineffable 'Japanese spirit.'" Robertson, *Takarazuka,* 94–95.
90. For a suggestive discussion of Takeuchi Yoshimi's thoughts on nationalism, see Satō Izumi, "Kindai bungaku shi no kioku/bōkyaku" (The remembering/forgetting of modern literary history), *Gendai shisō* 27, no. 1 (January 1999): 170–182.

CHAPTER 5

1. Kawakami Sadayakko, interview, "Meika shinsō roku 23" (True Records of Masters 23), *Engei gahō* (October 1908): 80–94; quote from 89. For Kawakami Otojirō's version of events, see *Kawakami Otojirō, Sadayakko man'yū ki* (Records of the wanderings of Kawakami Otojirō and Sadayakko), reprinted in Fujimori Ei'ichi, ed., *Autorō* (Outlaw), vol. 6 of *Dokyumento Nihonjin* (Documentaries of Japanese), 10 vols. (Tokyo: Gakugei Shorin, 1968), 6: 6–68.
2. Quoted in Kawakami Otojirō, *Jiden Otojirō, Sadayakko* (Autobiography: Otojirō, Sadayakko), ed. Fujii Sōtetsu (Tokyo: San'ichi Shobō, 1984), 65.
3. Kawakami Sadayakko, interview, "Meika shinsō roku 23," 92.
4. Ibid., 94.
5. In March of 1900, the troupe reached New York, and a full-length review praising "Otojirō Kawakami, who is considered the Henry Irving of Japan, and Sada Yacco, the most distinguished emotional actress of that empire" appeared in the *New York Times,* entitled "Plays in Japanese: Otojiro Kawakami and Sada Yacco Appear in Three Pieces at the Berkeley Lyceum," *New York Times,* 2 March 1900, 7:2.
6. "Japanese Plays in Boston: Actors and Dramatic Students from Tokio Present Two of Them," *New York Times,* 6 December 1899, 8:7.
7. Yamaguchi Reiko, *Joyū Sadayakko* (Actress Sadayakko) (Tokyo: Shinchōsha, 1982), 108–22.
8. Orientalism is defined here as the positing of a feminized, exotic object of knowledge and desire that secures the position of a masculinized, stable, Western subject. In a by now classic formulation, Edward Said has pointed out how "the Orient has helped to define Europe (or the West) as its contrasting image, idea, personality, experience." Edward Said, *Orientalism* (New York: Vintage, 1978), 1–2. The Orient has been feminized by Orientalists, with an insistence on "its silent indifference, its feminine penetrability, its supine malleability." Ibid., 206.
9. Louis Fournier, *Kawakami and Sada Yacco* (Paris: Brentano's, 1900), 17.
10. By lyricist William Schwenk Gilbert (1836–1911) and composer Arthur Seymour Sullivan (1842–1900).
11. Music by Giacomo Puccini (1858–1924) based on the 1900 play by David Belasco (1853–1931). For a fascinating exploration of the history of Orientalism and the reception of *Madame Butterfly,* see Colleen Lye, "*M. Butterfly* and the Rhetoric of Antiessentialism: Minority Discourse in an International Frame," in *The Ethnic Canon,* ed. David Palumbo-Liu (Minneapolis: University of Minnesota Press, 1995), 260–89.
12. Fournier, *Kawakami,* 34.
13. Both of these are elaborate and traditional styles of knotting hair.
14. "Kichō no shin haiyū Kawakami Otojirō" (The return of the new actor Kawakami Otojirō," *Chūō Shimbun* 4 January 1901 (Meiji 34); rpt. in Shirakawa Nobuo, ed., *Kawakami Otojirō, Sadayakko: shimbun ni miru jimbutsu zō* (Kawakami Otojirō, Sadayakko: Their personalities as seen in newspapers) (Tokyo: Yūshōdō, 1985), 341.

15. Kubota Beisai, "Parii no Kawakami shibai" (Kawakami's performances in Paris), 31 August to 4 September 1900 (Meiji 33); rpt. in Shirakawa, *Kawakami,* 324–27. For summaries of reactions to the Kawakami troupe's performances abroad, see the round-table discussion "Kawakami Otojirō Ichiza no kaigai kōen o megutte" (On Kawakami Otojirō troupe's performances abroad), *Nihon engeki gakkai kiyō* (Proceedings of the Japan Theater Studies Association) 16 (1976): 74–94. For reactions in the United States, see Jonah Salz, "Intercultural Pioneers: Otojirō Kawakami and Sada Yakko," *The Journal of Intercultural Studies* (Kansai University of Foreign Studies Publication, Japan) 20 (1993): 25–74. For reactions in France, see Shionoya Kei, *Shirano to samurai tachi* (Cyrano and the Samurais) (Tokyo: Hakusuisha, 1989). (This book was first published in French and is based on Shionoya's Ph.D. dissertation for the University of Paris.) For reactions in Britain, see Yoko Chiba, "Sada Yacco and Kawakami: Performers of *Japonisme,*" *Modern Drama* 35, no. 1 (March 1992): 35–53.
16. For background on the Japanese Villages and on the anxiety of the Japanese government about being represented abroad, see Kurata Yoshihiro, *1885 nen London Nihonjin mura* (1885 London Japanese Village) (Tokyo: Asahi Shimbunsha, 1983).
17. The tours of these acrobats have been studied in detail by Mihara Aya. See "Karuwaza shi no Rondon kōgyō: Roiyaru Raishiumu Gekijō, 1868 nen" (Japanese *artistes* at the Royal Lyceum 1868), *Geinōshi kenkyū* (History of the performing arts) no. 110 (July 1990): 44–66; "Gōhō to higōhō no hazama de: Tetsuwari Ichiza no San Furanshisuko kōgyō" (Between legal and illegal: The San Francisco performances of the Tetsuwari troupe), *Geinōshi kenkyū* no. 119 (October 1992): 25–46. The title of the latter article refers to the fact that the Tetsuwari troupe may have left Japan before they were issued official visas.
18. Kurata, *1885nen,* 96.
19. Four months after the opening, the Village burned down; the inhabitants moved to Berlin, where the response was on the whole negative, especially regarding the "ugliness of the women." Ibid., 87. After spending a few months each in Berlin and Munich, the Villagers returned to London, opening the Village again in December of 1885. Finally in 1887, the Village closed and the members dispersed.
20. Kurata, *1885nen,* 186–89.
21. The Japanese word used is "*hakurankai,*" and can cover small-scale local fairs as well as global events, which are called "world's fair" in the United States and "great exhibition" in Britain. The Japanese word for the latter kind of event is "*bankoku hakurankai*" (literally, exhibition of ten thousand nations). I will use the word "exhibition" to translate "*hakurankai*" in general, and the word "world's fair" to translate "*bankoku hakurankai*" in particular. For a definition of these terms, see Yoshimi Shun'ya, *Hakurankai no seijigaku: manazashi no kindai* (The politics of world's fairs: The modernity of vision), Chūkō Shinsho, no. 1090 (Tokyo: Chūō Kōronsha, 1992), 25.
22. Martin Jay, "Scopic Regimes of Modernity," in *Vision and Visuality,* ed. Hal Foster, Dia Art Foundation Discussions in Contemporary Culture, no. 2 (Seattle: Bay Press, 1988), 3–28.
23. Yoshimi, *Hakurankai,* 265.

24. Yoshimi, *Hakurankai,* 34–40.
25. Michel Foucault, *The Order of Things: An Archaeology of the Human Sciences* (New York: Vintage Books. 1973).
26. Yoshimi, *Hakurankai,* 76.
27. R. W. Rydell, *All the World's a Fair* (Chicago: University of Chicago Press, 1984). Quoted in Yoshimi, *Hakurankai,* 187–94.
28. Yoshimi analyzes the depiction in *The Illustrated London News* of May 20, 1862, of the first official Japanese fair-goers: Members of a delegation including Fukuzawa Yukichi and Fukuchi Gen'ichirō. In the illustrations, it appears that the Japanese visitors, clad in full samurai garb, themselves became curious spectacles for the European visitors.
29. Yoshimi, *Hakurankai,* 260.
30. Ibid., 212–14.
31. Michel Serres, *Jouvences sur Jules Verne* (Paris: Éditions de Minuit, 1974). On this topic, see also William Butcher, *Verne's Journey to the Centre of the Self: Space and Time in the* Voyages extraordinaires (New York: St. Martin's Press, 1990). For discussions of this novel, see also Kenneth Alcott, *Jules Verne* (New York: Macmillan, 1941), 169; Peter Costello, *Jules Verne: Inventor of Science Fiction* (London: Hodder and Stoughton, 1978), 118–21; I. O. Evans, *Jules Verne and His Work* (London: Arco, 1965), 69–71. Simone Vierne, *Jules Verne* (Paris: Balland, 1986) is the most thorough study of Verne's novels. For an admirable exception to the apolitical interpretations, see Jean Chesneaux, *Une lecture politique de Jules Verne* (Paris: Librarie François Maspero, 1971). For an English translation of Chesneaux, see *The Political and Social Ideas of Jules Verne,* trans. Thomas Wikeley (London: Thames and Hudson, 1972).
32. Pierre Macherey, "Quelques œuvres, Jules Verne ou le récit en défaut," *Pour une théorie de la production littérature* (Paris: Maspero, 1966). Quoted in Vierne, *Jules Verne,* 288.
33. "But Phileas Fogg, who was not traveling, but only describing a circumference, did not bother to inquire into these subjects; he was a solid body, traversing an orbit around the terrestrial globe according to the laws of rational mechanics. He was at this moment calculating in his mind the number of hours spent since his departure from London, and had it been in his nature to make a useless gesture, would have rubbed his hands in satisfaction." Jules Verne, *Around the World in Eighty Days,* trans. Jacqueline Rogers (New York: Signet-Penguin, 1991), chapter 11, 60.
34. Whereas Phileas Fogg is a passport circling the globe, Passepartout is all eyes, ears, and thumbs. Passepartout is representative of the traveler who engages with the local people, who talks to them, fights with them, and performs in theaters with them. Yet this open-eyed and open-mouthed mode of traveling is only made possible by his being Fogg's servant. While Passepartout's stance may be superficially more attractive to us, it is actually a clever camouflage that hides the exertion of power, discussed below, that makes any global travel possible.
35. It is important to note that while Verne the Frenchman is poking fun at British mentality through his portrayal of Fogg, he is not critical of the mode of the journey itself.

36. Although there were remarkable female travelers, including women who were inspired by Verne's novel to attempt traveling around the world in less than eighty days. In 1889–1890, Nellie Bly, an American journalist, made the round-trip in 72 days, 6 hours, 11 minutes and 14 seconds. In 1891, another journalist, Elizabeth Bisland, made the trip in 73 days. See Peter Costello, *Jules Verne,* 121.
37. Thurston Clarke, afterword, *Around the World in Eighty Days,* by Jules Verne, trans. Jacqueline Rogers (New York: Signet-Penguin, 1991), 246–53; quote from 246.
38. Chesneaux, *The Political and Social Ideas of Jules Verne,* 37.
39. Ibid., 112.
40. Chesneaux asserts that Verne never mentions the Meiji Restoration of 1868, but he is only partially right. Verne refers to the event, the return of the emperor (the Mikado) to power, though he does not specify the date: "At dawn on the 13th the *Carnatic* entered the port of Yokohama. This is an important way station in the Pacific, where all the mail steamers, and those carrying travelers between North America, China, Japan, and the Oriental islands, put in. It is situated in the bay of Yeddo, and at but a short distance from that second capital of the Japanese Empire, and the residence of the Tycoon, the civil Emperor, before the Mikado, the spiritual Emperor, absorbed his office in his own." Verne, *Around the World,* chapter 22, 142.
41. Ibid., 143. Emphasis mine.
42. For a provocative discussions of these concepts, see Mary Louise Pratt, *Imperial Eyes: Travel Writing and Transculturation* (London: Routledge, 1992).
43. Verne, *Around the World,* 151.
44. Chesneaux, *The Political and Social Ideas of Jules Verne,* 82.
45. Vierne, *Jules Verne,* 257.
46. Ibid., 245.
47. Most likely a translation by Inoue Tsutomu (1888). An earlier version of the play had been performed in 1897 (Meiji 30). The *Kabuki Shimpō* of February 1897 (no. 1666) reports that the play consisted of eight acts, reaching San Francisco in the fourth act, India in the fifth, Hong Kong in the sixth, returning to Japan in the seventh act. Compared to the version of 1910, it lacked the "London scene" described below and all female parts were performed by *onnagata.*
48. Benedict Anderson, *Imagined Communities: Reflections on the Origin and Spread of Nationalism,* 2d. ed. (London: Verso, 1991). Japan is discussed in 94–99.
49. Fukuhara Takeo is at once a samurai, a Westernized gentleman, and a loyal Japanese subject. That these identities do not contradict is emblematic of this historical moment. Using the example of Uchimura Kanzō, Karatani Kōjin points out how the process of a Tokugawa samurai becoming a Christian and a Meiji national subject exemplifies "the dialectical process through which the 'subject' emerges in the condition of 'being subject to the Lord.'" Karatani Kōjin, *Origins of Modern Japanese Literature,* 95.
50. Kawakami Otojirō, *Jiden,* 84–85.
51. "Joyū rekihō roku" (Records of visits with great actresses), *Engei gahō* (February 1911): 40–46.

52. Masuda Tarōkaja, *Oshi ryokō* (Dumb Travel) unpublished script, Theater Museum at Waseda University.
53. Quotes of actresses Hanaura Sakiko (Ms. Lily), Suzuki Utako (German officer), Miyashita Nobuko (Western lady and French officer), Kayano Kikuko (Japanese officer) Nishinaka Naoko (American officer); *Engei gahō* (October 1908): 70–74.
54. This is one solution, albeit a drastic and not very felicitous one, to the problem Suzuki Tadashi points out with regards to New Theater: the tension between speaking Japanese language, "a language in which the verb comes last," and imitating European physical movement. The Kawakami solution here is to simply drop the first and focus exclusively on the second. Suzuki's solution was to develop a new set of gestures that better match the rhythms of Japanese sentence structure. See Suzuki Tadashi, *The Way of Acting: The Theatre Writings of Tadashi Suzuki,* trans. J. Thomas Rimer (New York: Theatre Communications Group, 1986).
55. *Kokumin Shimbun,* 10 February 1903; rpt. in Shirakawa, *Kawakami,* 380–381.
56. For a provocative discussion of literary representation of "*shin heimin,*" also called "*burakumin*" or more officially "*hisabetsu buraku min,*" see Watanabe Naomi, *Nihon kindai bungaku to "sabetsu"* (Modern Japanese literature and "discrimination"), Hihyō Kūkan Sōsho, no. 2 (Tokyo: Ōta Shuppan, 1994).
57. *Yomiuri Shimbun,* 12 February 1903; rpt. in Shirakawa, *Kawakami,* 381–382.
58. *Yomiuri Shimbun,* 13 February 1903; rpt. in Shirakawa, *Kawakami,* 382.
59. In this chapter, I will refer to this play as *Korean King,* respecting the original title.
60. Kurata Yoshihiro, *Kindai geki no akebono: Kawakami Otojirō to sono shūhen* Mainichi Sensho, no. 4 (Tokyo: Mainichi Shimbunsha, 1981), 252–53.
61. Peter Duus, *The Abacus and the Sword: The Japanese Penetration of Korea, 1895–1910* (Berkeley: University of California Press, 1995), 400. Duus here is relying on Tsurumi Shunsuke, *Senjiki Nihon seishinshi: 1931–1945 nen* (Tokyo: Iwanami Shoten, 1982), 105.
62. Duus, *The Abacus and the Sword,* 339.
63. Ibid.
64. It is itself an adaptation of Meyer-Förster's novel *Karl Heinrich,* published in 1899. In the United States, the play is known through its adaptation into a musical called *The Student Prince,* with music by Sigmund Romberg. It was also made into a film entitled *The Student Prince in Old Heidelberg* in 1928, directed by Ernst Lubitsch.
65. This play has not been published. The quotes are from the manuscript stored in the Kawakami Archives at Waseda University's Theater Museum.
66. Kurata, in *Kindai geki no akebono,* mentions the police censorship of *Korean King* and the title-change to *New Nation's King* but does not discuss specific changes in the script.
67. Note, for example, that in 1907 a Korean prince was indeed sent to Japan; in 1920 a marriage was arranged between him and a Japanese woman from the aristocratic class. The Kawakami production of *Korean King* was undoubtedly inspired in part by the presence of this young Korean prince in Japan.

68. That is, the policy of imposing a Japanese education on colonized populations, modeled on the policy for education in India, proposed by Thomas Babington Macaulay in 1834. Macaulay wished to create "a class of persons, Indian in blood and colour, but English in taste, in opinion, in morals and in intellect." Benedict Anderson, *Imagined Communities,* 91.
69. Benedict Anderson, *Imagined Communities,* 98–99.
70. *Engei gahō* (November 1910): 199–202.
71. Oguma Eiji cites documents from the 1910s to 1940s, some of which strongly advocated intermarriage and some of which vehemently opposed it. Oguma Eiji, "Tsumazuita junketsu shugi: yūseigaku kei seiryoku no minzoku seisaku ron" (The pure-blood principle that stumbled: The ethnic policy discourse of eugenics advocates), *Jōkyō* (December 1994): 38–50. See also his book, Oguma Eiji, *Tan'itsu minzoku no shinwa: "Nihonjin" no jigazō no keifu* (The myth of the homogenous nation: Genealogy of the self-portrait of "the Japanese") (Tokyo: Shin'yōsha, 1995).
72. Kōseishō Kenkyūjo Jinkō Minzokubu (Ministry of health institute's population and ethnicity section), *Yamato minzoku o chūkaku to suru sekai seisaku no kentō* (Consideration of a global policy with the Yamato people as nucleus) (1943). Quoted in Oguma, "Tsumazuita junketsu shugi," 45. Although the statement is from a later historical moment and is referring to the marriage of Japanese women with Korean men brought to Japan as laborers, what I find suggestive is the logical contradiction between the racist "pure blood" principle and the realities of managing people in a colonial empire.
73. See, for example, the analysis of Isayama Yōtarō, *Ie, ai, sei: kindai Nihon no kazoku shisō* (Family, love, sex: Family ideology in modern Japan) (Tokyo: Keisō Shobō, 1994).
74. See Sakai Naoki, "'Jō' to 'kanshō': seiai no jōcho to kyōkan to shutai-teki gijutsu o megutte"("Feeling" and "sentiment": On sexual affections, common feeling, and subjective technology), in vol. 2 of *Jendā no Nihonshi,* ed. Wakita Haruko and Susan B. Hanley, 2 vols. (Tokyo: Tokyo University Press, 1995), 2: 137–77.
75. Laura Mulvey, "Afterthoughts on 'Visual Pleasure and Narrative Cinema' inspired by *Duel in the Sun*" in *Feminism and Film Theory,* ed. Constance Penley (New York: Routledge, 1988), 69–79; here 69.
76. For an article that offers suggestive parallels, see David Palumbo-Liu, "The *Bitter Tea* of Frank Capra," *positions: east asia cultures critique* 3, no. 3 (Winter, 1995): 759–789. Analyzing Frank Capra's 1933 film *The Bitter Tea of General Yen,* depicting an interracial romance between a white American woman and a Chinese warlord, Palumbo-Liu argues that "the film's failure may be attributed in part to the fact that it is unable to establish a stable identificatory position" (768). Using Laura Mulvey's well-known essay "Visual Pleasure and Narrative Cinema," Palumbo-Liu explains: "If we begin by accepting that the female character in this film is the object of the male gaze, then we have to adapt the position of the Asian male protagonist, that is, identify with him across conventional Hollywood racial lines. If we accept the position of the female protagonist, who is the orienting point of view, then we have to accept the Asian male protagonist as an object of sexual desire" (768).

CHAPTER 6

1. Matsumoto Kappei, "Kaisetsu," in Matsui Sumako, *Botanbake* (Peony Brush) (1914; reprint, Tokyo: Fuji Shuppan, 1986), 5.
2. Her second husband, Maezawa Seisuke, died in a fire at a school where he was school principal. Legend has it that he died protecting the photograph of the emperor and empress, which was enshrined at every school. Most biographies paint him as a sincere man who was discarded by self-centered Sumako after he had helped her begin her acting career.
3. After the director's death, there had been rumors of an affair between Sumako and a fellow actor of the troupe, but these died down with her death, which was seen as a form of *junshi:* suicide upon the death of one's master. Such suicides were common in feudal times, but more recently, a prominent example had seized the public imagination: General Nogi had committed suicide after the death of the Meiji emperor in 1912. Prominent writers, such as Mori Ōgai and Natsume Sōseki, had written about the suicide of General Nogi. Double suicides of couples had been a familiar topic in premodern Japanese theater as well. The death of Matsui Sumako, then, made perfect sense to the public: it was legible as an act of devotion and true love.
4. On the figure of the New Woman in Europe and America, see Gail Cunningham, *The New Woman and the Victorian Novel* (London: Macmillan, 1978); Carol Dyhouse, "The Role of Women: From Self-Sacrifice to Self-Awareness," in *The Victorians,* ed. Laurence Lerner (London: Methuen, 1978), 174–92; Patricia Marks, *Bicycles, Bangs, and Bloomers: The New Woman and the Popular Press* (Lexington: University Press of Kentucky, 1990); Elaine Showalter, *Sexual Anarchy: Gender and Culture at the Fin de Siècle* (New York: Penguin, 1990); Carroll Smith-Rosenberg, *Disorderly Conduct: Visions of Gender in Victorian America* (Oxford: Oxford University Press, 1985).
5. Rachel Bowlby, *Still Crazy After All These Years: Women, Writing and Psychoanalysis* (London: Routledge, 1992), 4–5. Bowlby, however, does not address the regressive step, only the progressive and transgressive. While it is important to point out the progressive or transgressive potential of even those steps that have been taken to be regressive, which I see as Bowlby's general strategy, I believe we cannot discount the regressive altogether.
6. On the New Woman and theater, see Vivien Gardner and Susan Rutherford, eds., *The New Woman and Her Sisters: Feminism and Theatre 1890–1914* (Ann Arbor: University of Michigan Press, 1992); Catherine Wiley, "The Matter with Manners: The New Woman and the Problem Play," in *Women in Theatre,* ed. James Redmond (Cambridge: Cambridge University Press, 1989), 109–127. Also, for a discussion of Ibsen's drama and the significance of actresses, see Gay Gibson Cima, *Performing Women: Female Characters, Male Playwrights, and the Modern Stage* (Ithaca, N.Y.: Cornell University Press, 1993).
7. Smith-Rosenberg, *Disorderly Conduct,* 245–96.
8. Tsubouchi Shōyō, "Atarashii onna," quoted on p. 212 of Yamada Keiko, "'Atarashii onna'" (The "New Woman"), in *Onna no imēji* (Women's image), ed. Joseigaku Kenkyūkai, vol. 1 of *Kōza joseigaku* (Lectures on women's studies), 4

vols. (Tokyo: Keisō Shobō, 1984), 1: 210–234. See also Nakamura Toshiko, "Ibsen in Japan: Tsubouchi Shōyō and His Lecture on New Women," *Edda: Nordisk Tiddskrift for Litteraturfoskning* (Scandinavian journal of literary research) no. 5 (1982): 261–272.

9. See Horiba Kiyoko, *Seitō no jidai: Hiratsuka Raichō to atarashii onnatachi* (Tokyo: Iwanami Shoten, 1988), 96–119.
10. *Chūō kōron* 28, no. 2 (1913). This manifesto was also translated into English as "The 'New Woman' in Japan" in *The Japan Times,* 11 January 1913.
11. The photograph and haiku are inserted between pages 224 and 225 of Matsui Sumako, *Botanbake.*
12. Judith Butler, *Excitable Speech: A Politics of the Performative* (New York: Routledge, 1997), 2.
13. On the historical origins and changes in the ideology of "good wife, wise mother" as well as resistances to the ideology, see Koyama Shizuko, *Ryōsai kenbo to iu kihan* (The norm of good wife, wise mother) (Tokyo: Keisō Shobō, 1991). Koyama's analysis carefully notes the overlaps and differences between the ideology of "good wife wise mother" and the various feminist ideas of women like Hiratsuka Raichō (who valorized motherhood and women's difference from men) and Yosano Akiko (who argued for women's economic independence through paid work outside the home).
14. The term "New Woman" was also appropriated by women who were primarily oriented toward gaining political power See, for example, the Shinfujin kyōkai (New Woman's Society) in Sharon L. Sievers, *Flowers in Salt: The Beginnings of Feminist Consciousness in Modern Japan* (Stanford: Stanford University Press, 1983), 187; Sheldon Garon, *Molding Japanese Minds: The State in Everyday Life* (Princeton: Princeton University Press, 1997), 123–4.
15. The following is a selective list of material examined:

1) Primary sources: Articles in *Engei gahō, Miyako Shimbun, Seitō.*
2) Post-mortem sources: Two major collections of essays are: Yasunari Jirō, ed. *Sumako gō* (Sumako issue), special issue of *Onna no sekai* (Women's world), 5, no. 2 (February 1919); Akita Ujaku and Nakagi Sadakazu, eds., *Koi no aishi: Sumako no isshō* (Love's sad history : Matsui Sumako's life) (Tokyo: Nihon Hyōronsha, 1919).

   The former will be hereafter referred to as *Onna no sekai.* The February 1919 issue of *Engei gahō* also contained a number of articles about Sumako's career and her suicide, written by people associated with the theater world.
3) Later sources: Kawamura Karyō, *Zuihitsu Matsui Sumako: Geijutsuza seisui ki* (Essay on Matsui Sumako: The rise and fall of the Geijutsuza theater) Seia Sensho, no. 25, (Tokyo: Seia Shobō, n.d.); Kawatake Shigetoshi, *Shōyō, Hōgetsu, Sumako no higeki: shingeki hiroku* (The tragedy of Shōyō, Hōgetsu, and Sumako: Secret records of the new theater) (Tokyo: Mainichi Shuppansha, 1966); Kōno Taeko, "Furui moraru to no tatakai ni inochi o kaketa koi no Kachūsha" (Love's Katusha who risked her life to fight old morals), in *Koi to geijutsu e no jōnen* (Passion for love and art), vol. 4 of *Jimbutsu kindai josei shi: onna no isshō* (Individuals in modern women's history: women's lives), ed. Setouchi Harumi, 8 vols. (Tokyo: Kōdansha, 1980), 4: 21–60; Mori Reiko,

"Matsui Sumako," *Geidō no hana hiraku toki* (When the flower of art boomed), vol. 5 of *Kindai Nihon josei shi* (History of women in modern Japan), ed. Enchi Fumiko, 12 vols. (Tokyo: Shūeisha, 1981), 5: 91–126; Murakami Nobuhiko, *Taishō joseishi: shimin seikatsu.* (History of Taishō women: Citizens' lives) (Tokyo: Rironsha, 1982); Ozaki Hirotsugu, "Matsui Sumako," in *Joyō no keizu* (Genealogy of actresses) (Tokyo: Asahi Shimbunsha, 1964), 71–141; Tanaka Sumie, "Engeki to shinjū shita 'Nihon no Nora': Matsui Sumako" (The "Japanese Nora" who committed love suicide with theater: Matsui Sumako), *Inu doshi hen* (Year of the Dog), vol. 11 of *Junishi-betsu ekigaku kaisetsu: josei geijutsuka no jinsei* (Fortune telling according to the twelve animal signs: lives of female artists), ed. Kinoshita Kazuo, 12 vols. (Tokyo: Shūeisha, 1980), 11: 9–44; Toita Kōji, *Joyū no ai to shi* (Love and death of an actress) (Tokyo: Kawade Shobō, 1963); also his "Matsui Sumako," *Monogatari kindai Nihon joyū shi* (Anecdotal history of modern Japanese actresses) (Tokyo: Chūō Kōronsha, 1980), 56–74; Wakashiro Kiiko, "Koi o shi ni yotte enjita Matsui Sumako" (Matsui Sumako who performed love through death), in *Kindai o irodotta onnatachi* (Women who colored modernity) (Tokyo: TBS Britanica, 1981), 191–206.

4) English language sources: Komiya Toyotaka, ed., Edward G. Seidensticker and Donald Keene, trans., *Japanese Music and Drama in the Meiji Era,* vol. 3 of *Japanese Culture in the Meiji Era,* 14 vols. (Tokyo: Ōbunsha, 1956); Brian Powell, "Matsui Sumako: Actress and Woman," in *Modern Japan: Aspects of History, Literature and Society,* ed. W. G. Beasley (Berkeley: University of California Press, 1975): 135–146. Powell's conclusion is that "Matsui Sumako by her behaviour only confirmed prejudices both of those who opposed female emancipation and those who regarded theatre artists in general as moral reprobates" (146). See also Phyllis Birnbaum, "Slamming the Door, Scaring the Neighbors" in her *Modern Girls, Shining Stars, the Skies of Tokyo,* 1–54. This biographical essay, though not an academic study in the traditional sense, is more sympathetic and nuanced than most other accounts.

5) Plays and scripts: Fujimori Seikichi, *Dokuhaku no onna: Shimamura Hōgetsu to Matsui Sumako* (Woman of monologues: Shimamura Hōgetsu and Matsui Sumako), *Higeki kigeki* 221 (March 1969): 93–138; Hōjō Hideji, *Joyū* (Actress), *Hōjō Hideji gikyoku senshū* (Selected plays of Hōjō Hideji) (Tokyo: Seia Shobō, 1971), 106–218; Kawaguchi Matsutarō, *Matsui Sumako* (Tokyo: Shimbashi Enbujō, 1963); Toita Kōji, *Joyū no ai to shi* (Love and death of an actress), *Higeki kigeki* 206 (December 1967): 76–138; Noguchi Tatsuji, *Joyū Sumako no koi* (Actress Sumako's love), *Noguchi Tatsuji Gikyoku Sen* (Selected plays of Noguchi Tatsuji) (Tokyo: Engeki Shuppansha, 1989), 439–527; Mizuki Kumio, *Wasure enu hitobito (dai jukkai): Matsui Sumako* (Unforgettable people (tenth installment): Matsui Sumako), produced by Dentsū Radio Station, recorded November 20, 1952, broadcast December 4, 1952. The date of recording and broadcast of this radio play is deduced from the stamped date on the script, given to the Waseda University's Theater Museum by Mizuki. See also the following film scripts: Hisaita Eijirō, *Joyū* (Actress), in *Hisaita Eijirō shinario shū* (Collected film scripts of Hisaita Eijirō) (Tokyo: Chūōsha, 1947), 3–89. This

was the script for Kinugasa Teinosuke's film, starring Yamada Isuzu. Also, Yoda Yoshikata, *Joyū Sumako no koi* (Actress Sumako's love), handwritten film script for Mizoguchi Kenji's film, starring Tanaka Kinuyo. My thanks to Shōchiku's Ōtani Library and Joanne Izbicki at Wake Forest University for allowing me to see this script.

16. Hasegawa Shigure, "Sumako san no koto" (About Ms. Sumako), *Engei gahō* (February 1919): 66–67. Also see her *Shimpen: kindai bijin den* (New edition: Legends of modern beauties) [1936], ed. Sugimoto Sonoko (Tokyo: Iwanami Shoten, 1985).
17. Okada Yachiyo, "Matsui Sumako-san" (Ms. Matsui Sumako), *Engei gahō* (February 1919): 81–83.
18. Hayashi Chitose, "Amari ni guchi rashikeredo" (Though it may seem too much like complaining) *Engei gahō* (February 1919): 80–81.
19. Kamiyama Uraji, "Magari zumai no koro" (When we lived in rented rooms) *Engai gahō* (February 1919): 72–74; quote from 74.
20. Ibid., 73. Mori Eijirō, a fellow actor at the Literary Society, also remembers how Sumako would review dances, rehearse plays, read texts aloud, and practice singing, from early in the morning to late at night; due to this awesome effort, says Mori, Sumako quickly memorized the choreography for her dances, and her elocution improved dramatically. Mori Eijirō, "Kobayashi-san" (Ms. Kobayashi), *Engei gahō* (June 1915): 37–41.
21. Mori Ritsuko, "Sumako no shi to joyū kai" (Sumako's death and the actress world), *Onna no sekai* 5, no. 2 (February 1919): 24–25; quote from 25. Mori was a former student at Kawakami Sadayakko's Actress Training Institute and an actress at the Imperial Theater (Teikoku Gekijō). It is interesting to compare Mori Ritsuko's cool view of Sumako with the more sympathetic views of fellow Literary Society (Bungei Kyōkai) actresses.
22. Mizushima Ryokusō, "Tōdai joyū getsutan: Matsui Sumako" (Monthly critique of contemporary actresses: Matsui Sumako), *Engei gahō* (February 1915): 46–49.

    Mizushima also notes, "I think it was Mr. Fukuzawa Momosuke who praised Sumako, saying that while most Japanese women's arms are narrow at the elbow and therefore unsightly, Sumako's arms are straight throughout." Mizushima, *Engei gahō* (January 1915): 210–213; quote from 213.
23. Kawamura Karyō, "Matsui Sumako no gigei" (The artistry of Matsui Sumako) *Engei gahō* (June 1915): 32–6.
24. Sōma Kokkō, "Sumako no otoko ni taishita taido to onna ni taishita taido" (Sumako's attitude towards men and attitude towards women," *Onna no sekai* 5, no. 2 (February 1919): 62–63.
25. Murata Eiko, "Matsui Sumako o kaibō su" (Dissecting Matsui Sumako), *Onna no sekai* 5, no. 2 (February 1919): 28–33.
26. They are attributed to different writers, but since both articles come up with the same five motivations, chances are they were written by one person with pseudonym(s), or one plagiarized from the other. Aoyagi Yūbi, "Sumako wa naniyue ni jisatsu seshiya" (Why did Sumako commit suicide?), *Engei gahō* (February 1919): 70–72. A longer version of the same argument appeared as Ōkubo Tōho,

"Sumako no jisatsu wa hentai seiyoku" (Sumako's suicide was due to perverse sexual desire), *Onna no sekai* 5, no. 2 (February 1919): 4–15. The five motivations given are: 1) her perverse sexual desire; 2) the introversion of one of her selfish tantrums; 3) living at the Geijutsuza Club, which lacked the warmth of a true home; 4) the increasing brusqueness in manner of the Geijutsuza troupe members toward her; 5) her failure to attract a large audience for the January performance at Yūrakuza.

27. Kuwano Tōka's book *Joyū ron* (On the actress), mentioned in chapter 2, started with a chapter on "Dissecting the actress/anatomy of actress" (*joyū no kaibō*). For a discussion of the reception of psychiatry, abnormal psychology, sexology, etc. see Kawamura Kunimitsu, "Onna no yamai, otoko no yamai: jendā to sekushuariti o meguru 'Fūkō no hensō"(Woman's illness, man's illness: A "variation on Foucault" concerning gender and sexuality), *Gendai shisō* (July 1993): 88–109; Furukawa Makoto, "Ren'ai to seiyoku no dai-san teikoku: tsūzokuteki seiyokugaku no jidai" (The Third Empire of romantic love and sexual desire: The age of popular sexology), *Gendai shisō* (July 1993): 110–127.
28. Akita Ujaku, "Hito oyobi haiyū to shite no Matsui Sumako" (Matsui Sumako as person and performer), *Engei gahō* (February 1919): 74–77.
29. In an intriguing parallel, Cima points out how the meaning of the theatrical term "action" changed in the nineteenth century, from denoting external patterns to be imitated to denoting the internal motivations of characters. Cima, *Performing Women,* 53.
30. Ihara Seiseien, "Inochi gake no gei" (Art that risks life), *Engei gahō* (February 1919): 64–5.
31. Ihara Seiseien, "Sumako no shi wa kūzen no kiroku" (Sumako's death is an unprecedented record), *Onna no sekai* 5, no. 2 (February 1919): 16–7.
32. Kawamura Karyō "Iki ga inochi datta," (Her spunk was her life), *Engei gahō* (February 1919): 83–4.
33. Nakai Tetsu, "Osuma-san no butai guse" (The stage habits of Sumako), *Engei gahō* (February 1919): 67–8.
34. Mori Reiko, "Matsui Sumako," 114.
35. Osanai Kaoru, "Kowareta sake game" (A broken wine bottle), *Engei gahō* (February 1919): 68–70; quote from 69.
36. Murakami, *Taishō josei shi,* 196–97.
37. Mori Reiko, "Matsui Sumako," 126.
38. Murakami, *Taishō josei shi,* 193.
39. Kitami Harukazu, *Tetteki to Shunsho;* quoted in Ōzasa, *Nihon gendai engeki shi* 1:86–87.
40. See Matsumoto Kappei, *Nihon shingeki shi: shingeki binbō monogatari* (History of Japanese new theater: A tale of poverty) (Tokyo: Chikuma Shobō, 1966). More recently, however, Matsumoto has argued for a feminist revision of Matsui Sumako, "having noticed how the critical views of her seem to be based on a highly feudalistic and masculine sense of superiority." See Matsumoto Kappei, "Matsui Sumako saikō" (Matsui Sumako reconsidered), in *Shingeki no yamanami* (Mountain ranges of new theater) (Tokyo: Asahi Shorin, 1991), 28–42.
41. Matsumoto, *Nihon shingeki shi,* 55.

42. For other examples illustrating the same process, including the political fate of actress Okada Yoshiko, who fled with her lover, Sugimoto Ryōkichi, across the border from Sakhalin to the Soviet Union in the 1930s, see the debate between Hirano Ken and Nakano Shigeharu, discussed in J. Victor Koschmann, *Revolution and Subjectivity in Postwar Japan* (Chicago: University of Chicago Press, 1996), 70–87.
43. Haino Shōhei, "Sumako ni kansuru taiwa" (Dialogue on Sumako), *Engei gahō* (June 1915): 28–32; quote from 29.
44. Kurawaka Umejirō, "Gokai no uchi ni ikita Sumako" (Sumako lived amidst misunderstanding), *Onna no sekai* 5, no. 2 (February 1919): 44–49; quote from 48.
45. Matsui Sumako, *Botanbake.* All further page references to this text will be given parenthetically in the text. This is a reprint, with an afterword by Matsumoto Kappei, published as part of the series *Seitō no onnatachi* (The Women of *Seitō*), vol. 18. "Peony brush" also refers to the large, round makeup brush used by actresses to put on facial powder.
46. In a review of the volume, Kobayashi Katsu writes that what she found most interesting were the photographs: "I found myself utterly fascinated with the way her face becomes artistically refined little by little." Kobayashi Katsu, "*Botanbake* o yonde" (On reading *Peony Brush*), *Seitō* 4, no. 9 (October 1914): 171.
47. Matsumoto, "Kaisetsu," 11.
48. Mori Reiko, "Matsui Sumako," 114.
49. For an exemplary analysis of female self-representation that takes into account recent feminist theories on autobiography, see Biddy Martin, *Woman and Modernity: The (Life)Styles of Lou Andreas-Salomé* (Ithaca, N.Y.: Cornell University Press, 1991), 24–60.
50. For a discussion of Higuchi's life and a translation of "Child's Play," see *In the Shade of Spring Leaves: The Life and Writings of Higuchi Ichiyō, a Woman of Letters in Meiji Japan,* ed. and trans. Robert Lyons Danly (New York: Norton, 1981).
51. For the figure of the *flâneur,* see Walter Benjamin, *Charles Baudelaire: A Lyric Poet in the Era of High Capitalism,* trans. Harry Zohn (London: Verso, 1983), 35–66.
52. Rachel Bowlby, "Walking, Women and Writing: Virginia Woolf as *flâneuse,*" in her *Still Crazy after All These Years: Women, Writing and Psychoanalysis* (London: Routledge, 1992), 1–33.
53. "I would like to add two more episodes that describe Sumako's tremendous jealousy," Matsumoto, *Nihon shingeki shi,* 211.

CHAPTER 7

1. Matsumoto Kappei, *Nihon shingeki shi: shingeki binbō monogatari* (A history of new theater: a tale of poverty) (Tokyo: Chikuma Shobō, 1966); Matsumoto Shinko, *Meiji engeki ron shi* (A history of Meiji theater discussions) (Tokyo: Engeki Shuppansha, 1980); Ōzasa Yoshio, *Nihon gendai engeki shi* (History of Japanese contemporary theater), 6 vols. (Tokyo: Hakusuisha, 1985–99).

2. J. Thomas Rimer, *Toward a Modern Japanese Theatre: Kishida Kunio* (Princeton: Princeton University Press, 1974), 75–77.
3. Ibid., 22.
4. Morinaga Maki, "Osanai Kaoru to shirōtoshugi: hiden no jissenkei ni taisuru hitei, muka, dakyō" (Osanai Kaoru and amateurism: denial, nullification, and compromise with the regime of esotericism), in *Nihon kinsei kokka no shosō* (Various appearances of premodern Japanese nation), ed. Nishimura Keiko (Tokyo: Tōkyōdō Shuppan, 1999), 271–97; quote from 281.
5. Jacques Derrida, "The Theater of Cruelty and the Closure of Representation," in *Writing and Difference,* trans. Alan Bass (Chicago: University of Chicago Press, 1978), 232–50; quote from 235.
6. One might note that many of the main New Theater advocates, including Shimamura Hōgetsu and Osanai Kaoru, had spent several years of study in Europe, the United States, and Russia, and that while earlier generations of Japanese sent abroad had either become successful extractors of practical knowledge (Mori Ōgai 1884–1888 in Germany) or become depressed at Japan's position vis-à-vis the West (Natsume Sōseki, 1900–1903 in Britain), this generation seems to have heartily imbibed and digested Western culture, embracing British, German, French, Russian, and Scandinavian drama as the embodiment of universal ideals. Note also that while the terms "Western" and "European" are often used interchangeably during this period, the status of "American" and "Russian" within "Western" remains somewhat contested.
7. Note that the West also understood itself and presented itself as universal. For an analysis of how the "narcissism" of the West and the non-West's cultural essentialism are caught up in a transferential relation, see Naoki Sakai, "Subject and Inscription of Cultural Difference" in *Translation and Subjectivity: On "Japan" and Cultural Nationalism* (Minneapolis: University of Minnesota Press, 1997), 117–152.
8. This basic system of theater censorship had been instituted in 1882, but increasingly strict rules were implemented after the turn of the century. The 1900 "Rules for Theater Control" (Engeki torishimari kisoku), the most comprehensive law up to that point, contained five sections ranging from the construction and maintenance of theater buildings to restrictions on topics for production. The following, for example, were topics to be summarily banned from the stage: 1) anything contrary to the spirit of rewarding good and punishing evil; 2) any words or gestures that border on obscenity or cruelty; 3) anything that can be construed as political discussion; 4) any other words or gestures that pose danger to public safety or morals. Saitō Yasuhide, "Dan'atsu to tōsei" (Suppression and control), in vol. 7 of *Nihon geinō shi* (Japanese performing arts history), ed. Geinōshi Kenkyūkai 7 vols. (Tokyo: Hōsei University Press, 1990), 7: 238–58; quote from 7: 241–42.
9. Matsumoto Shinko, *Meiji,* 645.
10. It is also interesting to note that cinema was not as carefully censored as the theater during this period, mostly because cinema was still too primitive technically to convey the dangerous sense of physical immediacy (*jikkan*) that a theater performance was generally thought to provoke. Matsumoto Shinko, *Meiji,* 670. The

"Rules for Motion Picture Exhibition Control" (Katsudō shashin kōgyō torishimari kisoku) of 1917 mostly sought to merely divide cinema between those pictures suitable for adults from those for children. A similar argument was made about the novel, which was also less strictly censored than the theater—the police superintendent in charge of censorship commented that the novel does not provide as much *jikkan* whereas a theater performance keeps flickering in front of the mind's eye and is therefore much more dangerous: "My opinion is that a script whose main focus is the romantic love [*ren'ai*] between adult men and women should absolutely never be allowed. . . . If you think my opinion is drastic, go over to Hibiya Park—you'll be able to see daily many examples of the living proof of the corruption of relations between male and female students." "Keishichō to shibai to geiki" (The Metropolitan Police Department, Theater, and Geisha), *Yorozu Chōhō,* July 14 and July 16, 1905. Here, amorous and injurious behavior on stage is directly linked to such behavior off stage.

11. Note that such demarcations existed also in the Edo period. In other words, "punishment" of transgressors of demarcating rules existed before the modern period, but not the "discipline" or internalization of these rules by individual bodies, which Foucault describes in *Discipline and Punish: The Birth of the Prison,* trans. Alan Sheridan, 2nd edition (New York: Vintage, 1995).
12. Foucault, *Discipline and Punish,* 141.
13. Ibid., 143.
14. This is often seen as the origin of the "shishōsetsu" or "I-novel" in Japan, though some recent criticism views caution us against seeing "shishōsetsu" in terms of retreat or pathology. See, for example, Watanabe Naomi, "Mokusetsuhō no seijigaku" (The politics of reticence), *Gendai shisō* 27 no. 2 (February 1999): 200–213. He sees in "shishōsetsu" a triumph of the rhetoric of "description" over that of "reticence," the latter being the rhetoric associated with the emperor system.
15. For an overview, see Laurel Rasplica Rodd, "Yosano Akiko and the Taishō Debate over the 'New Woman,'" in *Recreating Japanese Women, 1600–1945,* ed. Gail Lee Bernstein (Berkeley: University of California Press, 1991), 175–198. See also, Ayako Kano, "Nihon feminizumu ronsōshi 1: bosei to sekushuariti" (Japanese feminist debates 1: Motherhood and sexuality), in *Wādomappu feminizumu,* ed. Ehara Yumiko and Kanai Yoshiko (Wordmap feminism) (Tokyo: Shin'yōsha, 1997), 196–221.
16. Karatani Kōjin, *Origins of Modern Japanese Literature,* trans. Brett de Bary, et al. (Durham: Duke University Press, 1993), 70.
17. See Ōzasa, "Shokuminchi shugi to waga kuni no kindai gikyoku" (Colonialism and our nation's modern drama), *Shiatā ātsu* (Theater arts) 8 (1997): 50–55.
18. Ōzasa, "Shokuminchi shugi." This is a situation which Takeuchi Yoshimi has also castigated, with reference to the limitations of the cosmopolitanism of the White Birch School (Shirakaba-ha) of writing in the 1910s and 1920s—according to Takeuchi, these cosmopolitan writers' identification with the West and their representation of the universal "world" unmediated by ethnicity is itself the perfect manifestation of the mental colonization of Japan by the West. Takeuchi's devastating critique alerts us to the problems inherent in the New Theater's iden-

tification with the West and suggests one part of the mechanism through which imperialism and colonialism were reproduced. See Takeuchi Yoshimi, "Kindai to wa nani ka" (What is modernity?), in vol. 4 of *Takeuchi Yoshimi zenshū,* 17 vols. (Tokyo: Chūō Kōronsha, 1980), 130–57. See also pp. 179–81 of Satō Izumi, "Kindai Bungaku shi no kioku / bōkyaku" (The remembering / forgetting of modern literary history), *Gendai Shisō,* 27, no. 1 (January 1999): 170–82 for an interesting discussion of this issue. While Takeuchi's critique rightly targets the structure of Japan's reproduction of colonialism, there are several problems with his argument: One is that he assumes the positivity of a Japanese "self," that is, Japanese ethnic identity, which he sees as something that was lost due to mental colonization by the West. Close analysis of the formation of theater, as of other genres, would suggest that that kind of ethnic identity is precisely something that is created in reaction against and in dialogue with what Takeuchi sees as Western mental colonization: It is the linguistic, physical, cultural drag against the perfect identification with the West—whatever prevents a Kawakami Sadayakko from becoming an English lady—that becomes labeled as Japanese particularity and Japanese ethnicity. Second, by dismissing the cosmopolitan and utopian aspirations of the White Birch School, and by extension the kinds of people involved in New Theater, Takeuchi seems to throw away the baby with the bath water. Third, the position of women vis-à-vis men must be considered as an additional layer and complication in the colonial dialectic and the reproduction of imperialism.

19. See Maki Morinaga's discussion of Osanai Kaoru's attitude towards the West and towards translation in "Osanai Kaoru to shirōtoshugi," 286–90.
20. In "Osanai Kaoru to shirōtoshugi," Morinaga points out that Osanai Kaoru believed that complete imitation of the West would ultimately lead to complete originality of Japanese artists: If the West was universal and therefore the origin of everything, Japanese artists could become original by imitating the West completely. Shimamura Hōgetsu seems to have shared this view as well. The dialectical paradox of imitation and originality can be observed in the descriptions of Matsui Sumako's acting style discussed later in this chapter.
21. Karatani, *Origins,* 40.
22. Straightening does not yet arrive at the condition of "discipline" in the Foucauldian sense. Rather than being the disciplining of a docile body, straightening is the repudiation of the queered *kabuki* body. Through shouts that repudiate song and punches that repudiate dance, the "natural body" is constructed. Then, once such a body is constructed, it can be "expressed" by New Theater. And it will seem as if that natural body had always existed, merely repressed in *kabuki,* gradually discovered and liberated in the straightening of theater, and finally expressed freely in New Theater. This is the inversion that takes place. See Foucault, *Discipline and Punish,* 155.
23. Kitami Harukazu, *Tetteki to Shunsho: kindai engi no hajimari* (Tokyo: Shōbunsha, 1978), 36.
24. Gunji Masakatsu, "Hitotsu no kankyaku ron" in *Kabuki ronsō* (Kyoto: Shibunkaku, 1979), 671–79. Gunji describes this shift in terms of the change from "participating" to "looking" as the mode of the audience's experience of performance.

25. Chikamatsu Monzaemon (1653–1724) wrote a number of history plays (*jidaimono*) before turning to domestic plays (*sewamono*) for the first time in 1703 with *The Love Suicides at Sonezaki.* See vols. 43–44 of *Nihon koten bungaku zenshū,* ed. Torigoe Bunzō (Tokyo: Shōgakkan, 1975), which collects all 24 of Chikamatsu's domestic plays. Of these, 12 deal with the traffic of women in the pleasure quarters.
26. See for example, the special issue on "Kuruwa: Edo no sei kūkan" of *Kokubungaku: kaishaku to kyōzai no kenkyū* 38, no. 9 (August 1993) for an interpretation of the pleasure quarters as "sacred space," "cultural salon," and "realm of liberated sexuality"; see also Ogasawara Kyōko, *Toshi to gekijō: chū kinsei no chinkon, yūraku, kenryoku* (Tokyo: Heibonsha, 1992) for a contrasting interpretation of the pleasure quarters as the Tokugawa government's mechanism of social control.
27. Noah D. Zatz, "Sex Work/Sex Act: Law, Labor, and Desire in Constructions of Prostitution," *Signs: Journal of Women in Culture and Society,* 22, no. 2 (1997): 277–308.
28. See Nishiyama Matsunosuke, "Kuruwa," in *Kinsei fūzoku to shakai,* vol. 5 of *Nishiyama Matsunosuke chosakushū,* 8 vols. (Tokyo: Yoshikawa Kōbunkan, 1985), 5: 1–201. The various techniques cited in *Shikidō ōkagami* are discussed in pp. 98–100.
29. Drawing on Lacanian psychoanalytic theory, Takemura Kazuko demonstrates the "impossibility of love" in general. See Takemura Kazuko, "Ai ni tsuite" (On love), *Shisō* 886 (April 1998): 5–33. Takemura also notes that we dilute this impossibility through various mechanisms and fictions, including marriage, reproduction, and fantasy.
30. See Sakai Naoki, "'Jō' to 'kanshō': seiai no jōcho to kyōkan to shutaiteki gijutsu o megutte" ("Feeling" and "sentiment": On sexual affections, common feeling, and subjective technology), in *Jendā no Nihonshi,* ed. Wakita Haruko and Susan B. Hanley, 2 vols. (Tokyo: Tokyo University Press, 1995), 2: 137–77.
31. Donald Keene, trans., *Major Plays of Chikamatsu* (New York: Columbia University Press, 1961), 4–5.
32. Moriya Takeshi, "Geinōshi ni okeru kinseiteki naru mono" (What is early modern in performance history), in *Kinsei* (Early modern period), vol. 4 of *Nihon bungaku shinshi* (A new history of Japanese literature), ed. Matsuda Osamu, 6 vols. (Tokyo: Shibundō, 1990), 4: 169–92.
33. See Mark Rose, *Authors and Owners: The Invention of Copyright* (Cambridge: Harvard University Press, 1993).
34. See Noguchi Takehiko, "Sakusha," in *Nihon engeki shi no shiten,* vol. 1 of *Kōza Nihon no engeki,* ed. Suwa Haruo and Sugai Yukio, 8 vols. (Tokyo: Benseisha, 1992), 1: 110–124.
35. Matsumoto Shinko, *Meiji,* 440–46.
36. *Niroku Shimbun,* April 18, 1902; quoted in Matsumoto Shinko, *Meiji,* 443.
37. Matsumoto Shinko, *Meiji,* 440–46.
38. Sadoya Shigenobu, *Hōgetsu Shimamura Takitarō ron* (A study of Shimamura Hōgetsu) (Tokyo: Meiji Shoin, 1980), 464.

39. Roland Barthes, *Image, Music, Text,* trans. Stephen Heath (New York: The Noonday Press, 1988), 177.
40. Harold B. Segel points out that for modernist and avant-garde drama in Europe from the 1890s to the 1930s, the puppet and automaton became a metaphor for human helplessness in the face of powerful forces such as Eros, the supernatural, history, industrial society, and national myth. Segel, however, does not deal with Japanese puppet theater, except as a possible influence on Paul Claudel's theater. Harold B. Segel, *Pinocchio's Progeny: Puppets, Marionettes, Automatons, and Robots in Modernist and Avant-Garde Drama* (Baltimore, Md.: Johns Hopkins University Press, 1995), 100–101. One might speculate that even if it was a very different set of concerns that led turn-of-the-century Japanese theater practitioners to rediscover Chikamatsu, the metaphor of the puppet would have resonance with similar feelings of helplessness in Japanese intelligentsia, or at least with a sense of uncertainty about the locus of agency and subjectivity.
41. Katō Shūichi, "'Sei no shōhinka' o meguru nōto" (Notes concerning "commodification of sexuality") in *Sei no shōhinka* (Commodification of sexuality), ed. Ehara Yumiko, Feminizumu no shuchō, no. 2, (Tokyo: Keisō Shobō, 1995), 232–78. According to Katō, it is when both labor and sexuality become commodified that the concept of labor and sexuality per se—as either commodified or noncommodified—comes into being.
42. Rachel Bowlby, *Just Looking: Consumer Culture in Dreiser, Gissing, and Zola* (New York: Methuen, 1985). See also Otabe Tanehisa on the relation between notions of art and of property. Otabe, "Kindai teki 'shoyū' shisō to 'geijutsu' gainen: kindai bigaku no seijigaku e no joshō" (The modern philosophy of "property" and the concept of "art": Preface to a politics of modern aesthetics), in *Hihyō kūkan* 2, no.12 (1997): 51–66.
43. Pierre Bourdieu, *Practical Reason: On the Theory of Action* (Stanford: Stanford University Press, 1998), 85.
44. Ōzasa, *Nihon gendai engeki shi,* 1:22–24.
45. Actors in the premodern era were called "*ningaimono*": literally, "beings outside the law" or "outlaws."
46. Tsubouchi Shōyō, "Gekidan han jikan," *Kabuki* (January 1909).
47. Osanai Kaoru, "Gekiron shinsei," *Yomiuri Shimbun* (November 15, 1908; November 22, 1908).
48. Osanai Kaoru, "Haiyū D-kun e," *Engei gahō* (January 1909).
49. *Yorozu Chōhō* (November 27, 1907); quoted in Matsumoto Shinko, *Meiji,* 919.
50. In a highly perceptive analysis of Osanai Kaoru's writings on theater, Maki Morinaga has distinguished "amateurism" as characterized by 1) lack of experience and technique; 2) lack of possibility for income; 3) negation of existing institutions and value systems. It is the third criteria that is lacking in the literati theatricals. Morinaga Maki, "Osanai Kaoru to shirōtoshugi," 286–290.
51. Matsumoto Shinko, *Meiji,* 868–70.
52. *Yomiuri Shimbun* (May 22, 1911), quoted in Kawamura Karyō, *Zuihitsu Matsui Sumako: Geijutsuza seisuiki* (Essay on Matsui Sumako: The rise and fall of the Geijutsuza theater), Seia Sensho Series 25 (Tokyo: Seia Shobō, 1968), 264.

53. Matsumoto Kappei, *Nihon shingeki shi,* 42.
54. Takahashi Toyo, *Tagiru* (Boiling); quoted in Ōzasa, *Nihon gendai engeki shi,* 1:60.
55. Kawamura Karyō, *Zuihitsu Matsui Sumako,* 19–20.
56. Jennifer Robertson, *Takarazuka: Sexual Politics and Popular Culture in Modern Japan* (Berkeley: University of California Press, 1998), 151–86.
57. *Kōjien* defines *shirōto* as 1) an inexperienced person; 2) short for *shirōto onna,* woman who is not prostitute or geisha; 3) in the early modern period, private prostitutes (*shishō*) in the Kyoto-Osaka region. The vocabulary differentiates the two categories of *kurōto* and *shirōto* but implicitly recognizes that the difference is simply a matter of the amount of sexual experience, measured by the number of partners, or a matter of the degree of organization.
58. Tanaka Eizō, *Shingeki sono mukashi* (New theater once upon a time); quoted in Ōzasa, *Nihon gendai engeki shi,* 1:80–81.
59. *Tokyo Shimbun* (October 29, 1906); quoted in Matsumoto Shinko, *Meiji,* 925.
60. Matsumoto Shinko, *Meiji,* 986.
61. Osanai Kaoru, "Ningyō tare" (Be a puppet) in *Yomiuri Shimbun* (February 28, 1909).
62. See Michel Foucault, *Discipline and Punish,* 135–169, on the concept of "docile bodies."
63. Jennifer Robertson, *Takarazuka,* 186.
64. Ueda Kazutoshi, "Rien kōjōsaku" (Proposal for theater world improvement), *Engei gahō* (June 1907).
65. For a feminist analysis of the politics of adaptation that incorporates recent theories of translation, see Laura Grindstaff, "*La Femme Nikita* and the Textual Politics of 'The Remake,'" forthcoming in the journal *Camera Obscura.*
66. Suzuki Tadashi, *The Way of Acting: The Theatre Writings of Tadashi Suzuki,* trans. J. Thomas Rimer (New York: Theatre Communications Group, 1986), 3. Suzuki himself locates the source of the failure in language rather than in physique, but the two of course go together: "If an actor really wants to perform in the foreign fashion, then unnatural makeup alone will not suffice; Chekhov's words will have to be spoken in Russian, or Shakespeare's in English. . . . In contrast to a number of other languages, Japanese has a pitch accent, and sentences can be inordinately long. For better or for worse, such is the language that Japanese actors must speak, a language grammatically constructed so that the listener cannot fully understand what is said until the end of the sentence, a language in which the verb comes last. Yet our actors try to gesture along with this language as though they were Russians, Englishmen, or Frenchmen. Gesture is tied intimately to the words being spoken; indeed, words *represent* human gesture. There can be no words spoken that are not intimately connected to bodily sensations and rhythms. Therefore, however long our arms and legs may grow, however our physical appearance may improve, no Japanese actor can imitate the Chekhovian manner as well as his Russian counterpart—as long as he is speaking in Japanese." Suzuki Tadashi, *The Way of Acting,* 5. Suzuki went on to develop a new system of training the arms and legs and also wrote plays in a style that would take advantage of Japanese sentence constructions.

67. See Susan Blakeley Klein, *Ankoku Butō: The Premodern and Postmodern Influences on the Dance of Utter Darkness* (Ithaca, N.Y.: Cornell University East Asia Program, 1988). Note that Klein is careful to contextualize Hijikata's claims: "It is not, in fact, clear to me that the structure of the Japanese body is significantly different from a German or American body, or that modern dance and ballet training is any more 'natural' for an American than it is for a Japanese. . . . One might consider, however, the pervasive notion (only very recently challenged) that the Japanese body is unsuitable for classical ballet and modern dance. Although Hijikata's claim to have created a style of dance specifically for the Japanese body may not have been realistic, it was certainly ideologically persuasive, and must be taken into account on that basis." Klein, *Ankoku Butō,* 20.
68. For English-language discussion of *genbun itchi* see Karatani, *Origins.* For Japanese-language discussion, see Noguchi Takehiko, *Sanninshō no hakken made* (Until the discovery of the third person) (Tokyo: Chikuma Shobō, 1994); Suga Hidemi, *Shōsetsu teki kyōdo* (Novelistic force) (Tokyo: Fukutake Shoten, 1990).
69. Ōzasa, "Shokuminchi shugi," 1:38, 71–73. See also Kawatake Toshio, *Nihon engeki zenshi* (Complete history of Japanese theater) (Tokyo: Iwanami Shoten, 1959), 1032–37.
70. The importance of elocution for the educated student aspiring to be an actor may have been compounded by the denigration of film actors, who was not expected to speak any lines, since this was still the era of silent cinema. Most stage actors looked down on film actors as those incapable of making it on stage, but New Theater actors were particularly contemptuous of film actors as those incapable of elocution. Kawamura Karyō, one-time member of the Theater Institute, points out that he found many film actors to be riddled with speech impediments, heavy accents, and stuttering. Being able to read and articulate clearly was a distinguishing mark of the educated actor. Kawamura Karyō, *Zuihitsu Matsui Sumako,* 88–89.
71. For a detailed study of the various translations and stagings of *Hamlet* in Japan, see Kawatake Toshio, *Nihon no Hamuretto* (Hamlet in Japan) (Tokyo: Nansōsha, 1972).
72. *Tokyo Asahi Shimbun* (November 26, 1907); quoted in Matsumoto Shinko, *Meiji,* 914.
73. *Teikoku bungaku* (December 1907), quoted in Matsumoto Shinko, *Meiji,* 914.
74. He proposed the musical play (*gakugeki*) and the dance play *(buyō geki)* as the basis of the new national theater, music and dance being crucial ingredients of *kabuki* as well as Western opera. Ōzasa, *Nihon gendai engeki shi,* 1:74. His "Manifesto on New Musical Theater" (Shin gakugeki ron) was proposed on 1904, in the middle of the Russo-Japanese War, and his rhetoric manifests all the contradictions and compromises of the New Theater. He began by pointing out that all civilized nations of the world have a national theater or a national music. Japan used to have something equivalent in *noh* and *kabuki,* but both genres have declined. Once the Russo-Japanese War is over and the Japanese empire has attained a status equal to that of other civilized nations, it will also need a national theater or national music. At a moment when rumors of Yellow Peril

are alarming those abroad and sinister socialist trends are making inroads domestically, Tsubouchi Shōyō pleads, we need "to create something that will display externally the truth of our civilization, that is, our ideals and refinements, to Euro-American nations, and that will internally mediate the tastes of upper, middle, and lower classes, soothe and soften their emotions, and that will serve as the instrument of harmony between rich and poor on the one hand, as well as the instrument of education and enlightenment on the other hand." Quoted in Ōzasa, *Nihon gendai engeki shi,* 1:74.

75. Kawamura Karyō, *Zuihitsu Matsui Sumako,* 31–33.
76. Ōzasa, *Nihon gendai engeki shi,* 1:39. It is interesting to note that one of the realizations of Tsubouchi Shōyō's plans might have been the Takarazuka Revue. See Robertson, *Takarazuka,* 124–25.
77. On the Tsukiji Small Theater, see Akiba Tarō, *Nihon shingeki shi* (History of Japanese new theater), 2 vols. (Tokyo: Risōsha, 1955), 2:532–644.
78. Gay Gibson Cima, *Performing Women: Female Characters, Male Playwrights, and the Modern Stage* (Ithaca, N.Y.: Cornell University Press, 1993), 20–59.
79. Ibid., 25.
80. Antonin Artaud, *The Theater and its Double,* trans. Mary Caroline Richards (New York: Grove Press, 1958), 124.
81. Artaud, *The Theater,* 117–18. See also Jacques Derrida, "The Theater of Cruelty," 239.
82. Cima, *Performing Women,* 23.
83. Shimamura Hōgetsu, "Shingeki to serifu" (New Theater and lines), in vol. 2 of *Hōgetsu zenshū,* 639–43; quote from 640.
84. Ibid.
85. Shimamura, "Shingeki to serifu," 641.
86. Ibid.
87. Kawamura Karyō, *Zuihitsu Matsui Sumako,* 44–45.
88. Ibid., 45.
89. Matsui Shōyō, "Gekijutsu gakkō no hitsuyō" (The need for an acting school), *Waseda bungaku* (October 1907), quoted in Matsumoto Shinko, *Meiji,* 922.
90. Ibid., 923.
91. Matsui Shōyō, "Engeki kaishin saku" (Plans for theater innovation), quoted in Matsumoto Shinko, *Meiji,* 923.
92. Ryokurō Shujin, "Matsui Sumako to kataru: real conversation" (Talking with Matsui Sumako: Real conversation), *Engei gahō* (March 1911): 95–107; quote from 98. This interview with the actress, subtitled "Real Conversation" in English, is presented like a play set at the backstage of the Literary Society. The dialogue between the reporter and Sumako is presented with "stage directions" in brackets.
93. Ibid., 99.
94. Quoted in Akiba, *Nihon shingeki shi,* 2: 583. This was during rehearsals for Tsubouchi Shōyō's *En no gyōja* (The ascetic of En), a play that is said to represent the relationship between Tsubouchi himself, Shimamura Hōgetsu, and Matsui Sumako. In the play, a female demon lures a disciple away from the master ascetic. There are several versions of this play, published under different titles.

See, for example, *Onna mashin* (Female demon-god), *Shin engei* 1, no.7 (September 1916): 2–53; *Gyōja to joma* (The ascetic and the female demon), *Shin engei* 7, no. 8 (August 1922): 2–29. For a discussion of these various versions, see Kawatake Toshio, "Tsubouchi Shōyō to Ibsen: *En no gyōja, Brand* hikaku kō" (Tsubouchi Shōyō and Ibsen: Thoughts on a comparison between *En no gyōja* and *Brand*), in *Zoku hikaku engeki gaku* (Comparative study of theater, continued) (Tokyo: Nansōsha, 1974), 588–616.

95. Rimer, *Toward a Modern Japanese Theater,* 73.
96. Cima, *Performing Women,* 58.
97. In *Origins of Modern Japanese Literature,* Karatani Kōjin describes the reform of acting technique undertaken by Ichikawa Danjūrō. Karatani quotes Itō Sei's description of the *kabuki* actor's innovative techniques—using patterns of ordinary speech and bodily movements that conveyed a sense of psychology. See Itō Sei, *Nihon bundanshi* (A history of the Japanese bundan) (Tokyo: Kōdansha, 1953–73), 1:131–132. Karatani then summarizes

    The heavily made-up, boldly patterned face of the *kabuki* actor was nothing more than a mask. What Ichikawa brought to *kabuki,* and what can be seen even more clearly in later Shingeki performance, was the naked face. . . . Itō Sei describes how Ichikawa Danjūrō "struggled to create expressions that would convey a sense of psychology to his audience," but in fact it was the familiar naked ("realistic") face that emerged at this time as something that conveyed meaning, and that meaning—to be precise—was "interiority." Interiority was not something that had always existed, but only appeared as the result of the inversion of a semiotic constellation. No sooner had it appeared than it was seen as "expressed" by the naked face. In the process of this transformation the meaning of dramatic performance was reversed.

    Karatani, *Origins,* 56–57. Thus the naked face and the body of the actor came to be seen as transparent mediums for expressing "interior truths," a change that is often simply designated as a move towards "realism" and "mimesis" (*shajitsu*), but which involves a complicated rearticulation of what is real and what is mimed.
98. We can also think about New Theater as promoting the *genbun itchi* of gender: If *gen* (speech) is understood to be the internal essence expressed outward in *bun* (writing), then what New Theater tried to achieve was to unify gender expression (*bun*) with gender essence (*gen*), thereby helping to install essence as anterior to expression, rather than the other way around.
99. Derrida, "The Theater of Cruelty," 235. For an overview of scholarship on theater audiences see Susan Bennett, *Theatre Audiences: A Theory of Production and Reception,* 2d ed. (London: Routledge, 1997). For instructive discussions of spectatorship in cinema, see Judith Mayne, *Cinema and Spectatorship* (London: Routledge, 1993); Janet Staiger, *Interpreting Films: Studies in the Historical Reception of American Cinema* (Princeton: Princeton University Press, 1992).
100. Shimamura Hōgetsu, "Kono jijitsu o ika ni suru ka," *Engeki* (October 1915).
101. Osanai Kaoru, "Shingeki fukkō no tame ni," *Shin engei* (January 1917).

102. Morinaga, "Osanai Kaoru to shirōtoshugi," 285–86.
103. Bordieu, *Practical Reason,* 84.
104. Kawamura Karyō, *Zuihitsu Matsui Sumako,* 124–25.
105. Ibid., 129.
106. See Ōzasa, *Nihon gendai engeki shi,* vol. 3 for a detailed description of this process.

CHAPTER 8

1. See Mary Ann Doane, *Femmes Fatales: Feminism, Film Theory, Psychoanalysis* (New York: Routledge, 1991).
2. For a mapping of this process see Denise Riley, *"Am I That Name?": Feminism and the Category of "Women" in History* (Minneapolis: University of Minnesota, 1988). Also, see Bram Dijkstra, *Idols of Perversity: Fantasies of Feminine Evil in Fin-de-Siècle Culture* (New York: Oxford University Press, 1986).
3. Doane, *Femmes Fatales,* 3.
4. See Carol S. Vance, ed., *Pleasure and Danger: Exploring Female Sexuality* (London: Pandora, 1992).
5. For a list of plays performed by Matsui Sumako, see the appendix to Kawamura Karyō, *Zuihitsu Matsui Sumako: Geijutsuza seisui ki* (Essay on Matsui Sumako: Records of the rise and fall of the Geijutsuza), Seia Sensho, no. 25 (Tokyo: Seia Shobō, n.d.).
6. *Et Dukkehjem* should be translated as *A Doll House,* rather than *A Doll's House.* Rolf Fjelde, the English translator of Ibsen, uses the title *A Doll House* as well. The quotes from the play are taken from Rolf Fjelde, trans., *Ibsen: Four Major Plays* (New York: Signet, 1965).
7. See, for example, Katharine M. Rogers, "Feminism and *A Doll House: A Doll House* in a Course on Women in Literature," *Approaches to Teaching Ibsen's* A Doll House, ed. Yvonne Shafer (New York: MLA, 1985).
8. This is a topic of much speculation and the theme for many sequels and parodies, both in Europe and in Japan. See Nakamura Toshiko, "Three *A Doll's House* in Japan," *Edda: Nordisk Tidsskrift for Litteraturforskning* (Scandinavian journal for literary research), no.3 (1985): 163–71. Some flippant members of the public in Japan speculated that she might become an actress at the Teikoku Gekijō or a salesgirl at the Mitsukoshi department store, but in the end she would be reduced to poverty. Note that both the Teikoku Gekijō and the Mitsukoshi department store embodied the amalgamation of modernity, commodification, and femininity. See Mine Takashi, *Teikoku Gekijō kaimaku* (The opening of the Imperial Theater), Chūkō Shinsho, no. 1334 (Tokyo: Chūō Kōronsha, 1996), 211.
9. Joan Templeton attacks recent critical attempts to "rescue" *A Doll House* from feminist interpretation. See Joan Templeton, "The *Doll House* Backlash: Criticism, Feminism, and Ibsen," *PMLA* 104 (1989): 28–40.
10. Ibsen declared in his "Speech at the Banquet of the Norwegian League for Women's Rights" (1898) that he never consciously worked for the women's

rights movement, that he has merely sought to describe mankind in general. See Evert Spinchorn, ed. and trans., *Ibsen: Letters and Speeches* (New York: Hill and Wang, 1964).

11. Quoted in Siegfried Mandel, introduction, *Ibsen's Heroines,* by Lou Salomé (Redding Ridge, Conn.: Black Swan Books, 1985): 8–41; quote from 23.
12. Barbara Gentikow, *Skandinavien als präkapitalistische Idylle: Rezeption gesellschaftskritischer Literatur in deutschen Zeitschriften 1870 bis 1914* (Scandinavia as pre-capitalist idyll: Reception of socio-critical literature in German periodicals 1870 to 1914). Skandinavistische Studien 9 (Neumünster: Karl Wachholtz Verlag, 1978).
13. This ending appears in Wilhelm Lange's German translation, quoted in Gentikow, *Skandinavien,* 105.
14. Sadoya Shigenobu, *Hōgetsu Shimamura Takitarō ron* (Essay on Hōgetsu Shimamura Takitaro) (Tokyo: Meiji Shoin, 1980), 143.
15. Angela Livingstone, *Lou Andreas-Salomé* (London: G. Fraser, 1984), 235.
16. Ute Frevert, *Women in German History: From Bourgeois Emancipation To Sexual Liberation,* trans. Stuart McKinnon-Evans (Oxford: Berg, 1988), 126–27.
17. Shimaura Hōgetsu, *Kabuki* 137 (November 1911).
18. Matsumoto Shinko, *Meiji engeki ron shi* (A history of Meiji theater discussions) (Tokyo: Engeki Shuppansha, 1980), 1032.
19. Also due to the fact that, at the time, no one could figure out what the "Tarantella Dance" looked like. See Sadoya, *Hōgetsu Shimamura,* 416.
20. Matsui Sumako, "Nora to Maguda" (Nora and Magda), in *Botanbake* (Peony brush) (1914; reprint, Tokyo: Fuji Shuppan, 1986), 175–84.
21. Ibid., 175–76.
22. Ibid., 179–81.
23. Ibid., 181.
24. Matsui Sumako, "Ningyō no ie no omoide" (Memories of *A Doll House*), in her *Botanbake,* 144–57.
25. Matsui Sumako, "Nora to Maguda," 144–46.
26. One of three dance plays by Tsubouchi Shōyō.
27. Matsui Sumako, "Nora to Maguda," 148–150.
28. Ibid., 151–52.
29. Ibid., 157.
30. Ibid., 153–54.
31. Matsui Sumako, "Butai no ue de ichiban komatta koto" (What gave me the most trouble on stage), *Seitō* 2, no. 1 (1912): 162–63.
32. Matsui Sumako, "Nora to Maguda," 163.
33. Ihara Seisei'en, *Miyako Shimbun,* September 23, 1911, quoted in Kawamura Karyō, *Zuihitsu,* 266–67.
34. Kawamura Karyō, "Shienjō to ningyō no ie" (The private theater and *A Doll House*), *Kabuki,* November 1911.
35. Quoted in Murakami Nobuhiko, *Taishō joseishi: shimin seikatsu* (History of Taishō women: Citizen's lives) (Tokyo: Rironsha, 1982), 193.
36. For a more detailed discussion of the reception of *A Doll House* in Britain, Germany, and Japan, see Ayako Kano, "Acting Like a Woman in Modern Japan:

Gender, Performance, Nation, and the Roles of Kawakami Sadayakko and Matsui Sumako," (Ph.D. diss. Cornell University, 1995).

37. Li Takanori writes about "the new relation of reversibility" (*sōgo hanten teki na kankei*) between self and other that makes it possible for readers to identify with characters in the modern novel written in *genbun itchi* style. See Li Takanori, *Hyōshō kūkan no kindai: Meiji "Nihon" no media hensei* (The modernity of the space of representation: The media formation of Meiji "Japan") (Tokyo: Shin'yōsha, 1996), 106–8. For a relevant description of writings by fans of the Takarazuka theater, see Jennifer Robertson, who calls fan mail published in Takarazuka fan magazines "exercises in self-subjectivity and self-representation" and "interior monologues made public and visible." Jennifer Robertson, *Takarazuka: Sexual Politics and Popular Culture in Modern Japan,* (Berkeley: University of California Press, 1998), 191.
38. Her real name was Katō Kikuyo (1888–1922). She participated in *Seitō* from its first issue and wrote many novels as well as essays.
39. Katō Midori, "Ningyō no ie" (A Doll House), *Seitō* 2, no. 1 (1912): 115–25; quote from 123.
40. This probably refers to a lecture entitled "Tokyo ni okeru Nora geki no inshō" (Impressions of the Nora play in Tokyo), given in Osaka on March 13, 1911, in anticipation of the Osaka performances of *A Doll House.*
41. Katō Midori, "Ningyō no ie," 124.
42. Ibid., 117–19.
43. Ueno Yō(ko)'s real name was Ueno Tetsu (1886–1928). She was a teacher at a women's high school (*kōtō jogakko*), and wrote many essays and novels for *Seitō.*
44. Ueda Kimi(ko) (1886–1971) was a graduate of Japan Women's University (Nihon Joshi Daigaku) and published a number of novels and plays in *Seitō.*
45. Ueno Yōko, "*Ningyō no ie* yori josei mondai e" (From *A Doll House* to the Woman Question), *Seitō* 2, no.1 (1912): 62–114.
46. Ibid., 112.
47. Ibid., 94.
48. Ibid., 100–101.
49. Ueda Kimiko, "*Ningyō no ie* o yomu" (Reading *A Doll House*), *Seitō* 2, no. 1 (1912): 126–132; quote from 131.
50. Hiratsuka Raichō, *Chosakushū* (Collected works), 7 vols. (Tokyo: Ōtsuki Shoten, 1983), 1:79.
51. Ibid., 1:85.
52. Hiratsuka Raichō, vol. 2 of *Genshi josei wa taiyō de atta* (In ancient times woman was the sun), 4 vols (Tokyo: Ōtsuki Shoten, 1971), 2:350.
53. Hiratsuka, *Chosakushū,* 1:81.
54. Otake Kōkichi, "Akai tobira no ie yori" (From the house of red doors), *Seitō* 2, no. 5 (May 1912): 32–53; quote from 40.
55. Ibid., 46–47.
56. Horiba Kiyoko gives an account of Otake's relationship with Hiratsuka Raichō in the context of same-sex love in Meiji Japan. See Horiba Kiyoko, *Seitō no jidai,* 106–119. The presence and portrayal of female homosexual, homoerotic,

and homosocial relations in *Seitō* deserves more academic attention. Some of the essays and short stories published in the journal deal with "*dōseiai*" (same-sex love) between women. For instance, a translation of Havelock Ellis's chapter "Sexual Inversion of Women" from his *Studies in the Psychology of Sex* is included in volume 4 number 4 of *Seitō* (April 1914).

57. For an analysis of the different interpretations of this play by actresses, see Ellen Donkin, "The Problem of Interpretation: Bernhardt, Duse, Fiske and Modjeska Perform Magda," *Turn-of-the-Century Women* 4, no. 2 (Winter 1987): 48–59.
58. On the reception of Sudermann in Europe, the United States, and Japan, see Jean-Paul Mathieu Mannes, "Die Aufnahme der dramatischen Werke Hermann Sudermanns: Eine Untersuchung seines theatralischen Erfolgs," (Ph. D. diss., Utrecht University, 1976); Ingrid Nohl, "Das dramatische Werk Hermann Sudermanns: Versuch einer Darstellung seiner Gesellschaftskritik auf dem Theater im 19. und 20. Jahrhundert und im Film," (Ph. D. diss., University of Köln, 1973); Yokomizo Masahachiro, "Hermann Sudermann in Japan: Aspekte seines Einflusses auf Literatur und Geisteswelt der Meiji Periode (1868–1912)," in *Hermann Sudermann: Werk und Wirkung,* ed. Walter T. Rix (Würzburg: Königshausen und Neumann, 1980), 344–59.
59. Klaus Matthias, "Kerr und die Folgen: Analyse der Sudermann-Kritik als Perspektive einer Neubewertung seiner Dramen," in Rix. ed., *Hermann Sudermann,* 31–86; quote from 56.
60. The title of *Heimat* may also be referring to the "homeland" as an ethnically, culturally, and linguistically bounded space. It is significant that Magda must travel abroad in order to become a professional singer, and her acquired foreignness as Maddalena dall'Orto enables her freedom from the constraints of German domesticity.
61. This was one of the lines censored by Japanese authorities.
62. For overviews of the feminist movements in Germany, see Elke Frederiksen, ed., *Die Frauenfrage in Deutschland 1865–1915: Texte und Dokumente* (Stuttgart: Reclam, 1981); Ute Gerhard, *Unerhört: Die Geschichte der deutschen Frauenbewegung* (Hamburg: Rowohlt, 1990). "Geistige Mütterlichkeit" (Spiritual motherhood) became the program of moderate feminist associations such as the Allgemeine Deutsche Frauenverein.
63. For example, Paula Tanqueray in Arthur Wing Pinero's *The Second Mrs. Tanqueray.* See Elliott M. Simon, "Arthur Wing Pinero's *The Second Mrs. Tanqueray:* A Reappraisal," *The Ball State University Forum* 28, no. 1 (Winter 1987): 44–56.
64. "Introduction" to Hōgetsu's Japanese translation of *Heimat.* In *Hōgetsu zenshū,*8 vols. (Tokyo: Nihon Tosho Sentā, 1979), 5:1–130; quote from 3–4.
65. Both the female opera singer and the actress connoted freedom from family constraints as well as a loose morality in the Western context. See Susan Rutherford, "The Voice of Freedom: Images of the prima donna," in *The New Woman and her Sisters: Feminism and Theater 1850–1914,* ed. Vivien Gardner and Susan Rutherford (Ann Arbor: University of Michigan Press, 1992), 95–113. Also note that the line between opera and straight plays was not very distinct at this time in Japan: Operas such as *Carmen* and *Aïda* were often adapted and performed

as verse drama, while songs were often inserted into plays to display the vocal talents of the performers. On actresses as New Women, see Tracy C. Davis, *Actresses as Working Women: Their Social Identity in Victorian Culture* (London: Routledge, 1991).

66. In the same vein, *A Doll House* was often referred to as *Nora,* both in Europe and in Japan.
67. Charles Edward Amery Winslow, *Magda* (London: Lamson & Wolffe, 1896).
68. The translation was gently chastised by one critic as being too "conscientious" (*teinei*), that is, too faithful to the original and too wordy in its attempt to explicate the nuance of the original. This criticism is evidence that there is a sense of a master-text to be adhered to, that a translation should closely follow the original text, and that a performance should closely follow the written text. See Ikuta Chōkō, "Bungei Kyōkai no *Kokyō* o miru" (Seeing the Literary Society's *Heimat*), *Engei gahō* (June 1912): 108–115.
69. Matsui Sumako, "Maguda" (Magda), *Engei gahō* (June 1912): 126–127.
70. The staging also emphasized the theme of Magda's confinement in her father's home. The gray scenery contrasted with Magda's fiery red robe at her entrance in act 2. Thus, Terada Namiji begins his review of the play by conjuring up the image of a pretty little bug caught in a dull gray spider web: The image parallels that of Magda caught in the heavy atmosphere of her parental house. Terada Namiji, "*Kokyō* ni deru hitobito" (People who appear in *Heimat*), *Engei gahō* (June 1912): 101–108.
71. Kusuyama Masao, *Kokumin Shimbun,* May 10, 1912. Quoted in Sadoya, *Hōgetsu Shimamura,* 425.
72. Ikuta, "Bungei Kyōkai," 111.
73. Kawajiri Seitan, "Bungei Kyōkai *Kokyō* shokan" (Literary Society's *Heimat* review), *Engei gahō* (June 1912): 130–138; quote from 130.
74. Kawajiri Seitan, "Bungei Kyōkai," 137.
75. Ihara Seisei'en, *Miyako Shimbun,* May 6, 1912. Quoted in Sadoya, *Hōgetsu Shimamura,* 425.
76. Masamune Hakuchō, *Kokumin Shimbun,* May 10, 1912. Quoted in Kikuchi Akira, "Matsui Sumako butai kiroku," (Matsui Sumako's performance record), in *Zuihitsu Matsui Sumako: Geijutsuza seisui ki* (Essay on Matsui Sumako: The rise and fall of the Geijutsuza theater) (Tokyo: Seia Shobō, 1968), 257–91; quote from 269. Here, "actress-plays" (*joyū geki*) refers to performances by Teikoku Gekijō actresses; "old-plays" (*kyūgeki*) refers to *kabuki.*
77. Hasegawa Shigure, "Bungei Kyōkai no Magda" (Magda at the Literary Society), *Seitō* 2, no .6 (June 1912): 1–5.
78. Hiratsuka Raichō, "Yonda 'Magda'" (Reading "Magda"), *Seitō* 2, no. 6 (June 1912): 6–13.
79. Ibid., 11.
80. Ibid., 13.
81. Otake Kōkichi, "Magda ni tsuite" (On Magda), *Seitō* 2, no. 6 (June 1912): 14–16; quote from 16.
82. Kiuchi Tei, "Magda ni tsuite" (On Magda), *Seitō* 2, no. 6 (June 1912): 17.

83. Naganuma Chie, also known as Chieko, was later to achieve fame as the mad wife to whom the modernist poet Takamura Kōtarō dedicated his collection of poetry, *Chieko shō*. She was an artist responsible for much of the artwork in *Seitō,* but gave up her art after marriage.
84. Naganuma Chie, "Magda ni tsuite" (On Magda), *Seitō* 2.6 (June 1912): 14.
85. Police peace bureau director *(hoan kyokuchō)* Koga, quoted in *Waseda bungaku* no. 83 (October 1912), 288. The High Treason (*taigyaku*) incident, in which a large number of anarchists and socialists were accused of plotting the assassination of the emperor, had taken place only a few years prior to the performance of *Heimat*. Subsequent to the incident, the police strengthened its persecution of dissident activists, and ideological control was intensified in general. See Mikiso Hane, *Modern Japan: A Historical Survey,* 2d ed. (Colorado: Westview, 1992), 182–83 for a short summary of the incident and its impact.
86. Sadoya Shigenobu discusses the production and the controversy in some detail. See Sadoya, *Hōgetsu Shimamura,* 423–434.
87. Quoted in *Waseda bungaku* no. 83 (October 1912): 288.
88. Shimamura Hōgetsu, "Introduction" to his translation, in *Hōgetsu zenshū,* 5:5.
89. From Hōgetsu's Japanese translation in *Hōgetsu zenshū,* 5:129–30. The English translation is mine.
90. Magda's expressions of defiance such as "man weiß ja, was die Familie mit ihrer Moral von uns verlangt" (We all know what the family with its morality demands from us) had to be deleted, and other expressions softened. Several articles in *Engei gahō* (June 1912) about the play have also been censored: The offensive parts have been replaced by "O OOOOO OO OOO" in a common practice known as *fuseji.*
91. Shimamura Hōgetsu, "Introduction," 4.
92. Shimamura Hōgetsu, "Bungei Kyōkai no *Kokyō*" (The Literary Society's *Heimat*) and "*Maguda* no kinshi mondai" (The problem of the ban on *Magda*), both in *Hōgetsu zenshū* 2:405–7; and 2:415–417, respectively.
93. Quoted in *Waseda bungaku* no. 83 (October 1912): 296.
94. Ibid., 297.
95. Ibid., 296.
96. Interestingly, Tsubouchi Shōyō, founder of the Literary Society, felt that the alteration was minor: "It merely added a kind of solution to an ending that was left unresolved" (Ibid., 297). Ikuta Chōkō also reminded readers that the ending of *A Doll House* had likewise been changed for the first performance in Germany. He suggests that circumstances are similar in Germany and in Japan. He points out the significance of *Heimat* for the condition of women in Japan, and that in the conservative context of Japan, the middle-of-the-road ideas of the nonradical Sudermann hit just the right chord. See Ikuta, "Bungei Kyōkai," 108–115.
97. Matsui Sumako, *Botanbake,* 175–184.
98. Ibid., 184.
99. It is interesting to note that the genders of the protagonists reverse the gendered characterization of the two playwrights by Shimamura Hōgetsu. He was apparently echoing popular judgment in the West when he contrasted Sudermann and

Hauptmann, explaining the former to be the more masculine, flamboyant, philosophical, and technical artist, compared to the feminine, introspective, and poetic Hauptmann. "Sudermann no *Kokyō* ni egakaretaru shisō mondai" (The ideological problems portrayed in Sudermann's *Heimat*), *Hōgetsu zenshū,* 2:498.

100. *The Sunken Bell* was the most popularly successful work of Gerhart Hauptmann. See Gerhard Schulz, "Gerhart Hauptmanns dramatisches Werk," in *Handbuch des deutschen Dramas,* ed. Walter Hinck (Düsseldorf: Bagel, 1980), 311–26; Peter Sprengel, "Gerhart Hauptmann," in *Realismus, Naturalismus und Jugendstil,* ed. Gunter E. Grimm and Frank Rainer Max, vol. 6 of *Deutsche Dichter,* 8 vols. (Stuttgart: Reclam, 1989), 6:335–56. It was performed about two hundred times in the first three years after its premiere. See Eberhard Hilscher, *Gerhart Hauptmann: Leben und Werk: Mit bisher unpublizierten Materialen aus dem Manuskriptnachlaß des Dichters* (Frankfurt: Athenäum, 1988).
101. Hilscher, *Gerhart Hauptmann,* 224.
102. Gerhart Hauptmann, *Die versunkene Glocke,* in *Sämmtliche Werke,* ed. Hans-Egon Haas (Frankfurt: Propyläen Verlag, 1966), 1:757–869.
103. *The Sunken Bell,* the playwright's first complete break from naturalism and his most successful one, represents nonetheless a continuation of Hauptmann's thematic concerns. Schultz argues that the use of dialect and sociolect in Hauptmann was never intended to be a mere "*Naturnachahmung*" (mimesis of nature) but a form of artistic distancing. In this sense, the use of verse performed the same function.
104. Hauptmann's *Einsame Menschen* (Lonely people) was translated into Japanese by Mori Ōgai and performed by Osanai Kaoru's Jiyū Gekijō (Free Theater) troupe. All the roles, including the female roles, were performed by *kabuki* actors; the performance flopped and revealed the inadequacy of *kabuki* training for performing modern European plays in translation. See Ōzasa Yoshio, *Nihon gendai engeki shi* (History of Japanese contemporary theater), 6 vols. to date (Tokyo: Hakusuisha, 1985–1999), 1:111–112. See also Tamura Toshiko's quote in chapter 2, n.8.
105. Otto Mann, *Geschichte des deutschen Dramas* (History of German drama), Kröners Taschenausgabe Band 296 (Stuttgart: Alfred Kröner Verlag, 1963), 496–97.
106. Hilscher, *Gerhart Hauptmann,* 224–225.
107. Evelyn Weber, "Gerhart Hauptmann und die Frau" (Gerhart Hauptmann and woman), *Neue Deutsche Hefte* 31, no. 1 (1984): 79–96; in particular 84–88. A very different but persuasive interpretation by Marc A. Weiner explains the popular success of the play in terms of the cultural ideology of prefascist Germany. Weiner, "Gerhart Hauptmanns *Die versunkene Glocke* and the Cultural Vocabulary of Pre-Fascist Germany," *German Studies Review* 11, no. 3 (October 1988): 447–461.
108. See Sadoya, *Hōgetsu Shimamura,* 463–464.
109. Osanai Kaoru, director of a rival company, accused Hōgetsu of "stealing while giving alms" (quoted in Ibid., 475). For the rivalry between Shimamura Hōgetsu

and Osanai Kaoru, see Ochi Haruo, *Meiji Taishō no geki bungaku: Nihon kindai gikyoku shi e no kokoromi* (Dramatic literature in Meiji and Taisho: Towards a history of modern Japanese plays) (Tokyo: Hanawa Shobō, 1971), especially 39–52.

110. Shimamura Hōgetsu, "'Tsukuran to suru kokoro' to *Chinshō*" (The ideal to create and *Die versunkene Glocke*), in *Hōgetsu zenshū* 2: 637–638.
111. Ōzasa, *Nihon,* 1:168–171.
112. Ihara Seisei'en, *Miyako Shimbun,* August 11, 1918, quoted in Kawamura Karyō, *Zuihitsu,* 288.
113. Oka Kitarō, *Mainichi Shimbun,* n.d., quoted in Kawamura Karyō, *Zuihitsu,* 288.
114. *Tokyo Asahi Shimbun,* September 11, 1918, quoted in Kawamaura Karyō, *Zuihitsu,* 288.
115. My English translation borrows some phrasings from Charles Henry Meltzer, *The Sunken Bell: A Fairy Play in Five Acts by Gerhart Hauptmann: Freely Rendered into English Verse* (New York: R. H. Russell, 1899). This passage appears on p. 2.
116. Bram Dijkstra, *Idols of Perversity: Fantasies of Feminine Evil in Fin-de-Siècle Culture* (New York: Oxford University Press, 1986). See also pp. 135–137, where Dijkstra discusses representations of actresses who are "most relentlessly fixated on their mirrors." Dijkstra cites Zola's Nana, Theodore Dreiser's Carrie, and Mark Twain's Eve.
117. My translation borrows phrasings from Meltzer, *The Sunken Bell,* 64–65.
118. For the Japanese production, Nakayama Shimpei composed a song based on the Japanese lines of this song, to be sung by Matsui Sumako. On the songs performed by Sumako during her career, see Harris I. Martin, "Popular Music and Social Change in Prewar Japan," *The Japan Interpreter* 7, no. 3–4 (1972): 332–352; Komota Nobuo, et al., eds., *Nihon ryūkōka shi: senzen hen* (History of Japanese popular song: Prewar) (Tokyo: Shakai Shisōsha, 1981).
119. Watanabe Jun'ichi begins the prologue to his novelization of Matsui Sumako's biography with a description of the three recordings she made. She recorded two songs from *The Sunken Bell* and one song each from Tolstoy's *Resurrection* and his *Living Corpse.* "Katúsha's Song" from *Resurrection* became a tremendous hit, and 40,000 records were sold. See Watanabe Jun'ichi, *Joyū* (Actress) (Tokyo: Shūeisha, 1983).
120. Kusuyama Masao, "Haiyū to shite" (As a performer), *Engei gahō* (February 1919): 78–79. Kusuyama himself was rumored to have been Sumako's object of affection after Shimamura Hōgetsu's death—part of the mythology surrounding Sumako has her killing herself because Kusuyama spurned her advances.
121. Ibid., 79.
122. Kawamura Karyō, *Zuihitsu,* 195–96, 220.
123. Ibid., 187.
124. Ibid., 175–79.
125. Matsui Sumako's performances of the plays by Nakamura Kichizō, heavily influenced by Ibsen, Hauptmann, and other naturalist writers, but also by *shimpa* melodrama, ought to be the subject of another full-length study.

EPILOGUE

1. Kawakami Sadayakko's performance employed Matsui Shōyō's translation, with music composed by Yamada Kōsaku. See Imura Kimie, *Sarome no hen'yō: hon'yaku, butai* (Salomé's transformations: Translations and performances) (Tokyo: Shinshokan, 1990) for an extended discussion of Japanese receptions of the figure of Salomé.
2. Matsui Sumako's performance used Kusuyama Masao's translation. Matsui Sumako performed this play for the first time in 1913 (December 2 to 26), with Nakamura Kichizō's translation at the Teikoku Gekijō theater. The 1914 performances, which lasted from April to July, were part of a national tour. Matsui Sumako performed the role a total of 127 times; this was the third most-frequently performed play in her repertoire (after Tolstoy's *Resurrection* and Nakamura Kichizō's *The Razor* (Kamisori), another femme fatale play).
3. Parenthetical in-text page references are to Oscar Wilde, *Salomé,* trans. Alfred Douglas, in *The Importance of Being Earnest and Other Plays* (New York: Penguin, 1986), 315–348.
4. Gail Finney, "The (Wo)Man in the Moon: Wilde's *Salomé,*" in *Women in Modern Drama: Freud, Feminism, and European Theater at the Turn of the Century* (Ithaca, N.Y.: Cornell University Press, 1989), 55–78. Finney considers the femme fatale to be "as old as literature," with a lineage traceable to Helen of Troy. I am more convinced by Mary Ann Doane's historical explanation of the femme fatale as a figure of modernity, as discussed in the preceding chapter.
5. For a fuller discussion of the reception of *Salomé* in Japan, see Imura, *Sarome no hen'yō.* See also Kano, "Visuality and Gender in Modern Japan: Looking at Salome," *Japan Forum* 11, no. 1 (1999): 43–55.
6. Osanai Kaoru, "Hongōza no Sarome" (Hongōza Theater's *Salomé*), *Engei gahō* (June 1915): 148–63; quote from 150.
7. Honma Hisao, "Sendai hagi to Sarome" (Sendai Hagi and Salomé), *Engei gahō* (January 1914): 53.
8. Honma as quoted in Ōzasa, *Nihon gendai engeki shi* (History of contemporary Japanese theater) (Tokyo: Hakusuisha, 1985), 144.
9. Osanai, "Hongōza," 159.
10. Aoyagi Yumi, "Sumako wa naniyue ni jisatsu seshiya" (Why did Sumako commit suicide?), *Engei gahō* (February 1919): 70–72; Ōkubo Tōho, "Sumako no jisatsu wa hentai seiyoku" (Sumako's suicide was due to perverse desire), *Onna no sekai* 5, no.2 (February 1919): 4–15.
11. Imura, *Sarome no hen'yō,* 120–122.
12. The performance took place from March 20 to April 4, 1915, staged by a group that had split off from the troupe headed by Matsui Sumako and Shimamura Hōgetsu. This period saw the rise and fall of numerous small theater troupes in Japan.
13. Haino Shōhei, "Geijutsuza no Sarome" (Geijutsuza theater's Salomé), *Engei gahō* (June 1915): 140–147.

14. Kwaguchi Matsutarō, *Yaeko shō* (Tokyo: Chūō Kōronsha, 1981), quoted in Imura, *Sarome no hen'yō*, 146–47.
15. Tanaka Eizō, *Meiji Taishō shingeki shiryō shi* (Tokyo: Engeki Shuppansha, 1964), quoted in Imura, *Sarome no hen'yō*, 128.
16. Imura, *Sarome no hen'yō*, 96.
17. Mieke Bal, "His Master's Eye," in *Modernity and Hegemony of Vision*, ed. David Michael Levin (Berkeley: University of California Press, 1993), 382–83.
18. See Judith Butler, *Excitable Speech: A Politics of the Performative* (New York: Routledge, 1997).
19. Mizutani, as quoted in Imura, *Sarome no hen'yō*, 147.
20. Matsui Sumako, *Botanbake* (Peony brush) (1914; reprint, Tokyo: Fuji Shuppan, 1986), 160–62.

Bibliography

Adams, Hazard, and Leroy Searle, eds. *Critical Theory Since 1965*. Tallahassee: University Press of Florida; Florida State University Press, 1986.

Akashi Tetsuya. *Geinō chōhen shōsetsu: Kawakami Otojirō* (A grand novel about the performing arts: Kawakami Otojirō). Tokyo: Sankyō Shoin, 1943.

Akiba Tarō. *Nihon shingeki shi* (History of Japanese new theater). 2 vols. Tokyo: Risōsha, 1955.

Akita Ujaku. "Hito oyobi haiyū to shite no Matsui Sumako" (Matsui Sumako as person and performer). *Engei gahō* (February 1919): 74–77.

Akita Ujaku, and Nakagi Sadakazu, eds. *Koi no aishi: Sumako no isshō* (Love's sad history: Matsui Sumako's life). Tokyo: Nihon Hyōronsha, 1919.

Alcott, Kenneth. *Jules Verne*. New York: Macmillan, 1941.

Allison, Anne. *Permitted and Prohibited Desires: Mothers, Comics, and Censorship in Japan*. Boulder, Colo.: Westview Press, 1996.

Anderson, Benedict. *Imagined Communities: Reflections on the Origin and Spread of Nationalism*. 2d. ed. London: Verso, 1991.

Andreas-Salomé, Lou. *Henrik Ibsens Frauen-Gestalten: Nach seinen sechs Familiendramen* (Henrik Ibsen's female figures: On his six family dramas). 2d ed. Jena: Eugen Diederichs, 1906.

———. *Ibsen's Heroines*. Translated by Siegfried Mandel. Redding Ridge, Conn.: Black Swan Books, 1985.

———. *Lebensrückblick: Grundrisse einiger Lebenserinnerungen* (Looking back on life: Outline of a few memories). Edited by Ernst Pfeiffer. Frankfurt: Insel Verlag, 1968.

Aoyagi Yūbi. "Sumako wa naniyue ni jisatsu seshiya" (Why did Sumako commit suicide?). *Engei gahō* (February 1919): 70–72.

Artaud, Antonin. *The Theater and Its Double*. Translated by Mary Caroline Richards. New York: Grove Press, 1958.

Asano Miwako. "Geinō ni okeru josei" (Women in performing arts). *Ranjuku suru onna to otoko: kinsei* (Ripening women and men: Early modern). Vol. 4 of *Onna to otoko no jikū: Nihon joseishi saikō* (The space-time of women and men: Rethinking Japanese women's history), edited by Fukuda Mitsuko, 31–68. 7 vols. Tokyo: Fujiwara Shoten, 1995.

Austin, Gayle. *Feminist Theories for Dramatic Criticism*. Ann Arbor: University of Michigan Press, 1990.

Bal, Mieke. "His Master's Eye." In *Modernity and the Hegemony of Vision*, edited by David Michael Levin, 379–404. Berkeley: University of California Press, 1993.

Barthes, Roland. *Camera Lucida: Reflections on Photography.* Translated by Richard Howard. New York: Noonday, 1981.

———. *Empire of Signs.* New York: Noonday, 1982.

———. *Image, Music, Text.* Translated by Stephen Heath. New York: The Noonday Press, 1988.

Beasley, W. G. *Japanese Imperialism, 1894–1945.* Oxford: Clarendon, 1987.

Belsey, Catherine. *Critical Practice.* London: Routledge, 1980.

Benhabib, Seyla. "Epistemologies of Postmodernism: A Rejoinder to Jean-François Lyotard." In *Feminism/Postmodernism,* edited by Linda Nicholson, 107–32. New York: Routledge, 1990.

Benjamin, Walter. *Charles Baudelaire: A Lyric Poet in the Era of High Capitalism.* Translated by Harry Zohn. London: Verso, 1983.

Bennett, Milton J. "A Developmental Approach to Training for Intercultural Sensitivity." *International Journal of Intercultural Relations* 10, no. 2 (1986): 179–96.

Bennett, Susan. *Theatre Audiences: A Theory of Production and Reception.* 2d ed. London: Routledge, 1997.

Bernstein, Gail Lee, ed. *Recreating Japanese Women, 1600–1945.* Berkeley: University of California Press, 1991.

Binion, Rudolph. *Frau Lou: Nietzsche's Wayward Disciple.* Princeton: Princeton University Press, 1968.

Birnbaum, Phyllis. *Modern Girls, Shining Stars, the Skies of Tokyo: 5 Japanese Women.* New York: Columbia University Press, 1999.

Böttger, Claudia. "Androgynität und Kreativität bei Lou Andreas-Salomé" (Androgyny and creativity in Lou Andreas-Salomé). In *Andreas-Salomé,* edited by Rilke-Gesellschaft, 23–25. Karlsruhe: von Loeper Verlag, 1986.

Bourdieu, Pierre. *In Other Words: Essays Towards a Reflexive Sociology.* Translated by Matthew Adamson. Stanford: Stanford University Press, 1990.

———. *Practical Reason: On the Theory of Action.* Stanford: Stanford University Press, 1998.

Bowlby, Rachel. *Just Looking: Consumer Culture in Dreiser, Gissing, and Zola.* New York: Methuen, 1985.

———. *Still Crazy After All These Years: Women, Writing and Psychoanalysis.* London: Routledge, 1992.

Brandon, James R., William P. Malm, and Donald H. Shively. *Studies in Kabuki: Its Acting, Music, and Historical Context.* Honolulu: University of Hawaii Press, 1978.

Britain, Ian. "A Transplanted Dolls House: Ibsenism, Feminism, and Socialism in Late-Victorian and Edwardian England." In *Transformations in Modern European Drama,* 14–54. Atlantic Highlands, N.J.: Humanities Press, 1983.

Butcher, William. *Verne's Journey to the Centre of the Self: Space and Time in the* Voyages extraordinaires. New York: St. Martins, 1990.

Butler, Judith. *Bodies that Matter: On the Discursive Limits of Sex.* New York: Routledge, 1993.

———. *Excitable Speech: A Politics of the Performative.* New York: Routledge, 1997.

———. *Gender Trouble: Feminism and the Subversion of Identity.* New York: Routledge, 1990.

———. "Gender Trouble, Feminist Theory, and Psychoanalytic Discourse." In *Feminism/Postmodernism,* edited by Linda Nicholson, 324–40. New York: Routledge, 1990.

———. "Performative Acts and Gender Constitution: An Essay in Phenomenology and Feminist Theory." In *Performing Feminisms: Feminist Critical Theory and Theatre,* edited by Sue-Ellen Case, 270–82. Baltimore, Md.: Johns Hopkins University Press, 1990.

Case, Sue-Ellen. *Feminism and Theatre.* New York: Methuen, 1988.

———, ed. *Performing Feminisms: Feminist Critical Theory and Theatre.* Baltimore, Md.: Johns Hopkins University Press, 1990.

Chesneaux, Jean. *The Political and Social Ideas of Jules Verne.* Translated by Thomas Wikeley. London: Thames and Hudson, 1972.

Chance, Frank. "Images of Victory: Woodblock Prints from the Sino-Japanese War." Paper presented at the Mid-Atlantic Regional Conference of the Association for Asian Studies, Towson State University, October 1995.

Chiba, Yoko. "Sada Yacco and Kawakami: Performers of *Japonisme.*" *Modern Drama* 35, no. 1 (March 1992): 35–53.

Chow, Rey. "Its you, and not me: Domination and Othering in Theorizing the Third World." In *Coming to Terms: Feminism, Theory, Politics,* edited by Elizabeth Weed, 152–61. New York: Routledge, 1989.

———. *Women and Chinese Modernity: The Politics of Reading Between West and East.* Minneapolis: Minnesota University Press, 1991.

———. *Writing Diaspora.* Bloomington: Indiana University Press, 1993.

Cima, Gay Gibson. "Elizabeth Robins: The Genesis of an Independent Manageress." *Theatre Survey: The American Journal of Theatre History* 21, no. 2 (November 1980): 145–63.

———. *Performing Women: Female Characters, Male Playwrights, and the Modern Stage.* Ithaca, N.Y.: Cornell University Press, 1993.

Cixous, Hélène. "The Laugh of the Medusa." Translated by Keith Cohen and Paula Cohen. In *Critical Theory Since 1965,* edited by Hazard Adams and Leroy Searle, 309–320. Tallahassee: University Press of Florida; Florida State University Press, 1986.

Clarke, Thurston. "Afterword." In *Around the World in Eighty Days* by Jules Verne, translated by Jacqueline Rogers, 246–53. New York: Signet-Penguin, 1991.

Coaldrake, Angela Kimi. *Women's Gidayū and the Japanese Theatre Tradition.* London: Routledge, 1997.

Costello, Peter. *Jules Verne: Inventor of Science Fiction.* London: Hodder and Stoughton, 1978.

Cunningham, Gail. *The New Woman and the Victorian Novel.* London: Macmillan, 1978.

Dale, Peter. *The Myth of Japanese Uniqueness.* London: Croom Helm, 1986.

Danly, Robert Lyons, ed. and trans. *In the Shade of Spring Leaves: The Life and Writings of Higuchi Ichiyō, a Woman of Letters in Meiji Japan.* New York: Norton, 1981.

Davis, Tracy C. "Actresses and Prostitutes in Victorian London." *Theatre Research International* 13, no. 3 (1988): 221–34.

———. *Actresses as Working Women: Their Social Identity in Victorian Culture.* London: Routledge, 1991.

———. "Questions for a Feminist Methodology in Theatre History." In *Interpreting the Theatrical Past: Essays in the Historiography of Performance,* edited by Thomas Postlewait and Bruce A. McConachie, 59–81. Iowa City: University of Iowa Press, 1989.

de Bary, Brett, and Karatani Kōjin. "Feminizumu to kindai hihyō" (Feminism and modern criticism). *Subaru* 13, no. 11 (November 1991): 214–35.

de Lauretis, Teresa. *Alice Doesn't: Feminism, Semiotics, Cinema.* Bloomington: Indiana University Press, 1984.

———. "Sexual Indifference and Lesbian Representation." In *Performing Feminisms: Feminist Critical Theory and Theatre,* edited by Sue-Ellen Case, 17–39. Baltimore, Md.: Johns Hopkins University Press, 1990.

———. *Technologies of Gender: Essays on Theory, Film and Fiction.* Bloomington: Indiana University Press, 1987.

Derrida, Jacques. *Margins of Philosophy.* Translated by Alan Bass. Chicago: University of Chicago Press, 1982.

———. "The Theater of Cruelty and the Closure of Representation." In *Writing and Difference,* translated by Alan Bass, 232–50. Chicago: University of Chicago Press, 1978.

Diamond, Elin. "Brechtian Theory/Feminist Theory: Toward a Gestic Feminist Criticism." *Drama Review* 32, no. 1 (1988): 82–94.

Dijkstra, Bram. *Idols of Perversity: Fantasies of Feminine Evil in Fin-de-Siècle Culture.* New York: Oxford University Press, 1986.

Doane, Mary Ann. *Femmes Fatales: Feminism, Film Theory, Psychoanalysis.* New York: Routledge, 1991.

Dolan, Jill. "Breaking the Code: Musings on Lesbian Sexuality and the Performer." *Modern Drama* 32, no. 1 (March 1989): 146–58.

———. *The Feminist Spectator as Critic.* Ann Arbor: UMI Research Press, 1988.

———. "Lesbian Subjectivity in Realism: Dragging at the Margins of Structure and Ideology." In *Performing Feminisms: Feminist Critical Theory and Theatre,* edited by Sue-Ellen Case, 40–53. Baltimore, Md.: Johns Hopkins University Press, 1990.

Donkin, Ellen. "The Problem of Interpretation: Bernhardt, Duse, Fiske and Modjeska Perform Magda." *Turn-of-the-Century Women* 4, no. 2 (Winter 1987): 48–59.

Dudden, Faye. *Women in American Theater: Actresses and Audiences, 1790–1870.* New Haven: Yale University Press, 1994.

Dunn, Charles J., and Torigoe Bunzō, ed. and trans. *The Actors' Analects (Yakusha Rongo).* New York: Columbia University Press, 1969.

Durbach, Errol. "Ibsen's Liberated Heroines and the Fear of Freedom." In *Contemporary Approaches to Ibsen Vol. 5: Reports from the Fifth International Ibsen Seminar, Munich 1983,* edited by Daniel Haakonsen, 11–23. Oslo: Universitetsforlaget, 1985.

Dusinberre, Juliet. *Shakespeare and the Nature of Women.* London: Macmillan, 1975.

Duus, Peter. *The Abacus and the Sword: The Japanese Penetration of Korea, 1895–1910.* Berkeley: University of California Press, 1995.

Duus, Peter, Ramon H. Myers, and Mark. R. Peattie, eds. *The Japanese Informal Empire in China, 1895–1937*. Princeton: Princeton University Press, 1989.

———, eds. *The Japanese Wartime Empire, 1931–1945*. Princeton: Princeton University Press, 1996.

Dyhouse, Carol. "The Role of Women: From Self-Sacrifice to Self-Awareness." In *The Victorians,* edited by Laurence Lerner, 174–92. London: Methuen, 1978.

Egusa Mitsuko. "Watashi no shintai, watashi no kotoba: *Baien, Futon* no shūhen" (My body, my words: On *Smoke* and *The Quilt*). *Kindai 1* (Modern 1). Vol. 5 of *Nihon bungaku shi o yomu* (Reading Japanese literary history), edited by Yūseidō Henshūbu, 177–208. 6 vols. Tokyo: Yūseidō, 1990.

Egusa Mitsuko, and Seki Reiko, eds. *Dansei sakka o yomu: feminizumu hihyō no seijuku e* (Reading male writers: Towards the maturation of feminist criticism). Tokyo: Shin'yōsha, 1994.

———, eds. *Onna ga yomu Nihon kindai bungaku: feminizumu hihyō no kokoromi* (Women reading modern Japanese literature: Experiments in feminist criticism). Tokyo: Shin'yōsha, 1992.

Ehara Yumiko. *Feminizumu to kenryoku sayō* (Feminism and the workings of power). Tokyo: Keisō Shobō, 1988.

———. *Josei kaihō to iu shisō* (The ideology of women's liberation). Tokyo: Keisō Shobō, 1985.

———. *Radikaru feminizumu saikō* (Radical feminism's renaissance). Tokyo: Keisō Shobō, 1991.

Enami Shigeyuki, and Mitsuhashi Toshiaki. *Modan toshi kaidoku dokuhon: arui wa kindai no chikaku o ōdan suru chishiki/kenryoku no keifugaku* (A reader to decode the modern city: Or, a genealogy of knowledge/power traversing the senses of the modern). Bessatsu Takarajima, no. 75. Tokyo: JICC, 1988.

Evans, I. O. *Jules Verne and His Work*. London: Arco, 1965.

Ezaki Atsushi. *Jitsuroku Kawakami Sadayakko: sekai o kaketa honoo no onna* (The true records of Kawakami Sadayakko: A fiery woman who spanned the world). Tokyo: Shin Jimbutsu Ōraisha, 1985.

Feldstein, Richard, and Judith Roof, eds. *Feminism and Psychoanalysis*. Ithaca, N.Y.: Cornell University Press, 1989.

Felski, Rita. *Beyond Feminist Aesthetics: Feminist Literature and Social Change*. Cambridge: Harvard University Press, 1989.

Ferris, Lesley. *Acting Women: Images of Women in Theatre*. New York: New York University Press, 1989.

Field, Norma. *In the Realm of a Dying Emperor: Japan at Century's End*. New York: Pantheon, 1991.

Finney, Gail. *Women in Modern Drama: Freud, Feminism, and European Theater at the Turn of the Century*. Ithaca, N.Y.: Cornell University Press, 1989.

Fjørtoft, Kari. "The Reception Given to Hedda Gabler by Ibsen's Contemporaries: A Comparison between Women's and Men's Critical Evaluation." In *Contemporary Approaches to Ibsen Vol. 5: Reports from the Fifth International Ibsen Seminar, Munich 1983,* edited by Daniel Haakonsen, 58–69. Oslo: Universitetsforlaget, 1985.

Fleischhacker, Sabine. "Ibsen im Lichte der Münchner Presse (1876–1891)" (Ibsen in the light of Munich's press (1876–1891)). In *Contemporary Approaches to Ibsen Vol. 5: Reports from the Fifth International Ibsen Seminar, Munich 1983*, edited by Daniel Haakonsen, 113–31. Oslo: Universitetsforlaget, 1985.

Foster, Susan Leigh. "Choreographies of Gender." *Signs* 24, no. 1 (Autumn 1998): 1–34.

Foucault, Michel. *Discipline and Punish: The Birth of the Prison*. 1977. Translated by Alan Sheridan. 2d ed. New York: Vintage, 1995.

———. *The History of Sexuality Vol. 1*. Translated by Robert Hurley. New York: Vintage, 1980.

———. *The Order of Things: An Archaeology of the Human Sciences*. New York: Vintage Books. 1973.

Fournier, Louis. *Kawakami and Sada Yacco*. Paris: Brentanos, 1900.

Fowler, Edward. *The Rhetoric of Confession: Shishōsetsu in Early Twentieth-Century Japanese Fiction*. Berkeley: University of California Press, 1988.

Fredriksen, Elke, ed. *Die Frauenfrage in Deutschland 1865–1915: Texte und Dokumente* (The woman question in Germany 1865–1915: Texts and documents). Stuttgart: Reclam, 1981.

Freedman, Barbara. "Frame-Up: Feminism, Psychoanalysis, Theatre." In *Performing Feminisms: Feminist Critical Theory and Theatre,* edited by Sue-Ellen Case, 54–76. Baltimore, Md.: Johns Hopkins University Press, 1990.

———. *Staging the Gaze: Postmodernism, Psychoanalysis and Shakespearean Comedy.* Ithaca, N.Y.: Cornell University Press, 1991.

Frevert, Ute. *Women in German History: From Bourgeois Emancipation To Sexual Liberation*. Translated by Stuart McKinnon-Evans. Oxford: Berg, 1988.

Friese, Wilhelm. "Das deutsche Theater und Henrik Ibsen: ein historisches Panorama" (The German theater and Henrik Ibsen: A historical panorama). In *Contemporary Approaches to Ibsen Vol. 5: Reports from the Fifth International Ibsen Seminar, Munich 1983,* edited by Daniel Haakonsen, 132–42. Oslo: Universitetsforlaget, 1985.

Fujii, James. *Complicit Fictions: The Subject in the Modern Japanese Prose Narrative.* Berkeley: University of California Press, 1992.

Fujii Sōtetsu, "Hajimeni: kaisetsu ni kaete" (Introduction: In place of a commentary). In *Jiden Otojirō, Sadayakko* (Autobiography of Otojirō, Sadayakko), edited by Fujii Sōtetsu. Tokyo: San'ichi Shobō, 1984.

Fujimori Seikichi. *Dokuhaku no onna: Shimamura Hōgetsu to Matsui Sumako* (Woman of monologues: Shimamura Hōgetsu and Matsui Sumako). *Higeki kigeki* (Tragedies and comedies) 221 (March 1969): 93–138.

Fukuda Yoshiyuki. "Oppekepe" (Oppekepe). *Shingeki* (New theater) 11, no. 1 (January 1964): 56–124.

Fukuzawa, Yukichi. *The Autobiography of Fukuzawa Yukichi*. Translated by Eiichi Kiyooka. Lanham: Madison Books, 1992.

Funabashi Kuniko. "Dansei kaihō no susume" (An encouragement of men's liberation). *Gunzō* 46, no. 11 (November 1991): 155.

Furukawa Makoto. "Dōseiaisha no shakai shi" (The social history of homosexuals). In *Wakaritai anata no tame no shakaigaku nyūmon* (An introduction to sociology for those of you who want to know), 218–22. Bessatsu Takarajima, no. 176. Tokyo: Takarajimasha, 1993.

———. "Ren'ai to seiyoku no dai-san teikoku: tsūzoku-teki seiyoku-gaku no jidai" (The Third Empire of romantic love and sexual desire: The age of popular sexology). *Gendai shisō* (July 1993): 110–127.

Gainor, J. Ellen. *Shaw's Daughters: Dramatic and Narrative Constructions of Gender.* Ann Arbor: University of Michigan Press, 1991.

Garber, Marjorie. *Vested Interests: Cross-Dressing and Cultural Anxiety.* New York: Routledge, 1992.

Gardner, Vivien, and Susan Rutherford, eds. *The New Woman and Her Sisters: Feminism and Theatre, 1850–1914.* Ann Arbor: University of Michigan Press, 1992.

Garon, Sheldon. *Molding Japanese Minds: The State in Everyday Life.* Princeton: Princeton University Press, 1997,

Garten, H. F. *Modern German Drama.* 2d ed. London: Methuen, 1964.

Geertz, Clifford. *Local Knowledge: Further Essays in Interpretive Anthropology.* New York: Basic Books, 1983.

Gentikow, Barbara. *Skandinavien als präkapitalistische Idylle: Rezeption gesellschaftskritischer Literatur in deutschen Zeitschriften 1870 bis 1914* (Scandinavia as precapitalist idyll: Reception of socio-critical literature in German periodicals 1870 to 1914). Skandinavistische Studien 9. Neumünster: Karl Wachholtz Verlag, 1978.

George, David E. R. *Henrik Ibsen in Deutschland: Rezeption und Revision* (Henrik Ibsen in Germany: reception and revision). Palaestra Band 251. Göttingen: Vandenhoeck & Ruprecht, 1968.

———. "A Question of Method: Ibsen's Reception in Germany." In *Transformations in Modern European Drama,* edited by Ian Donaldson, 55–79. Atlantic Highlands, N.J.: Humanities Press, 1983.

Gerhard, Ute. *Unerhört: Die Geschichte der deutschen Frauenbewegung* (Unheard of: The history of the German women's movement). Hamburg: Rowohlt, 1990.

Giesing, Michaela. *Ibsens Nora und die wahre Emanzipation der Frau: Zum Frauenbild im Wilhelminischen Theater* (Ibsen's Nora and the true emancipation of woman: On the image of women in Wilhelminian theater). Studien zum Theater, Film und Fernsehen 4. Frankfurt: Peter Lang, 1984.

Girard, René. *Deceit, Desire, and the Novel: Self and Other in Literary Structure.* Translated by Yvonne Freccero. Baltimore, Md.: Johns Hopkins University Press, 1965.

Gluck, Carol. *Japan's Modern Myths: Ideology in the Late Meiji Period.* Princeton: Princeton University Press, 1985.

Goodman, David. *Japanese Drama and Culture in the 1960s: The Return of the Gods.* London: M. E. Sharpe, 1988.

Griffis, William Elliot. *The Mikado's Empire.* 11th ed. 2 vols. New York: Harper, 1906.

Grimm, Gunter E., and Frank Rainer Max, eds. *Realismus, Naturalismus und Jugenstil* (Realism, naturalism, and Jugendstil). Vol. 6 of *Deutsche Dichter* (German writers). 8 vols. Stuttgart: Reclam, 1989.

Grindstaff, Laura. "*La Femme Nikita* and the Textual Politics of 'The Remake.'" *Camera Obscura,* forthcoming.

Gropp, Rose-Maria. "Das Weib existiert nicht" (Woman does not exist). In *Lou Andreas-Salomé,* edited by Rilke-Gesellschaft, 46–54. Karlsruhe: von Loeper Verlag, 1986.

Gunji Masakatsu. "Hitotsu no kankyaku ron" (A theory of audience). In *Kabuki ronsō* (Essays on kabuki), 671–79. Kyoto: Shibunkaku, 1979.

Haakonsen, Daniel, ed. *Contemporary Approaches to Ibsen Vol. 5: Reports from the Fifth International Ibsen Seminar, Munich 1983.* Oslo: Universitetsforlaget, 1985.

Hagii Kōzō. *Shimpa no gei* (The art of shimpa). Tokyo: Tokyo Shoseki, 1984.

Haino Shōhei. "Geijutsuza no Sarome" (Geijutsuza theater's Salomé). *Engei gahō* (June 1915): 140–47.

———. "Sumako ni kansuru taiwa" (Dialogue on Sumako). *Engei gahō* (June 1915): 28–32.

Hamaguchi Eshun. *Nihonrashisa no saihakken* (The rediscovery of Japanliness). Tokyo: Nihon Keizai Shimbunsha, 1977.

Hane, Mikiso. *Modern Japan: A Historical Survey.* 2d ed. Boulder, Colo.: Westview, 1992.

Hanna, Judith Lynne. *Dance, Sex and Gender: Signs of Identity, Dominance, Defiance, and Desire.* Chicago: University of Chicago Press, 1988.

———. *To Dance Is Human: A Theory of Nonverbal Communication.* Chicago: University of Chicago Press, 1987.

Hanson, Katherine. "Ibsen's Women Characters and Their Feminist Contemporaries." *Theatre History Studies* 2 (1982): 86–87.

Haraway, Donna. "A Manifesto for Cyborgs: Science, Technology, and Socialist Feminism in the 1980s." In *Coming to Terms: Feminism, Theory, Politics,* edited by Elizabeth Weed, 173–204. New York: Routledge, 1989.

Harding, Sandra. "Feminism, Science, and the Anti-Enlightenment Critiques." In *Feminism/Postmodernism,* edited by Linda Nicholson, 83–106. New York: Routledge, 1990.

———. *Whose Science? Whose Knowledge?: Thinking from Women's Lives.* Ithaca, N.Y.: Cornell University Press, 1991.

Hardwick, Elizabeth. *Seduction and Betrayal: Women and Literature.* New York: Random House, 1970.

Hart, Lynda, ed. *Making a Spectacle: Feminist Essays on Contemporary Women's Theatre.* Ann Arbor: University of Michigan Press, 1988.

Hasegawa Shigure. "Bungei Kyōkai no Maguda" (Magda at the Literary Society). *Seitō* 2, no. 6 (June 1912): 1–5.

———. "Kyūgeki wa onnagata" (Old plays are for onnagata). *Engei gahō* (January 1912): 50–52.

———. "Madamu Sadayakko" (Madame Sadayakko). In *Shimpen: kindai bijin den* (New edition: Legends of modern beauties), edited by Sugimoto Sonoko, 49–99. Tokyo: Iwanami Shoten, 1985 [1936].

———. "Matsui Sumako." In *Shimpen: kindai bijin den* (New edition: Legends of modern beauties), edited by Sugimoto Sonoko, 277–316. Tokyo: Iwanami Shoten, 1985 [1936].

———. "Sumako san no koto" (About Ms. Sumako). *Engei gahō* (February 1919): 66–67.

Hatoyama Kazuo. "Engeki kairyō" (Theater reform). *Engei gahō* (January 1907): 69–71.

Hauptmann, Gerhart. *Die versunkene Glocke* (The sunken bell). In vol. 1 of *Sämmtliche Werke* (Complete works), edited by Hans-Egon Haas, 57–869. Frankfurt: Propyläen Verlag, 1966.

Hayashi Chitose. "Amari ni guchi rashikeredo" (Though it may seem too much like complaining). *Engei gahō* (February 1919): 80–81.

Helms, Lorraine. "Playing the Woman's Part: Feminist Criticism and Shakespearean Performance." In *Performing Feminisms: Feminist Critical Theory and Theatre,* edited by Sue-Ellen Case, 196–206. Baltimore, Md.: Johns Hopkins University Press, 1990.

———. "Roaring Girls and Silent Women: The Politics of Androgyny on the Jacobean Stage." In *Women in Theatre,* edited by James Redmond, 9–73. London: Cambridge University Press, 1989.

Herrmann, Anne. "Travesty and Transgression: Transvesticism in Shakespeare, Brecht and Churchill." In *Performing Feminisms: Feminist Critical Theory and Theatre,* edited by Sue-Ellen Case, 294–315. Baltimore, Md.: Johns Hopkins University Press, 1990.

Hijiya-Kirschnereit, Irmela. *Rituals of Self-Revelation : Shishōsetsu as Literary Genre and Socio-Cultural Phenomenon.* Cambridge: Council on East Asian Studies, Harvard University, 1996.

Hilscher, Eberhard. *Gerhart Hauptmann: Leben und Werk: Mit bisher unpublizierten Materialen aus dem Manuskriptnachlass des Dichters* (Gerhart Hauptmann: Life and work: With hitherto unpublished material from the writer's manuscripts). Frankfurt: Athenäum, 1988.

Hiratsuka Raichō. *Chosakushū* (Collected works). 7 vols. Tokyo: Ōtsuki Shoten, 1983.

———. *Genshi josei wa taiyō de atta* (In ancient times woman was the sun). 4 vols. Tokyo: Otsuki Shoten, 1971.

———. "Yonda Maguda" (Reading Magda). *Seitō* 2, no. 6 (June 1912): 6–13.

Hisaita Eijirō. *Joyū* (Actress). In *Hisaita Eijirō shinario shū* (Collected film scripts of Hisaita Eijirō), 3–89. Tokyo: Chūōsha, 1947.

Hoefert, Sigfrid. "Zur Wirkung Gerhart Hauptmanns in Asien" (On Gerhart Hauptmanns impact in Asia). *Jahrbuch der Schlesischen Friedrich-Wilhelms-Universität zu Breslau* 27 (1985): 135–51.

Honma Hisao. "Sendai hagi to Sarome" (*Sendai Hagi* and *Salomé*). *Engei gahō* (January 1914): 53.

Horiba Kiyoko. *Seitō no jidai: Hiratsuka Raichō to atarashii onnatachi* (The era of the Blue Stockings: Hiratsuka Raichō and new women). Tokyo: Iwanami Shoten, 1988.

Horiba Kiyoko, ed. *Seitō josei kaihō ron shū* (Seitō essays on women's liberation). Tokyo: Iwanami Shoten, 1991.

Howe, Elizabeth. *The First English Actress: Women and Drama 1660–1700.* Cambridge: Cambridge University Press, 1992.

Hōjō Hideji. *Joyū* (Actress). In *Hōjō Hideji gikyoku senshū* (Selected plays of Hōjō Hideji). Tokyo: Seia Shobō, 1971. 106–218.

Hyland, Peter. "A Kind of Woman: The Elizabethan Boy-Actor and the Kabuki Onnagata." *Theatre Research International* 12.1 (1987): 1–8.

Hyōdō Hiromi. *"Koe" no kokumin kokka: Nihon* ("Voice" and nation-state: Japan). Tokyo: NHK Books, 2000.

Ibsen, Henrik. *Ibsen: Four Major Plays.* Translated by Rolf Fjelde. New York: Signet, 1965.

———. *The Complete Prose Plays.* Translated by Rolf Fjelde. New York: Farrar Straus Giroux, 1965.

Ichikawa Fusae, et al. eds. *Nihon fujin mondai shiryō shūsei* (Collection of documents on Japanese women's issues). 10 vols. Tokyo: Domesu Shuppan, 1976–1981.

Ihara Seisei'en. "Inochi gake no gei" (Art that risks life). *Engei gahō* (February 1919): 64–65.

———. "Sumako no shi wa kūzen no kiroku" (Sumako's death is an unprecedented record). *Onna no sekai* 5, no. 2 (February 1919): 16–17.

Ihara Toshio. *Meiji engeki shi* (History of Meiji theater). Tokyo: Hōō Shuppan, 1975 [1933].

Iizuka Tomoichirō. *Kabuki gairon* (Overview of kabuki). Tokyo: Hakubunkan, 1928.

Ikuta Chōkō. "Bungei Kyōkai no *Kokyō* o miru" (Seeing the Literary Society's *The Home*). *Engei gahō* (June 1912): 108–15.

Imura Kimie. *Sarome no hen'yō: hon'yaku, butai* (Salomé's transformations: Translations and performances). Tokyo: Shinshokan, 1990.

Inoue Seizō. *Kawakami Otojirō no shōgai* (The life of Kawakami Otojirō). Tokyo: Ashi Shobō, 1985.

Irigaray, Luce. *This Sex Which is Not One.* Translated by Catherine Porter with Carolyn Burke. Ithaca, N.Y.: Cornell University Press, 1985.

Isayama Yōtarō. *Ie, ai, sei: kindai Nihon no kazoku shisō* (Family, love, sex: Family ideology in modern Japan). Tokyo: Keisō Shobō, 1994.

Ishikawa Mikiaki. "Yonkajō no yōkyū" (Four demands). *Engei gahō* (May 1907): 1–3.

Itō Sei. *Nihon bundanshi* (A history of the Japanese *bundan*). 8 vols. Tokyo: Kōdansha, 1953–73.

Ivy, Marilyn. "Critical Texts, Mass Artifacts: The Consumption of Knowledge in Postmodern Japan." In *Postmodernism and Japan,* edited by Masao Miyoshi, and H. D. Harootunian, 21–46. Durham, N.C.: Duke University Press, 1989.

———. *Discourses of the Vanishing: Modernity, Phantasm, Japan.* Chicago: University of Chicago Press, 1995.

Iwamoto Kenji. "Sekkin to hedatari: close-up no shisō" (Nearness and distance: The ideology of the close-up). In *Nihon eiga no tanjō* (The birth of Japanese cinema). Vol. 1 of *Kōza Nihon eiga* (Lectures on Japanese cinema), 250–59. 7 vols. Tokyo: Iwanami Shoten, 1985.

Jardine, Alice A. *Gynesis: Configurations of Woman and Modernity.* Ithaca, N.Y.: Cornell University Press, 1985.

Jardine, Lisa. *Still Harping on Daughters: Women and Drama in the Age of Shakespeare.* Brighton: Harvester, 1983.

Jay, Martin. "Scopic Regimes of Modernity." In *Vision and Visuality,* edited by Hal Foster, 3–28. Dia Art Foundation Discussions in Contemporary Culture No. 2. Seattle: Bay Press, 1988.

Johnson, Barbara. *A World of Difference.* Baltimore, Md.: Johns Hopkins University Press, 1987.

Josei Shi Sōgō Kenkyūkai (Women's history general study group), ed. *Nihon josei shi* (Japanese women's history). 5 vols. Tokyo: Tōdai Shuppankai, 1982.

Kamata Tadayoshi, "Tabi geinintachi no kaigai jungyō" (The overseas tours of traveling players). *Rekishi e no shōtai* (Invitation to history) 12 (1981): 82–85.

Kameda Atsuko. "Shūzoku ni miru josei kan: sekushizumu no shintō to shūzoku no hen'yō" (Views of women in folk customs: The permeation of sexism and the transformation of folk customs). In *Onna no imēji* (Women's images). Vol. 1 of *Kōza joseigaku* (Lectures in women's studies), edited by Joseigaku Kenkyūkai (Women's studies study group), 162–83. 4 vols. Tokyo: Keisō Shobō, 1984.

Kamiyama Uraji. "Magari zumai no koro" (When we lived in rented rooms). *Engei gahō* (February 1919): 72–74.

Kang Sang-jung. "Datsu orientarizumu no shikō" (Thinking of de-orientalism). In *Nashonariti no datsukōchiku* (Deconstructing nationality), edited by Sakai Naoki, Brett de Bary, and Iyotani Toshio, 137–58. Tokyo: Kashiwa Shobō, 1996.

Kanai Yoshiko. *Posutomodan feminizumu: sai to josei.* (Postmodern feminism: Difference and women). Tokyo: Keisō Shobō, 1989.

Kanai Yoshiko. *Tenki ni tatsu feminizumu* (Feminism at a turning point). Tokyo: Mainichi Shimbunsha, 1985.

Kanai Yoshiko, and Biddy Martin. "Rezubian feminizumu to Fūkō riron" (Lesbian feminism and Foucauldian theory). Translated by Ayako Kano. *Jōkyō* (June 1993): 127–55.

Kano, Ayako. "Acting Like a Woman in Modern Japan." Ph. D. diss., Cornell University, 1995.

———. "Feminist Criticism of Theater: An Overview of the Field." *The Round Table* 8 (1993): 20–29.

———. "Japanese Theater and Imperialism: Romance and Resistance." *U.S.-Japan Women's Journal.* English version 12 (1997): 17–47.

———. "Nihon feminizumu ronsōshi 1: bosei to sekushuariti" (Japanese feminist debates 1: Motherhood and sexuality). In *Wādomappu feminizumu* (Wordmap feminism), edited by Ehara Yumiko and Kanai Yoshiko, 196–221. Tokyo: Shin'yōsha, 1997.

———. Review of *Takarazuka: Sexual Politics and Popular Culture in Modern Japan,* by Jennifer Robertson. *Journal of Japanese Studies* 25, no. 2 (1999): 473–78.

———. "The Roles of the Actress in Modern Japan." In *New Directions in the Study of Meiji Japan,* edited by Helen Hardacre, 189–202. Leiden: E. J. Brill, 1997.

———. "Seishinbunseki to feminizumu" (Psychoanalysis and feminism). In *Wādomappu feminizumu* (Wordmap feminism), edited by Ehara Yumiko and Kanai Yoshiko, 146–71. Tokyo: Shin'yōsha, 1997.

———. "Visuality and Gender in Modern Japanese Theater: Looking at Salome." *Japan Forum* 11, no. 1 (1999): 43–55.

Kant, Immanuel. *Critique of Judgment.* Translated by J. H. Bernard. New York: Hafner; London: Macmillan, 1951.

Karasuyakko. "Onna yakusha to joyū" (Female players and actresses). *Engei gahō* (January 1912): 151–54.

Karatani Kōjin. *Nihon kindai bungaku no kigen* (Origins of Modern Japanese literature). Tokyo: Kōdansha, 1980.

———. "Nihon seishin bunseki" (Psychoanalysis of Japan). *Hihyō kūkan* 1, no. 4 (1992): 271–81; 1, no. 5 (1992): 336–45; 1, no. 7 (1992): 246–61; 1, no. 8 (1993): 241–55; 1, no. 9 (1993): 242–51.

———. *Origins of Modern Japanese Literature.* Translated by Brett de Bary, et al. Durham, N.C.: Duke University Press, 1993.

———. "Sōkei-sei o megutte" (On bilinearity). In *Senzen no shikō* (Thoughts of prewar), 157–83. Tokyo: Bungei Shunjū, 1994.

———, et al. "Edo shisō-shi e no shiten" (A perspective towards Edo intellectual history). *Hihyō kūkan* 1, no. 5 (1992): 6–36.

Kasza, Gregory J. *The State and the Mass Media in Japan, 1918–1945.* Berkeley: University of California Press, 1988.

Katō Midori. "Ningyō no ie" (A Doll House). *Seitō* 2, no. 1 (1912): 115–25.

Katō Norihiro, and Takeda Seiji. *Futatsu no sengo kara* (From the two post-war periods). Tokyo: Chikuma Shobō, 1998.

Katō Shūichi. "'Sei no shōhinka' o meguru nōto" (Notes concerning 'commodification of sexuality'). In *Sei no shōhinka* (Commodification of sexuality), edited by Ehara Yumiko, 222–78. Feminizumu no shuchō (Feminist claims), no. 2. Tokyo: Keisō Shobō, 1995.

Kawaguchi Matsutarō. *Matsui Sumako.* Tokyo: Shimbashi Enbujō, 1963.

———. *Yaeko shō* (On Yaeko). Tokyo: Chūō Kōronsha, 1981.

Kawajiri Seitan. "Bungei Kyōkai *Kokyō* shokan" (Literary Society's *The Home* review). *Engei Gahō* (June 1912): 130–38.

Kawakami Otojirō, and Kawakami Sadayakko. *Jiden Otojirō, Sadayakko* (Autobiography of Otojirō, Sadayakko), edited by Fujii Sōtetsu. Tokyo: San'ichi Shobō, 1984.

———. *Kawakami Otojirō, Sadayakko manyū ki* (Records of the wanderings of Kawakami Otojirō and Sadayakko). Rpt. in *Autorō* (Outlaw), edited by Fujimori Eiichi. Vol. 6 of *Dokyumento Nihonjin* (Documentaries of Japanese), 6–68. 10 vols. Tokyo: Gakugei Shorin, 1968.

Kawakami Sadayakko. "Joyū rekihō roku" (Records of visits with great actresses). With Azuma Gakusei. *Engei gahō* (February 1911): 40–46.

———. "Meika shinsō roku" (Records of the true nature of master artists). With Kawajiri Seitan. *Engei gahō* (October 1908): 80–94.

———. "Otto ni wakarete nochi" (After my husband's departure). *Engei gahō* (November 1912): 169–72.

Kawakami Tomiji. "Gibo Sadayakko no omoide" (Memories of fostermother Sadayakko). *Rekishi e no shōtai* (Invitation to history) 12 (1981): 80–81.

Kawamura Karyō. "Matsui Sumako no gigei" (The artistry of Matsui Sumako). *Engei gahō* (June 1915): 32–36.

———. "Osuma san no butai guse" (Stage habits of Sumako). *Engei gahō* (February 1919): 67–68.

———. *Zuihitsu Matsui Sumako: Geijutsuza seisui ki* (Essay on Matsui Sumako: The rise and fall of the Geijutsuza theater). Seia Sensho, no. 25. Tokyo: Seia Shobō, 1968.

Kawamura Kunimitsu. "Onna no yamai, otoko no yamai: jendā to sekushuariti o meguru Fūkō no hensō" (Woman's illness, man's illness: A variation on Foucault concerning gender and sexuality). *Gendai shisō* (July 1993): 88–109.

Kawasaki Kenko. *Takarazuka: shōhi shakai no supekutakuru* (Takarazuka: Spectacle of consumer society). Tokyo: Kōdansha, 1999.

Kawatake Shigetoshi. *Nihon Engeki zenshi* (Complete history of Japanese theater). Tokyo: Iwanami Shoten, 1959.

———. *Shōyō, Hōgetsu, Sumako no higeki: shingeki hiroku* (The tragedy of Shōyō, Hōgetsu, and Sumako: Secret records of the new theater). Tokyo: Mainichi Shuppansha, 1966.

Kawatake Toshio. *Hikaku engeki gaku* (Comparative theater studies). Tokyo: Nansōsha, 1967.

———. *Nihon no Hamuretto* (Hamlet in Japan). Tokyo: Nansōsha, 1972.

———. *Zoku hikaku engeki gaku* (Comparative theater studies continued). Tokyo: Nansōsha, 1974.

———, et al. "Kawakami Otojirō ichiza no kaigai kōen o megutte" (On Kawakami Otojirō troupe's performances abroad). *Nihon Engeki Gakkai kiyō* (Proceedings of the Japan Theater Studies Association) 16 (1976): 74–94.

Kawazoe Kunimoto. *Shimamura Hōgetsu: hito oyobi bungakusha to shite* (Shimamura Hōgetsu: As man and as literary scholar). Tokyo: Waseda Sensho, 1953.

Keene, Donald, trans. *Major Plays of Chikamatsu*. New York: Columbia University Press, 1961.

Kema Namboku. "Joyū to onnagata no kachi" (The values of actresses and onnagata). *Engei Gahō* (March 1912): 95.

Kent, Christopher. "Image and Reality: The Actress and Society." In *A Widening Sphere: Changing Role of Victorian Women*, edited by Martha Vicinus, 94–116. Bloomington: Indiana University Press, 1977.

Kikuchi Akira, "Matsui Sumako butai kiroku" (Matsui Sumako's performance record). In Kawamura Karyō, *Zuihitsu Matsui Sumako: Geijutsuza seisui ki* (Essay on Matsui Sumako: The rise and fall of the Geijutsuza theater), 257–91. Seia Sensho, no. 25. Tokyo: Seia Shobō, n.d.

Kiuchi Tei. "Maguda ni tsuite" (On Magda). *Seitō* 2, no. 6 (June 1912): 17.

Kimura Ki. *Kaigai ni katsuyaku shita Meiji no josei* (Meiji women who succeeded abroad). Tokyo: Shibundō, 1963.

Kishii Yoshie. *Onna geisha no jidai* (The era of the female geisha). Tokyo: Seiabō, 1972.

Kitami Harukazu. *Tetteki to Shunsho: kindai engi no hajimari* (Tetteki and Shunsho: The beginnings of modern acting). Tokyo: Shōbunsha, 1978.

Klein, Susan Blakeley. *Ankoku Butō: The Premodern and Postmodern Influences on the Dance of Utter Darkness*. Ithaca, N.Y.: Cornell University East Asia Program, 1988.

Kobayashi Katsu. "*Botanbake* o yonde" (On reading *Peony Brush*). *Seitō* 4, no. 9 (October 1914): 171.

Kohama Itsuo. "Wakaritai otoko no tame no feminizumu nyūmon: onna wa hontō ni sabetsu sarete iru no ka?" (An introduction to feminism for men who want to know: Do women really suffer from discrimination?). In *Onna ga wakaranai!* (We can't understand women!), 146–59. Bessatsu Takarajima, no. 107. Tokyo: JICC, 1990.

Kohama Itsuo, Ehara Yumiko, and Kōno Kiyomi. "Onna wa doko ni iru no ka" (Where are women?). *Gunzō* 46.10 (October 1991): 144–74.

Kojève, Alexandre. *Introduction to the Reading of Hegel: Lectures on the Phenomenology of Spirit,* edited by Allan Bloom. Ithaca, N.Y.: Cornell University Press, 1969.

Kojima Koshū. "Geki no ikan ni yoru" (Depends on the kind of play). *Engei gahō* (January 1912): 147–51.

Kolodny, Annette. "Dancing Through the Minefield: Some Observations on the Theory, Practice, and Politics of a Feminist Literary Criticism." In *The New Feminist Criticism: Essays on Women, Literature and Theory,* edited by Elaine Showalter, 144–67. New York: Pantheon Books, 1985.

Komiya Toyotaka, ed. Edward G. Seidensticker and Donald Keene, trans. *Japanese Music and Drama in the Meiji Era.* Vol. 3 of *Japanese Culture in the Meiji Era.* 14 vols. Tokyo: Ōbunsha, 1956.

Komota Nobuo, et al. eds. *Nihon ryūkōka shi: senzen hen* (History of Japanese popular songs: Prewar). Tokyo: Shakai Shisōsha, 1981.

Kōno Taeko. "Furui moraru to no tatakai ni inochi o kaketa koi no Kachūsha" (Love's Katusha who risked her life to fight old morals). *Koi to geijutsu e no jōnen* (Passion for love and art). Vol. 4 of *Jimbutsu kindai josei shi: onna no isshō* (Individuals in modern women's history: women's lives), edited by Setouchi Harumi, 21–60. 8 vols. Tokyo: Kōdansha, 1980.

Koschmann, J. Victor. *Revolution and Subjectivity in Postwar Japan.* Chicago: University of Chicago Press, 1996.

Koshō Yukiko, ed. *Shiryō: josei-shi ronsō* (Documents: Women's history debate). Tokyo: Domesu Shuppan, 1984.

Kōuchi Nobuko, ed. *Shiryō: bosei hogo ronsō* (Documents: Motherhood protection debate). Tokyo: Domesu Shuppan, 1984.

Koyama Shizuko. *Ryōsai kenbo to iu kihan* (The norm of good wife wise mother). Tokyo: Keisō Shobō, 1991.

Kristeva, Julia. "Woman Can Never Be Defined." Translated by Marilyn A. August. In *New French Feminisms,* edited by Elaine Marks and Isabelle de Courtivron, 137–41. Brighton: Harvester, 1980.

———. "Women's Time." Translated by Alice Jardine and Harry Blake. In *Critical Theory Since 1965,* edited by Hazard Adams and Leroy Searle, 471–484. Tallahassee: University Press of Florida; Florida State University Press, 1986.

Kruger, Loren. *The National Stage: Theatre and Cultural Legitimation in England, France, and America.* Chicago: University of Chicago Press, 1992.

Kuhn, Annette. *The Power of the Image: Essays on Representation and Sexuality.* London: Routledge, 1985.

Kurata Yoshihiro. *Kindai geki no akebono* (The dawn of modern drama). Mainichi Sensho, no. 4. Tokyo: Mainichi Shimbunsha, 1981.

———. *1885 nen London Nihonjin mura* (1885 London Japanese Village). Tokyo: Asahi Shimbunsha, 1983.

Kurawaka Umejirō. "Gokai no uchi ni ikita Sumako" (Sumako lived amidst misunderstanding). *Onna no sekai* 5, no. 2 (February 1919): 44–49.

Kusuyama Masao. "Haiyū to shite" (As a performer). *Engei gahō* (February 1919): 78–79.

Kuwano Tōka. *Joyū ron* (On actresses). Tokyo: Sampōdō Shoten, 1913.

Laderrière, Mette. "The Technique of Female Impersonation in Kabuki." *Maske und Kothurn: Internationale Beiträge zur Theaterwissenschaft* 27 (1981): 30–35.

Layoun, Mary N. *Travels of a Genre: The Modern Novel and Ideology.* Princeton: Princeton University Press, 1990.

Leiter, Samuel, ed. *Japanese Theater in the World.* New York: Japan Society, 1997.

Leupp, Gary P. *Male Colors: The Construction of Homosexuality in Tokugawa Japan.* Berkeley: University of California Press, 1995.

Li, Takanori. *Hyōshō kūkan no kindai: Meiji "Nihon" no media hensei* (The modernity of the space of representation: The media formation of Meiji "Japan"). Tokyo: Shin'yōsha, 1996.

Livingstone, Angela. *Lou Andreas-Salomé.* London: G. Fraser, 1984.

Lye, Colleen. "*M. Butterfly* and the Rhetoric of Antiessentialism: Minority Discourse in an International Frame." In *The Ethnic Canon,* edited by David Palumbo-Liu, 260–89. Minneapolis: University of Minnesota Press, 1995.

Mackie, Vera. *Creating Socialist Women in Japan: Gender, Labour and Activism, 1900–1937.* Cambridge: Cambridge University Press, 1997.

Mandel, Siegried. "Introduction." In *Ibsen's Heroines,* by Lou Salomé, 8–41. Redding Ridge, Conn.: Black Swan Books, 1985.

Mann, Otto. *Geschichte des deutshcen Dramas* (History of German drama). Kröners Taschenausgabe Band 296. Stuttgart: Alfred Kröner Verlag, 1963.

Mannes, Jean-Paul Mathieu. "Die Aufnahme der dramatischen Werke Hermann Sudermanns: Eine Untersuchung seines theatralischen Erfolgs" (The reception of Hermann Sudermann's dramatic works: An examination of his theatrical success). Ph.D. diss., Utrecht University, 1976.

Marks, Patricia. *Bicycles, Bangs, and Bloomers: The New Woman and the Popular Press.* Lexington: University Press of Kentucky, 1990.

Marshall, Alan. *The German Naturalists and Gerhart Hauptmann: Reception and Influence.* European University Studies Series 1: German Language and Literature 556. Frankfurt: Peter Lang, 1982.

Martin, Biddy. *Femininity Played Straight: The Significance of Being Lesbian.* New York: Routledge, 1996.

———. *Woman and Modernity: The (Life)Styles of Lou Andreas-Salomé.* Ithaca, N.Y.: Cornell University Press, 1991.

Martin, Harris I. "Popular Music and Social Change in Prewar Japan." *The Japan Interpreter* 7, no. 3–4 (1972): 332–52.

Marukawa Kayoko. "Saishō o patoron to shita meigi kara ichiyaku kokusai joyū ichigō e" (From famed geisha patronized by prime minister in a single leap to the first international actress). In *Meiji ni kaika shita saien tachi* (Talented women blossoming in Meiji). Vol. 2 of *Jimbutsu kindai josei shi: onna no isshō* (Individuals in modern women's history: women's lives), edited by Setouchi Harumi, 19–62. 8 vols. Tokyo: Kōdansha, 1980.

Masao Miyoshi, and H. D. Harootunian, eds. *Postmodernism and Japan.* Durham, N.C.: Duke University Press, 1989.

Matsui Sumako. *Botanbake* (Peony brush). 1914. Reprint. Tokyo: Fuji Shuppan, 1986.

———. "Butai no ue de ichiban komatta koto" (What gave me the most trouble on stage). *Seitō* 2, no. 1 (1912): 162–63.

———. "Maguda" (Magda). *Engei gahō* (June 1912): 127.

Matsui Yayori. *Ajia no onnatachi* (Women of Asia). Tokyo: Iwanami Shoten, 1987.

Matsumoto Kappei. "Kaisetsu" (Afterword). In *Botanbake* (*Peony Brush*), by Matsui Sumako. Tokyo: Fuji Shuppan, 1986 [1914].

———. "Matsui Sumako saikō" (Matsui Sumako reconsidered). In *Shingeki no yamanami* (Mountain ranges of new theater), 28–42. Tokyo: Asahi Shorin, 1991.

———. *Nihon Shingeki shi: Shingeki binbō monogatari* (A history of Japanese new theater: A tale of poverty). Tokyo: Chikuma Shobō, 1966.

Matsumoto Shinko. *Meiji engeki ron shi* (A history of Meiji theater discussions). Tokyo: Engeki Shuppansha, 1980.

Matthias, Klaus. "Kerr und die Folgen: Analyse der Sudermann-Kritik als Perspektive einer Neubewertung seiner Dramen" (Kerr and the results: Analysis of Sudermann-criticism as perspective for a re-evaluation of his dramas). In *Hermann Sudermann: Werk und Wirkung* (Hermann Sudermann: Work and impact), edited by Walter T. Rix, 31–86. Würzburg: Königshausen und Neumann, 1980.

Mayama Seika. "Onnagata wa nagaki kenkyū no kekka" (Onnagata is the result of long study). *Engei gahō* (January 1912): 52–53.

Mayne, Judith. *Cinema and Spectatorship*. London: Routledge, 1993.

McDowell, Deborah. "New Directions for Black Feminist Criticism." In *The New Feminist Criticism: Essays on Women, Literature and Theory,* edited by Elaine Showalter, 186–99. New York: Pantheon Books, 1985.

Meltzer, Charles Henry. *The Sunken Bell: A Fairy Play in Five Acts by Gerhart Hauptmann: Freely Rendered into English Verse.* New York: R. H. Russell, 1899.

Meyer, Michael. *Ibsen: A Biography.* Garden City, N.Y.: Doubleday, 1971.

Mihara Aya. "*Geisha to samurai:* ikoku de umareta Dōjōji" (*Geisha and the Knight:* A Dōjōji born in a foreign land). *Gekkan geinō* 35, no. 4 (April 1993): 26–30.

———. "Gōhō to higōhō no hazama de: Tetsuwari Ichiza no San Furanshisuko Kōgyō" (Between legal and illegal: The San Francisco performances of the Tetsuwari troupe). *Geinōshi kenkyū* (Studies in the history of performing arts) 119 (October 1992): 25–46.

———. "Karuwaza shi no Rondon kōgyō: Roiyaru Raishiumu Gekijō, 1868nen" (Japanese *artistes* at the Royal Lyceum 1868). *Geinōshi kenkyū* (Studies in the history of performing arts) 110 (July 1990): 44–66.

Minaguchi Biyō. "Onnagata to joyū" (Onnagata and actresses). *Engei gahō* (October 1909): 76–80.

Mine Takashi. *Teikoku Gekijō kaimaku* (The opening of the Imperial Theater). Chūkō Shinsho 1334. Tokyo: Chūō Kōronsha, 1996.

Mishō Kingo. "Kawakami Sadayakko no kaigai de no hyōka" (Kawakami Sadayakko's reputation abroad). *Rekishi e no shōtai* (Invitation to history) 12 (1981): 77–79.

Mitsuda Kyōko. "Kindaiteki bosei-kan no juyō to hen'yō: kyōiku suru hahaoya kara ryōsai kenbo e" (The reception and transformation of modern views of motherhood: From educating mother to good wife, wise mother). In vol. 2 of *Bosei o tou: rekishiteki hensen* (Questioning motherhood: Historical changes), edited by Wakita Haruko, 100–129. 2 vols. Kyoto: Bunkōsha, 1985.

Miyaoka Kenji. *Ikoku henro tabi geinin shimatsu sho* (A report on travelling players who toured in foreign lands). Tokyo: Shūdōsha, 1959.

Mizuki Kumio. *Wasure enu hitobito (dai jukkai): Matsui Sumako* (Unforgettable people (tenth installment): Matsui Sumako). Radio-script. Tokyo: Dentsū Rajio Kyoku (Radio station), 1952.

Mizushima Ryokusō. "Tōdai joyū getsutan: Matsui Sumako" (Monthly critique of contemporary actresses: Matsui Sumako). *Engei gahō* (January 1915): 210–13; *Engei gahō* (February 1915): 46–49.

Mohanty, Chandra Talpade, et al., eds. *Third World Women and the Politics of Feminism.* Bloomington: Indiana University Press, 1991.

Mohanty, Satya P. "Us and Them: On the Philosophical Bases of Political Criticism." *Yale Journal of Criticism* 2, no. 2 (Spring 1989): 1–31.

Moi, Toril. *Sexual/Textual Politics: Feminist Literary Theory.* London: Routledge, 1985.

Molony, Barbara, and Kathleen Uno, eds. *Gendering Modern Japanese History.* Cambridge: Harvard University Press, forthcoming.

Mori Eijirō. "Kobayashi-san" (Ms. Kobayashi). *Engei gahō* (June 1915): 37–41.

Mori Reiko. "Matsui Sumako." *Geidō no hana hiraku toki* (When the flower of art bloomed). Vol. 5 of *Kindai Nihon josei shi* (A history of women in modern Japan), edited by Enchi Fumiko, 91–126. 12 vols. Tokyo: Shūeisha, 1981.

Mori Ritsuko. "Sumako no shi to joyū kai" (Sumako's death and the actress world). *Onna no sekai* 5, no. 2 (February 1919): 24–25.

Morinaga, Maki. "The Gender of Onnagata as the Imitating Imitated: Its Historicity, Performativity, and Involvement in the Circulation of Femininity." *positions: east asia cultures critique*, forthcoming.

———. "Osanai Kaoru to shirōtoshugi: hiden no jissenkei ni taisuru hitei, muka, dakyō" (Osanai Kaoru and amateurism: Denial, nullification, and compromise with the regime of esotericism). In *Nihon kinsei kokka no shosō* (Various appearances of premodern Japanese nation), edited by Nishimura Keiko, 271–97. Tokyo: Tōkyōdō Shuppan, 1999.

Morita Sōhei. "Joshi wa oshiu bekarazu" (Women should not be taught). *Engei gahō* (January 1912): 48–50.

Moriya Takeshi. "Geinōshi ni okeru kinseiteki naru mono" (What is early modern in performance history). In *Kinsei* (Early modern period. Vol. 4 of *Nihon bungaku shinshi* (A new history of Japanese literature), edited by Matsuda Osamu, 169–92. 6 vols. Tokyo: Shibundō, 1990.

Murakami Hatsu. "Sangyō kakumeiki no joshi rōdō" (Women's labor during the industrial revolution era). In *Kindai* (Modern period). Vol. 4 of *Nihon joseishi* (Japanese women's history), edited by Joseishi Sōgō Kenkyūkai, 77–114. 5 vols. Tokyo: Tōdai Shuppankai, 1982.

Murakami Nobuhiko. *Meiji joseishi* (History of Meiji women). 4 vols. Tokyo: Rironsha, 1969–1972.

———. *Taishō joseishi: shimin seikatsu.* (A history of Taishō women: Citizens lives). Tokyo: Rironsha, 1982.

Murata Eiko. "Matsui Sumako o kaibō su" (Dissecting Matsui Sumako). *Onna no sekai* 5, no. 2 (February 1919): 8–33.

Murphy, Joseph A. "Approaching Japanese Melodrama." *East-West Film Journal* 7, no. 2 (July 1993): 1–38.

Muta Kazue. *Senryaku to shite no kazoku: kindai Nihon no kokumin kokka keisei to josei* (Family as strategy: Women and the formation of the modern Japanese nation-state). Tokyo: Shin'yōsha, 1996.

Naganuma Chie. "Maguda ni tsuite" (On Magda). *Seitō* 2, no. 6 (June 1912): 14.

Nakai Tetsu. "Osuma san no butai guse" (Stage habits of Sumako). *Engei gahō* (February 1919): 67–68.

Nakamura Toshiko, "Ibsen in Japan: Tsubouchi Shoyo and His Lecture on New Women." *Edda: Nordisk Tiddskrift for Litteraturfoskning* (Scandinavian journal of literary research) 5 (1982): 261–72.

———. "Three *A Dolls House* in Japan." *Edda: Nordisk Tidsskrift for Litteraturforskning* (Scandinavian journal for literary research) 3 (1985): 163–71.

Nakayama Hakuhō. "Joyū wa fuhitsuyō" (Actresses are unnecessary). *Engei gahō* (January 1912): 146–47.

Nicholson, Linda J., ed. *Feminism/Postmodernism.* New York: Routledge, 1990.

Nishiyama Matsunosuke. "Kuruwa." (The pleasure quarter). In *Kinsei fūzoku to shakai* (Early modern customs and society). Vol. 5 of *Nishiyama Matsunosuke chosakushū* (Collected writings of Nishiyama Matsunosuke), 1–201. 8 vols. Tokyo: Yoshikawa Kōbunkan, 1985.

Noguchi Takehiko. "Sakusha" (Author). In *Nihon engeki shi no shiten* (The viewpoint of Japanese theater history). Vol. 1 of *Kōza Nihon no engeki* (Lectures on Japanese theater), edited by Suwa Haruo and Sugai Yukio, 110–24. 8 vols. Tokyo: Benseisha, 1992.

———. *Sanninshō no hakken made* (Until the discovery of the third person). Tokyo: Chikuma Shobō, 1994.

Noguchi Tatsuji. *Joyū Sumako no koi* (Actress Sumakos love). In *Noguchi Tatsuji gikyoku sen* (Selected plays of Noguchi Tatsuji), 439–527. Tokyo: Engeki Shuppansha, 1989.

Nohl, Ingrid. "Das dramatische Werk Hermann Sudermanns: Versuch einer Darstellung seiner Gesellschaftskritik auf dem Theater im 19. und 20. Jahrhundert und im Film" (The dramatic works of Hermann Sudermann: An attempt to represent his social criticism in 19th and 20th century theater and film). Ph.D. diss., University of Köln, 1973.

Nolte, Sharon H., and Sally Ann Hastings. "The Meiji State's Policy Toward Women, 1890–1910." In *Recreating Japanese Women, 1600–1945,* edited by Gail Lee Bernstein, 151–70. Berkeley: University of California Press, 1991.

Ochi Haruo. *Meiji Taishō no geki bungaku: Nihon kindai gikyoku shi e no kokoromi* (Dramatic literature in Meiji and Taishō: Towards a history of modern Japanese plays). Tokyo: Hanawa Shobō, 1971.

Ochiai Emiko. *Kindai kazoku to feminizumu* (The modern family and feminism). Tokyo: Keisō Shobō, 1989.

Ogasawara Kyōko. *Toshi to gekijō: chū kinsei no chinkon, yūraku, kenryoku* (Cities and theaters: Soul-quelling, play, and power from the middle ages to the early modern period). Heibonsha Sensho, no. 14. Tokyo: Heibonsha, 1992.

Ōgoshi Aiko. "Feminizumu wa towarete iru: jūgun ianfu to Nihon teki sei fūdo" (Feminism is being interrogated: Military comfort women and the Japanese sexual climate). *Jōkyō* (June 1992): 15–33.

———. *Kindai Nihon no jendā: gendai Nihon no shisōteki kadai o tou* (Modern Japanese gender: Interrogating the philosophical task of contemporary Japan). Tokyo: San'ichi Shobō, 1997.

Ōgoshi Aiko, Minamoto Junko, and Yamashita Akiko. *Nihon-teki sekushuariti: feminizumu kara no sei fūdo hihan* (Japanese sexuality: A feminist critique of sexual climate). Tokyo: Hōzōkan, 1991.

———. *Sei sabetsu suru bukkyō: feminizumu kara no kokuhatsu* (Sexual discrimination in Buddhism: A feminist indictment). Tokyo: Hōzōkan, 1990.

Oguma Eiji. *Tan'itsu minzoku no shinwa: "Nihonjin" no jigazō no keifu* (The myth of the homogenous nation: Genealogy of the self-portrait of "the Japanese"). Tokyo: Shin'yōsha, 1995.

———. "Tsumazuita junketsu shugi: yūseigaku kei seiryoku no minzoku seisaku ron" (The pure-blood principle that stumbled: The ethnic policy discourse of eugenics advocates). *Jōkyō* (December 1994): 38–50.

Okada Yachiyo. "Matsui Sumako san" (Ms. Matsui Sumako). *Engei gahō* (February 1919): 81–83.

Ōkubo Tōho. "Sumako no jisatsu wa hentai seiyoku" (Sumako's suicide was due to perverse sexual desire). *Onna no sekai* 5, no. 2 (February 1919): 4–15.

Ooms, Herman. *Tokugawa Village Practice: Class, Status, Power, Law.* Berkeley: University of California Press, 1996.

Origuchi Shinobu. "Nyōbō bungaku kara inja bungaku e" (From the literature of ladies in waiting to the literature of hermits). In vol. 1 of *Origuchi Shinobu zenshū* (Complete works of Origuchi Shinobu), 265–320. 31 vols. Tokyo: Chūō Kōronsha, 1986.

Ortolani, Benito. *The Japanese Theatre: From Shamanistic Ritual to Contemporary Pluralism.* Revised edition. Princeton: Princeton University Press, 1995.

Osanai Kaoru. "Hongōza no Sarome" (Hongōza theater's Salomé). *Engei gahō* (June 1915): 148–63.

———. "Kowareta sake game" (A broken wine bottle). *Engei gahō* (February 1919): 68–70.

Ōsawa Yoshihiro. "Hikaku: Nihonjin wa saru ni mieru ka" (Comparison: Do Japanese look like apes?), In *Chi no gihō* (Techniques of knowledge), edited by Kobayashi Yasuo and Funabiki Takeo, 172–83. Tokyo: Tokyo University Press, 1993.

Otabe Tanehisa. "Kindai teki 'shoyū' shisō to 'geijutsu' gainen: kindai bigaku no seijigaku e no joshō" (The modern philosophy of "property" and the concept of "art": Preface to a politics of modern aesthetics). *Hihyō kūkan* 2, no. 12 (1997): 51–66.

Otake Kōkichi. "Akai tobira no ie yori" (From the house of red doors). *Seitō* 2, no. 5 (May 1912): 32–53.

———. "Maguda ni tsuite" (On Magda). *Seitō* 2, no. 6 (June 1912): 14–16.

Ōwaki Masako. "Hōritsu ni okeru josei kan" (Views of women in law). In *Onna no imēji* (Women's images). Vol. 1 of *Kōza joseigaku* (Lectures in women's studies), edited by Joseigaku Kenkyūkai (Women's studies study group), 102–28. 4 vols. Tokyo: Keisō Shobō, 1984.

Ozaki Hirotsugu. *Joyū no keizu* (Genealogy of actresses). Tokyo: Asahi Shimbunsha, 1964.

———. *Shimamura Hōgetsu*. Vol. 1 of *Nihon Kindai geki no sōshishatachi* (The pioneers of modern Japanese theater). 3 vols. Tokyo: Miraisha, 1965.

Ōzasa Yoshio. *Nihon gendai engeki shi* (History of Japanese contemporary theater). 6 vols. to date. Tokyo: Hakusuisha, 1985–1999.

———. "Shokuminchi shugi to waga kuni no kindai gikyoku" (Colonialism and our nation's modern drama). *Shiataa Aatsu* (Theater Arts) 8 (1997): 50–55.

Paul, Fritz. "Sechs Antworten und Sechs Geschichten: Lou Andreas-Salomé interpretiert Ibsen" (Six answers and six stories: Lou Andreas-Salomé interprets Ibsen). In *Contemporary Approaches to Ibsen Vol. 5: Reports from the Fifth International Ibsen Seminar, Munich 1983,* edited by Daniel Haakonsen, 99–112. Oslo: Universitetsforlaget, 1985.

Pflugfelder, Gregory M. *Cartographies of Desire: Male-Male Sexuality in Japanese Discourse, 1600–1950* (Berkeley: University of California Press, 1999).

Pollack, David. *Reading Against Culture: Ideology and Narrative in the Japanese Novel.* Ithaca, N.Y.: Cornell University Press, 1992.

Powell, Brian. *Japan's Modern Theatre: A Century of Change and Continuity.* New York: St. Martin's Press, 2001.

———. "Matsui Sumako: Actress and Woman." In *Modern Japan: Aspects of History, Literature and Society,* edited by W. G. Beasley, 135–46. Berkeley: University of California Press, 1975.

Pratt, Mary Louise. *Imperial Eyes: Travel Writing and Transculturation.* London: Routledge, 1992.

Pribram, E. Deidre, ed. *Female Spectators: Looking At Film and Television.* London: Verso, 1988.

Probyn, Elspeth. "Travels in the Postmodern: Making Sense of the Local." In *Feminism/Postmodernism,* edited by Linda Nicholson, 176–89. New York: Routledge, 1990.

Rackin, Phyllis. "Androgyny, Mimesis, and the Marriage of the Boy Heroine on the English Renaissance Stage." *PMLA* 102, no. 1 (1987): 29–41.

Rilke-Gesellschaft, ed. *Lou Andreas-Salomé.* Karlsruhe: von Loeper Verlag, 1986.

Riley, Denise. *"Am I That Name?": Feminism and the Category of 'Women' in History.* Minneapolis: University of Minnesota Press, 1988.

Rimer, J. Thomas. *Toward a Modern Japanese Theatre: Kishida Kunio.* Princeton: Princeton University Press, 1974.

Riviere, Joan. "Womanliness as a Masquerade." In *Formations of Fantasy,* edited by Victor Burgin, James Donald, and Cora Kaplan, 35–44. London: Methuen, 1986.

Rix, Walter. "Hermann Sudermann." In *Realismus, Naturalismus und Jugenstil* (Realism, naturalism, and Jugendstil). Vol. 6 of *Deutsche Dichter* (German writers), edited by Gunter E. Grimm and Frank Rainer Max, 298–308. 8 vols. Stuttgart: Reclam, 1989.

———, ed. *Hermann Sudermann: Werk und Wirkung* (Hermann Sudermann: Work and impact). Würzburg: Königshausen und Neumann, 1980.

Robertson, Jennifer. "Gender-Bending in Paradise: Doing Female and Male in Japan." *Genders* 5 (July 1989): 50–69.

———. "The Magic If: Conflicting Performances of Gender in the Takarazuka Revue of Japan." In *Gender in Performance: The Presentation of Difference in the Performing Arts,* edited by Laurence Senelick, 46–67. Hanover, N.H.: University Press of New England, 1992.

———. "The Shingaku Woman: Straight from the Heart." In *Recreating Japanese Women, 1600–1945,* edited by Gail Lee Bernstein, 88–107. Berkeley: University of California Press, 1991.

———. *Takarazuka: Sexual Politics and Popular Culture in Modern Japan.* Berkeley: University of California Press, 1998.

Rodd, Laurel Rasplica. "Yosano Akiko and the Taisho Debate over the 'New Woman'." In *Recreating Japanese Women, 1600–1945,* edited by Gail Lee Bernstein, 175–98. Berkeley: University of California Press, 1991.

Rogers, Katharine M. "A Doll House in a Course on Women in Literature." In *Approaches to Teaching Ibsen's* A Doll House, edited by Yvonne Shafer, 81–85. New York: MLA, 1985.

Rorty, Richard. "The Historiography of Philosophy: Four Genres." In *Philosophy in History: Essays on the Historiography of Philosophy,* edited by Richard Rorty, et al. Cambridge: Cambridge University Press, 1984.

———. "Solidarity or Objectivity?" In *Post-Analytic Philosophy,* edited by John Rajchman and Cornel West. New York: Columbia University Press, 1985.

Rose, Jacqueline. *Sexuality in the Field of Vision.* London: Verso, 1986.

Rose, Mark. *Authors and Owners: The Invention of Copyright.* Cambridge: Harvard University Press, 1993.

Rubin, Gayle. "Thinking Sex: Notes for a Radical Theory of the Politics of Sexuality." In *Pleasure and Danger: Exploring Female Sexuality,* edited by Carole S. Vance, 267–319. London: Pandora, 1992.

———. "The Traffic in Women: Notes on the Political Economy of Sex." In *Toward an Anthropology of Women,* edited by Rayna Reiter, 157–210. New York: Monthly Review Press, 1975.

Rubin, Jay. *Injurious to Public Health: Writers and the Meiji State.* Seattle: University of Washington, 1984.

Rutherford, Susan. "The Voice of Freedom: Images of the prima donna." In *The New Woman and her Sisters: Feminism and Theatre 1850–1914,* edited by Vivien Gardner and Susan Rutherford, 95–113. Ann Arbor: University of Michigan Press, 1992.

Ryokurō Shujin. "Matsui Sumako to kataru: real conversation" (Talking with Matsui Sumako: Real conversation). *Engei gahō* (March 1911): 95–107.

Sadoya Shigenobu. *Hōgetsu Shimamura Takitarō ron* (A Study of Shimamura Hōgetsu). Tokyo: Meiji Shoin, 1980.

Saeki Junko. "Hanasaku Edo no bishōnen: ai no zankoku bigaku" (Blooming Edo's beautiful boys: The cruel aesthetics of love). In *Edo no shinjitsu: dare mo idomanakatta kinsei Nihon no wakarikata* (Edo's truth: An unprecedented way of understanding early modern Japan), edited by Ishii Shinji, 218–232. Bessatsu Takarajima, no. 126. Tokyo: JICC, 1991.

———. *Yūjo no bunkashi: hare no onnatachi* (A cultural history of the Japanese courtesan: Sacred women). Chūkō Shinsho, no. 853. Tokyo: Chūō Kōronsha, 1987.

Said, Edward. *Orientalism*. New York: Vintage, 1978.

Saitō Yasuhide. "Dan'atsu to tōsei" (Suppression and control). In vol. 7 of *Nihon geinō shi* (Japanese performing arts history), edited by Geinōshi Kenkyūkai, 238–58. 7 vols. Tokyo: Hōsei University Press, 1990.

Sakai, Naoki. "Feeling and Sentiment: On Fujitani Mitsue's Poetics of Choreography." Translated by Holly Sanders. In vol. 2 of *Gender and Japanese History*, edited by Wakita Haruko, Anne Bouchy, and Ueno Chizuko, 163–95. 2 vols. Osaka: Osaka University Press, 1999.

———. "'Jō' to 'kanshō': seiai no jōcho to kyōkan to shutai-teki gijutsu o megutte" ("Feeling" and "sentiment": On sexual affections, common feeling, and subjective technology). In vol. 2 of *Jendā no Nihonshi*, edited by Wakita Haruko and Susan B. Hanley, 137–77. 2 vols. Tokyo: Tokyo University Press, 1995.

———. "Modernity and Its Critique: The Problem of Universalism and Particularism." In *Postmodernism and Japan*, edited by Masao Miyoshi and H. D. Harootunian, 93–122. Durham, N.C.: Duke University Press, 1989.

———. "Nashonariti to bo(koku)go no seiji," (Nationality and the politics of mother (nation's) tongue) in *Nashonariti no datsukōchiku* (Deconstructing nationality), edited by Sakai Naoki, Brett de Bary, and Iyotani Toshio, 9–53. Tokyo: Kashiwa Shobō, 1996.

———. "Return to the West / Return to the East: Watsuji Tetsuro's Anthropology and Discussions of Authenticity." In *Japan in the World*, edited by Masao Miyoshi and H. D. Harootunian, 237–70. Durham, N.C.: Duke University Press, 1993.

———. *Translation and Subjectivity: On "Japan" and Cultural Nationalism*. Minneapolis: University of Minnesota Press, 1997.

———. *Voices of the Past: The Status of Language in Eighteenth-Century Japanese Discourse*. Ithaca, N.Y.: Cornell University Press, 1992.

Salz, Jonah. "Intercultural Pioneers: Otojirō Kawakami and Sada Yakko." *The Journal of Intercultural Studies* (Kansai University of Foreign Studies Publication, Japan) 20 (1993): 25–74.

Sano Mitsuo. "Machiai saron shi no onna: Hanai Ume to Meiji no geiki" (Women in the history of salons: Hanai Ume and the Meiji geisha). In *Meiji no onna* (Women of Meiji), edited by Kida Jun'ichirō, 131–51. Vol. 9 of *Meiji no gunzō* (Meiji group portrait). 10 vols. Tokyo: San'ichi Shobō, 1969.

Satake Shingo. *Sadayakko: honoo no shōgai* (Sadayakko: A life in flames). Tokyo: Kōfūsha, 1984.

Satō Izumi. "Kindai bungaku shi no kioku / bōkyaku" (The remembering/forgetting of modern literary history) *Gendai shisō* 27, no. 1 (January 1999): 170–82.

Satō Tadao. "Nihon eiga no seiritsu shita dodai" (The foundation of Japanese cinema). In *Nihon eiga no tanjō* (The birth of Japanese cinema). Vol. 1 of *Kōza Nihon eiga* (Lectures on Japanese cinema), 2–52. 7 vols. Tokyo: Iwanami Shoten, 1985.

Schalow, Paul Gordon, trans. *The Great Mirror of Male Love*, by Ihara Saikaku. Stanford: Stanford University Press, 1990.

Schalow, Paul Gordon, and Janet A. Walker, eds. *The Woman's Hand: Gender and Theory in Japanese Women's Writing*. Stanford: Stanford University Press, 1996.

Schanke, Robert A. *Ibsen in America: A Century of Change*. Metuchen, N.J.: Scarecrow Press, 1988.

Schulz, Gerhard. "Gerhart Hauptmanns dramatisches Werk" (Gerhart Hauptmann's dramatic works). In *Handbuch des deutschen Dramas* (Handbook of German drama), edited by Walter Hinck, 311–26. Düsseldorf: Bagel, 1980.

Scott, Joan W. "Gender: A Useful Category of Historical Analysis." In *Coming to Terms: Feminism, Theory, Politics,* edited by Elizabeth Weed, 81–100. New York: Routledge, 1989.

Sedgwick, Eve. *Between Men: English Literature and Male Homosocial Desire*. New York: Columbia University Press, 1985.

———. *Epistemology of the Closet*. Berkeley: University of California Press, 1990.

Segel, Harold B. *Pinocchio's Progeny: Puppets, Marionettes, Automatons, and Robots in Modernist and Avant-Garde Drama*. Baltimore, Md.: Johns Hopkins University Press, 1995.

Seigle, Cecilia Segawa. *Yoshiwara: The Glittering World of the Japanese Courtesan*. Honolulu: University of Hawaii Press, 1993.

Senelick, Laurence. "Changing Sex in Public: Female Impersonation as Performance." *Theater* 20, no. 2 (1989): 6–11.

———, ed. *Gender in Performance: The Presentation of Difference in the Performing Arts*. Hanover, NH: University Press of New England, 1992.

Serres, Michel. *Jouvences sur Jules Verne*. Paris: Éditions de Minuit, 1974.

Shaw, Bernard. *The Quintessence of Ibsenism: Now Completed to the Death of Ibsen*. New York: Brentanos, 1913.

Shibusawa Ei'ichi. *The Autobiography of Shibusawa Ei'ichi: From Peasant to Entrepreneur,* translated, with an introduction and notes, by Teruko Craig. Tokyo: University of Tokyo Press, 1994.

Shimamura Hōgetsu. *Hōgetsu zenshū* (Collected works of Hōgetsu). 8 vols. 1919. Reprint. Tokyo: Nihon Tosho Sentā, 1979.

Shimokawa Enji. *Joyū no ai to shi* (Love and death of an actress). (Adaptation of Toita Kōji's original). *Higeki kigeki* 206 (December 1967): 6–138.

Shionoya Kei, *Shirano to samurai tachi* (Cyrano and the Samurais). Tokyo: Hakusuisha, 1989.

Shiraishi Masayoshi. "Saisho no shingeki joyū: Matsui Sumako" (The first new theater actress: Matsui Sumako). *Denden jidai* 8, no. 3 (May 1979): 14–21.

Shirakawa Nobuo, ed. *Kawakami Otojirō, Sadayakko: shimbun ni miru jimbutsu zō* (Kawakami Otojirō, Sadayakko: Their personalities as seen in newspapers). Tokyo: Yūshōdō, 1985.

Shively, Donald. "The Social Environment of Tokugawa Kabuki." In *Studies in Kabuki: Its Acting, Music, and Historical Context,* edited by James R. Brandon, William P. Malm, and Donald H. Shively, 1–61. Honolulu: University of Hawaii Press, 1978.

Showalter, Elaine, ed. *The New Feminist Criticism: Essays on Women, Literature and Theory*. New York: Pantheon Books, 1985.

———. "Representing Ophelia: Women, Madness, and Responsibilities of Feminist Criticism." In *Shakespeare and the Question of Theory,* edited by Patricia Parker and Geoffrey Hartman, 77–94. New York: Methuen, 1985.

———. *Sexual Anarchy: Gender and Culture at the Fin de Siècle.* New York: Penguin, 1990.

Sievers, Sharon L. *Flowers in Salt: The Beginnings of Feminist Consciousness in Modern Japan.* Stanford: Stanford University Press, 1983.

Simon, Elliott M. "Arthur Wing Pinero's *The Second Mrs. Tanqueray:* A Reappraisal." *The Ball State University Forum* 28, no. 1 (Winter 1987): 44–56.

Smith, Barbara. "Toward a Black Feminist Criticism." In *The New Feminist Criticism: Essays on Women, Literature and Theory,* edited by Elaine Showalter, 168–85. New York: Pantheon Books, 1985.

Smith, Robert J., and Ella Lury Wiswell. *The Women of* Suye Mura. Chicago: University of Chicago Press, 1982.

Smith-Rosenberg, Carroll. *Disorderly Conduct: Visions of Gender in Victorian America.* Oxford: Oxford University Press, 1985.

Sōma Kokkō. "Sumako no otoko ni taishita taido to onna ni taishita taido" (Sumako's attitude towards men and attitude towards women). *Onna no sekai* 5, no. 2 (February 1919): 62–63.

Sōya Shinji. *Honoo to niji no fūkei: joyū Kawakami Sadayakko* (The landscape of flames and rainbows: Actress Kawakami Sadayakko). Chiba: Ron Shobō, 1982.

Spivak, Gayatri Chakravorty. *In Other Worlds: Essays in Cultural Politics.* New York: Routledge, 1988.

———. "The Political Economy of Women as Seen by a Literary Critic." In *Coming to Terms: Feminism, Theory, Politics,* edited by Elizabeth Weed, 218–29. New York: Routledge, 1989.

———. *The Post-Colonial Critic: Interviews, Strategies, Dialogues,* edited by Sarah Harasym. New York: Routledge, 1990.

Sprengel, Peter. "Gerhart Hauptmann." In *Realismus, Naturalismus und Jugenstil* (Realism, naturalism, and Jugendstil), edited by Gunter E. Grimm and Frank Rainer Max, 335–56. Vol. 6 of *Deutsche Dichter* (German writers). 8 vols. Stuttgart: Reclam, 1989.

Sprinchorn, Evert, ed. and trans. *Ibsen: Letters and Speeches.* New York: Hill and Wang, 1964.

———. "Ibsen, Strindberg, and the New Woman." In *The Play and Its Critic: Essays for Eric Bentley,* edited by Michael Bertin, 45–66. Lanham, Md.: University Press of America, 1986.

Staiger, Janet. *Interpreting Films: Studies in the Historical Reception of American Cinema.* Princeton: Princeton University Press, 1992.

Stam, Robert, Robert Burgoyne, and Sandy Flitterman-Lewis. *New Vocabularies in Film Semiotics: Structuralism, Post-Structuralism and Beyond.* London: Routledge, 1992.

Stephens, Judith. "Gender Ideology and Dramatic Convention in Progressive Era Plays, 1890–1920." In *Performing Feminisms: Feminist Critical Theory and Theatre,* edited by Sue-Ellen Case, 283–93. Baltimore, Md.: Johns Hopkins University Press, 1990.

Sterner, Mark H. "The Changing Status of Women in Late Victorian Drama." In vol. 6 of *Within the Dramatic Spectrum: The University of Florida Department of Clas-*

sics Comparative Drama Conference Papers, edited by Karelisa Hartigan, 199–212. Lanham, Md.: University Press of America, 1986.

Stokes, John, Michael R. Booth, and Susan Bassnett. *Bernhardt, Terry, Duse: The Actress in Her Time.* Cambridge: Cambridge University Press, 1988.

Stowell, Sheila. *A Stage of Their Own: Feminist Playwrights of the Suffrage Era.* Ann Arbor: University of Michigan Press, 1992.

Sudermann, Hermann. *Die Heimat* (The home). In vol. 4 of *Gesamt-Ausgabe* (Complete works), 245–348. Stuttgart: J. G. Cottasche Buchhandlung, 1923.

Suga Hidemi. *Nihon kindai bungaku no "tanjō": genbun itchi undō to nashonarizumu* (The "birth" of Japanese modern literature: The *genbun itchi* movement and nationalism). Tokyo: Ōta Shuppan, 1995.

———. *Shōsetsu-teki kyōdo* (Novelistic force). Tokyo: Fukutake Shoten, 1990.

———. "Shōsetsu-teki modaniti no kōzō" (The structure of novelistic modernity). *Hihyō kūkan* 1, no. 3 (1991): 52–76; 1, no. 5 (1992): 108–28; 1, no. 6 (1992): 213–33; 1, no. 7 (1992): 148–69; 1, no. 10 (1993): 232–50; 1, no. 11 (1993): 229–48; 2, no. 3 (1994): 141–60.

———. "Sōshitsu no jimeisei: hachijū-nendai feminizumu to bungaku" (The self-evidence of loss: 1980s feminism and literature). *Gunzō* 47, no. 11 (October 1992): 296–318.

Sugimoto Sonoko, "Bunmei kaika ki no maboroshi no stā: Kawakami Sadayakko" (The elusive star of the civilization-and-enlightenment period: Kawakami Sadayakko). In *Ranse no shomin* (The populace in an age of strife), edited by Ozaki Hideki, 41–59. Vol. 10 of *Meiji no gunzō* (Meiji group portrait). 10 vols. Tokyo: San'ichi Shobō, 1969.

———. *Madamu Sadayakko* (Madame Sadayakko). Tokyo: Shūeisha, 1980.

Sugimoto Sonoko, and Kawatake Toshio. "Kawakamiza umi o wataru: joyū dai ichi gō Sadayakko" (The Kawakami troupe crosses the seas: Actress number one Sadayakko). *Rekishi e no shōtai* (Invitation to history) 12 (1981): 45–85.

Suwa Haruo and Sugai Yukio, eds. *Kōza Nihon no engeki* (Lectures on Japanese theater). 8 vols. Tokyo: Benseisha, 1992.

Suzuki Naoko, ed. *Shiryō: sengo bosei no yukue* (Documents: Directions for post-war motherhood). Tokyo: Domesu Shuppan, 1984.

Suzuki Tadashi. *The Way of Acting: The Theatre Writings of Tadashi Suzuki.* Translated by J. Thomas Rimer. New York: Theatre Communications Group, 1986.

Suzuki, Tomi. *Narrating the Self: Fictions of Japanese Modernity.* Stanford: Stanford University Press, 1996.

Tachi Kaoru. "Ryōsai kenbo" (Good wife, wise mother). In *Onna no imēji* (Women's images). Vol. 1 of *Kōza joseigaku* (Lectures in women's studies), edited by Joseigaku Kenkyūkai (Women's studies study group), 184–209. 4 vols. Tokyo: Keisō Shobō, 1984.

Takaya, Ted. *Modern Japanese Drama: An Anthology.* New York: Columbia University Press, 1979.

Takayasu Gekkō. "Shōrai wa joyū" (The future belongs to actresses). *Engei gahō* (January 1912): 53–54.

Takemura Kazuko. "Ai ni tsuite" (On love). *Shisō* 886 (April 1998): 5–33.

Takemura Tamio. *Haishō undō: kuruwa no josei wa dō kaihō sareta ka* (The prostitution abolition movement: How the women of the pleasure quarters were liberated). Chūkō Shinsho, no. 663. Tokyo: Chūō Kōronsha, 1982.

Takeuchi Yoshimi. *Takeuchi Yoshimi zenshū* (Complete works of Takeuchi Yoshimi). 17 Vols. Tokyo: Chūō Kōronsha, 1980.

Tamura Toshiko. "Ne hanashi" (Ne story). *Engei gahō* (January 1912): 144–46.

Tanaka Eizō. *Joyū mandan* (Random talk on actresses). Mandan Sōsho, no. 3. Tokyo: Shūeikaku, 1927.

———. *Meiji Taishō shingeki shi shiryō* (Meiji Taishō new theater history documents). Tokyo: Engeki Shuppansha, 1964.

Tanaka Sumie. "Engeki to shinjū shita Nihon no Nora: Matsui Sumako" (The Japanese Nora who committed love suicide with theater). In *Inu doshi hen* (Year of the dog). Vol. 11 of *Jūnishi-betsu ekigaku kaisetsu: josei geijutsuka no jinsei* (Fortune telling according to the twelve animal signs: Lives of female artists), edited by Kinoshita Kazuo, 9–44. 12 vols. Tokyo: Shūeisha, 1980.

Tanaka, Stefan. *Japan's Orient: Rendering Pasts into History.* Berkeley: University of California Press, 1993.

Tanji Ai. "Fikushon to shite no tasha: orientarizumu no kōzō" (The other as fiction: The structure of Orientalism). In *Chi no ronri* (Logics of knowledge), edited by Kobayashi Yasuo and Funabiki Takeo, 173–83. Tokyo: Tokyo University Press, 1993.

Templeton, Joan. "The *Doll House* Backlash: Criticism, Feminism, and Ibsen." *PMLA* 104 (1989): 28–40.

Terada Namiji. "*Kokyō* ni deru hitobito" (People who appear in *Heimat*). *Engei gahō* (June 1912): 101–8.

Toita Kōji. *Joyū no ai to shi* (Love and death of an actress). Tokyo: Kawade Shobō, 1963.

———. *Monogatari kindai Nihon joyū shi* (An anecdotal history of modern Japanese actresses). Tokyo: Chūō Kōronsha, 1980.

Tsurumi, Patricia. *Factory Girls: Women in the Thread Mills of Meiji Japan.* Princeton: Princeton University Press, 1990.

Tsurumi, Shunsuke. *Senjiki Nihon seishinshi: 1931–1945 nen* (History of Japanese wartime mentality: 1931–1945). Tokyo: Iwanami Shoten, 1982.

Uchida Roan. "Joyū mondai" (Actress question). *Kabuki* (November 1908): 32.

Ueda Kazutoshi. "Rien kōjōsaku" (Proposals for theater world improvement). *Engei Gahō* (June 1907): 13–14.

Ueda Kimiko. "Ningyō no ie o yomu" (Reading *A Doll House*). *Seitō* 2, no. 1 (1912): 126–32.

Ueno Chizuko. *Kafuchōsei to shihonsei: Marukusushugi feminizumu no chihei* (Patriarchy and capitalism: The horizon of marxist feminism). Tokyo: Iwanami Shoten, 1990.

———. "Kaisetsu" (Commentary). In *Fūzoku, sei* (Folk customs and sexuality), edited by Ogi Shinzō, Kumakura Isao, and Ueno Chizuko, 505–50. Vol. 23 of *Nihon kindai shisō taikei* (Collected Japanese modern thought). 24 vols. Tokyo: Iwanami Shoten, 1990.

———. *Nashonarizumu to jendā* (Engendering nationalism). Tokyo: Seidosha, 1998.

———. *Onna wa sekai o sukueru ka* (Can women save the world?). Tokyo: Keisō Shobō, 1986.

———. *Shihonsei to kaji rōdō.* (Capitalism and domestic labor). Tokyo: Kaimeisha, 1985.

Ueno Chizuko, Mizuta Noriko, Karatani Kōjin, Asada Akira. "Nihon bunka to jendā" (Japanese culture and gender). *Hihyō kūkan* 2, no. 3 (1994): 6–43.

Ueno Chizuko, and Nakamura Yūjirō. *Ningen o koete: idō to chakuchi.* (Beyond human: Transit and landing). Tokyo: Seidosha, 1989.

Ueno Chizuko, Ogura Chikako, and Tomioka Taeko. *Danryū bungaku ron* (Theory of men's literature). Tokyo: Chikuma Shobō, 1992.

Ueno Ichirō. "*Joyū* hyō" (Review of *The Actress*),[1948]. In *Sengo eiga no shuppatsu* (The beginnings of post-war cinema), edited by Ogawa Tetsu et al. Vol. 1 of *Gendai Nihon eiga ron taikei* (An outline of contemporary Japanese writings on film). 6 vols. Tokyo: Tōkisha, 1971.

Ueno Yōko "Ningyō no ie yori josei mondai e" (From *A Doll House* to the Woman Question). *Seitō* 2, no. 1 (1912): 62–114.

Uno, Kathleen S. "The Origins of 'Good Wife, Wise Mother' in Modern Japan." In *Japanische Frauengeschichte(n)* (Japanese women's histories), edited by Erich Pauer and Regine Mathias, 31–46. Marburg: Förderverein Marburger Japan Reihe, 1995.

———. *Passages to Modernity: Motherhood, Childhood, and Social Reform in Early Twentieth Century Japan.* Honolulu: University of Hawaii Press, 1999.

Vance, Carole S., ed. *Pleasure and Danger: Exploring Female Sexuality.* London: Pandora, 1992.

Varner, Richard. "The Organized Peasant: The *Wakamonogumi* in the Edo Period." *Monumenta Nipponica* 32, no. 4 (Winter 1977): 459–83.

Verne, Jules. *Around the World in Eighty Days.* Translated by Jacqueline Rogers. New York: Signet-Penguin, 1991.

Vierig, Jürgen. "Die Schauspielerin als Vertreterin der Modernität: Über die Darstellung der Schauspielerin im Frühwerk Heinrich Manns und das Bild der modernen Schauspielerin in der zeitgenössischen Theaterkritik" (The Actress as representative of modernity: On the portrayal of the actress in the early works of Heinrich Mann and the image of the modern actress in contemporary theater criticism). *Jahrbuch für Internationale Germanistik* 18, no. 2 (1986): 8–75.

Vierne, Simone. *Jules Verne.* Paris: Balland, 1968.

Wakakuwa Midori. *Sensō ga tsukuru josei zō: dainiji sekai taisen ka no Nihon josei dōin no shikaku teki puropaganda* (Image of women created by war: Visual propaganda for the mobilization of Japanese women under World War Two). Tokyo: Chikuma Shobō, 1995.

Wakashiro Kiiko. "Koi o shi ni yotte enjita Matsui Sumako" (Matsui Sumako who performed love through death). In *Kindai o irodotta onnatachi* (Women who colored modernity), 191–206. Tokyo: TBS Britannica, 1981.

Wakita Haruko et al. eds. *Nihon josei shi* (Japanese women's history). Tokyo: Yoshikawa Kōbunkan, 1987.

Walthall, Anne. "Devoted Wives/Unruly Women: Invisible Presence in the History of Japanese Social Protest." *Signs* 20, no. 1 (Autumn 1994): 106–36.

Watanabe Jun'ichi. *Joyū* (Actress). Tokyo: Shūeisha, 1983.

Watanabe Naomi. "Deai sobireta danjo: bungei jihyō to feminizumu" (The man and woman who should have met and never did: Literary criticism and feminism). *Gunzō* 48, no. 4 (April 1993): 330–35.

Watanabe Naomi. *Nihon kindai bungaku to sabetsu* (Modern Japanese literature and discrimination). Hihyō kūkan sensho, no. 2. Tokyo: Ōta Shuppan, 1994.

Watanabe Shōichi. "Onna mosunaru shakai shinshutsu no bunmei-ron-teki kōsatsu" (A study of women's social advancement from a civilizational perspective). *Chūō kōron* 104, no. 9 (September 1989): 149–59.

Watsuji Tetsurō. *Climate and Culture: A Philosophical Study.* Translated by Geoffrey Bownas. Tokyo: Hokuseidō, 1961.

Watsuji Tetsurō. *Fūdo* (Climate). Vol. 8 of *Watsuji Tetsurō zenshū* (Complete works of Watsuji Tetsurō). 20 vols. Tokyo: Iwanami Shoten, 1977.

Weber, Evelyn. "Gerhart Hauptmann und die Frau" (Gerhart Hauptmann and woman). *Neue Deutsche Hefte* 31, no. 1 (1984): 76–96.

Weed, Elizabeth, ed. *Coming to Terms: Feminism, Theory, Politics.* New York: Routledge, 1989.

Weiner, Marc A. "Gerhart Hauptmanns *Die versunkene Glocke* and the Cultural Vocabulary of Pre-Fascist Germany." *German Studies Review.* 11, no. 3 (October 1988): 447–61.

Weiner, Michael. *Race and Migration in Imperial Japan.* New York: Routledge, 1994.

Whitford, Margaret, ed. *The Irigaray Reader.* Oxford: Basil Blackwell, 1991.

Wiesenthal, J. L., ed. *Shaw and Ibsen: Bernard Shaw's The Quintessence of Ibsenism and Related Writings.* Toronto: University of Toronto Press, 1979.

Wiesner, Michaela. "Leben in seinem Ursinn: Lou Andreas-Salomés Essays zur Erotik" (Life in its original sense: Lou Andreas-Salomés essays on erotics). In *Lou Andreas-Salomé,* edited by Rilke-Gesellschaft, 36–45. Karlsruhe: von Loeper Verlag, 1986.

Wiley, Catherine. "The Matter with Manners: The New Woman and the Problem Play." In *Women in Theatre,* edited by James Redmond, 109–27. Cambridge: Cambridge University Press, 1989.

Winch, Peter. "Understanding a Primitive Society." In *Rationality,* edited by Bryan R. Wilson. Oxford: Blackwell, 1985.

Woodbridge, Linda. *Women and the English Renaissance: Literature and the Nature of Womankind, 1540–1620.* Urbana: University of Illinois Press, 1984.

Wright, Elizabeth, ed. *Feminism and Psychoanalysis: A Critical Dictionary.* Oxford: Basil Blackwell, 1992.

Yamada Keiko. "Atarashii onna" (The new woman). In *Onna no imēji* (Women's images). Vol. 1 of *Kōza joseigaku* (Lectures in women's studies), edited by Joseigaku Kenkyūkai (Women's studies study group), 210–34. 4 vols. Tokyo: Keisō Shobō, 1984.

Yamaguchi Reiko. *Joyū Sadayakko* (Actress Sadayakko). Tokyo: Shinchōsha, 1982.

Yamashita Etsuko. *Josei no jidai to iu shinwa: Ueno Chizuko wa onna o sukueru ka* (The myth of the woman's era: Can Ueno Chizuko save women?). Tokyo: Seikyūsha, 1991.

———. *Mazakon bungakuron: jubaku to shite no haha* (The mother complex in literature: Mother as a binding curse). Tokyo: Shin'yōsha, 1991.

———. *Nihon josei kaihō shisō no kigen: posuto-feminizumu shiron* (Origins of women's liberation ideology in Japan: A post-feminist essay). Tokyo: Kaimeisha, 1988.

———. *Takamure Itsue-ron: haha no arukeorogī* (On Takamure Itsue: An archaeology of the mother). Tokyo: Kawade Shobō Shinsha, 1988.

Yanagawa Shun'yō. "Joyū wa ōi ni yūbō" (There is much hope for actresses). *Engei gahō* (January 1912): 45–48.

Yano Seiichi, ed. *Miyako Shimbun geinō shiryō shūsei: Taishō hen* (Miyako newspaper performance art materials collected: Taishō era). Tokyo: Hakusuisha, 1991.

Yasumochi Yoshiko. "Ningyō no ie ni tsuite" (About *A Doll House*). *Seitō* 2, no. 1 (1912): 143–54.

Yasunari Jirō, ed. *Sumako gō* (Sumako issue), special issue of *Onna no sekai* (Women's world) 5, no. 2 (February 1919).

Yoda Yoshitaka. *Joyū Sumako no koi* (Actress Sumako's love). Filmscript. Shōchiku Library.

Yokomizo Masahachiro. "Hermann Sudermann in Japan: Aspekte seines Einflusses auf Literatur und Geisteswelt der Meiji Periode (1868–1912)" (Hermann Sudermann in Japan: Aspects of his influence on the literature and the intellectual world of the Meiji period). In *Hermann Sudermann: Werk und Wirkung*, edited by Walter T. Rix, 344–59. Würzburg: Königshausen und Neumann, 1980.

Yoshimi Shun'ya. *Hakurankai no seijigaku: manazashi no kindai* (The politics of worlds fairs: The modernity of vision). Chūkō Shinsho, no. 1090. Tokyo: Chūō Kōronsha, 1992.

Young, Louise. *Japan's Total Empire: Manchuria and the Culture of Wartime Imperialism.* Berkeley: University of California Press, 1998.

Zatz, Noah D. "Sex Work/Sex Act: Law, Labor, and Desire in Constructions of Prostitution." *Signs: Journal of Women in Culture and Society* 22, no. 2 (1997): 277–308.

Zimmerman, Bonnie. "What Has Never Been: An Overview of Lesbian Feminist Criticism." In *The New Feminist Criticism: Essays on Women, Literature and Theory,* edited by Elaine Showalter, 200–224. New York: Pantheon Books, 1985.

Index

act, various meanings of, 232n10, 261n29
actors (*haiyū*): amateur *vs.* professional, 164–70; as interpretive slaves, 152, 165–66, 169, 181; as puppets, 132–34, 142, 169, 176–77, 267n40; separation from spectators, 155; theater reform and, 6–7
actresses (*joyū*): agency of, 132–33, 227–30; as "female players" *(onna yakusha)* 32; and geisha compared, 24–26, 43, 167–68; as New Women, 125; and *onnagata* compared, 16–24, 27; pure, 168; subjectivity of, 177; Matsui Sumako's uniqueness among, 131; in Tokugawa period, 31–32; training of, 39–40, 73–75, 140, 166, 167, 170, 181; use of terminology, 231n1. *See also specific actresses*
actress plays (*joyū geki*), 75, 104–5
Actress Question (*joyū mondai*), 15–27, 182, 203–4; arguments against, 21–23; eclectic position on, 20, 23; feminist position on, 18–19; geisha/prostitute and, 25–26; modern Western plays and, 20–21; sexuality and, 24–27; voice and body of, 20–21. *See also onnagata* (female impersonator)
adaptation (*hon'an*). *See* translation
Alt Heidelberg (Meyer-Förster), 12, 111, 112, 116, 117
amateur-professional (*shirōto-kurōto*) debate, 164–70, 181, 267n50, 268n57
Anderson, Benedict, 99, 114
Around the World in Eighty Days (Verne), 78, 95–104, 253nn33–34; colonialism in, 110; Japanese version of, 99–104, 248n52
art, and commercialism, 179–81, 214–15
Artaud, Antonin, 160, 175, 247n40, n42
art for art's sake, 164, 180–81
Art Theater (Geijutsuza), 124
audience: as consumer, 179–80; New Theater and, 160; and war plays, 66. *See also* spectator

Barthes, Roland, 71, 163, 247n37
battle scenes, 61–66, 68–69, 88, 103
Bernhardt, Sarah, 9, 90, 149, 177, 200, 203
biological motherhood, 28
bodily display, in Wilde's *Salomé,* 219–30; linguistic *vs.* voyeuristic modes in, 227–30; parodies of, 224–25; of Sadayakko and Sumako compared, 221–24; as striptease, 221, 226–27
body: of actress, 31, 130; female voice and, 20–21; inner emotions and, 177; Japanese *vs.* Western, 21, 172, 269n67; nature and, 27, 265n22; and sensuality, 130, 223–24, 225; theatrical deployment of, 141
Botanbake (Sumako). *See Peony Brush*
Bourdieu, Pierre, 164
Bowlby, Rachel, 164
boy-actors, 5, 8, 31. *See also wakashu*
Bungei Kyōkai. *See* Literary Society
bunraku. See puppet theater
bunshigeki (literati theatricals), 166
Butler, Judith: *Bodies that Matter,* 4, 237n27; *Gender Trouble,* 4, 73, 238n47; *Excitable Speech,* 127–28, 227
butō (dance genre), 171–72

Carmen (Bizet), 217
censorship, 110, 153, 154–55, 263n8, n10; of Sudermann's *Heimat,* 209–12
Chicago Fair (1893), 94
Chikamatsu Monzaemon, 161, 162–63. *See also* puppet theater
children: gendering of, 29–30; theater for, 52; literary representations of, 141–42. *See also* motherhood
China, 61, 63, 64–65
Chitose Beiha, 32
Chōsen ō. See Korean King
Cima, Gay Gibson, 175
cinema. *See* film
class hierarchy, 29, 55, 78
colonialism, 94, 110, 265n18; and *Korean King,* 112–15; and New Theater, 158; and travel plays, 95–97. *See also* imperialism; Orientalism
colonial plays, 12–13, 106–9, 111; romance in, 110, 114–16, 118
commercialism, of art, 179–81, 240n70
commodified sexuality, 160–61, 163–64, 168–69, 170, 226, 227. *See also* prostitution
communication modes, 227–30
consumer, spectator as, 33–34, 179–80
consumerism, 93–94. *See also* commercialism
costumes, 127, 192–93, 204–5, 222–24, 276n70; as metaphor for gender, 3–4
Craig, Gordon, 169
cross-gender performance, 102–3, 145–46, 238n50. *See also onnagata;* male impersonation
crying, release in, 131, 145
cultural colonization, 9, 264n18
cultural practices, and imperialism, 11

dance and song, 67–68, 69, 174, 178, 217
"Dance of the Seven Veils," 220, 224, 226–27
dance play (*buyō geki*), 174, 269n74
dancing, 108, 172, 177–78, 222, 269n67.
Danjūrō. *See* Ichikawa Danjūrō IX
Delsarte, François, 177
D'Ennery, Adolphe, 64, 65
Derrida, Jacques, 13, 152, 159, 175, 187
différance, 72, 168, 172
direct *vs.* indirect speech and action, 68–73, 176–77, 247n38
disguise. *See* transformation
Doane, Mary Ann, 184
Dōjōji (dance play), 53, 69, 87, 88, 92, 100
Doll House, A (Ibsen), 133, 167, 178, 184–99; alternative ending for, 186–87; author's intentions for, 185–86; critical response to, 193–99; *Heimat* compared to, 201, 208–9, 212; Matsui Sumako as Nora in, 188–91. *See also* Nora *(A Doll House)*
Dumb Travel (Masuda), 75, 81, 104–5
Duse, Eleonora, 9, 200
duty, 185. *See also* obligation
Duus, Peter, 111, 112, 114–15

eclecticism, 20, 23
educational system, 29–30
elocution *(rōdoku),* 142–43, 173, 174, 269n70
emotions: body movement and, 177; crying and, 145; real feelings, 138, 161–62; voice and, 19
Enchi Fumiko, ix, 236n10
Engei gahō (magazine), 15
engeki (extending drama), 33, 240n63
enunciation, and enunciated, 72, 246n35
essentialism, 8, 21, 22, 23, 35, 156, 171, 177, 195, 230
ethnicity, 65, 83–84, 264n18
Euro-American context: and New Woman, 124–26
European actresses, 9. *See also specific actresses*
European theater, 107. *See also* modern European drama; Shakespearean drama
European tour, 88–90, 94–95
exhibition. *See* world's fairs
extraordinary action, dance as, 68
Ezaki Atsushi, 49

faithfulness to original text, 158–59, 170–78, 205–6; and speech-writing unity 172, 177–78, 194
female body. *See* body
"Female Butterfly" (Sumako), 141–42
female impersonators. *See onnagata*
female players (*onnna yakusha*), 32. *See also* actresses
femininity: ideal of, 28, 31, 41; as performed, 72–73; stylized, 5; transhistorical, 10; *vs.* masculinity, 138–40
feminism, 8, 133, 156, 227, 230; in Germany, 187
feminist journal. *See Seitō*
feminists: *A Doll House* and, 184–85, 194–98; femme fatale and, 184, 216; Magda in *Heimat,* 200–212; Matsui Sumako as, 127, 134, 148–49; as New Women, 127–28. *See also* New Women; Nora *(A Doll House);* suffragettes
femme fatale, 123, 280n4; ambivalent power of, 183–84; feminism and, 184, 216; New Woman as, 128; Rautendelein *(The Sunken Bell),* 213–16; Salomé as, 220, 230; Sumako as, 132, 142
film, 31, 239n57, 263n8, 269n70
Finney, Gail, 220
Fjelde, Rolf, 186
flâneur (writer-as-walker), 146–48
Fogg, Phileas *(Around the World in 80 Days),* 96, 110, 253nn33–35
Foucault, Michel, 81, 155, 264n11, 265n22, 268n62
freedom, personal, 156
Free Theater (Jiyū Gekijō), 151, 164, 166
Fukuhara Takeo *(Around the World in 70 Days),* 100, 101–2, 103, 254n49
Fukuzawa Momosuke, 46, 48–49, 74, 260n22
Fukuzawa Yukichi, 46, 253n28
Furukawa Makoto, 30

Geijutsuza. *See* Art Theater
geisha, 32, 77, 116, 146–47, 167–68; actresses compared to, 25–26, 167–68; as actress students, 74; marriage of, 46–47; prostitutes compared to, 42–43, 44, 242n13; Sadayakko as 42–43, 44, 46, 116
Geisha and the Knight, The (play) 87–88
genbun itchi (unity of speech and writing), 172, 177–78, 194, 271n98, 274n37
gender and perfomance: 3–5, 8, 11, 27–35, 131; binary division of 30–31; bodily display and, 219; différance and, 72; *genbun itchi* of, 271n98; historicity of, 4–5; identity, 73; modern formation of, 10; politics of, 83; sex and, 28–29, 30; *shibai* to *engeki* shift in, 33–35; subjectivity and, 177. *See also* Actress Question
Germany, 112, 186, 187
good wife, wise mother (*ryōsai kenbo*), 12, 41, 42, 128, 195–96, 197, 258n13. *See also* motherhood; wifeing
government, 92–93, 154. *See also* censorship; nation-state
Great Exhibition of London (1851), 94
Griffis, William Elliot, 6

Hamada Kame, 46
Hamlet (Shakespeare), 69, 108–9, 167, 173–74, 269n71
Hana *(Korean King),* 113, 116
Hanabusa Ryūgai, 162
Hasegawa Shigure, 19–21, 23, 54, 129, 208, 236n10
Hatoyama Kazuo, 79
Hatsuta Jōji (*Around the World in Seventy Days*), 99–100, 101, 103
Hauptmann, Gerhart, 19, 213, 214, 278nn99, 103–4
Hayashi Chitose, 129
Heimat (Sudermann), 200–212, 213, 275n60; alternative ending for, 210–12; banning of, 209–10; Shimamura's translation of, 204, 205–6; motherhood *vs.* career in, 202–3. *See also* Magda *(Heimat)*
Heinrich *(The Sunken Bell),* 213, 214
Helmer *(A Doll House),* 186–87

heterosexuality, 27, 30, 83
High Treason Incident (Taigyaku Jiken), 154, 155, 277n85
Higuchi Ichiyō, 142
Hiratsuka Raichō, 127, 157, 197–98, 208, 236n20
historicity, of gender, 4–5
Hōgetsu. *See* Shimamura Hōgetsu
home, confinement in, 200–201, 275n60
homosexuality, 27, 30, 250n86; homosociality and, 82–83; *kabuki* and, 58–60; women and, 274n56
homosocial theater, 12, 62, 77, 82–84
Honma Hisao, 222

Ibsen, Henrik, 185–86, 187
Ichikawa Danjūrō IX, 32, 66, 80, 271n97
Ichikawa Enjaku, 19–20
Ichikawa Kumehachi, 32, 69, 169, 239n59
Ichikawa Sadanji, 164
iemoto. *See* school master system
Ihara Seisei'en, 193, 207, 215
Ii Yōhō, 32, 162
Ikuta Chōkō, 206
Imperial Actress Training Institute (Teikoku Joyū Yōseijo), 39–40, 73–75, 167
imperialism, reproduction of, 11, 61, 84, 99, 249n72, 250n89, 265n18; in Japanese-Korean relations, 110–11, 117, 118; world's fairs and, 93–94. *See also* colonialism
Imperial Theater (Teikoku Gekijō), 73, 167, 173–74, 192, 194, 249n75, 272n8; theater reform and, 75, 232n15, 240n70
independence of women, 201, 209, 212
Indian princess (*Around the World in Eighty Days)* 98–99, 101
indirect *vs*. direct speech and action, 68–73
"In Place of a Preface" (Sumako), 137–40
interior essence, 160, 198
interiority, 138, 195, 206
interior purity, 138. *See also* purity, theater of
intermarriage, 115, 256n71
interpretive slave, actor as, 152, 165–66, 169, 181. *See also* puppet, actor as
Irigaray, Luce, 72
Irving, Henry, 106, 251n5
Ishibashi Tanzan, 212
Ishikawa Takuboku, 156
Itō Hirobumi, 46
Iwasaki Momosuke, 46. *See also* Fukuzawa Momosuke

Japanese body, 171–72
Japanese essence, 140, 171
Japanese government. *See* imperialism, reproduction of; nation-state
Japanese Noras, 133, 197. *See also* Nora *(A Doll House)*
Japanese Theater in the World (exhibit), 10
Japanese Village exhibitions, 92–93
Japan-Korean relations, 110–11, 115, 117, 118, 155
Jay, Martin, 93
Jiyū Gekijō. *See* Free Theater
Jokanaan *(Salomé)*, 220, 223
Joyū Yōseijo. *See* Imperial Actress Training Institute

kabuki actors, 6–7, 61–62, 66, 69, 165–66, 207, 271n97, 278n104; and geisha, 47; improvisation by, 71, 175. *See also onnagata*
kabuki theater, 6–7, 240n64; commodification of, 162, 181; modern theater compared to, 80, 181; as national theater, 60, 249n70; *onnagata* tradition in, 22–23, 24; performance length of, 79; *as queered theater,* 58–60; *shimpa* and, 57; as song-dance-mime, 67; stylization in, 71; war plays and, 61, 62, 66. *See also* patterns, pseudo-*kabuki* plays
Kabukiza theater, 78
Kamiyama Uraji, 129
Karatani Kōjin, 159, 271n97
Katō Midori, 195
Katō Shūichi, 163
Kawajiri Seitan, 206–7
Kawakami Otojirō, 12, 41, 57, 67–68, 80; death of, 51; Sadayakko as wife

to, 39, 46–48, 52–54; theater reform and, 75–77, 78–81
Kawakami Sadayakko, 7, 32, 39–119; acting career of, 12, 49–52; actress training and, 40, 73, 168; in *Dōjōji,* 53, 69, 83, 88, 92, 100; as feminist, 230; as geisha, 42–43, 44, 46–47,116; in *Korean King,* 113, 116; life and role parallels of, 105–6; male impersonation by, 49, 50, 102–3; marriage to Otojirō, 46–48, 52–54; Matsui Sumako compared to, 13, 217, 221–24; as mistress, 42, 44–45, 48–49; as oriental woman on tour, 85–90, 94–95; private life of, 45–49; roles of, 12–13, 39–40, 69, 118–19; in *Salomé,* 219, 221–24; Shakespearean roles of, 106–9; western fashions and, 90–91. *See also* wifeing, Kawakami Sadayakko's
Kawakami troupe, 57, 67, 249n77; colonial plays of, 106–9, 118; European tour, 88–90, 98; in *Sino-Japanese War* (play), 12, 61–66, 68–69, 84; U.S. tour, 85–88
Kawamura Karyō, 130, 269n70
Keller *(Heimat),* 200, 201–2
Kema Namboku, 24, 25
Kitamura Rokurō, 32
Kiuchi Tei, 209
Kobayashi Masako. *See* Matsui Sumako
kōgyō. See show business system
Kojima Koshū, 22, 26–27, 236n15
Kojima Takanori (play), 86
Kokyō. See Heimat (Sudermann)
Komiya Toyotaka, 211
Korea-Japan relations, 110–11, 115, 117, 118, 155
Korean King (play), 110–18, 255n65; censorship of, 110, 113–14, 155; colonialism and, 112–13, 114
Koyama Sada. *See* Kawakami Sadayakko
Kubota Beisai, 92
Kurakawa Umejirō, 134
Kusuyama Masao, 205, 216, 279n120
Kuwano Tōka, 25
kyōgen (medieval comic theater), ix

labor, sexual division of, 28–29
language, 71, 268n66. *See also* direct *vs.* indirect speech; *genbun itchi;* translation
Literary Society (Bungei Kyōkai), 109, 165, 192, 211. *See also* Theater Institute of the Literary Society
loyalty *(chūkō)* 83

Macherey, Pierre, 96
Mackie, Vera, 41–42
Maeterlinck, Maurice, 134
Magda *(Heimat),* 146, 147, 200–212, 276n70; feminist reactions to, 208–9; Matsui Sumako as, 203–6; motherhood *vs.* career of, 202–3; Nora *(A Doll House)* compared, 203, 207–8
male actors, in female roles, 5. *See also onnagata* (female impersonators)
male impersonation, by actress, 49, 50, 102–3
male prostitution, 24, 25
male same-sex relations, 60. *See also* homosexuality
manteau (cape), 127, 135, 205; photographs with, 193, 207, 237
marriage, 157; intermarriage, 115, 256n71; geisha, 46–47. *See also* wifeing
Marukawa Kayoko, 54
Masamune Hakuchō, 208
masculinity: and theater reform, 76–77; *vs.* femininity, 138–40
masses, 93–94, 155, 240n69
Masuda Tarōkaja, 75, 104
Matsui Shōyō, 177
Matsui Sumako, x, 7–8, 32; ambiguous status of, 148; competition with Kawakami Sadayakko, 13, 221–24; costume of, 127; family background of, 124; femininity *vs.* masculinity and, 138–40; as feminist, 127, 134, 148–49; as femme fatale, 132, 142, 183–84; as *flâneur,* 146–48; as Magda *(Heimat),* 203–6; 163; memoirs and essays, 135–49, 189–92; motivation for acting, 143–45; as natural woman, 131, 156–57; and New

Theater, 216; as New Woman, 123–24, 127–49, 169, 205; as Nora *(A Doll House),* 19, 188–91, 192–95; as Ophelia *(Hamlet),* 109, 167, 173–74; as puppet, 132–34; reaction to suicide of, 129–30; as Salomé, 219, 221–24, 225, 228–29; sexuality and, 125; Shimamura Hōgetsu's defense of, 137–40; and song and dance, 217; theatricality of, 125–27
Matsumoto Kappei, 133, 136, 261n40
Mayama Seika, 21
Meiji Period (1868–1912), 5–6, 15, 34, 67, 254n40
melodrama, 69, 217
memorization, 71, 175–77
Merchant of Venice (Shakespeare), 106
merchants, 74, 248n52
Meyer-Förster, Wilhelm, 12, 111
Michel Strogoff (Verne), 63
middle class, New Woman as, 124, 125
military, represented in theater, 61–66; as model for theater, 81, 246n30
mimicry: femininity as, 72; as imitation of imperialism, 99; *of The Merchant of Venice,* 106; and originality, 265n20. *See also* parody; patterns
Minaguchi Biyō, 18, 23, 26, 235n3
mistress, and wife compared, 43, 44–45, 47
Mizushima Ryokusō, 130
Mizutani Yaeko, 225, 228
modern European drama: New Woman in, 19, 125, 127; problems in translation of, 172, 174. *See also specific plays*
modern formation of theater, 33–35. *See also* New Theater, straightening theater
modernity of vision, and imperialism, 93–94
Monna Vanna (Maeterlinck), 134
morality, 24, 157, 210. *See also* censorship
Mori Reiko, 131, 132, 133, 137
Mori Ritsuko, 74, 130, 168
Morita Sōhei, 22, 236n20
Moritaza theater, 78
Moriya Takeshi, 33–35, 240n69
motherhood: biological, 28; duty of, 185, 187; ideology of, 41; *vs.* career, 202–3. *See also* good wife, wise mother
motivation, for acting, 49–51, 143–45
Mulvey, Laura, 117
Murakami Nobuhiko, 132–33
Murata Eiko, 130
Muro Washirō *(Othello),* 107–8
musical play (*gakugeki*), 269n74. *See also* song and dance
music and dance, 75, 174. *See also* song and dance
"My Hometown" (Sumako), 145–46

Naganuma Chie, 209
Nakamura Kichizō, 279n125, 280n2
Nakayama Hakuhō, 24–25
naked face, in theater, 62, 271n97
narration (*katari*). *See* (in)direct speech and action
narrator (*chobo*), 174
nationalism, 84, 99, 153–54
national theater (*kokugeki*), 153, 174. *See also* New Theater
nation-state, 95, 153; actors and, 51; building of, 5–6, 26, gender and, 10–11, 29–30; theater and, 15–16
natural womanhood, 131, 156–57, 219
nature *vs.* artifice, 23, 27, 139
Nazimova, Alla, 190, 191
New Nation's King, 110, 113. *See also Korean King*
New Othello (parody), 107–8
new school drama. *See shimpa*
New Theater (*shingeki*), 13, 34, 123, 151–82, 198, 255n54; actor as puppet in, 163, 169, 176–77; assumptions of, 151; colonialism and, 158; faithfulness to origins debate in, 158–59, 170–78, 194; feminist expression and, 199; gender and sexuality in, 160; intense rehearsal for, 190; Matsui Sumako and, 216; memorization in, 175–77; modern European plays in, 184; New Woman and, 13, 123, 129, 156–57; professionals *vs.* amateurs in, 164–70; spectators as consumers in, 179–80; song and dance in, 174,

178, 217; state censorship of, 153, 154–55; as theater of purity, 160–62; Westernization and, 152–54, 157–59; womanhood in, 156–57. *See also* theater of logos
New Woman (*atarashii onna*), 13, 19, 116, 124–28, 142; Euro-American, 124–26, 204; in Japan, 126–27; New Theater and, 13, 123, 129, 156–57; Salomé as, 227–28, 230; sexuality of, 128, 183. *See also* Matsui Sumako, as New Woman
Ningyō no ie. See A Doll House
Nisshin sensō. See Sino-Japanese War
noh theater, 6, 70
Nora *(A Doll House)*,19, 184–99; actress training for, 140; alternative ending and, 186–87; critical response to, 193–99; Magda *(Heimat)* compared to, 203, 207–8, 212; motherhood and, 185; self-awareness of, 192–93, 195, 196; Matsui Sumako as, 188–91
"Nora and Magda" (Sumako), 212
"Notes for a Modern Tragedy" (Ibsen), 185–86

obligation, 77, 83, 84, 101
Okada Yachiyo, 129
Okada Yoshiko, 262n42
Oka Kitarō, 215
Onna daigaku (treatise), 28
onnagata (female impersonators), 5, 6, 16–17, 26, 220, 233n20; as feminine ideal, 31; homosexuality and, 60; marginalization of, 8, 26; set patterns of, 18–19, 149; sexual attractiveness of, 24; suitability of, in *kabuki,* 19–20, 22–23; voice of, 19, 20, 145. *See also* Actress Question
onna yakusha. See female players
Ophelia *(Hamlet),* 109, 167, 173–74
Orientalism, 64, 89, 95, 99, 251n8
Osanai Kaoru, 132, 152, 174, 178, 221–23, 265n20; amateur *vs.* professional debate, 164–70; art *vs.* commerce debate, 179–81
Otake Kōkichi, 198–99, 208
Othello (Shakespeare), 12, 69, 106–8

Ōzasa Yoshio, 158

Paris World's Fair, 89, 93, 94–95, 98
parody: of actress training, 75; of *Othello,* 107–8; of *Salomé,* 224–25. *See also* mimicry; translation.
Passepartout *(Around the World in 80 Days),* 96, 98, 253n34
patterns (*kata*), in acting, 19, 149, 166, 177, 178, 190, 250n89
Peony Brush (Matsui Sumako), 135, 136–37, 140, 148, 189, 228–29. *See also specific essays*
People's Rights Movement (*minken undō*), 84, 239n53
performance: as commodity, 161, 162; hours for, 79–80; *See also* gender and performance
performers, as teachers, 34. *See also* actors; actresses, training of
personal *vs.* political, 155–57
Pflugfelder, Gregory, 30
playwright's intentions, 165, 194, 195
pleasure quarters (*yūkaku*), 78, 161, 181, 242n13, 249n66, 266n26. *See also* prostitution
political theater (*sōshi shibai*), 46–48, 62, 154
politics: of gender, 83; women's prohibition from, 27, 30
popular theater (*taishū engeki*), 181; *Salomé* as, 220, 224–26
postmodern genres, 171–72
Prise de Pékin, Le (D'Ennery), 64, 65
professional-amateur debate, 164–70, 181, 267n50
proletarian theater, 181
propaganda play, 65. *See also Sino-Japanese War*
prostitute, and geisha compared, 26–27, 42–43, 44, 242n13
prostitution, 5, 24, 161
pseudo-*kabuki* plays, 39, 75, 87–88, 91–95
puppet, actor as, 132–34, 142, 163, 169, 176–77, 267n40
puppet theater, 70–71, 162, 163
pure actress, 168
pure art, 164
purity, theater of, 138, 160–62

queer, *kabuki* understood as, 58–60

racism: against Chinese, 64–65; against Koreans, 115
Rautendelein *(The Sunken Bell),* 213–16
reader, spectator as, 159, 160, 175, 187, 195
real feelings (*jō*), 136, 138, 161–2, 250n88. *See also* emotion, sentimentality (*kanshō*)
real sensations *(jikkan),* 25, 130, 195, 263n10
"Recent Complaints" (Sumako), 148
"Reflections" (Sumako), 148–49
Reformed Theater Management (*kakushin kōgyō*), 81
Renaissance-Restoration theater (England), 8
reproduction. *See* imperialism, reproduction of
Riviere, Joan, 72
Robertson, Jennifer, 170, 237n31, 250n89
rōdoku. See elocution
romance, 46, 76, 114–16, 118, 163
Rosi, Giovanni Vittorio, 222, 229
Russo-Japanese War, 114, 153–54, 243n23, 269n74
ryōsai kenbo. See good wife, wise mother

Sadayakko. *See* Kawakami Sadayakko
Sakai, Naoki, 68, 70, 72, 82–83, 232n10, 246n25, n29, 250n88
Salomé (Wilde). *See* bodily display, in *Salomé*
sameness, and empire, 84
school master system (*iemoto*), 34
schools, for actors/actresses, 39–40, 73–75, 166–70
scopic regime, 93
Sedgwick, Eve Kosofsky, 82
Seibikan troupe, 32
Seitō (feminist journal), 48, 127, 133, 194–99
self-awareness (*jikaku*), 19, 192–93, 195, 212
self-centeredness, 53–54, 133, 230
sensuality, 130, 223–25
sentimentality (*kanshō*), 84, 115, 116, 118, 250n88. *See also* real feelings
sex role, 231n5
sexual difference, 28–29, 183
sexual freedom, 126
sexuality: and actress question, 24–27; difference in, 83; and femme fatale, 183–84, 215–16; and gender, 28; homosexuality, 27, 30, 58–60, 82–83; and New Woman, 123, 125, 128, 130, 156, 183; and theatricality, 141, 237n27; and womanhood, 30
sexuality, commodification of, 160–61, 163–64, 168–69, 170, 226, 227. *See also* prostitution
sexual subject, 128
Shakespeare, Japanese. *See* Chikamatsu Monzaemon
Shakespearean drama, 69, 106–9, 166–67, 173–74
shasei (sketching from life), 172, 177–78
Shaw, George Bernard, 125
shibai (premodern performance), 33–34, 239n62
Shibusawa Ei'ichi, 74
Shimamura Hōgetsu, 124, 152; death of, 124, 131, 163, 224; debate with Osanai, 179–81; debate with Tsubouchi, 172–78, 188–89; *A Doll House* and, 124, 187–88; as ghost writer for Sumako, 136–40, 229; *Heimat* and, 203–4, 210–11; as Monna Vanna, 134; as puppet master of Sumako, 132–34, 229; *The Sunken Bell* and, 214–15
Shimazaki Tōson, 156
Shimoyama Kyōko, 224–25
shimpa (new school drama), 10, 32, 57–58, 77, 175, 182, 217, 244n1, 250n85
shin'engeki. See straightening theater
shingeki, 58, 151. *See also* New Theater
shin heimin (new commoner), 61, 107, 245n14
Shin Koku ō. See Korean King
Shintomiza theater, 78
Shōchiku (production company), 167, 215
Shōkyokusai Tenkatsu, 224
"Shop Keeper" (Matsui Sumako), 142–43

show business system (*kōgyō*), 33–34, 75–82
Sino-Japanese War (play), 12, 61–66, 68–69, 71, 83–84, 85
sketching from life *(shasei),* 172, 177–78
social class, 29
social context, 21
social hierarchy, 78
socialist movement, 41–42
social movements, 154–56
social outcasts, actors as, 6–7, 78
Sōda Usuke (*Dumb Travel*), 104
song and dance, 67–69, 75, 174, 178, 217, 275n65, 279n118, n119
sōshi shibai. See political theater
space, abstract, 78, 93, 96–97,
spatial and temporal confining of theater, 77–80
spectator, as consumer, 33–34, 179–80
spectator-actor separation, 155
speech, direct *vs.* indirect, 68–73, 176–77
speech-writing unity, 172. *See also genbun itchi*
state censorship, 110, 153, 154–55
straightening theater (*seigeki*), 12, 57–84, 95, 110, 182; actress training and, 73–75; homosocial theater and, 62, 77, 82–84; (in)direct speech and action in, 68–73; *kabuki* as queered theater and, 58–60, 265n22; New Theater compared to, 158, 159, 162; rejection of song and dance by, 67–68, 69; Sino-Japanese war play, 61–66; theater reform and, 75–82; wifeing and, 106
Strauss, Richard, 220
striptease, 221, 226–27. *See also* dance
students, 34, 152, 154
student types *(shosei),* 47–48
subject, modern and national, 15, 29, 58, 64, 83, 95, 103, 107, 108, 110, 113, 118, 254n49,
Sudermann, Hermann, 146–47, 200, 213, 277n99
Suematsu Kenchō, 232n15
suffragettes, 125
Sugimoto Sonoko, 53–54
suicide, 236n20, 257n3; of Sumako, 129, 130–31, 163, 224, 261n26; in puppet theater 162
Sumako. *See* Matsui Sumako
"Summer in Kyoto" (Matsui Sumako), 146–48
Sunken Bell, The (Hauptmann), 213–16, 278n103
Suzuki Tadashi, 171–72, 255n54, 268n66

Taigyaku Jiken. *See* High Treason Incident
Takarazuka Revue, 10, 168, 170, 182, 237n31, 250n89, 274n37
Takeuchi Yoshimi, 84, 264n18
Tamura Toshiko, 18–19, 145
Tanaka Eizō, 226
Tayama Katai, 156
teachers, performers as, 34
Teikoku Gekijō theater. *See* Imperial Theater
Teikokuza theater, 78
Terry, Ellen, 9, 106
text, 175, 246n25. *See also* language
theater: diplomacy and, 6; nation building and, 15–16; prostitution and, 5
theater of cruelty, 175, 247n42
theater districts (*shibai machi*), 77–78, 249n66
Theater Institute of the Literary Society (Engeki Kenkyūjo), 124, 166–67, 170, 173, 177, 188
theater of logos, 152–53, 163, 170, 172, 178; Derrida and, 13, 152, 159, 175. *See also* New Theater
theater of purity, 160–62
theater reforms, 6–7, 34–35, 198, 249n77; actor's motivation and, 144; by Kawakami, 75–82, 248n63; Imperial Theater and, 75, 232n15, 240n70; masculinity and, 76–77; reducing hours of performance, 79–80; theater districts and, 77–78; Western theater and, 78, 170–71. *See also* New Theater; straightening theater
Theater Reform Society (Engeki Kairyōkai), 6–7
theatricality, 4; and sexuality, 141, 237n27

Tokyo Actors' School (Tokyo Haiyū Gakkō), 168, 169
Tolstoy, Leo, 217
tour system, 81. *See also* Kawakami troupe
training, for actors/actresses, 39–40, 73–75, 140; and amateur-professional debate, 166–67, 170, 181. *See also* Imperial Actress Training Institute; Theater Institute of the Literary Society
transculturation, 9
transformation (plot device), 65, 83–84, 101
translation, 158–59, 171, 172, 189, 204, 205–6, 276n68. *See also* faithfulness to origins
transparency, 27, 35, 59, 68, 94, 123, 129, 159, 177, 178, 181, 195, 199, 204, 206, 216
travel plays. *See Around the World in Eighty Days; Dumb Travel*
Tsubouchi Shōyō, 127, 152, 163, 195, 269n74; debate with Osanai, 164–70; debate with Shimamura, 172–78, 188–89
Tsukiji Small Theater, 174, 178

Über-Marionette, actor as, 169, 176. *See also* interpretive slave; puppet
Ueda Kazutoshi, 170
Ueda Kimiko, 196–97
Ueno Chizuko, 28
Ueno Yōko, 195–96
United States: Kawakami troupe tour of, 85–88; New Woman in, 126; Kawakami Sadayakko's debut in, 50
universalism, 153, 158, 171, 263n7

Verne, Jules, 63, 95, 99, 254n40
Vierne, Simone, 98
violence, staged, 103. *See also* battle scenes
virginity, 48
vision, and visuality, 78, 79, 93, 227
voice, 216, 230; elocution and, 142–43, 173; female body and, 20–21; of actress *vs. onnagata,* 19, 145
voyeurism, 130, 224, 225, 227–28

wakashu (youths), as boy-actors, 5, 16, 31
war plays. *See Sino-Japanese War* play
Western drama, 76, 174, 263n6. *See also* modern European drama
Western fashions, 90–91
Westernization, 64, 99, 104–5, 139, 140, 265n20; faithfulness to origins debate and, 170–72; Japanese essence and, 140; New Theater and, 152–54, 157–59
Western-style theaters, 78. *See also* Imperial theater
wifeing, 57, 64, 83, 106, 196
wifeing, Kawakami Sadayakko's, 41–55; acting career and, 49–52; ideology of, 41–42, 52–53, 55; mistress compared to, 43, 44–45; private life and, 45–49
Wilde, Oscar, 125, 219, 225, 228
Winslow, Charles E. A., 204
womanhood, 10; essence of, 8; ideal of, 53; natural, 131, 156–57; New Woman and, 128; physical body and, 219. *See also* femininity; New Woman
womanliness, as masquerade, 72
Woman Question (*fujin mondai*), 184–85, 203–4
women: independence of, 201, 209, 212; mental capacity of, 22; objectification of, 9, 228; politics and, 30; social standing of, 145; theater reform and, 7; war effort and, 64. *See also* actresses; femininity; geisha
women's movement, 187. *See also* feminism
world's fairs, 89, 92, 93–95, 252n21

Yanagawa Shun'yō, 23
Yano Fumio, 92
Yoda Gakkai, 32
"Young Tears" (Matsui Sumako), 143–45
Yūrakuza theater, 78